# LOVE is LOVE is LOVE is LOVE is LOVE is LOVE is LOVE is LOVE is LOVE is LOVE

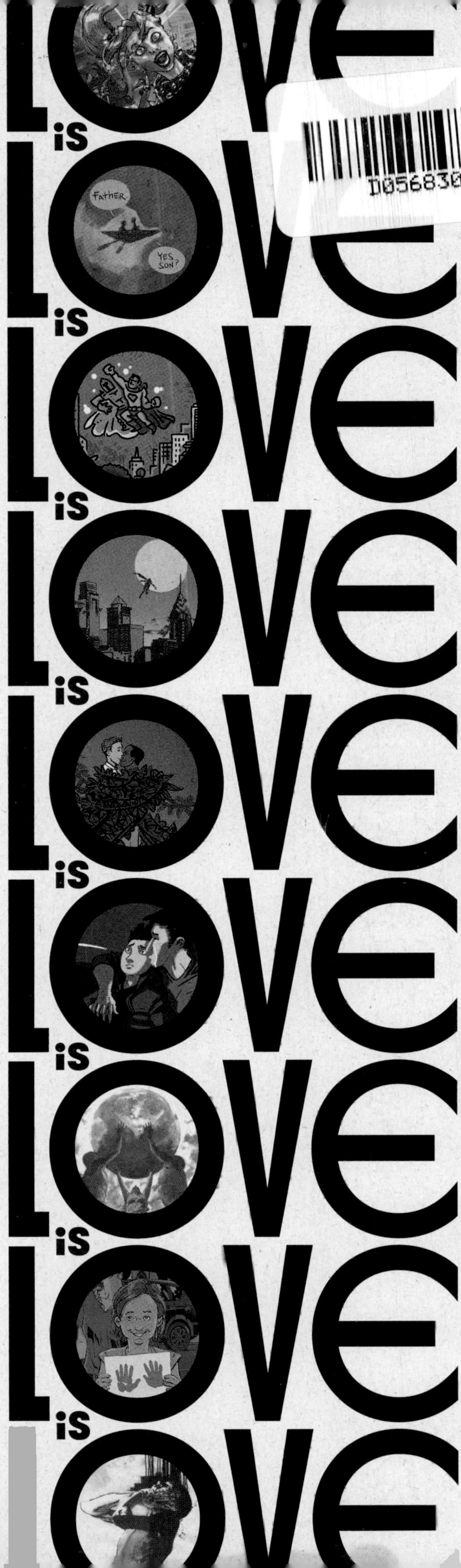
FATHER.
YES SON?

***A comic book anthology to benefit the survivors of the Orlando Pulse shooting***

**IDW PUBLISHING**

Editorial and Related Services Provided by

**DC ENTERTAINMENT**

**For more information and to make your own donation, please contact Equality Florida Institute: www.eqfl.org**

Project originated by **Marc Andreyko**

Logo created by **Steve Cook** of DC Comics

Edited by IDW Publishing's **Sarah Gaydos** and DC Comics' **Jamie S. Rich**

Assistant-edited by **Maggie Howell** of DC Comics

Design by **Amie Brockway-Metcalf** of DC Comics

### IDW PUBLISHING
TED ADAMS CEO & Publisher
GREG GOLDSTEIN President & COO
ROBBIE ROBBINS EVP/Sr. Graphic Artist
CHRIS RYALL Chief Creative Officer
DAVID HEDGECOCK Editor-in-Chief
LAURIE WINDROW Senior Vice President of Sales & Marketing
MATTHEW RUZICKA CPA, Chief Financial Officer
DIRK WOOD VP of Marketing
LORELEI BUNJES VP of Digital Services
JEFF WEBBER VP of Licensing, Digital and Subsidiary Rights
JERRY BENNINGTON VP of New Product Development

### DC COMICS
BOB HARRAS Senior VP - Editor-in-Chief, DC Comics
DIANE NELSON President
DAN DiDIO Publisher
JIM LEE Publisher
GEOFF JOHNS President & Chief Creative Officer
AMIT DESAI Executive VP - Business & Marketing Strategy, Direct to Consumer & Global Franchise Management
SAM ADES Senior VP - Direct to Consumer
BOBBIE CHASE VP - Talent Development
MARK CHIARELLO Senior VP - Art, Design & Collected Editions
JOHN CUNNINGHAM Senior VP - Sales & Trade Marketing
ANNE DePIES Senior VP - Business Strategy, Finance & Administration
DON FALLETTI VP - Manufacturing Operations
LAWRENCE GANEM VP - Editorial Administration & Talent Relations
ALISON GILL Senior VP - Manufacturing & Operations
HANK KANALZ Senior VP - Editorial Strategy & Administration
JAY KOGAN VP - Legal Affairs
THOMAS LOFTUS VP - Business Affairs
JACK MAHAN VP - Business Affairs
NICK J. NAPOLITANO VP - Manufacturing Administration
EDDIE SCANNELL VP - Consumer Marketing
COURTNEY SIMMONS Senior VP - Publicity & Communications
JIM (SKI) SOKOLOWSKI VP - Comic Book Specialty Sales & Trade Marketing
NANCY SPEARS VP - Mass, Book, Digital Sales & Trade Marketing

# LOVE IS LOVE

## INTRODUCTION
### BY PATTY JENKINS

When I first heard about the shooting in Orlando, I was struck with the deep sense of devastation shared by so many. For something so awful to happen in a place of celebration and acceptance made that all the worse. And in my case, my own familiarity with the warm and loving acceptance I had witnessed in the Orlando LGBT community made it painful to imagine.

In 2003 I wrote and directed the film *Monster* about Aileen Wuornos, the female serial killer who'd made headlines for killing seven men in the state of Florida. I had watched Aileen's story unfold like some awful Greek tragedy thirteen years earlier, when she was apprehended for murdering a series of her johns while working as a highway prostitute. When her story broke, she made headlines as the "man-hating lesbian who killed for the thrill of it" and was thrown into the pantheon of famous and perverted serial killers without a second thought. But that was not what I saw.

As I started to read more about Aileen Wuornos, what I learned about her horrified me. Here was a woman who had been prostituting herself on the street as her only means of survival since the age of 9. Who left a trail of hospital records documenting a lifetime of rape and abuse from every avenue she turned toward for help and survival, including her own grandfather and family. Who had carried a gun for 20-plus years before she ever used it, despite having been shot, beaten, and raped during that time. And who kept trying to explain that the first person she killed was in self-defense after he raped and attacked her (this information was never even presented at her trial, despite her first victim being a serial rapist who had just been released from prison for aggravated rape). To me, all of this painted quite a different portrait than "man-hating lesbian who killed for thrills," but no amount of clarification seemed to bring the world around to considering her as anything more.

Thirteen years later, I ended up making a film about her—not because

I wanted to apologize for what she had done or dismiss its gravity, but because I could not accept the lack of compassion and understanding that was being applied to this incredibly tragic case of damage and destruction. Aileen had clearly crossed a line and finally turned into exactly the same kind of victimizer that had created her; I wanted to state that clearly, and did so with the title *Monster*. Here is one. Let's come in and see. But if only she had found more compassion in the world, if only our world could have looked a little more deeply at her story a little sooner, maybe this could have been avoided.

The reason the Orlando shooting was so painfully reminiscent of all of this was twofold. First, after a lifetime of pain and rejection, the Orlando and Central Florida LGBT community was one of the first and only communities to ever finally embrace Aileen and give her shelter from her lonely existence, and would be one of the only she ever experienced in her entire life. Second, because it appears more clear all the time that the perpetrator of the Pulse shooting was himself struggling with his own sexuality and the same kind of homophobia, xenophobia, and cycle of violence that created Aileen Wuornos. Everything about that circle of pain hurts my heart.

Unfortunately for all the victims and victors in both of these stories, no one was able to escape the damage that a world without compassion and acceptance creates. But what all of the artists in this book have done, and what I so believe in, is try to turn these moments of darkness into some glimmer of light by expressing them through art that finally brings them the compassion they deserve.

When I first saw the beautiful pages in this book, I was moved beyond words to see so many personal and specific sentiments expressed with so much compassion. The story I read on the news reflected hate, but its result is reflected back in this book, and comes out only as love. I hope you enjoy these pieces of art as much as I did. And here is to continuing the tradition of turning darkness into light through art.

PATTY JENKINS

*Patty Jenkins is an acclaimed film and television director whose credits include* Monster, *the pilot for* The Killing, *and the forthcoming* Wonder Woman.

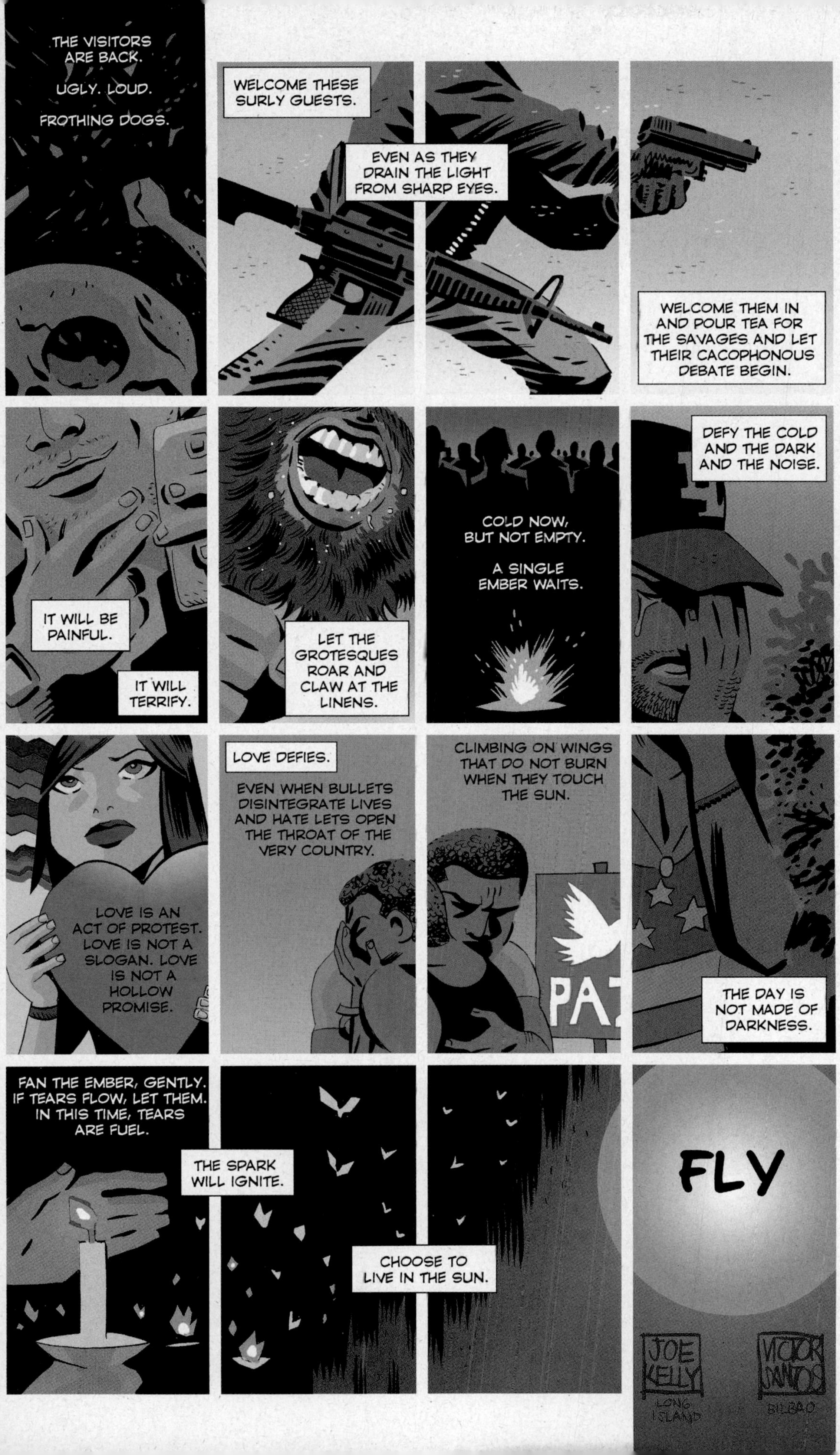
THE VISITORS ARE BACK.
UGLY. LOUD.
FROTHING DOGS.
WELCOME THESE SURLY GUESTS.
EVEN AS THEY DRAIN THE LIGHT FROM SHARP EYES.
WELCOME THEM IN AND POUR TEA FOR THE SAVAGES AND LET THEIR CACOPHONOUS DEBATE BEGIN.
IT WILL BE PAINFUL.
IT WILL TERRIFY.
LET THE GROTESQUES ROAR AND CLAW AT THE LINENS.
COLD NOW, BUT NOT EMPTY.
A SINGLE EMBER WAITS.
DEFY THE COLD AND THE DARK AND THE NOISE.
LOVE IS AN ACT OF PROTEST. LOVE IS NOT A SLOGAN. LOVE IS NOT A HOLLOW PROMISE.
LOVE DEFIES.
EVEN WHEN BULLETS DISINTEGRATE LIVES AND HATE LETS OPEN THE THROAT OF THE VERY COUNTRY.
CLIMBING ON WINGS THAT DO NOT BURN WHEN THEY TOUCH THE SUN.
PAZ
THE DAY IS NOT MADE OF DARKNESS.
FAN THE EMBER, GENTLY. IF TEARS FLOW, LET THEM. IN THIS TIME, TEARS ARE FUEL.
THE SPARK WILL IGNITE.
CHOOSE TO LIVE IN THE SUN.
FLY
JOE KELLY
LONG ISLAND
VICTOR SANTOS
BILBAO

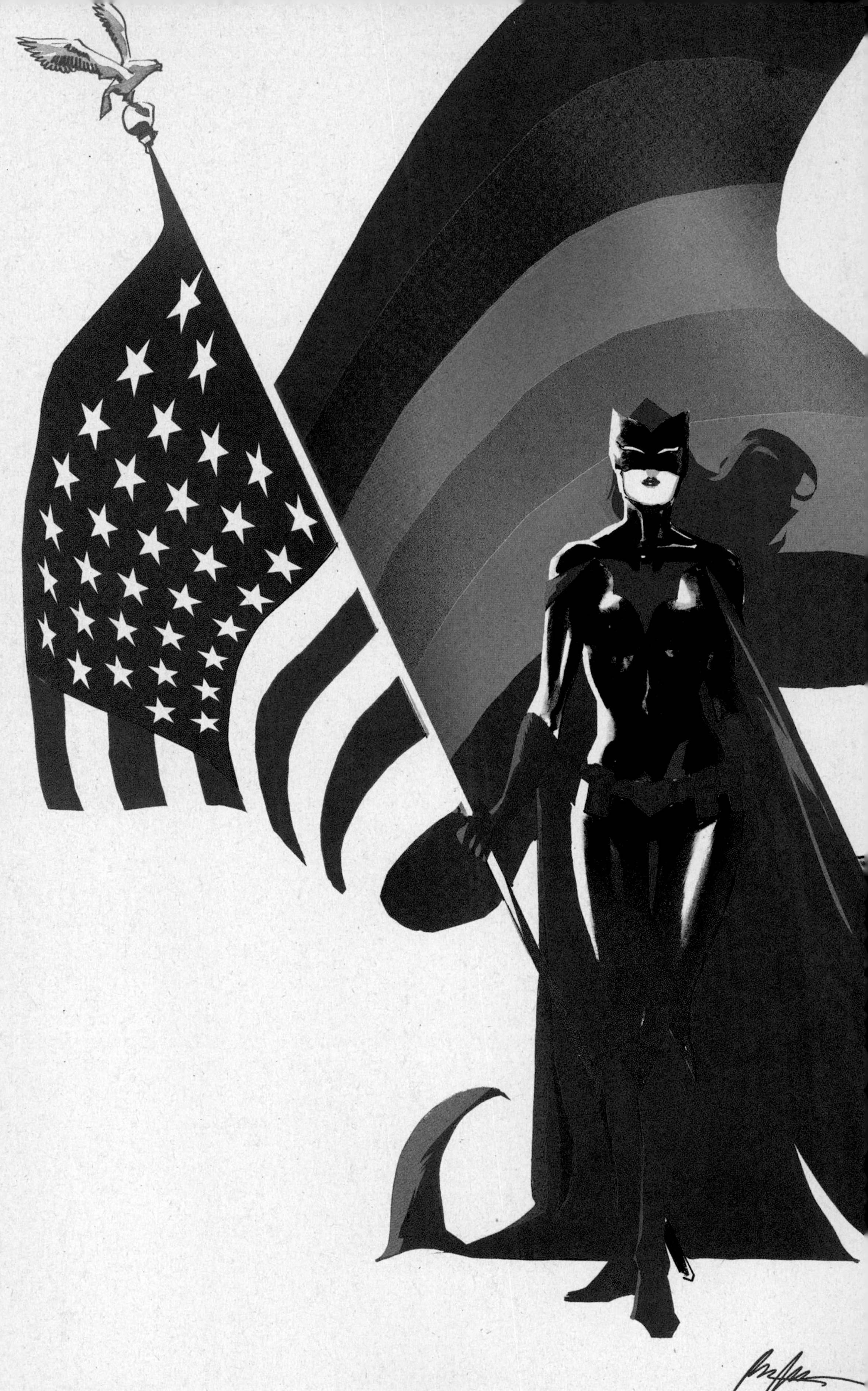

Art by Rafael Albuquerque

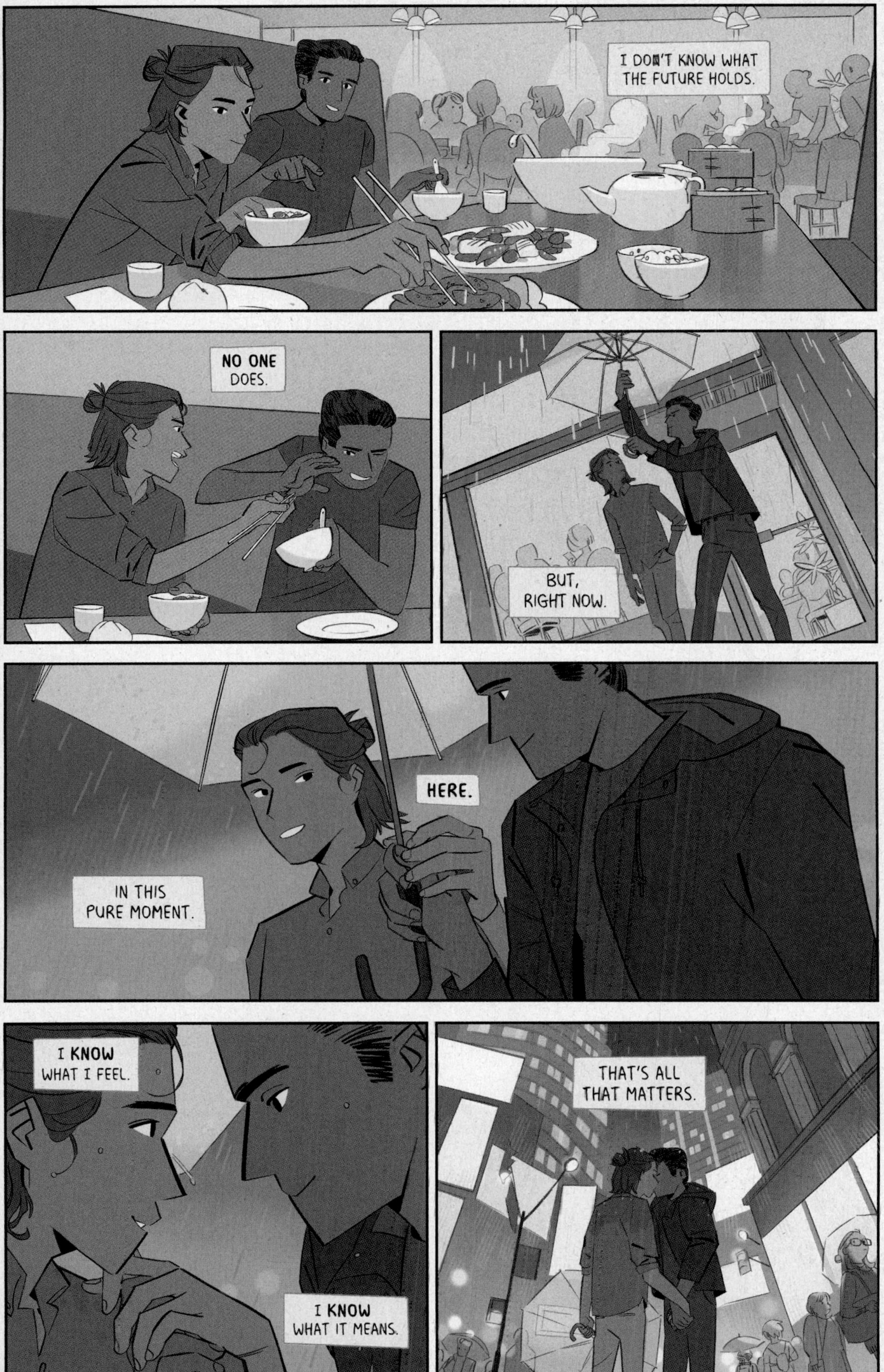
I DON'T KNOW WHAT THE FUTURE HOLDS.
NO ONE DOES.
BUT, RIGHT NOW.
HERE.
IN THIS PURE MOMENT.
I KNOW WHAT I FEEL.
I KNOW WHAT IT MEANS.
THAT'S ALL THAT MATTERS.

Written & lettered by Jim Zub • Art by Vivian Ng

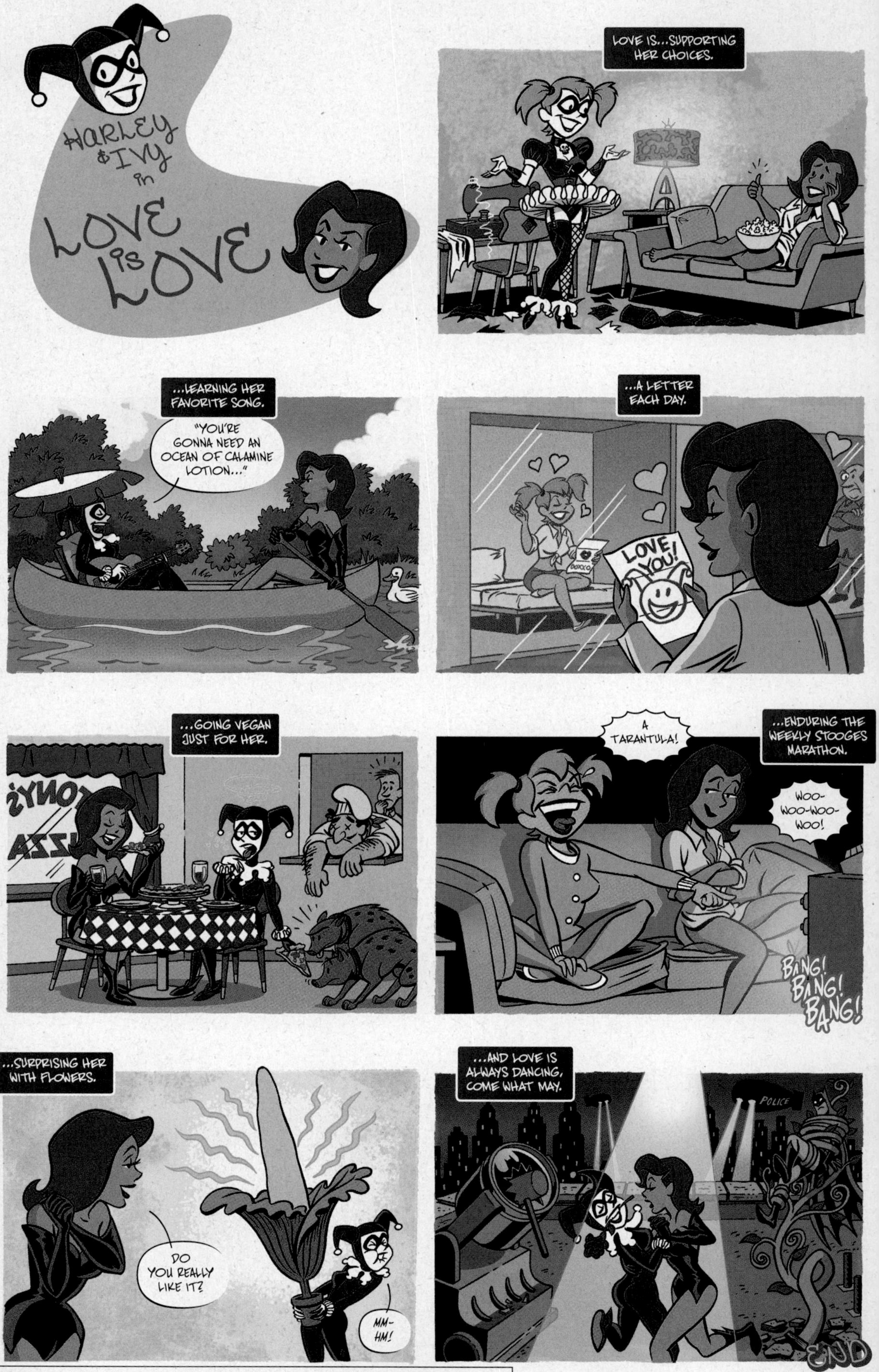
HARLEY & IVY in
LOVE is LOVE
LOVE IS...SUPPORTING HER CHOICES.
...LEARNING HER FAVORITE SONG.
"YOU'RE GONNA NEED AN OCEAN OF CALAMINE LOTION..."
...A LETTER EACH DAY.
LOVE YOU!
...GOING VEGAN JUST FOR HER.
...ENDURING THE WEEKLY STOOGES MARATHON.
A TARANTULA!
WOO-WOO-WOO-WOO!
BANG! BANG! BANG!
...SURPRISING HER WITH FLOWERS.
DO YOU REALLY LIKE IT?
MM-HM!
...AND LOVE IS ALWAYS DANCING, COME WHAT MAY.
POLICE
END

Written by Paul Dini • Illustrated by Bill Morrison • Colored by Robert Stanley • Lettered by Sal Cipriano

MY DAUGHTER IS OBSESSED WITH SPACE. WELL, TECHNICALLY, SPACE AND POKEMON. BUT, SHE READS BOOKS ABOUT MARS AND JUPITER, ABOUT BLACK HOLES, AND ABOUT THE SCIENCE OF THE STARS. WHEN WE TALK ABOUT IT, WE TALK ABOUT HOW GREAT MANKIND CAN BE. HOW COMPASSION AND TEAMWORK CAN ACHIEVE MORE THAN FEAR AND CLOSED-MINDEDNESS. WE'VE STOOD IN MISSION CONTROL AT THE JET PROPULSION LAB, AND SEEN THE PROFOUNDNESS OF OUR KNOWLEDGE, AND THE VASTNESS OF OUR MYSTERIES. WE TALK ABOUT ALL OF THESE THINGS WITH EASE AND JOY.

THEN THERE WAS THAT MORNING. WE'D GONE TO IOWA FOR MY NIECE'S BAT MITZVAH, AND EARLY IN THE MORNING, MY WIFE AND I WATCHED THE NEWS, TEARS STREAMING DOWN OUR FACES. THE HORROR OF IGNORANCE AND FEAR. AND SHE CAME INTO THE ROOM AND SAW US CRYING AND ASKED WHAT WAS WRONG. WE TRIED, FEEBLY, TO EXPLAIN WHAT HAPPENED, THAT A MAN TOOK GUNS INTO A NIGHTCLUB AND KILLED PEOPLE. WHY? SHE ASKED. BECAUSE THEY WERE DIFFERENT FROM HIM. SHE FURROWED HER BROW AND STARED AT US, DUMBFOUNDED. BUT, BEING DIFFERENT IS WHAT MAKES US SPECIAL, SHE SAID. AND WE TOLD HER THAT NOT EVERYBODY THOUGHT THAT.

SHE SAT ON THE BED AND WATCHED WITH US FOR A FEW MINUTES AND THEN POINTED OUT THE PEOPLE HELPING. THE PARAMEDICS. THE POLICE. THE FIREMEN. SHE FACED US, THE TEARS IN OUR EYES, AND SHE SAID THAT IT WOULD BE OKAY, BECAUSE THERE'S PROBABLY MORE PEOPLE WHO CARED, THAN PEOPLE WHO HATED. NORMALLY, I'D SAY I WISH SHE WAS RIGHT. BUT, THE LOOK IN HER EYES, THE HOPE IN HER HEART, MAYBE, JUST MAYBE, SHE SIMPLY IS RIGHT.

Written by Joshua Hale Fialkov • Art and lettering by Gabriel Bautista

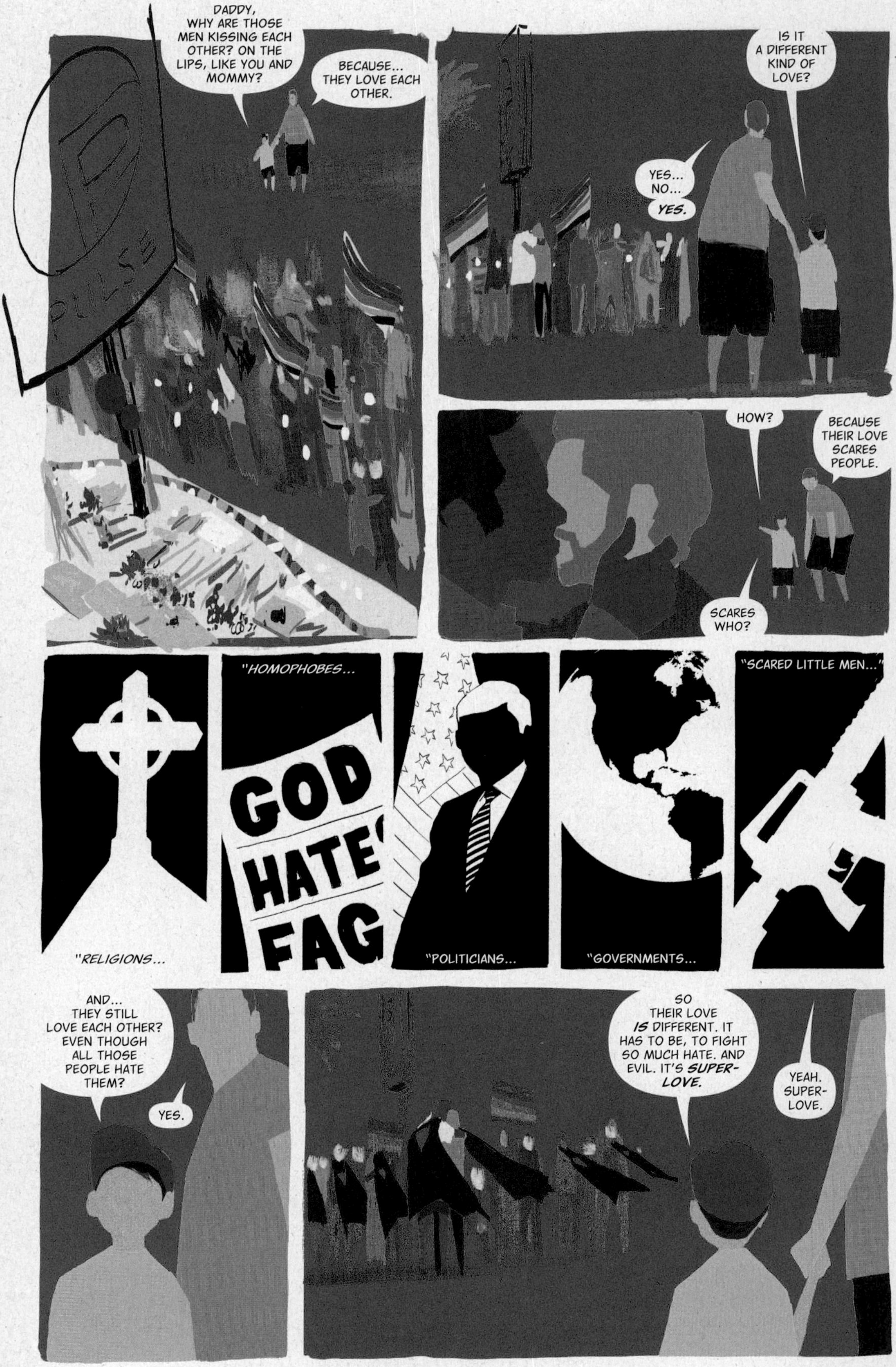
DADDY, WHY ARE THOSE MEN KISSING EACH OTHER? ON THE LIPS, LIKE YOU AND MOMMY?
BECAUSE... THEY LOVE EACH OTHER.
PULSE
IS IT A DIFFERENT KIND OF LOVE?
YES... NO... *YES.*
HOW?
BECAUSE THEIR LOVE SCARES PEOPLE.
SCARES WHO?
"RELIGIONS...
"HOMOPHOBES...
GOD HATES FAG
"POLITICIANS...
"GOVERNMENTS...
"SCARED LITTLE MEN..."
AND... THEY STILL LOVE EACH OTHER? EVEN THOUGH ALL THOSE PEOPLE HATE THEM?
YES.
SO THEIR LOVE *IS* DIFFERENT. IT HAS TO BE, TO FIGHT SO MUCH HATE. AND EVIL. IT'S *SUPER-LOVE.*
YEAH. SUPER-LOVE.

WORDS BY
TEDDY TENENBAUM

ART BY
MIKE HUDDLESTON

LETTERS BY
COREY BREEN

Judd Winick 6/12/16

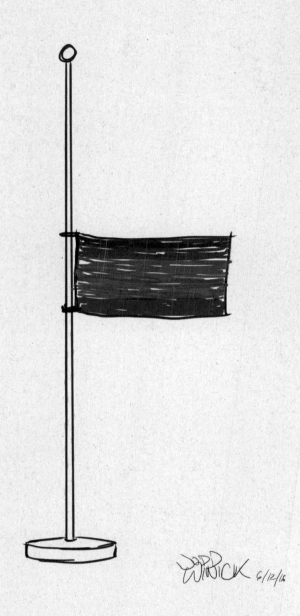

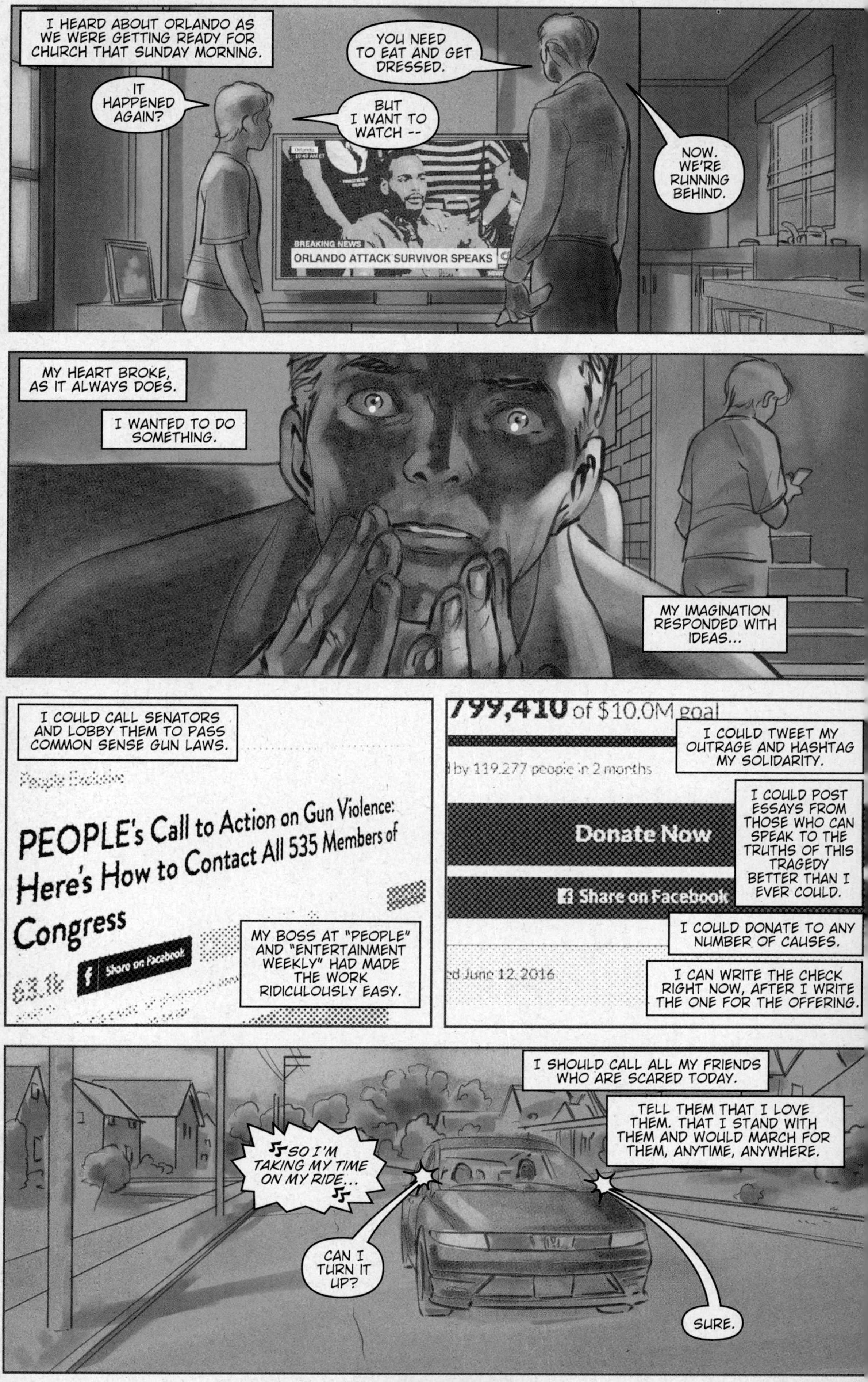
I HEARD ABOUT ORLANDO AS WE WERE GETTING READY FOR CHURCH THAT SUNDAY MORNING.
IT HAPPENED AGAIN?
YOU NEED TO EAT AND GET DRESSED.
BUT I WANT TO WATCH --
BREAKING NEWS
ORLANDO ATTACK SURVIVOR SPEAKS
NOW. WE'RE RUNNING BEHIND.
MY HEART BROKE, AS IT ALWAYS DOES.
I WANTED TO DO SOMETHING.
MY IMAGINATION RESPONDED WITH IDEAS...
I COULD CALL SENATORS AND LOBBY THEM TO PASS COMMON SENSE GUN LAWS.
PEOPLE's Call to Action on Gun Violence: Here's How to Contact All 535 Members of Congress
Share on Facebook
63.1k
MY BOSS AT "PEOPLE" AND "ENTERTAINMENT WEEKLY" HAD MADE THE WORK RIDICULOUSLY EASY.
799,410 of $10.0M goal
I COULD TWEET MY OUTRAGE AND HASHTAG MY SOLIDARITY.
by 119,277 people in 2 months
I COULD POST ESSAYS FROM THOSE WHO CAN SPEAK TO THE TRUTHS OF THIS TRAGEDY BETTER THAN I EVER COULD.
Donate Now
Share on Facebook
I COULD DONATE TO ANY NUMBER OF CAUSES.
ed June 12, 2016
I CAN WRITE THE CHECK RIGHT NOW, AFTER I WRITE THE ONE FOR THE OFFERING.
I SHOULD CALL ALL MY FRIENDS WHO ARE SCARED TODAY.
TELL THEM THAT I LOVE THEM. THAT I STAND WITH THEM AND WOULD MARCH FOR THEM, ANYTIME, ANYWHERE.
SO I'M TAKING MY TIME ON MY RIDE...
CAN I TURN IT UP?
SURE.

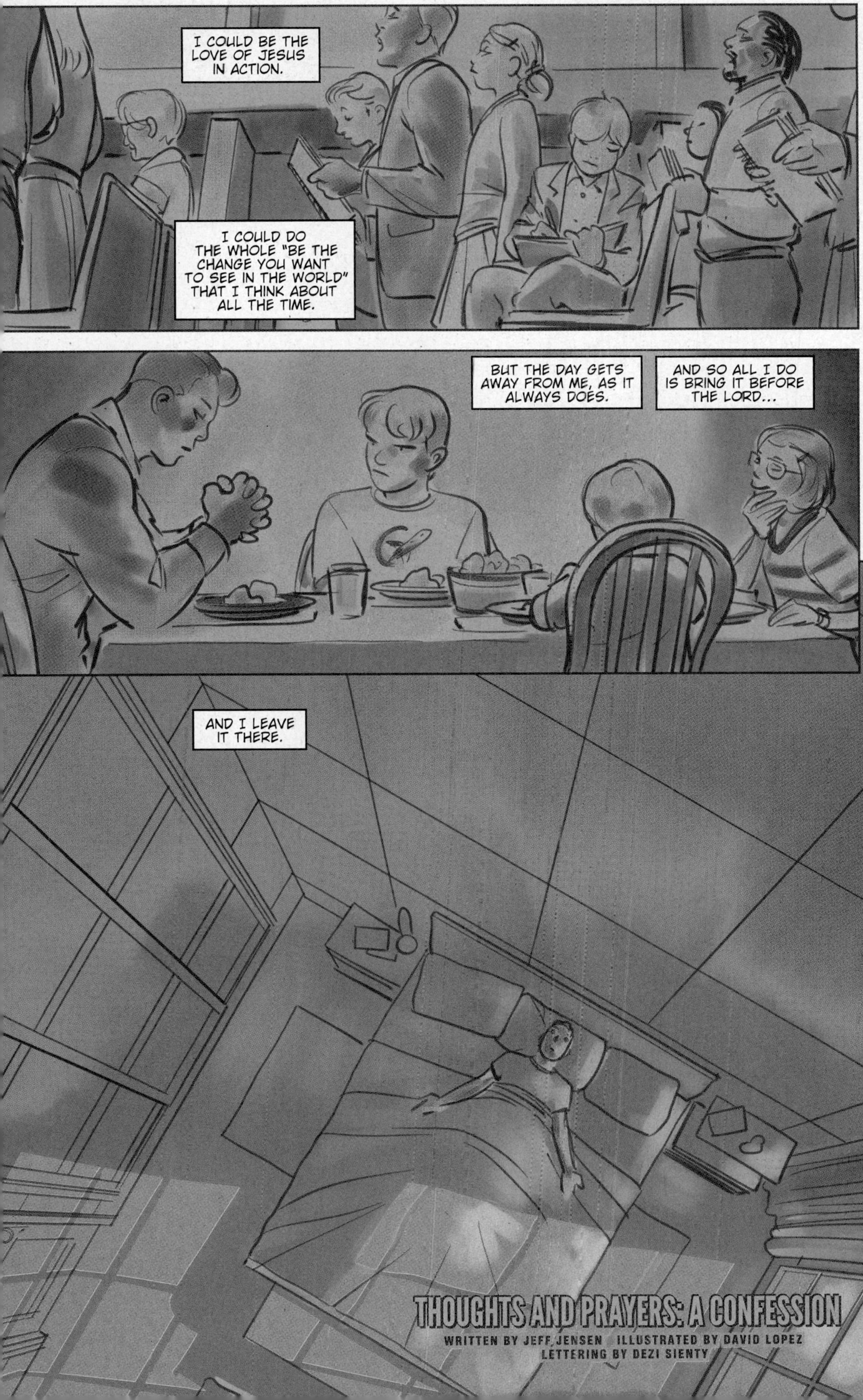

I COULD BE THE LOVE OF JESUS IN ACTION.
I COULD DO THE WHOLE "BE THE CHANGE YOU WANT TO SEE IN THE WORLD" THAT I THINK ABOUT ALL THE TIME.
BUT THE DAY GETS AWAY FROM ME, AS IT ALWAYS DOES.
AND SO ALL I DO IS BRING IT BEFORE THE LORD...
AND I LEAVE IT THERE.
THOUGHTS AND PRAYERS: A CONFESSION
WRITTEN BY JEFF JENSEN ILLUSTRATED BY DAVID LOPEZ
LETTERING BY DEZI SIENTY

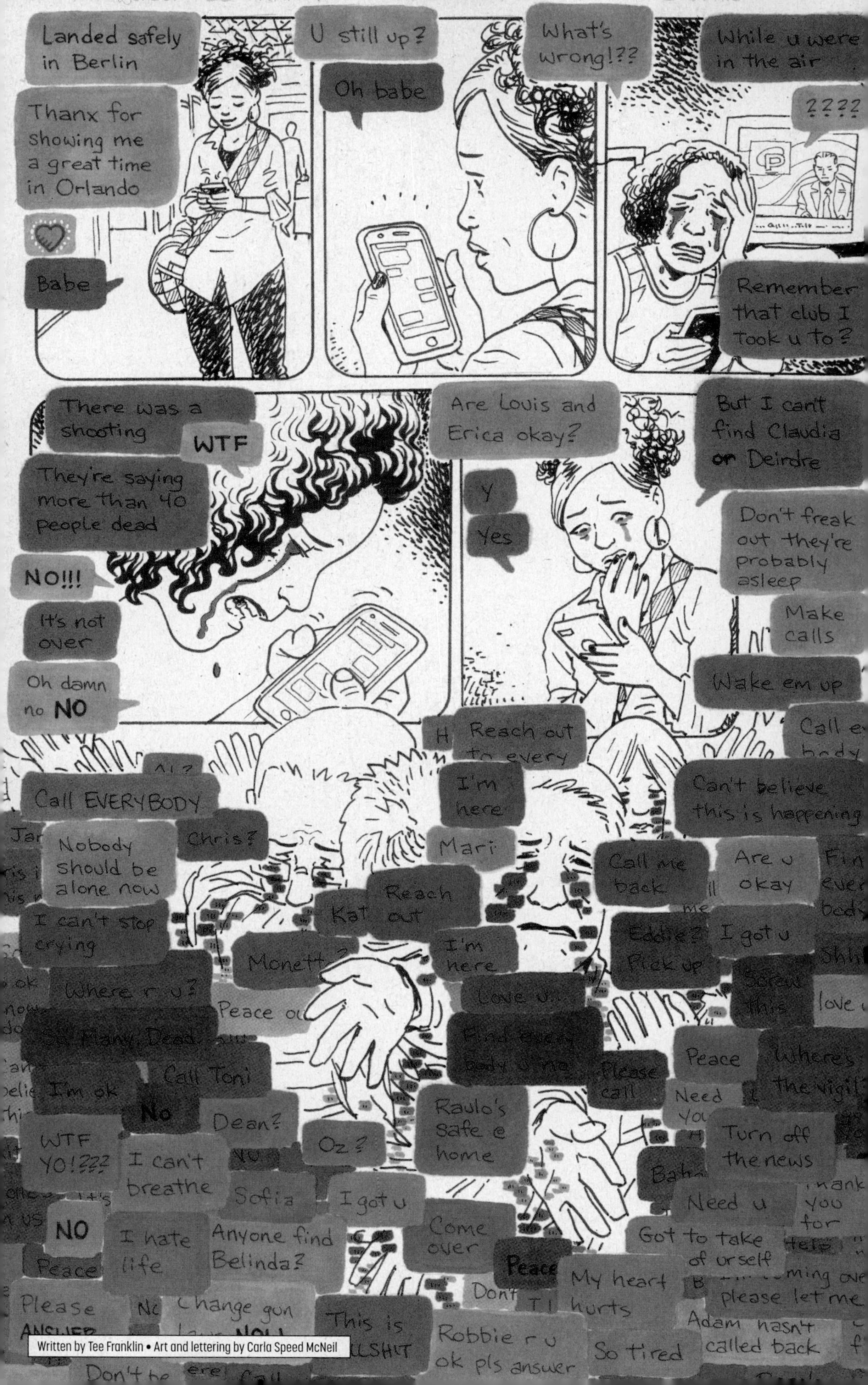
Landed safely in Berlin
Thanx for showing me a great time in Orlando
Babe
U still up?
Oh babe
What's wrong!??
While u were in the air
????
Remember that club I took u to?
There was a shooting
WTF
They're saying more than 40 people dead
NO!!!
It's not over
Oh damn no NO
Are Louis and Erica okay?
Y
Yes
But I can't find Claudia or Deirdre
Don't freak out they're probably asleep
Make calls
Wake em up
Call EVERYBODY
I'm here
Can't believe this is happening
Nobody should be alone now
Chris?
Mari
Call me back
Are u okay
I can't stop crying
Reach out
Eddie? Pick up
I got u
Monett?
I'm here
Where r u?
Peace out
Love u
So Many Dead
Peace
Call Toni
Please call
I'm ok
No
Dean?
Raulo's safe @ home
Turn off the news
WTF YO!???
I can't breathe
Oz?
Sofia
I got u
Need u
Got to take of urself
NO
I hate life
Anyone find Belinda?
Come over
Peace
Peace
My heart hurts
please let me
Please
Change gun
This is
Robbie r u ok pls answer
So tired
Adam hasn't called back

Written by Tee Franklin • Art and lettering by Carla Speed McNeil

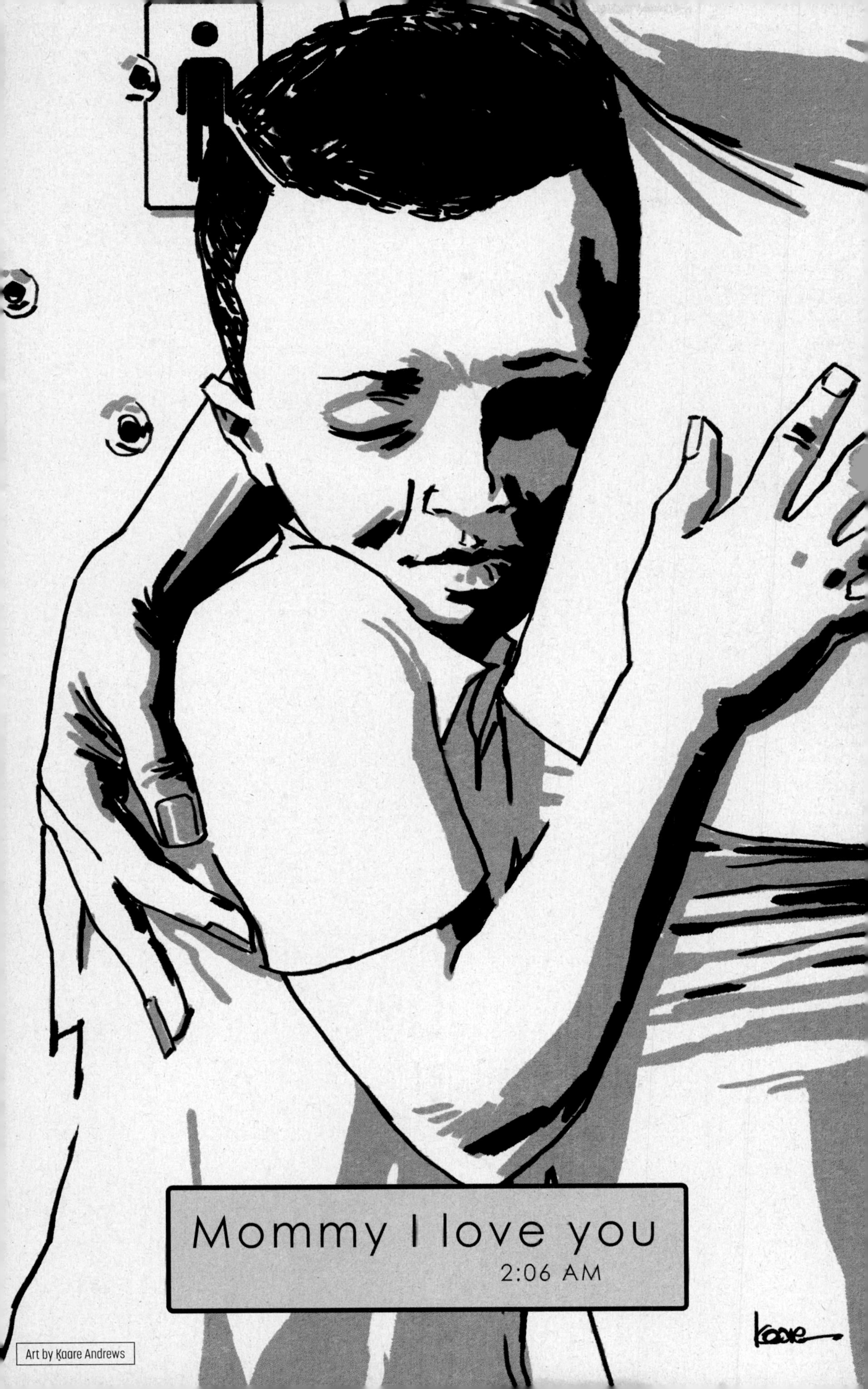
Mommy I love you
2:06 AM
kaare

Art by Kaare Andrews

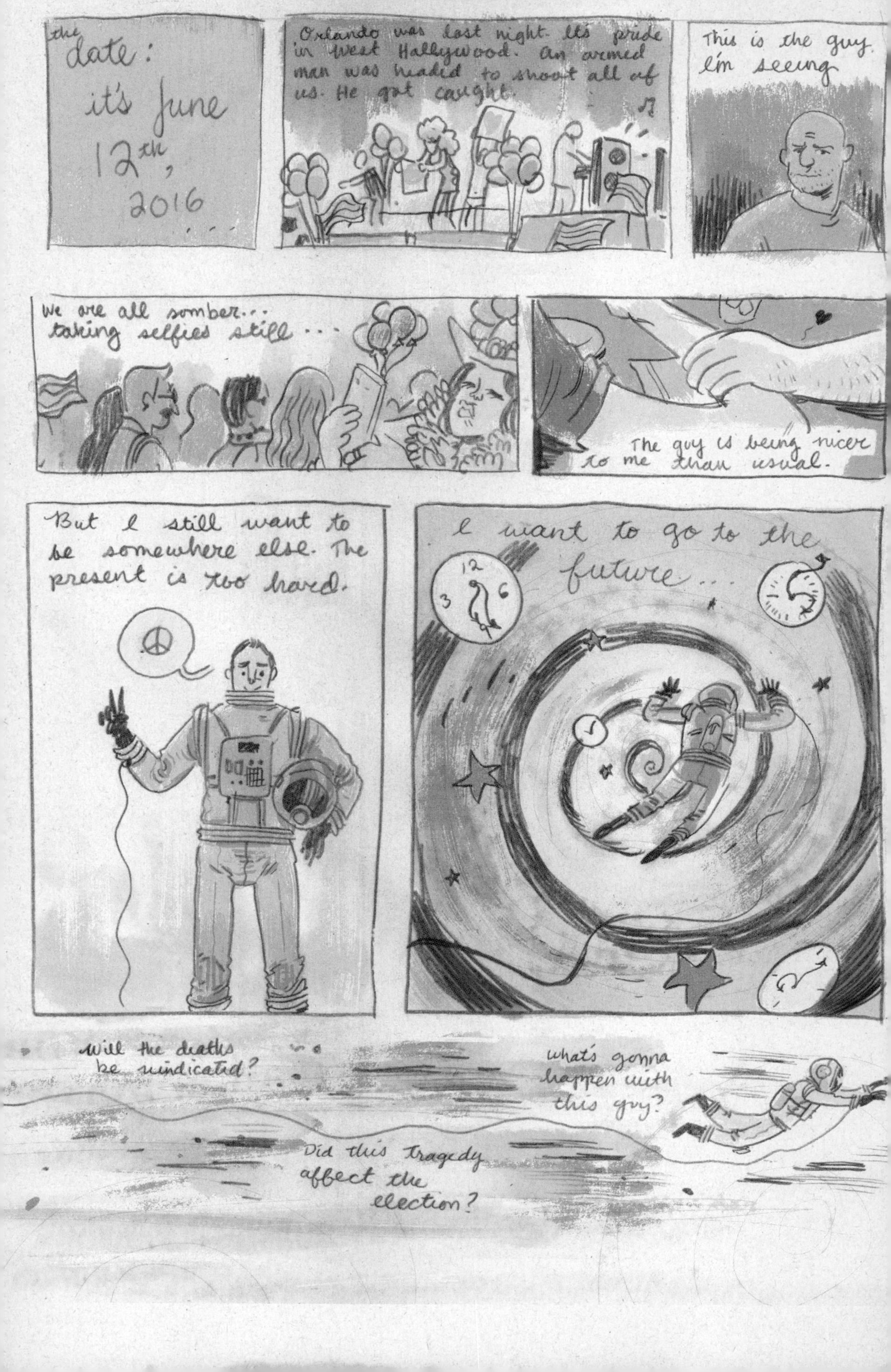
the date: it's June 12th, 2016 . . .
Orlando was last night. It's pride in West Hollywood. An armed man was headed to shoot all of us. He got caught.
This is the guy I'm seeing
We are all somber... taking selfies still...
The guy is being nicer to me than usual.
But I still want to be somewhere else. The present is too hard.
I want to go to the future...
Will the deaths be vindicated?
What's gonna happen with this guy?
Did this tragedy affect the election?

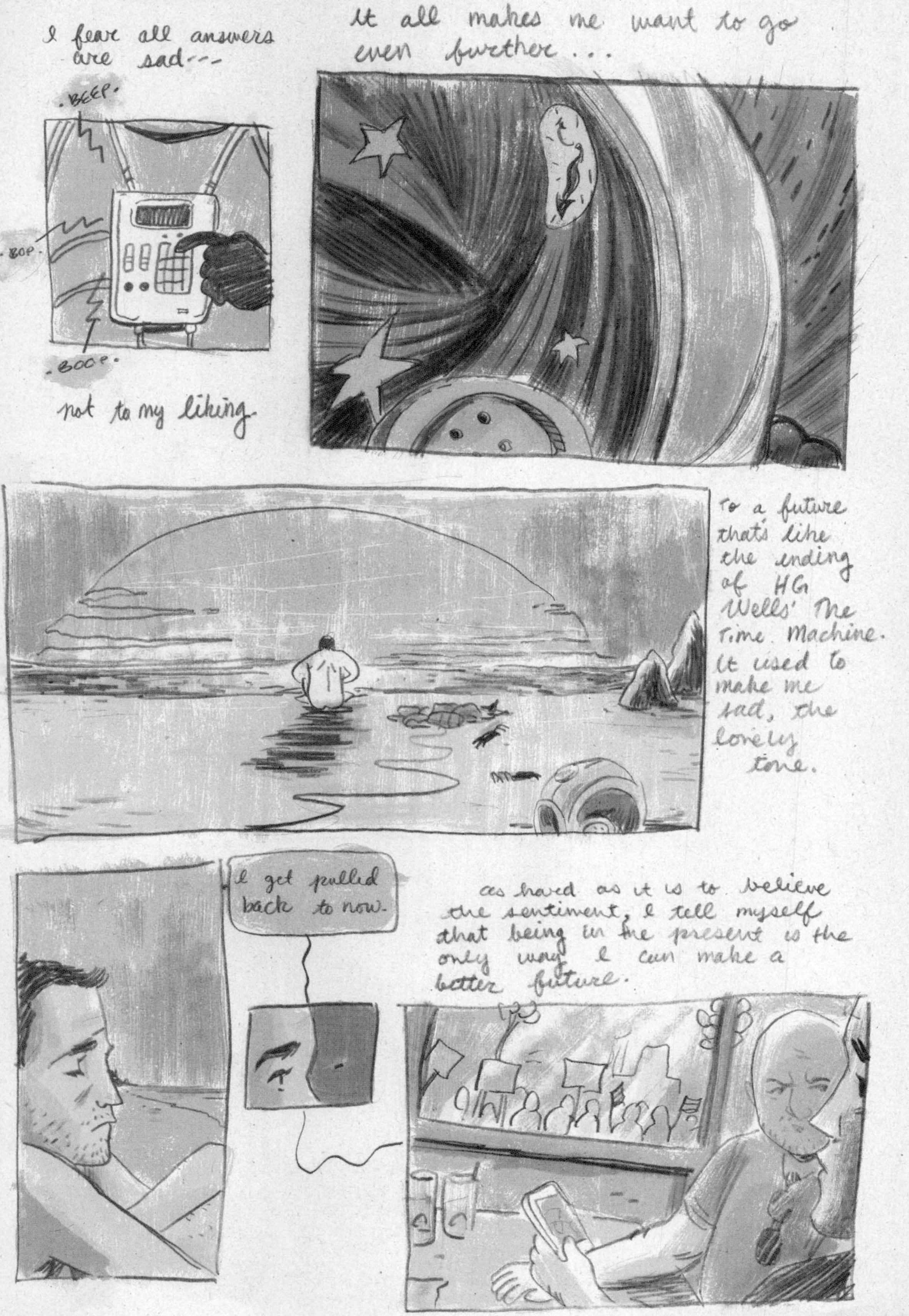
I fear all answers are sad---
BEEP
BOP
BOOP
not to my liking.
It all makes me want to go even further...
To a future that's like the ending of HG Wells' The Time Machine. It used to make me sad, the lonely tone.
I get pulled back to now.
as hard as it is to believe the sentiment, I tell myself that being in the present is the only way I can make a better future.

Writing, art, and lettering by Sina Grace

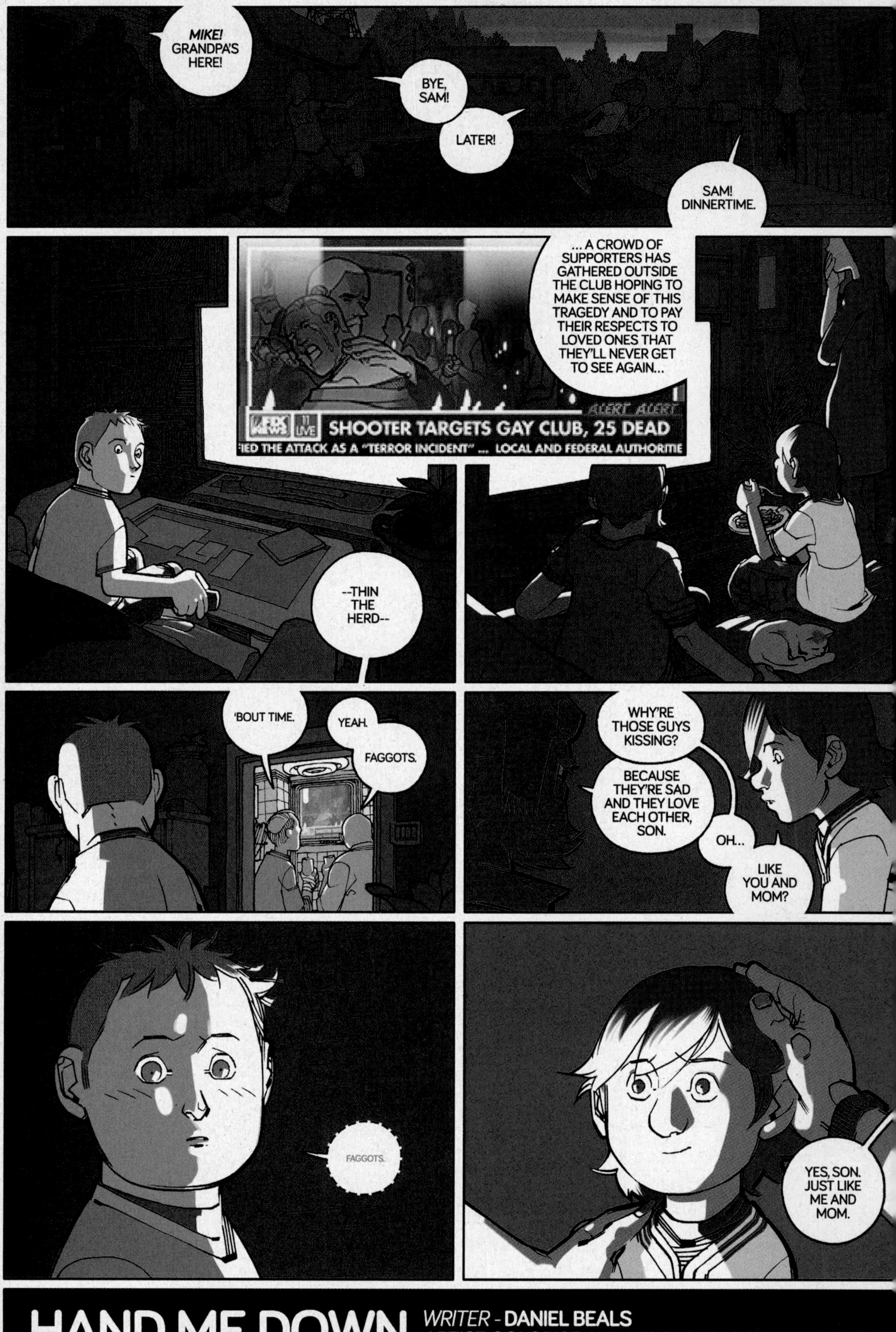
MIKE! GRANDPA'S HERE!
BYE, SAM!
LATER!
SAM! DINNERTIME.
... A CROWD OF SUPPORTERS HAS GATHERED OUTSIDE THE CLUB HOPING TO MAKE SENSE OF THIS TRAGEDY AND TO PAY THEIR RESPECTS TO LOVED ONES THAT THEY'LL NEVER GET TO SEE AGAIN...
ALERT ALERT
SHOOTER TARGETS GAY CLUB, 25 DEAD
IED THE ATTACK AS A "TERROR INCIDENT" ... LOCAL AND FEDERAL AUTHORITIE
--THIN THE HERD--
'BOUT TIME.
YEAH.
FAGGOTS.
WHY'RE THOSE GUYS KISSING?
BECAUSE THEY'RE SAD AND THEY LOVE EACH OTHER, SON.
OH...
LIKE YOU AND MOM?
FAGGOTS.
YES, SON. JUST LIKE ME AND MOM.

# HAND ME DOWN

*WRITER* - **DANIEL BEALS**
*ARTIST, COLORIST AND LETTERER* - **DAVID LAFUENTE**

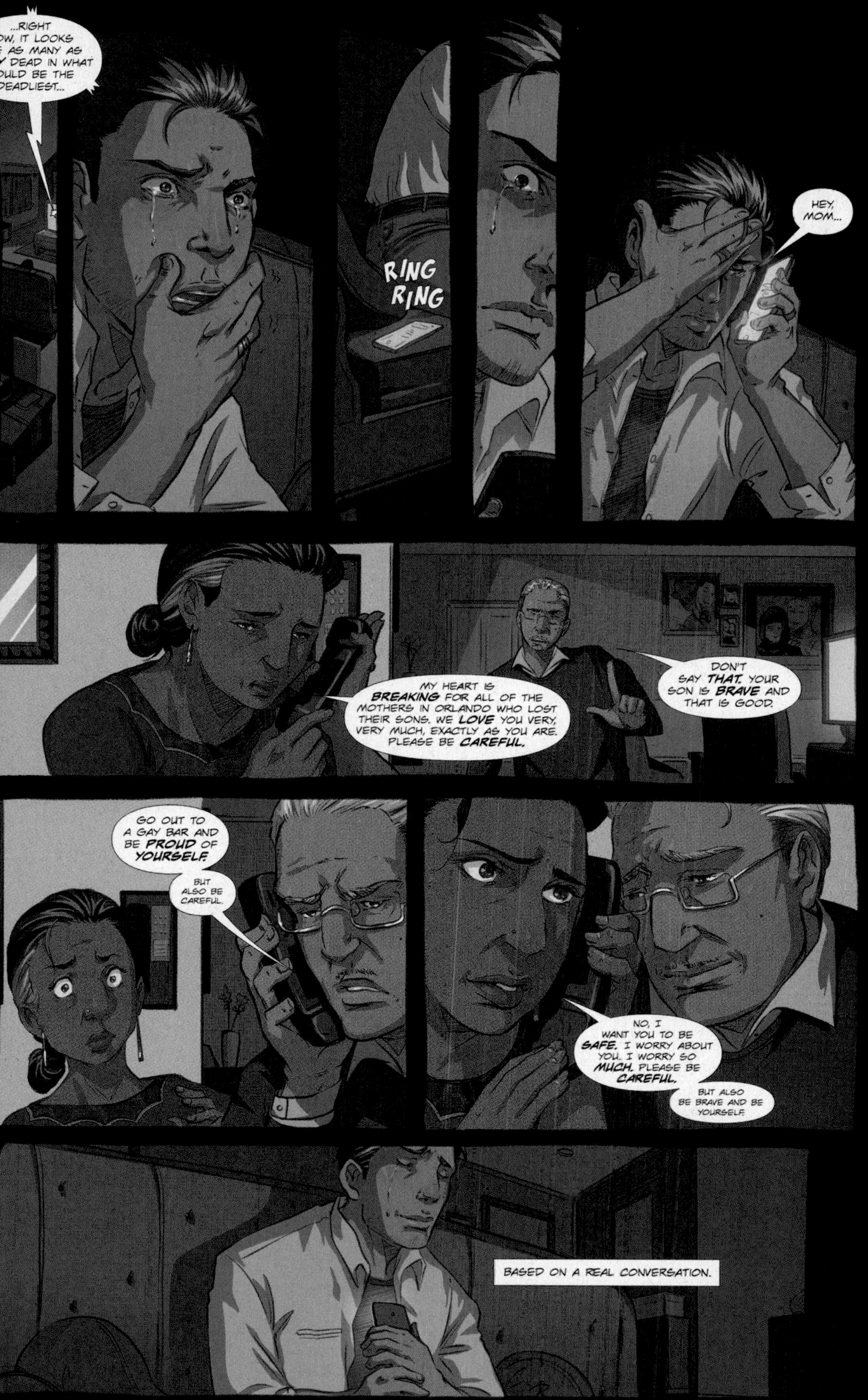
...RIGHT OW, IT LOOKS E AS MANY AS Y DEAD IN WHAT OULD BE THE DEADLIEST...
RING RING
HEY, MOM...
MY HEART IS BREAKING FOR ALL OF THE MOTHERS IN ORLANDO WHO LOST THEIR SONS. WE LOVE YOU VERY, VERY MUCH, EXACTLY AS YOU ARE. PLEASE BE CAREFUL.
DON'T SAY THAT. YOUR SON IS BRAVE AND THAT IS GOOD.
GO OUT TO A GAY BAR AND BE PROUD OF YOURSELF.
BUT ALSO BE CAREFUL.
NO, I WANT YOU TO BE SAFE. I WORRY ABOUT YOU. I WORRY SO MUCH. PLEASE BE CAREFUL.
BUT ALSO BE BRAVE AND BE YOURSELF.
BASED ON A REAL CONVERSATION.

Written by Nunzio DeFilippis & Christina Weir • Illustrated by Emma Vieceli • Colored by Christina Strain • Lettered by Neal Bailey

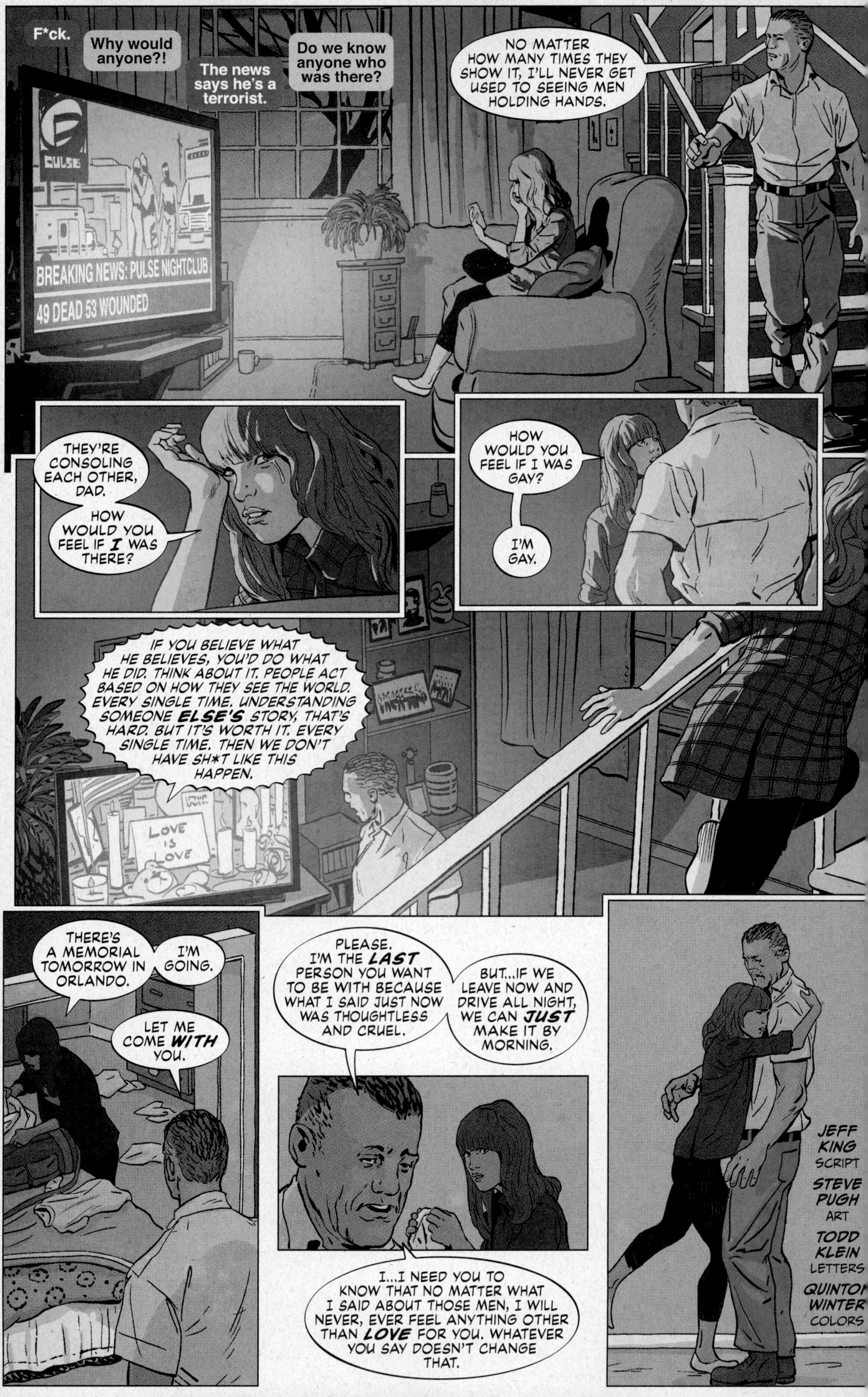
F*ck.
Why would anyone?!
The news says he's a terrorist.
Do we know anyone who was there?
NO MATTER HOW MANY TIMES THEY SHOW IT, I'LL NEVER GET USED TO SEEING MEN HOLDING HANDS.
BREAKING NEWS: PULSE NIGHTCLUB
49 DEAD 53 WOUNDED
THEY'RE CONSOLING EACH OTHER, DAD.
HOW WOULD YOU FEEL IF *I* WAS THERE?
HOW WOULD YOU FEEL IF I WAS GAY?
I'M GAY.
IF YOU BELIEVE WHAT HE BELIEVES, YOU'D DO WHAT HE DID. THINK ABOUT IT. PEOPLE ACT BASED ON HOW THEY SEE THE WORLD. EVERY SINGLE TIME. UNDERSTANDING SOMEONE **ELSE'S** STORY, THAT'S HARD. BUT IT'S WORTH IT. EVERY SINGLE TIME. THEN WE DON'T HAVE SH*T LIKE THIS HAPPEN.
LOVE IS LOVE
THERE'S A MEMORIAL TOMORROW IN ORLANDO.
I'M GOING.
LET ME COME **WITH** YOU.
PLEASE. I'M THE **LAST** PERSON YOU WANT TO BE WITH BECAUSE WHAT I SAID JUST NOW WAS THOUGHTLESS AND CRUEL.
BUT...IF WE LEAVE NOW AND DRIVE ALL NIGHT, WE CAN **JUST** MAKE IT BY MORNING.
I...I NEED YOU TO KNOW THAT NO MATTER WHAT I SAID ABOUT THOSE MEN, I WILL NEVER, EVER FEEL ANYTHING OTHER THAN **LOVE** FOR YOU. WHATEVER YOU SAY DOESN'T CHANGE THAT.
JEFF KING SCRIPT
STEVE PUGH ART
TODD KLEIN LETTERS
QUINTO WINTER COLORS

## Helpless/Not Helpless

Story: Rob Williams - Art: Mike Dowling
Letters: Corey Breen

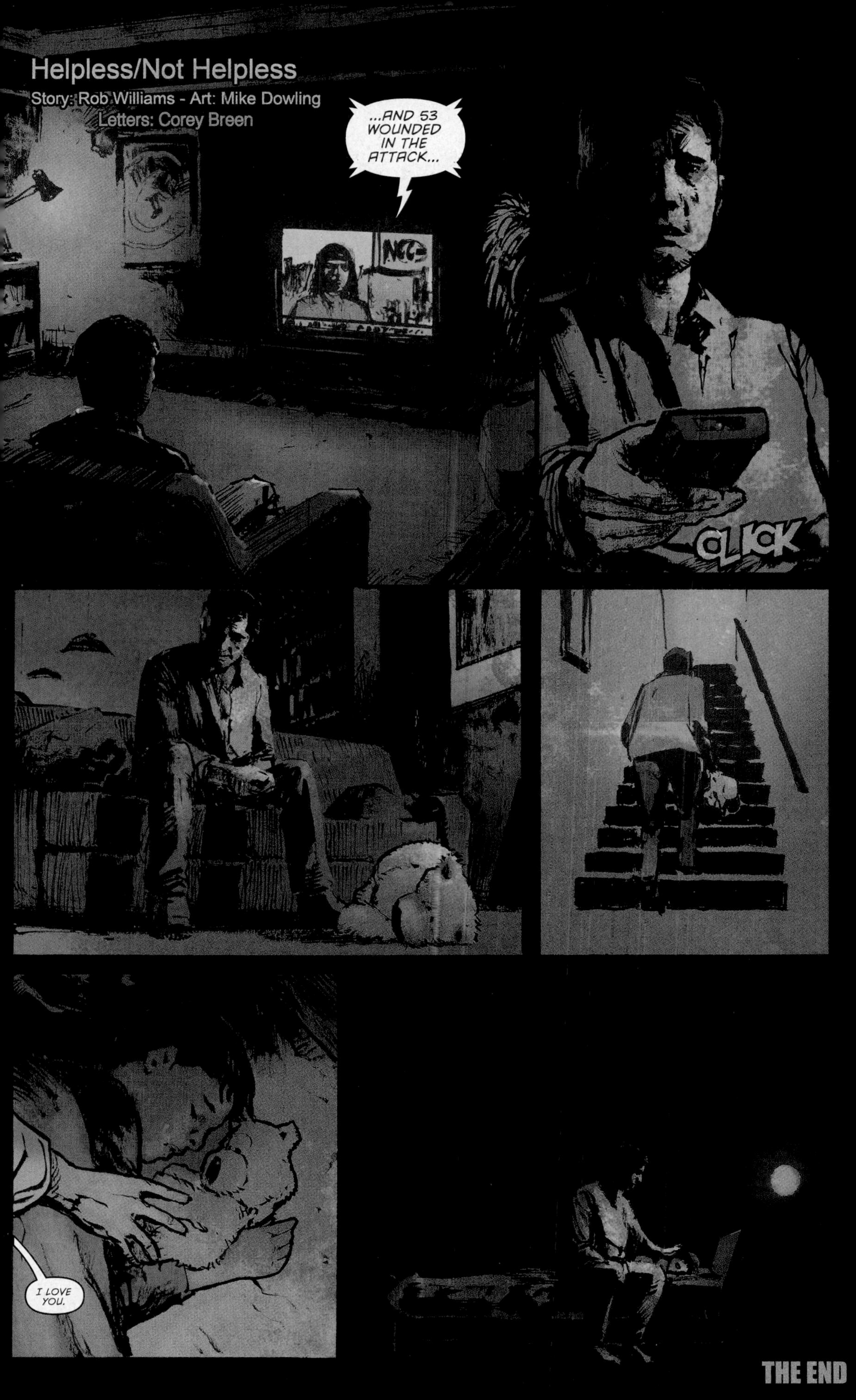
...AND 53 WOUNDED IN THE ATTACK...
CLICK
I LOVE YOU.
THE END

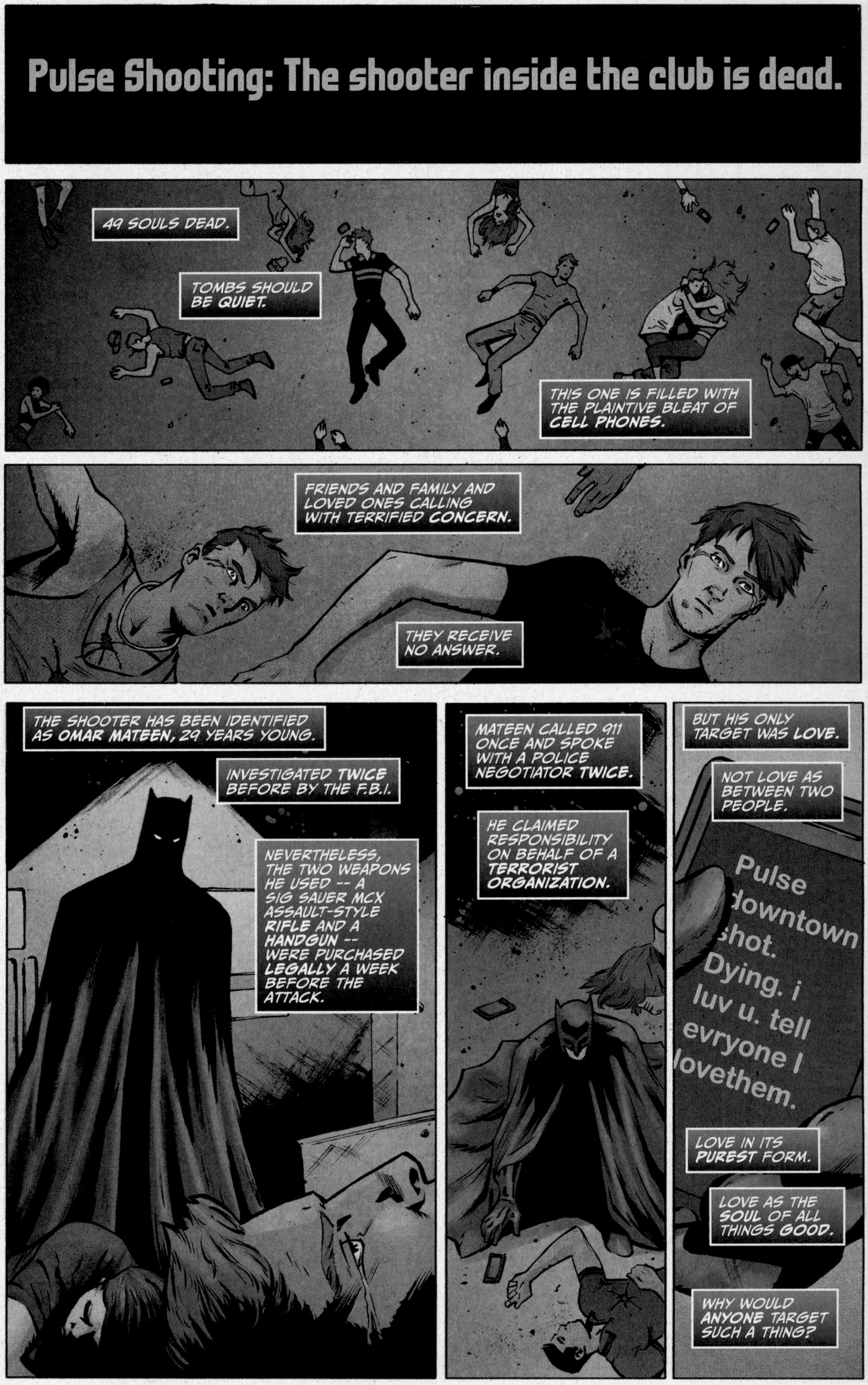
Pulse Shooting: The shooter inside the club is dead.
49 SOULS DEAD.
TOMBS SHOULD BE QUIET.
THIS ONE IS FILLED WITH THE PLAINTIVE BLEAT OF CELL PHONES.
FRIENDS AND FAMILY AND LOVED ONES CALLING WITH TERRIFIED CONCERN.
THEY RECEIVE NO ANSWER.
THE SHOOTER HAS BEEN IDENTIFIED AS OMAR MATEEN, 29 YEARS YOUNG.
INVESTIGATED TWICE BEFORE BY THE F.B.I.
NEVERTHELESS, THE TWO WEAPONS HE USED -- A SIG SAUER MCX ASSAULT-STYLE RIFLE AND A HANDGUN -- WERE PURCHASED LEGALLY A WEEK BEFORE THE ATTACK.
MATEEN CALLED 911 ONCE AND SPOKE WITH A POLICE NEGOTIATOR TWICE.
HE CLAIMED RESPONSIBILITY ON BEHALF OF A TERRORIST ORGANIZATION.
BUT HIS ONLY TARGET WAS LOVE.
NOT LOVE AS BETWEEN TWO PEOPLE.
Pulse downtown shot. Dying. i luv u. tell evryone I lovethem.
LOVE IN ITS PUREST FORM.
LOVE AS THE SOUL OF ALL THINGS GOOD.
WHY WOULD ANYONE TARGET SUCH A THING?

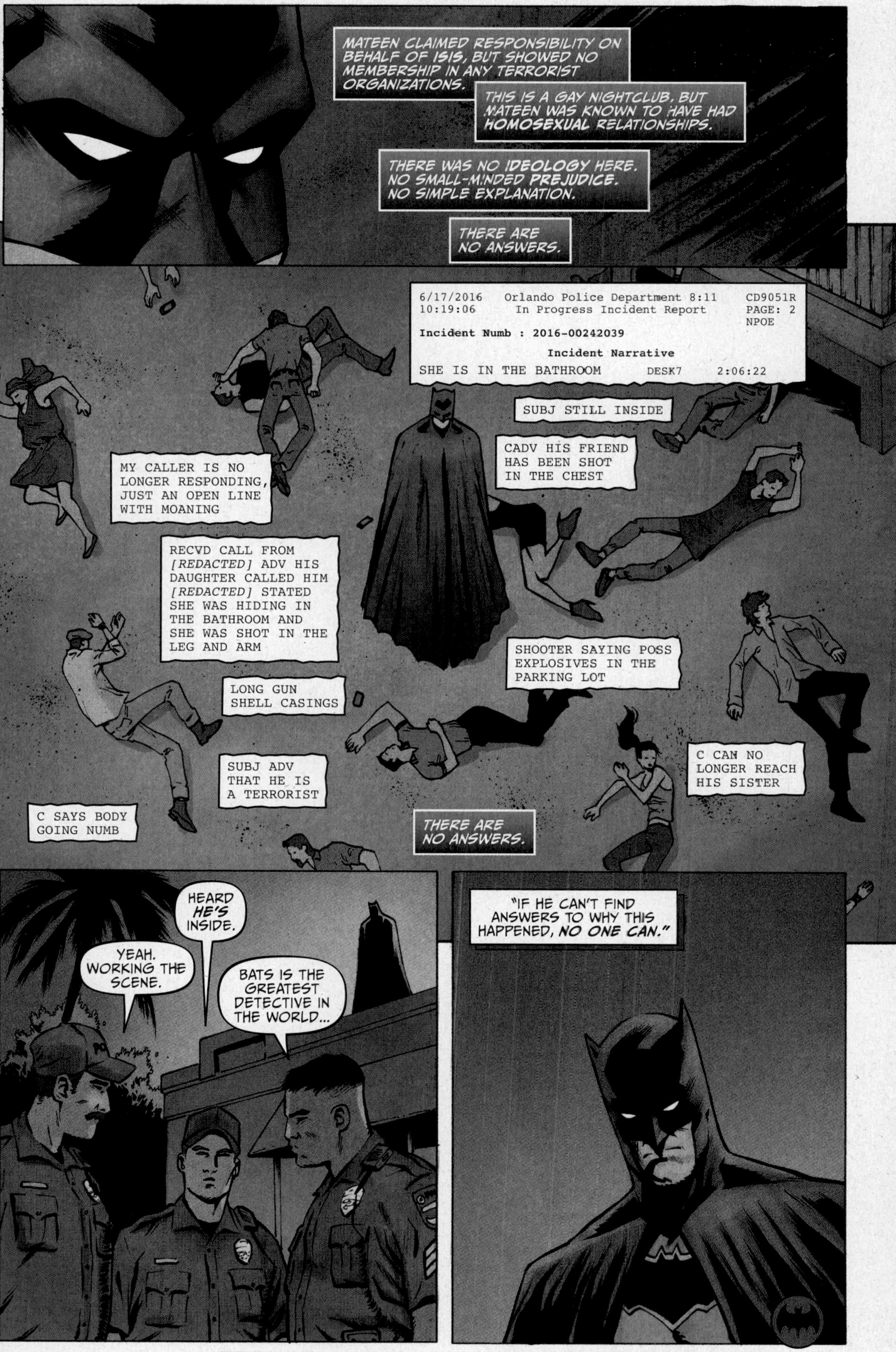
MATEEN CLAIMED RESPONSIBILITY ON BEHALF OF ISIS, BUT SHOWED NO MEMBERSHIP IN ANY TERRORIST ORGANIZATIONS.
THIS IS A GAY NIGHTCLUB, BUT MATEEN WAS KNOWN TO HAVE HAD HOMOSEXUAL RELATIONSHIPS.
THERE WAS NO IDEOLOGY HERE. NO SMALL-MINDED PREJUDICE. NO SIMPLE EXPLANATION.
THERE ARE NO ANSWERS.
6/17/2016 Orlando Police Department 8:11 CD9051R
10:19:06 In Progress Incident Report PAGE: 2
NPOE
Incident Numb : 2016-00242039
Incident Narrative
SHE IS IN THE BATHROOM DESK7 2:06:22
SUBJ STILL INSIDE
CADV HIS FRIEND HAS BEEN SHOT IN THE CHEST
MY CALLER IS NO LONGER RESPONDING, JUST AN OPEN LINE WITH MOANING
RECVD CALL FROM [REDACTED] ADV HIS DAUGHTER CALLED HIM [REDACTED] STATED SHE WAS HIDING IN THE BATHROOM AND SHE WAS SHOT IN THE LEG AND ARM
SHOOTER SAYING POSS EXPLOSIVES IN THE PARKING LOT
LONG GUN SHELL CASINGS
SUBJ ADV THAT HE IS A TERRORIST
C CAN NO LONGER REACH HIS SISTER
C SAYS BODY GOING NUMB
THERE ARE NO ANSWERS.
HEARD HE'S INSIDE.
YEAH. WORKING THE SCENE.
BATS IS THE GREATEST DETECTIVE IN THE WORLD...
"IF HE CAN'T FIND ANSWERS TO WHY THIS HAPPENED, NO ONE CAN."

Written by Marc Guggenheim • Illustrated by Brent Peeples • Colored by Chris Sotomayor • Lettered by Comicraft's John Roshell

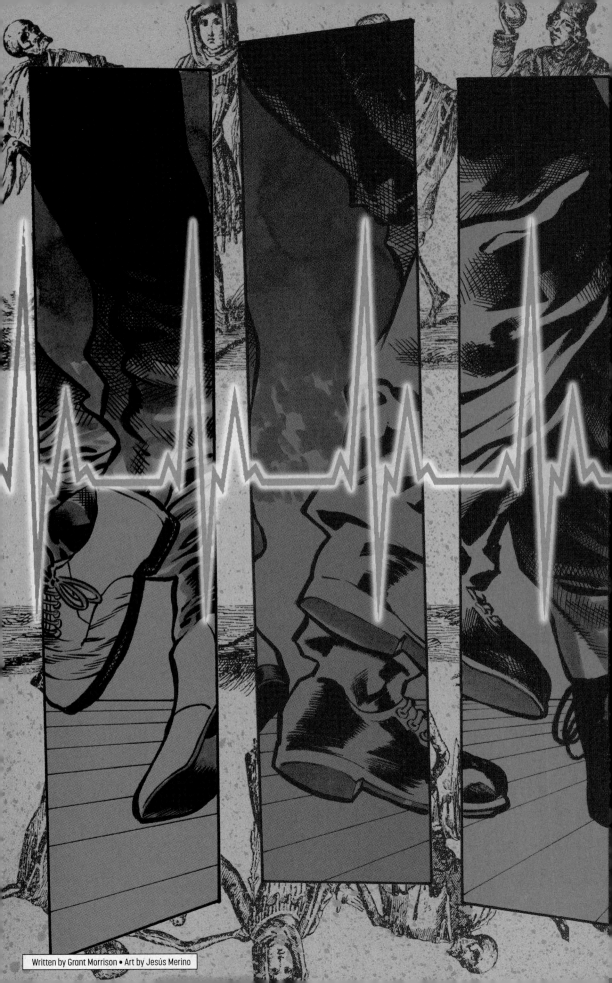

Written by Grant Morrison • Art by Jesús Merino

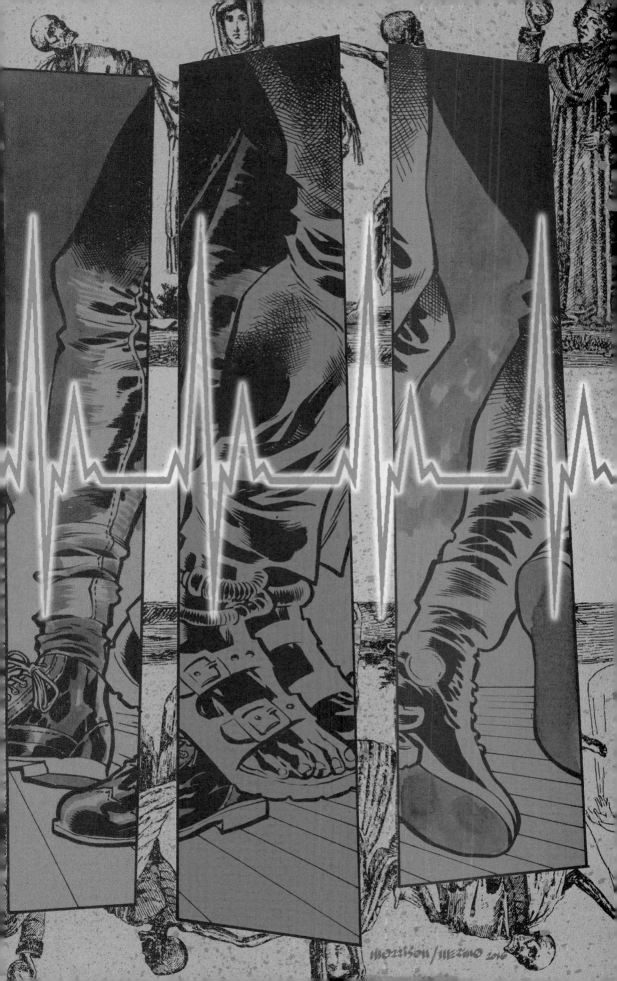

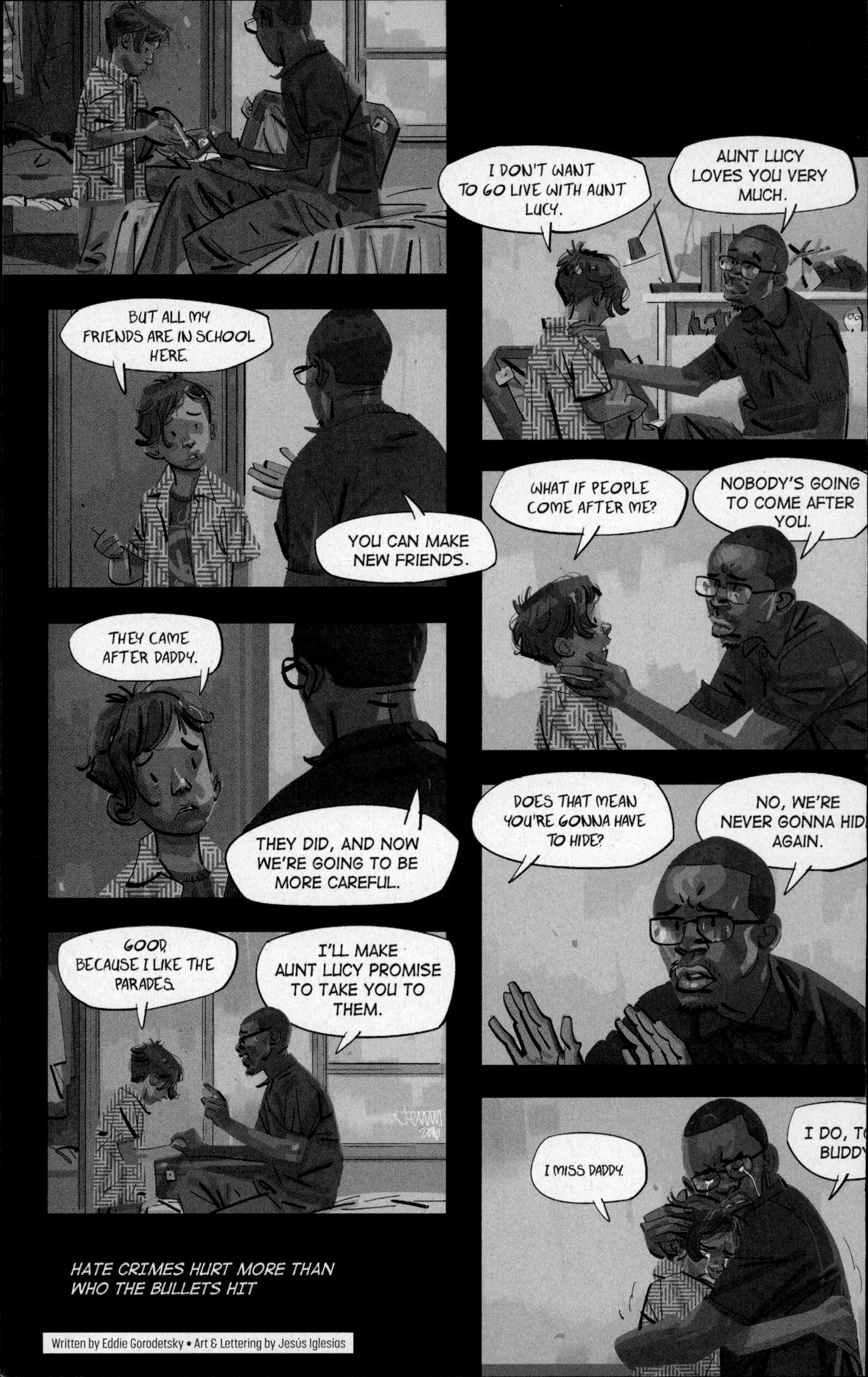

I DON'T WANT TO GO LIVE WITH AUNT LUCY.
AUNT LUCY LOVES YOU VERY MUCH.
BUT ALL MY FRIENDS ARE IN SCHOOL HERE.
YOU CAN MAKE NEW FRIENDS.
WHAT IF PEOPLE COME AFTER ME?
NOBODY'S GOING TO COME AFTER YOU.
THEY CAME AFTER DADDY.
THEY DID, AND NOW WE'RE GOING TO BE MORE CAREFUL.
DOES THAT MEAN YOU'RE GONNA HAVE TO HIDE?
NO, WE'RE NEVER GONNA HID
AGAIN.
GOOD, BECAUSE I LIKE THE PARADES.
I'LL MAKE AUNT LUCY PROMISE TO TAKE YOU TO THEM.
I MISS DADDY.
I DO, T
BUDDY
HATE CRIMES HURT MORE THAN WHO THE BULLETS HIT
Written by Eddie Gorodetsky • Art & Lettering by Jesús Iglesias

RITER - DEVON T.W. MORALES ARTIST - RAGS MORALES

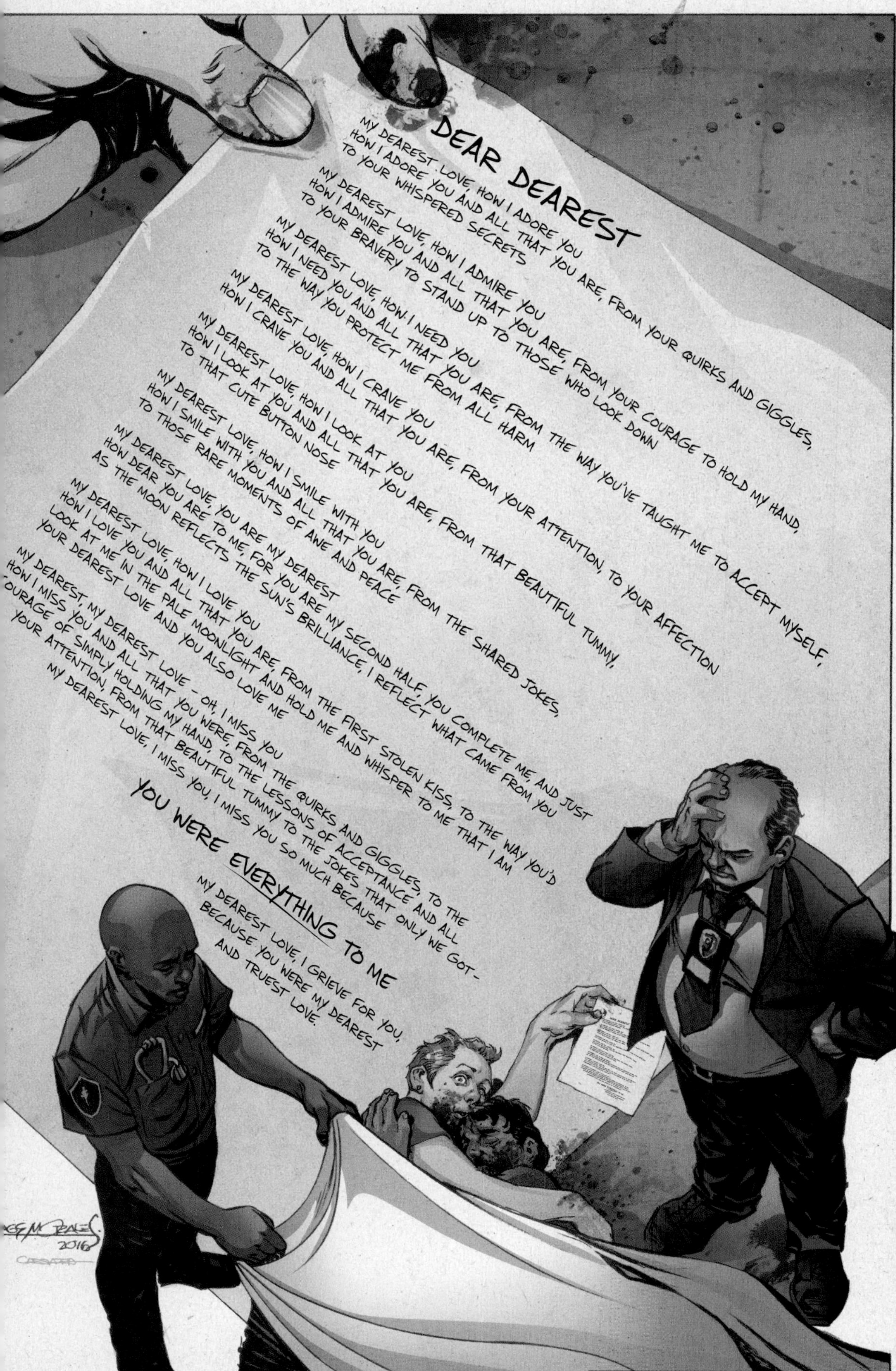
DEAR DEAREST
MY DEAREST LOVE, HOW I ADORE YOU
HOW I ADORE YOU AND ALL THAT YOU ARE, FROM YOUR QUIRKS AND GIGGLES,
TO YOUR WHISPERED SECRETS
MY DEAREST LOVE, HOW I ADMIRE YOU
HOW I ADMIRE YOU AND ALL THAT YOU ARE, FROM YOUR COURAGE TO HOLD MY HAND,
TO YOUR BRAVERY TO STAND UP TO THOSE WHO LOOK DOWN
MY DEAREST LOVE, HOW I NEED YOU
HOW I NEED YOU AND ALL THAT YOU ARE, FROM THE WAY YOU'VE TAUGHT ME TO ACCEPT MYSELF,
TO THE WAY YOU PROTECT ME FROM ALL HARM
MY DEAREST LOVE, HOW I CRAVE YOU
HOW I CRAVE YOU AND ALL THAT YOU ARE, FROM YOUR ATTENTION, TO YOUR AFFECTION
MY DEAREST LOVE, HOW I LOOK AT YOU
HOW I LOOK AT YOU AND ALL THAT YOU ARE, FROM THAT BEAUTIFUL TUMMY,
TO THAT CUTE BUTTON NOSE
MY DEAREST LOVE, HOW I SMILE WITH YOU
HOW I SMILE WITH YOU AND ALL THAT YOU ARE, FROM THE SHARED JOKES,
TO THOSE RARE MOMENTS OF AWE AND PEACE
MY DEAREST LOVE, YOU ARE MY DEAREST
HOW DEAR YOU ARE TO ME, FOR YOU ARE MY SECOND HALF, YOU COMPLETE ME, AND JUST
AS THE MOON REFLECTS THE SUN'S BRILLIANCE, I REFLECT WHAT CAME FROM YOU
MY DEAREST LOVE, HOW I LOVE YOU
HOW I LOVE YOU AND ALL THAT YOU ARE, FROM THE FIRST STOLEN KISS, TO THE WAY YOU'D
LOOK AT ME IN THE PALE MOONLIGHT AND HOLD ME AND WHISPER TO ME THAT I AM
YOUR DEAREST LOVE AND YOU ALSO LOVE ME
MY DEAREST, MY DEAREST LOVE - OH, I MISS YOU
HOW I MISS YOU AND ALL THAT YOU WERE, FROM THE QUIRKS AND GIGGLES, TO THE
COURAGE OF SIMPLY HOLDING MY HAND, TO THE LESSONS OF ACCEPTANCE AND ALL
YOUR ATTENTION, FROM THAT BEAUTIFUL TUMMY TO THE JOKES THAT ONLY WE GOT-
MY DEAREST LOVE, I MISS YOU, I MISS YOU SO MUCH BECAUSE
YOU WERE EVERYTHING TO ME
MY DEAREST LOVE, I GRIEVE FOR YOU,
BECAUSE YOU WERE MY DEAREST
AND TRUEST LOVE.

Coloring by Gabriel Cassata • Lettered by Steve Wands

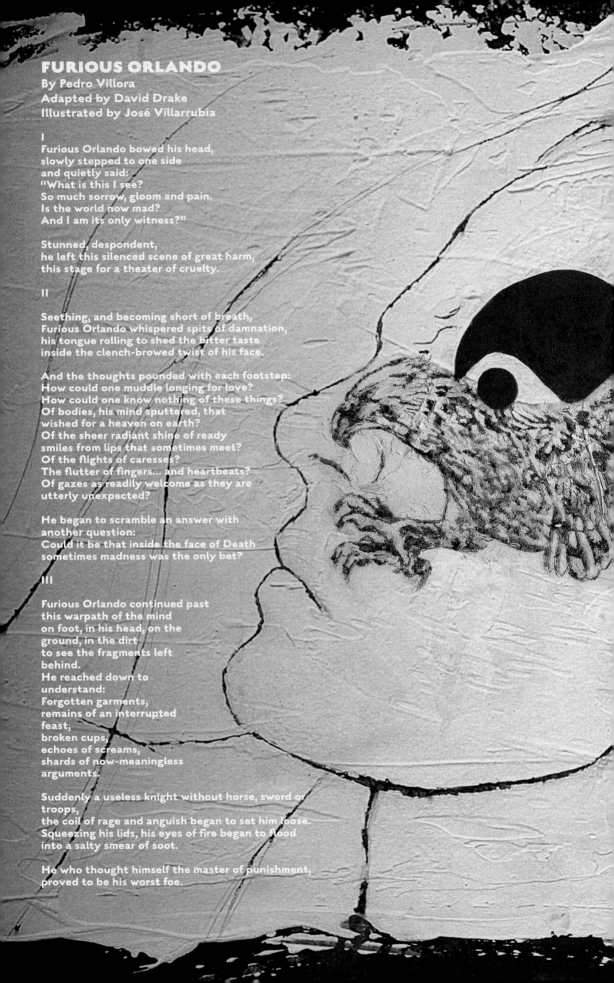

# FURIOUS ORLANDO
By Pedro Villora
Adapted by David Drake
Illustrated by José Villarrubia

I
Furious Orlando bowed his head,
slowly stepped to one side
and quietly said:
"What is this I see?
So much sorrow, gloom and pain.
Is the world now mad?
And I am its only witness?"

Stunned, despondent,
he left this silenced scene of great harm,
this stage for a theater of cruelty.

II

Seething, and becoming short of breath,
Furious Orlando whispered spits of damnation,
his tongue rolling to shed the bitter taste
inside the clench-browed twist of his face.

And the thoughts pounded with each footstep:
How could one muddle longing for love?
How could one know nothing of these things?
Of bodies, his mind sputtered, that
wished for a heaven on earth?
Of the sheer radiant shine of ready
smiles from lips that sometimes meet?
Of the flights of caresses?
The flutter of fingers... and heartbeats?
Of gazes as readily welcome as they are
utterly unexpected?

He began to scramble an answer with
another question:
Could it be that inside the face of Death
sometimes madness was the only bet?

III

Furious Orlando continued past
this warpath of the mind
on foot, in his head, on the
ground, in the dirt
to see the fragments left
behind.
He reached down to
understand:
Forgotten garments,
remains of an interrupted
feast,
broken cups,
echoes of screams,
shards of now-meaningless
arguments.

Suddenly a useless knight without horse, sword or
troops,
the coil of rage and anguish began to set him loose.
Squeezing his lids, his eyes of fire began to flood
into a salty smear of soot.

He who thought himself the master of punishment,
proved to be his worst foe.

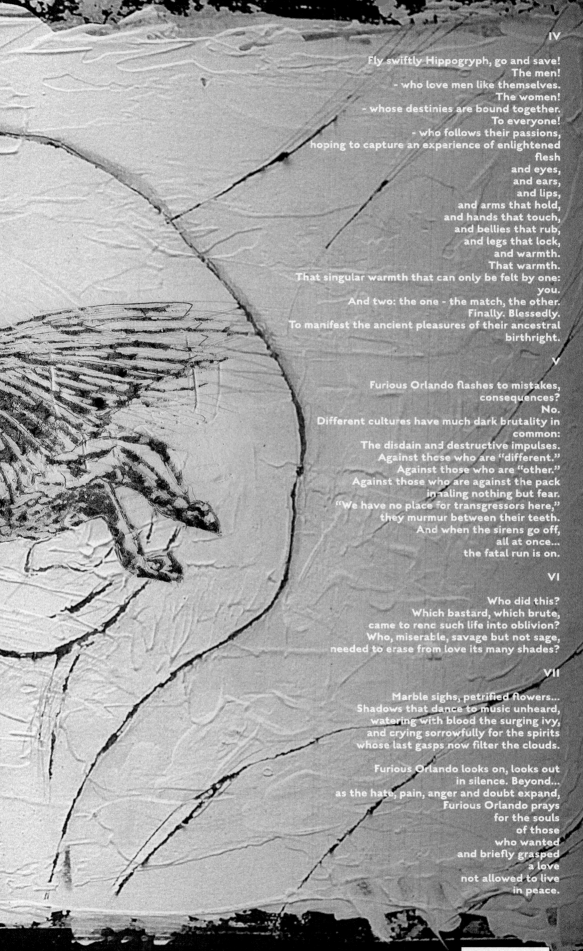

## IV

Fly swiftly Hippogryph, go and save!
The men!
- who love men like themselves.
The women!
- whose destinies are bound together.
To everyone!
- who follows their passions,
hoping to capture an experience of enlightened
flesh
and eyes,
and ears,
and lips,
and arms that hold,
and hands that touch,
and bellies that rub,
and legs that lock,
and warmth.
That warmth.
That singular warmth that can only be felt by one:
you.
And two: the one - the match, the other.
Finally. Blessedly.
To manifest the ancient pleasures of their ancestral
birthright.

## V

Furious Orlando flashes to mistakes,
consequences?
No.
Different cultures have much dark brutality in
common:
The disdain and destructive impulses.
Against those who are "different."
Against those who are "other."
Against those who are against the pack
inhaling nothing but fear.
"We have no place for transgressors here,"
they murmur between their teeth.
And when the sirens go off,
all at once...
the fatal run is on.

## VI

Who did this?
Which bastard, which brute,
came to rend such life into oblivion?
Who, miserable, savage but not sage,
needed to erase from love its many shades?

## VII

Marble sighs, petrified flowers...
Shadows that dance to music unheard,
watering with blood the surging ivy,
and crying sorrowfully for the spirits
whose last gasps now filter the clouds.

Furious Orlando looks on, looks out
in silence. Beyond...
as the hate, pain, anger and doubt expand,
Furious Orlando prays
for the souls
of those
who wanted
and briefly grasped
a love
not allowed to live
in peace.

Layout by Lou Prandi

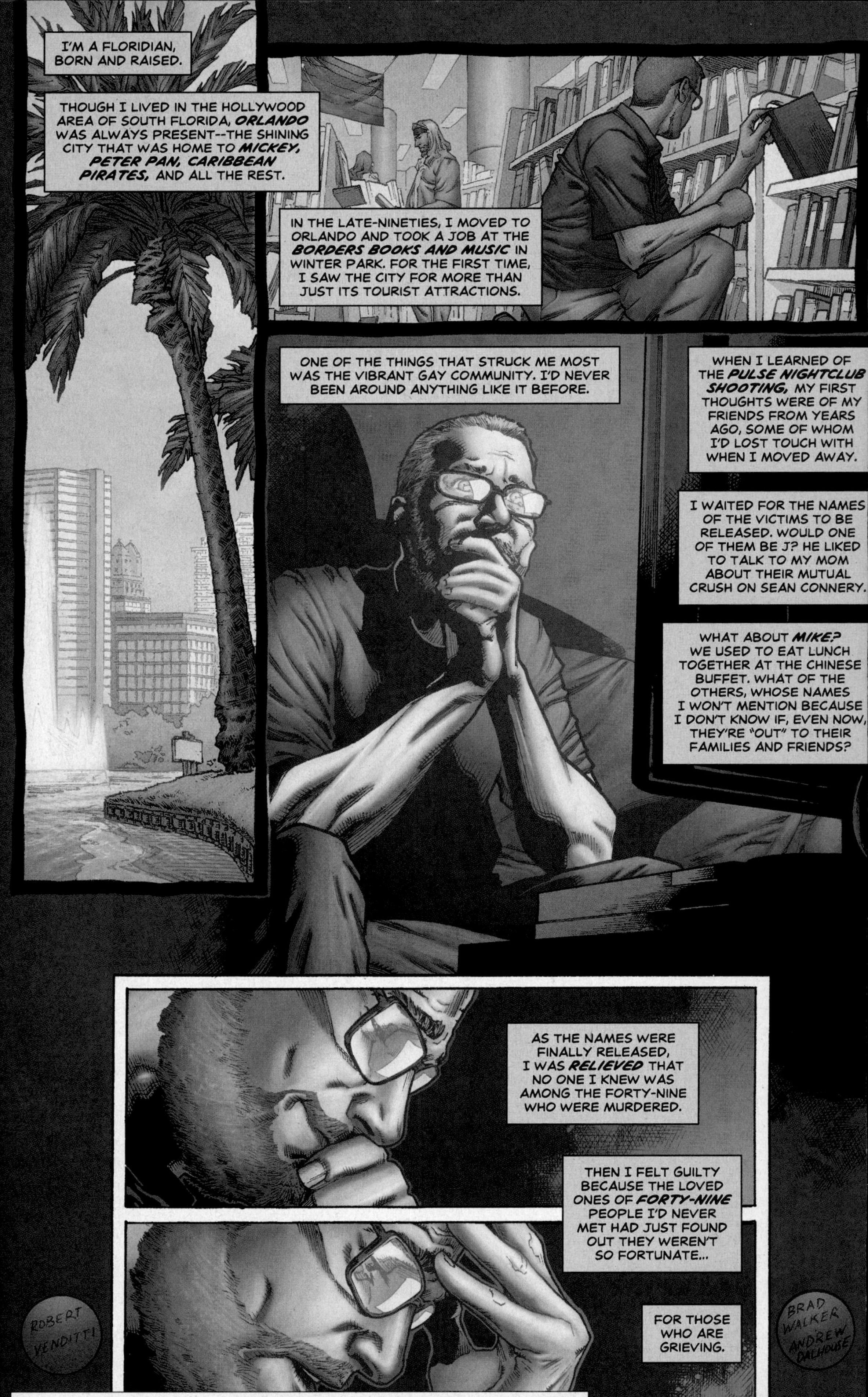
I'M A FLORIDIAN, BORN AND RAISED.
THOUGH I LIVED IN THE HOLLYWOOD AREA OF SOUTH FLORIDA, ***ORLANDO*** WAS ALWAYS PRESENT--THE SHINING CITY THAT WAS HOME TO ***MICKEY, PETER PAN, CARIBBEAN PIRATES,*** AND ALL THE REST.
IN THE LATE-NINETIES, I MOVED TO ORLANDO AND TOOK A JOB AT THE ***BORDERS BOOKS AND MUSIC*** IN WINTER PARK. FOR THE FIRST TIME, I SAW THE CITY FOR MORE THAN JUST ITS TOURIST ATTRACTIONS.
ONE OF THE THINGS THAT STRUCK ME MOST WAS THE VIBRANT GAY COMMUNITY. I'D NEVER BEEN AROUND ANYTHING LIKE IT BEFORE.
WHEN I LEARNED OF THE ***PULSE NIGHTCLUB SHOOTING,*** MY FIRST THOUGHTS WERE OF MY FRIENDS FROM YEARS AGO, SOME OF WHOM I'D LOST TOUCH WITH WHEN I MOVED AWAY.
I WAITED FOR THE NAMES OF THE VICTIMS TO BE RELEASED. WOULD ONE OF THEM BE J? HE LIKED TO TALK TO MY MOM ABOUT THEIR MUTUAL CRUSH ON SEAN CONNERY.
WHAT ABOUT ***MIKE?*** WE USED TO EAT LUNCH TOGETHER AT THE CHINESE BUFFET. WHAT OF THE OTHERS, WHOSE NAMES I WON'T MENTION BECAUSE I DON'T KNOW IF, EVEN NOW, THEY'RE "OUT" TO THEIR FAMILIES AND FRIENDS?
AS THE NAMES WERE FINALLY RELEASED, I WAS ***RELIEVED*** THAT NO ONE I KNEW WAS AMONG THE FORTY-NINE WHO WERE MURDERED.
THEN I FELT GUILTY BECAUSE THE LOVED ONES OF ***FORTY-NINE*** PEOPLE I'D NEVER MET HAD JUST FOUND OUT THEY WEREN'T SO FORTUNATE...
FOR THOSE WHO ARE GRIEVING.
ROBERT VENDITTI
BRAD WALKER ANDREW DALHOUSE

Written by Robert Venditti • Illustrated by Brad Walker • Colored by Andrew Dalhouse • Lettered by Jared K. Fletcher

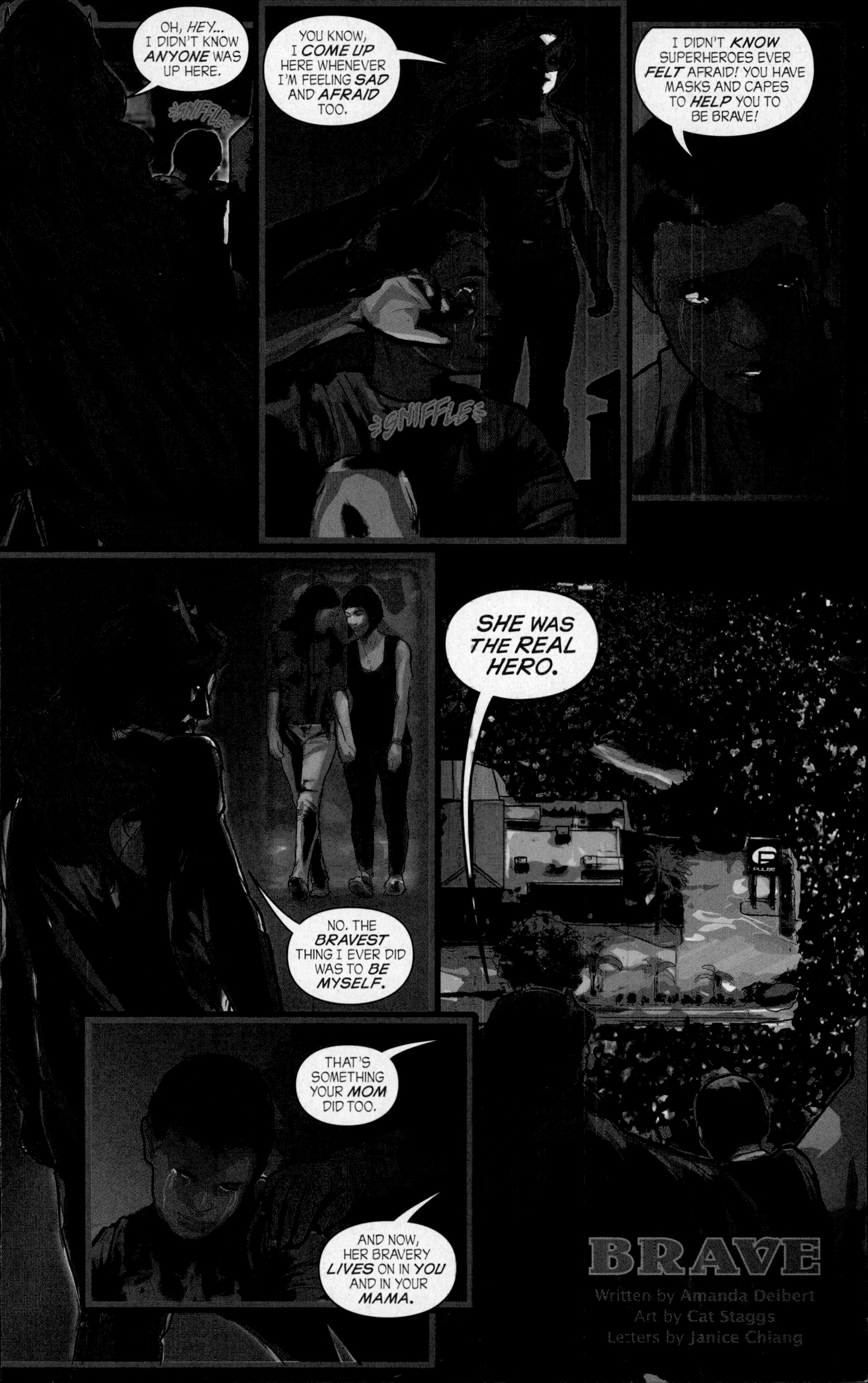
OH, HEY... I DIDN'T KNOW ANYONE WAS UP HERE.
SNIFFLE
YOU KNOW, I COME UP HERE WHENEVER I'M FEELING SAD AND AFRAID TOO.
SNIFFLE
I DIDN'T KNOW SUPERHEROES EVER FELT AFRAID! YOU HAVE MASKS AND CAPES TO HELP YOU TO BE BRAVE!
NO. THE BRAVEST THING I EVER DID WAS TO BE MYSELF.
THAT'S SOMETHING YOUR MOM DID TOO.
AND NOW, HER BRAVERY LIVES ON IN YOU AND IN YOUR MAMA.
SHE WAS THE REAL HERO.
BRAVE
Written by Amanda Deibert
Art by Cat Staggs
Letters by Janice Chiang

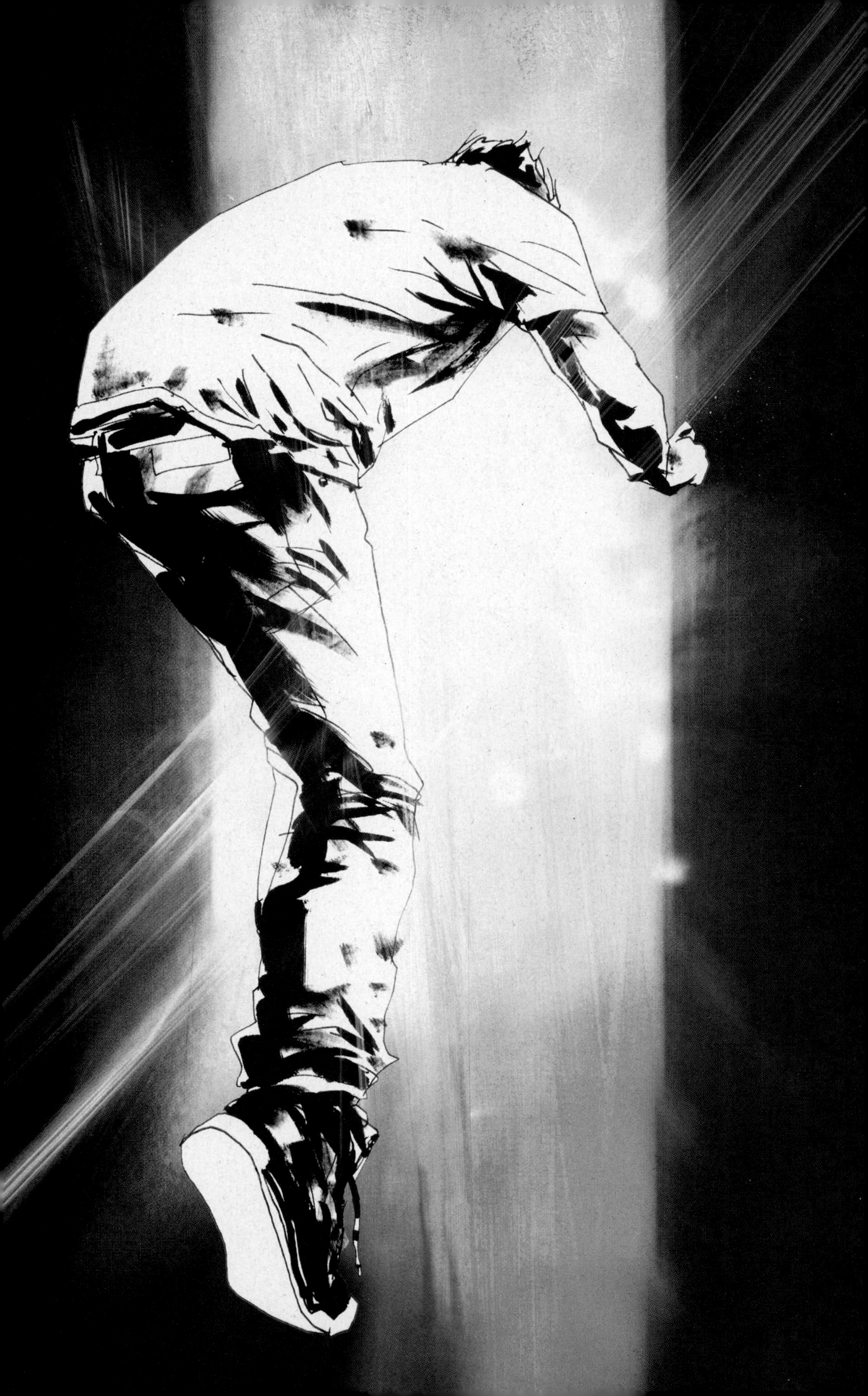

# The door was open to us.

I was 22 when I moved to Orlando. I was just out of college, and I was on fire with the idea of becoming a writer. Most people I knew who wanted to be writers were applying for jobs at publishing houses, magazines. But I figured I'd travel the country, work odd jobs, meet inspiring people. Basically, I had no idea who the hell I was.

I took a job at Disney World as a janitor. The community was rough. No one's dream job is being a janitor for minimum wage, even at Disney World. These were the people I wanted to meet. Tough, with stories. They were a conservative crowd.

Across the way, in the tunnels, was Characters. People from custodial didn't really talk to people in Characters. Characters was theatrical; it was silly. Also, many of the cast members in Characters were gay. Custodial wasn't like that; that was fairy tales, as custodial sometimes called it. That was happy land. This, pushing garbage carts that weighed a ton in the sun...

Still, every Thursday, a few folks from Characters would invite us all to come out to a club called Mannequins over at Pleasure Island. It was a gay club, as much as one could be on Pleasure Island. Sometimes we would swing by Mannequins on our way home, after going out to the sports-bar-themed place or the rock-show-themed place, but if so it was mostly to watch from the corners. Some of my coworkers were religious, some made disparaging comments about the people dancing. We were there to differentiate ourselves. Strong, weak.

Still, the invitation always came on Thursdays.

Eventually I injured my shoulder, and pushing the big garbage carts became difficult. I started having problems with a couple guys in management, a couple other custodians. I didn't say anything, but I started looking for a transfer. The first invite I got was to audition for Characters.

I was given a job in fur, as Pluto, Eeyore, and Buzz Lightyear. My old custodial friends didn't really want much to do with me after that. And I understood that the folks in Characters would recognize me from that group of custodial folks who sometimes came to Mannequins and gawked and laughed. I was ready to just be on my own.

But my first Thursday, the invitation came as usual.

The door was open to me.

I made some real friends in Characters. Every Thursday we'd go to Mannequins, or sometimes to clubs downtown, and dance together. One friend had been disowned by his parents but paid for their house himself. Another spent her free time lobbying with her partner for marriage equality, often under withering criticism and sometimes threats of violence. Characters was one of the toughest crowds I've ever encountered, and when writing superheroes, I have often drawn inspiration from the people I met while there. Not just for their fortitude, but for their generosity of spirit, their greatness of heart.

Sometimes I think about how that door was always open, to people who were not always kind, who were fearful and angry, and I think about what happened on June 12. They took him in and he opened fire. I think of dancing in those clubs with my friends, think of that dance floor, that crowd, defiant, celebratory, brave, welcoming...people who knew who the hell they were at that moment.

The door should close.

That's how I feel in the aftermath. Don't let another one like him in. Don't let anyone in.

But it won't close. It'll stay open. And that's the thing I keep coming back to. How the door will stay open, because the people in that club are better than that, better than I am. They are the strongest of us, the heroes.

The door is open to walk through and show support.

The invitation will be there Thursday.

# Love is love.

Written by Scott Snyder • Art by Jock • Layout by Steve Cook

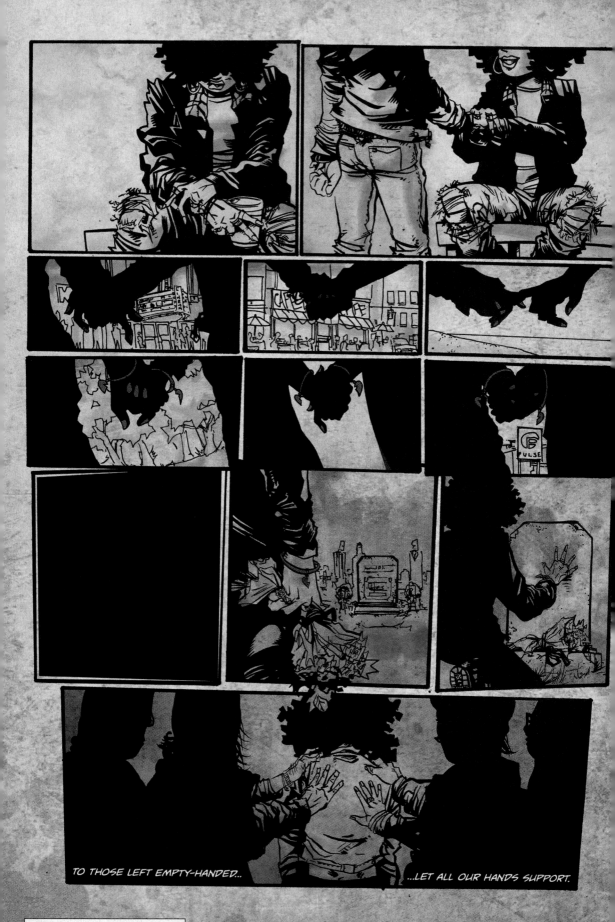

TO THOSE LEFT EMPTY-HANDED...

...LET ALL OUR HANDS SUPPORT.

Written by Jeff Dixon • Art by Karl Slominski

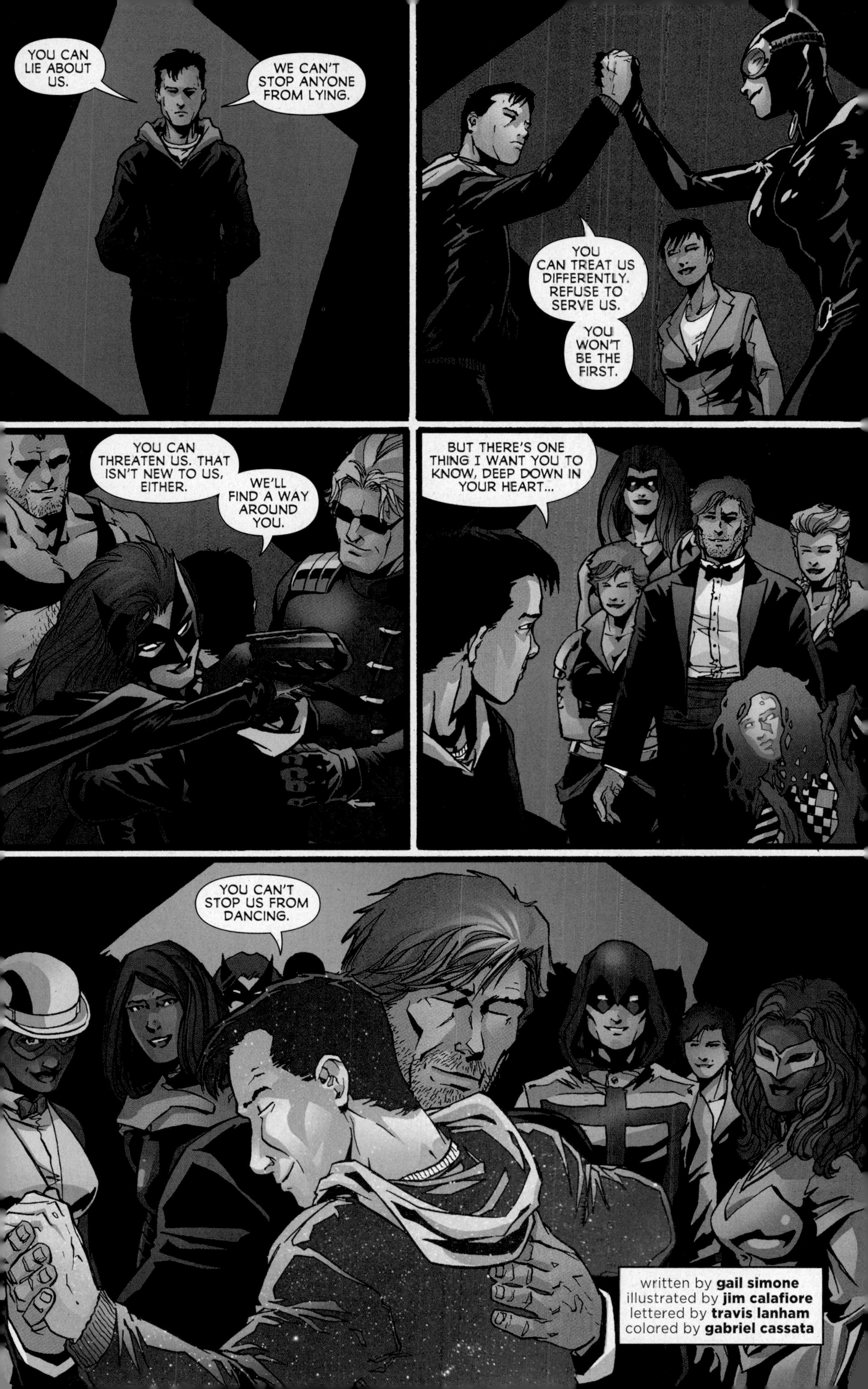
YOU CAN LIE ABOUT US.
WE CAN'T STOP ANYONE FROM LYING.
YOU CAN TREAT US DIFFERENTLY. REFUSE TO SERVE US.
YOU WON'T BE THE FIRST.
YOU CAN THREATEN US. THAT ISN'T NEW TO US, EITHER.
WE'LL FIND A WAY AROUND YOU.
BUT THERE'S ONE THING I WANT YOU TO KNOW, DEEP DOWN IN YOUR HEART...
YOU CAN'T STOP US FROM DANCING.
written by gail simone
illustrated by jim calafiore
lettered by travis lanham
colored by gabriel cassata

# Still

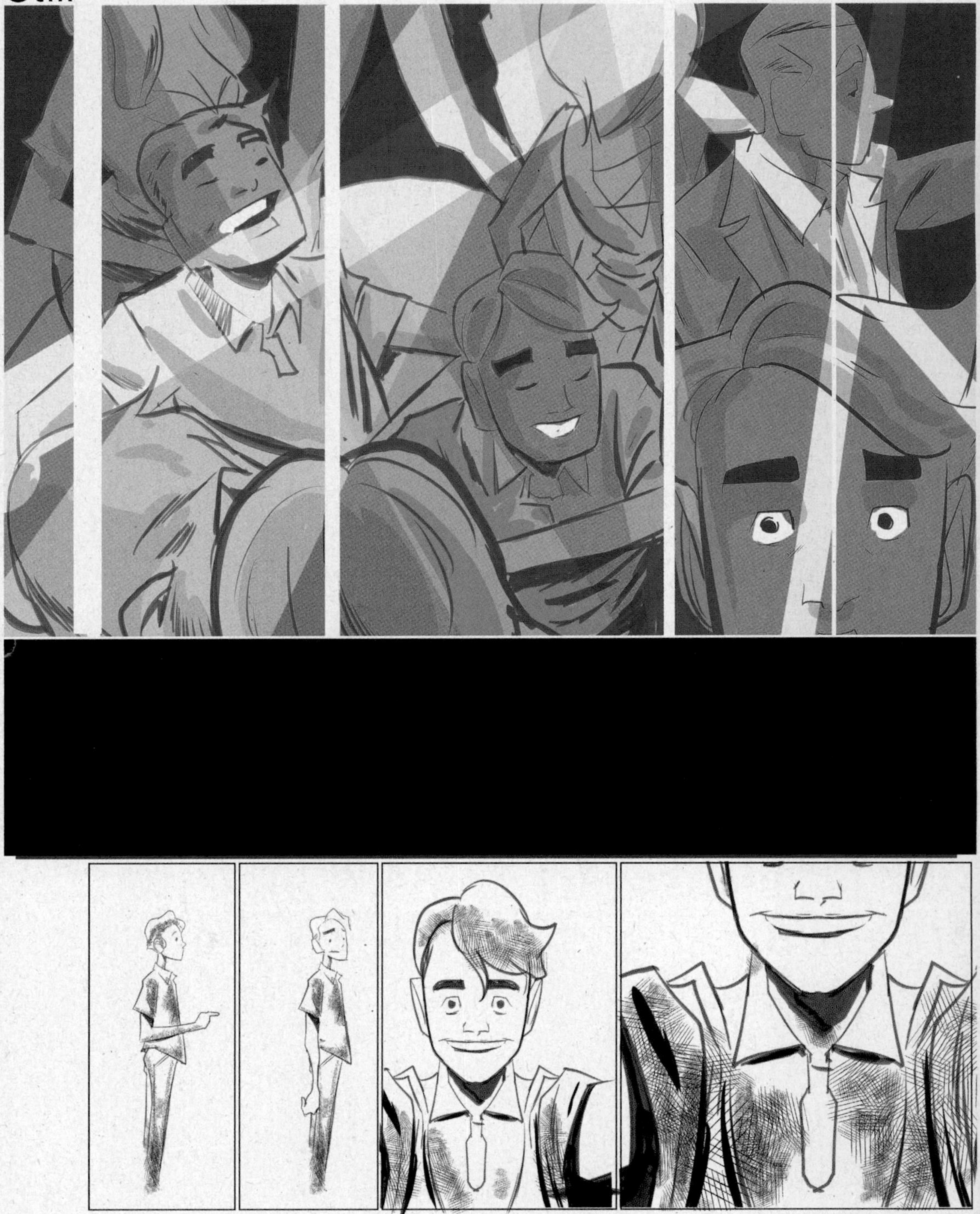

Written by Justin Zimmerman • Art by Robbi Rodriguez

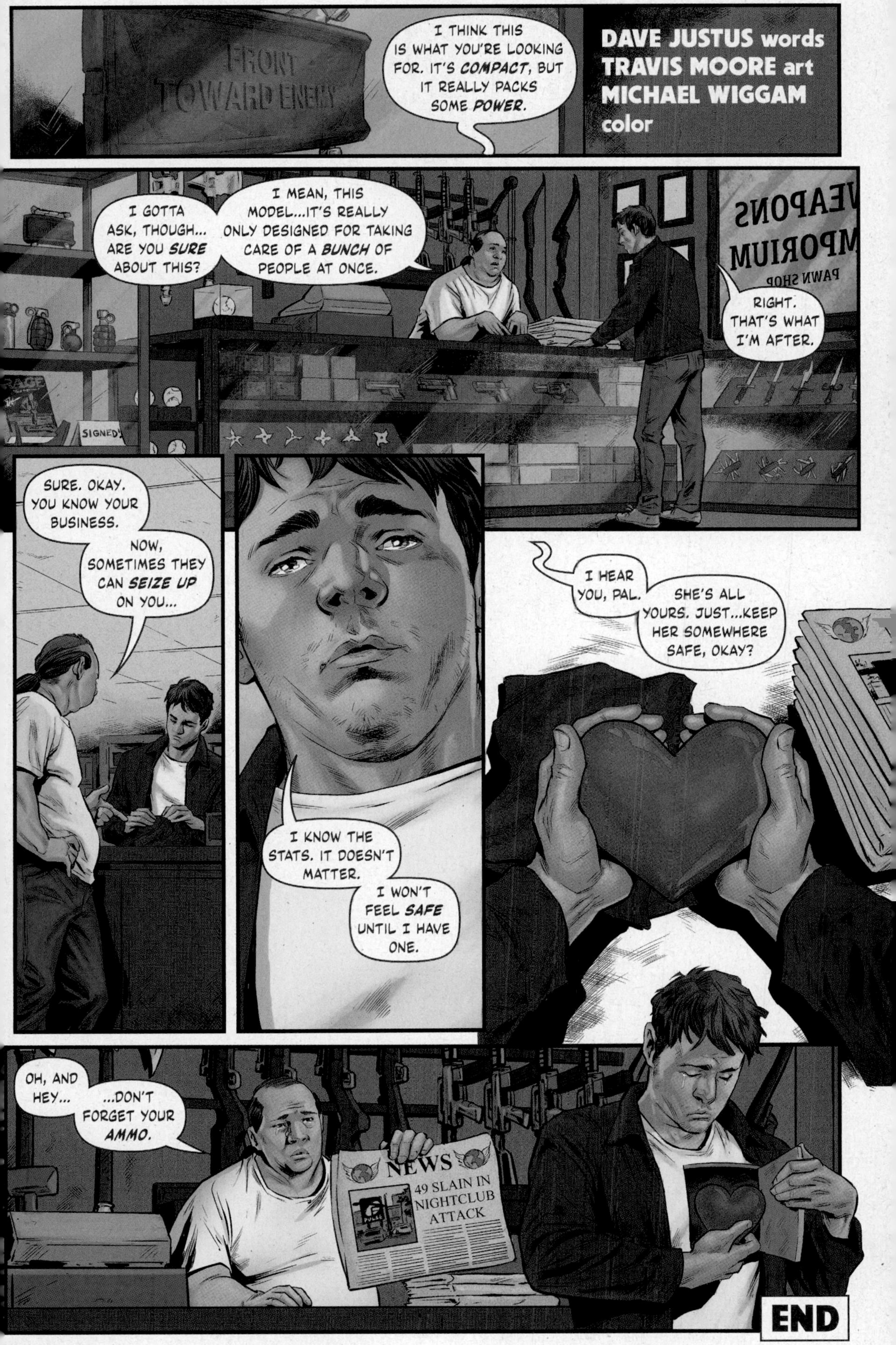
FRONT TOWARD ENEMY
I THINK THIS IS WHAT YOU'RE LOOKING FOR. IT'S *COMPACT*, BUT IT REALLY PACKS SOME *POWER*.
**DAVE JUSTUS** words **TRAVIS MOORE** art **MICHAEL WIGGAM** color
I GOTTA ASK, THOUGH... ARE YOU *SURE* ABOUT THIS?
I MEAN, THIS MODEL...IT'S REALLY ONLY DESIGNED FOR TAKING CARE OF A *BUNCH* OF PEOPLE AT ONCE.
WEAPONS EMPORIUM PAWN SHOP
RIGHT. THAT'S WHAT I'M AFTER.
SIGNED!
SURE. OKAY. YOU KNOW YOUR BUSINESS.
NOW, SOMETIMES THEY CAN *SEIZE UP* ON YOU...
I KNOW THE STATS. IT DOESN'T MATTER.
I WON'T FEEL *SAFE* UNTIL I HAVE ONE.
I HEAR YOU, PAL.
SHE'S ALL YOURS. JUST...KEEP HER SOMEWHERE SAFE, OKAY?
OH, AND HEY...
...DON'T FORGET YOUR *AMMO*.
NEWS
49 SLAIN IN NIGHTCLUB ATTACK
END

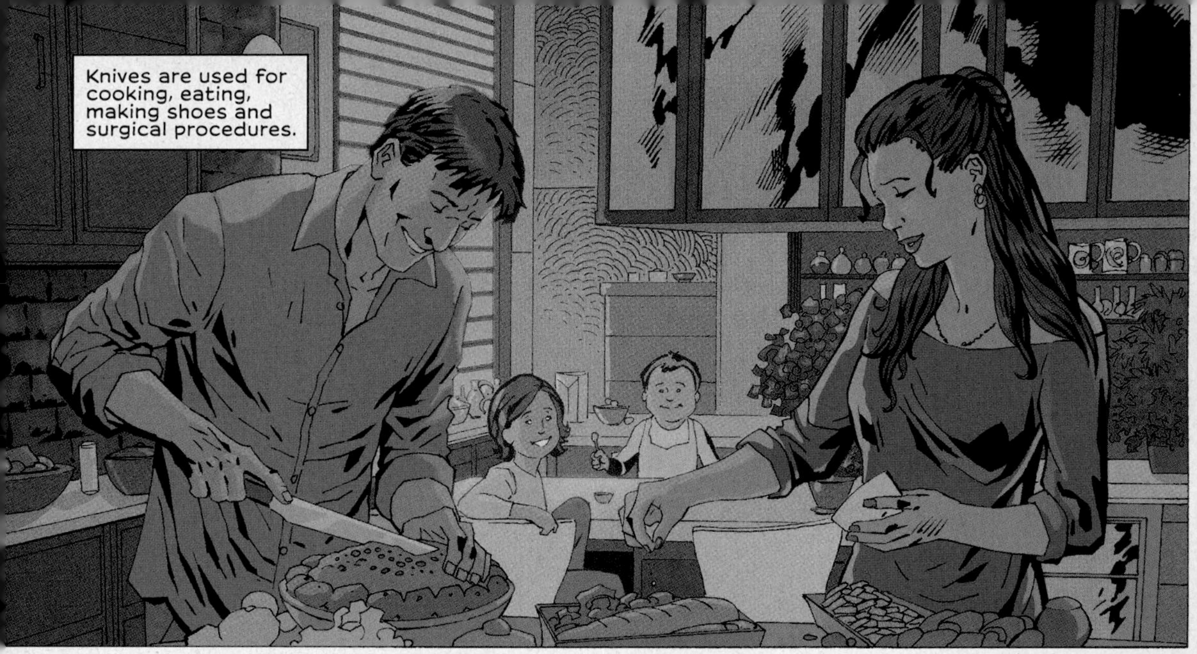
Knives are used for cooking, eating, making shoes and surgical procedures.
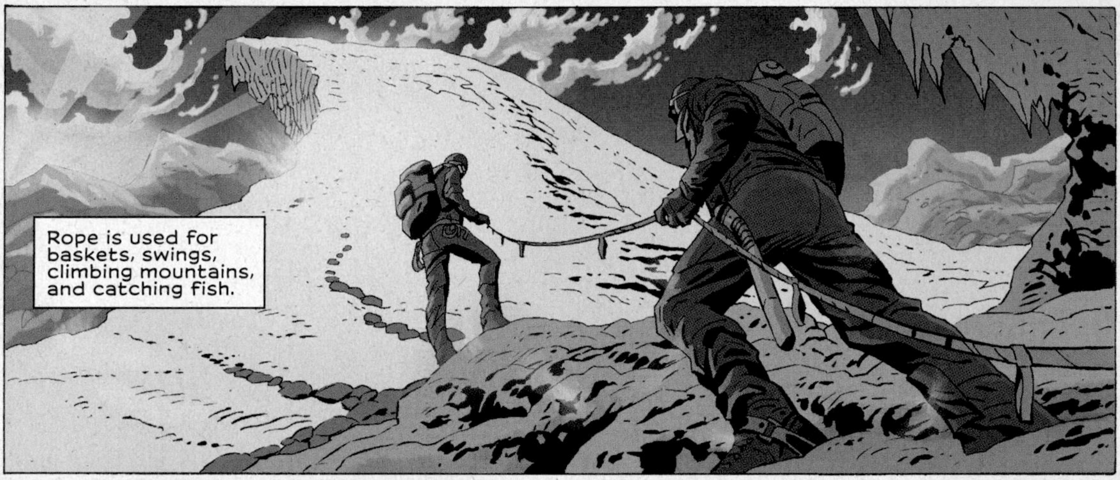
Rope is used for baskets, swings, climbing mountains, and catching fish.
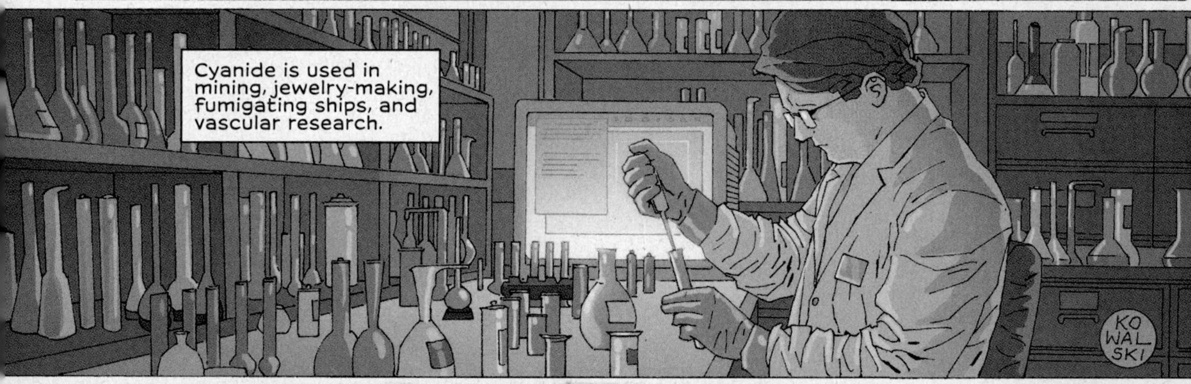
Cyanide is used in mining, jewelry-making, fumigating ships, and vascular research.
KO WAL SKI
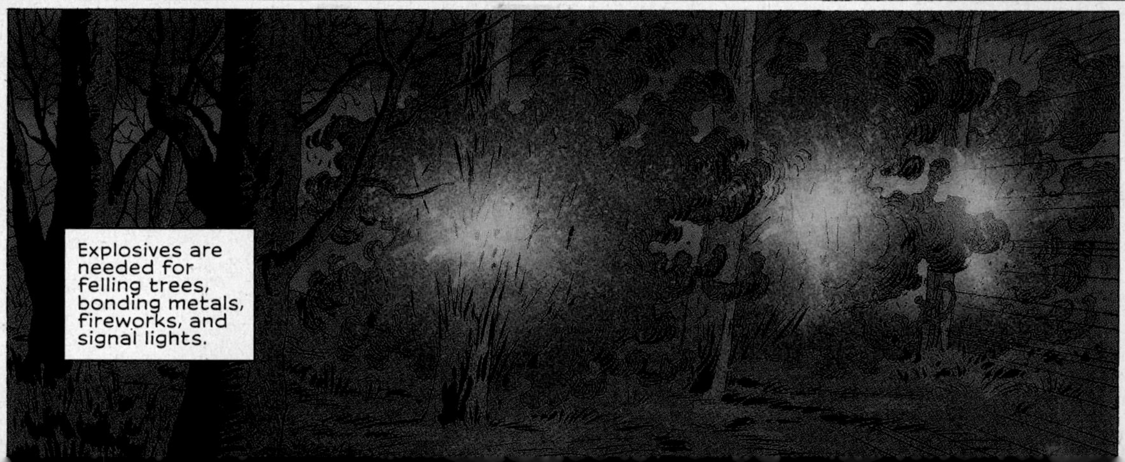
Explosives are needed for felling trees, bonding metals, fireworks, and signal lights.

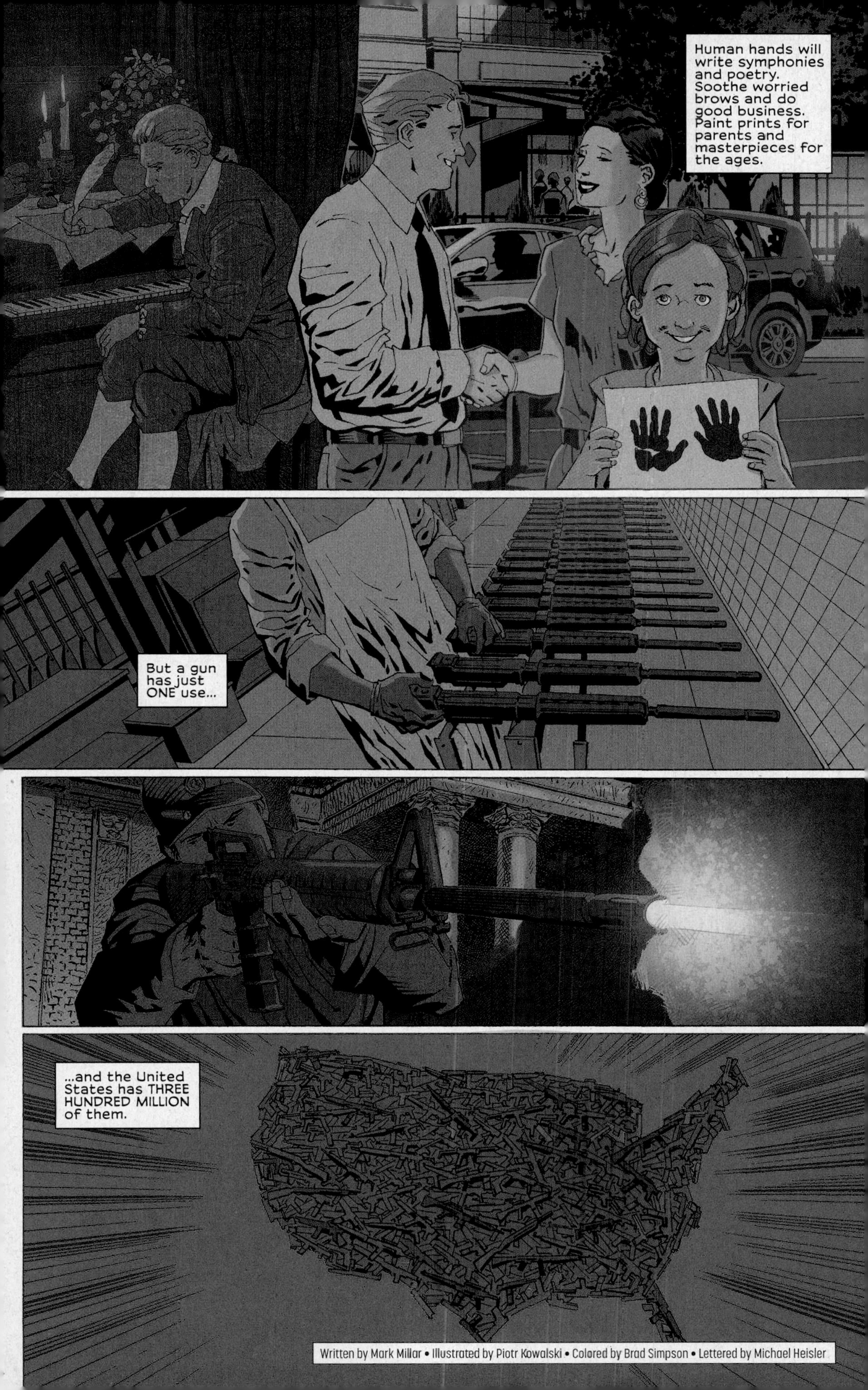
Human hands will write symphonies and poetry. Soothe worried brows and do good business. Paint prints for parents and masterpieces for the ages.
But a gun has just ONE use...
...and the United States has THREE HUNDRED MILLION of them.
Written by Mark Millar • Illustrated by Piotr Kowalski • Colored by Brad Simpson • Lettered by Michael Heisler

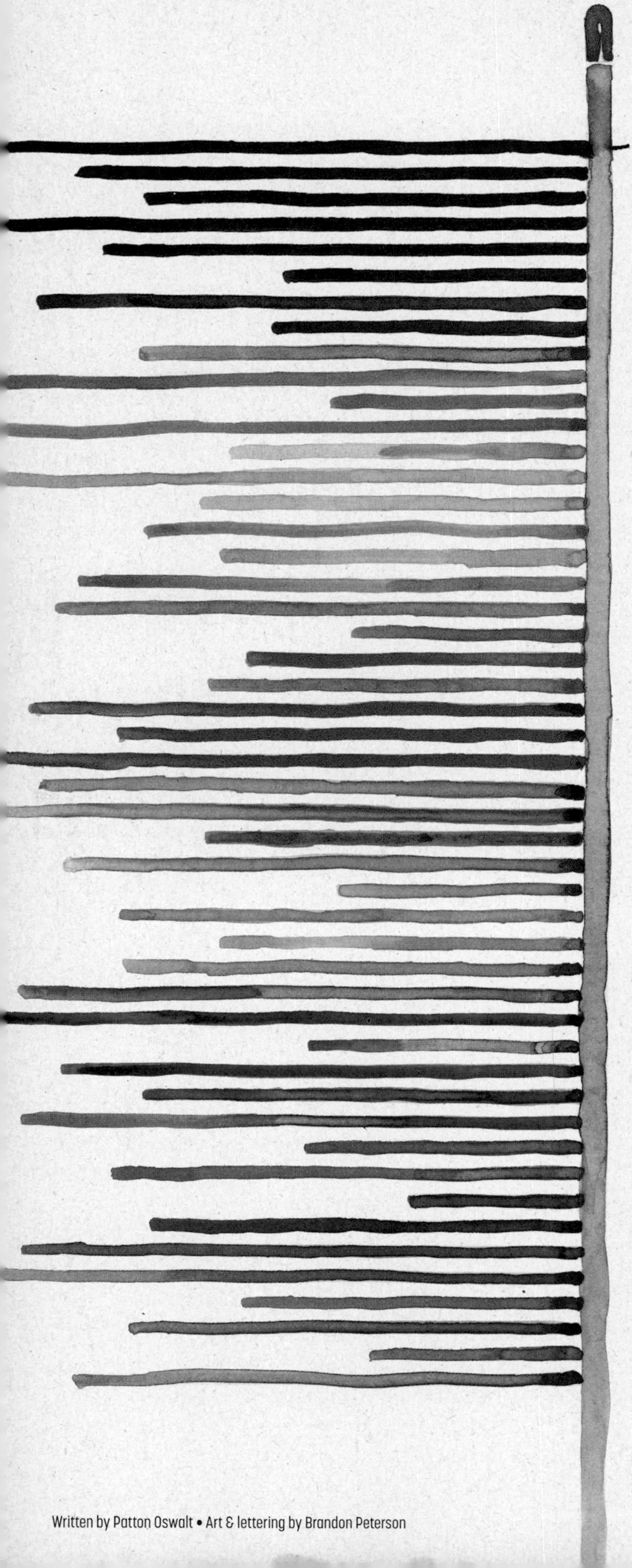

ALL DIFFERENT BIRTHDAYS
ALL DIFFERENT PEOPLE
ALL DIFFERENT PLANS
ALL DIFFERENT DREAMS

ONE KIND OF BULLET
ONE KIND OF GUN
ONE KIND OF LONELINESS

June 12th, 2016

OSWALT +
BRANDO 2016

Written by Patton Oswalt • Art & lettering by Brandon Peterson

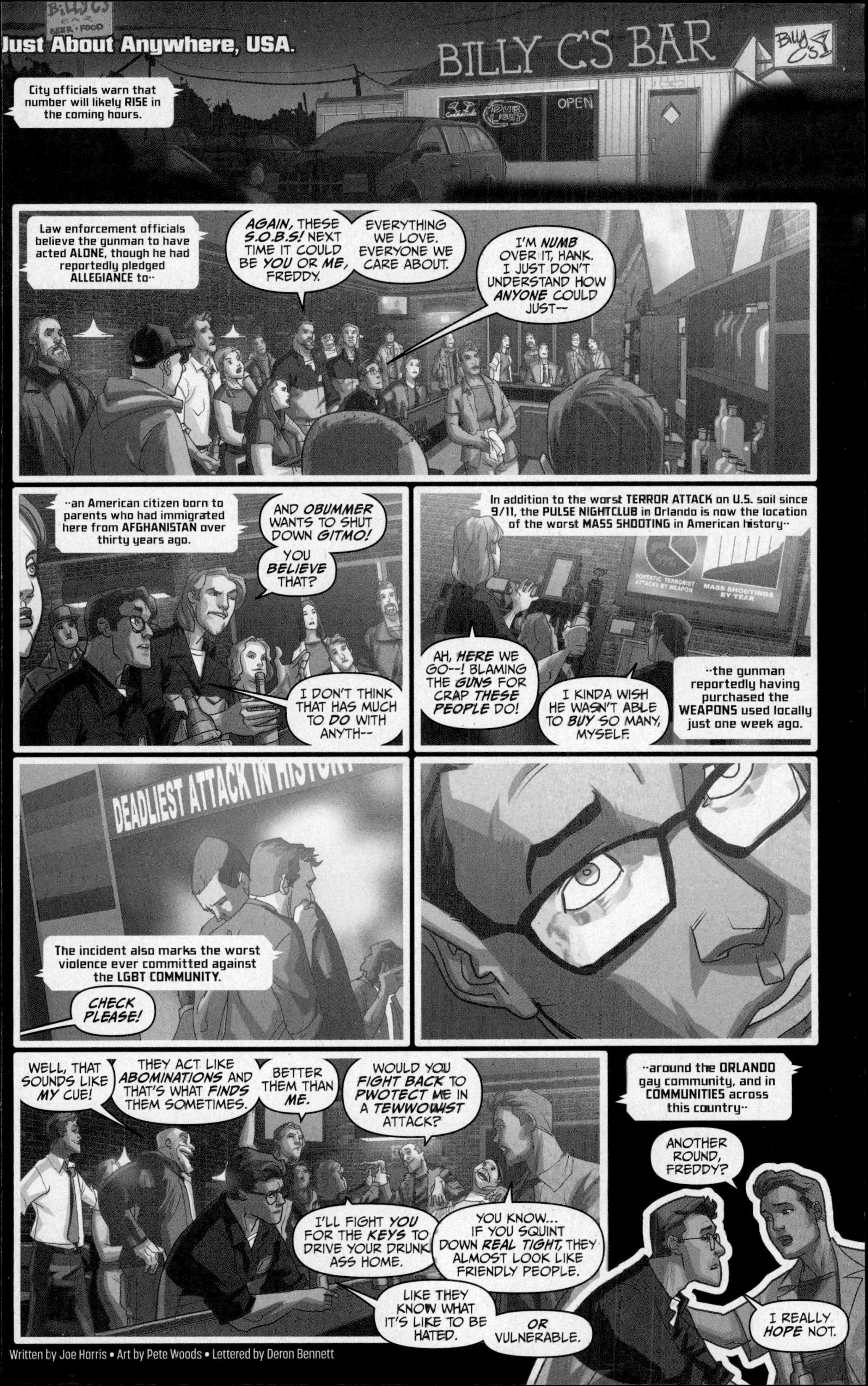
BILLY C'S BAR BEER • FOOD
Just About Anywhere, USA.
BILLY C'S BAR
OPEN
City officials warn that number will likely RISE in the coming hours.
Law enforcement officials believe the gunman to have acted ALONE, though he had reportedly pledged ALLEGIANCE to--
AGAIN, THESE S.O.B.S! NEXT TIME IT COULD BE YOU OR ME, FREDDY.
EVERYTHING WE LOVE. EVERYONE WE CARE ABOUT.
I'M NUMB OVER IT, HANK. I JUST DON'T UNDERSTAND HOW ANYONE COULD JUST--
--an American citizen born to parents who had immigrated here from AFGHANISTAN over thirty years ago.
AND OBUMMER WANTS TO SHUT DOWN GITMO!
YOU BELIEVE THAT?
I DON'T THINK THAT HAS MUCH TO DO WITH ANYTH--
In addition to the worst TERROR ATTACK on U.S. soil since 9/11, the PULSE NIGHTCLUB in Orlando is now the location of the worst MASS SHOOTING in American history--
DOMESTIC TERRORIST ATTACKS BY WEAPON
MASS SHOOTINGS BY YEAR
AH, HERE WE GO--! BLAMING THE GUNS FOR CRAP THESE PEOPLE DO!
I KINDA WISH HE WASN'T ABLE TO BUY SO MANY, MYSELF.
--the gunman reportedly having purchased the WEAPONS used locally just one week ago.
DEADLIEST ATTACK IN HISTORY
The incident also marks the worst violence ever committed against the LGBT COMMUNITY.
CHECK PLEASE!
WELL, THAT SOUNDS LIKE MY CUE!
THEY ACT LIKE ABOMINATIONS AND THAT'S WHAT FINDS THEM SOMETIMES.
BETTER THEM THAN ME.
WOULD YOU FIGHT BACK TO PWOTECT ME IN A TEWWOWIST ATTACK?
I'LL FIGHT YOU FOR THE KEYS TO DRIVE YOUR DRUNK ASS HOME.
YOU KNOW... IF YOU SQUINT DOWN REAL TIGHT, THEY ALMOST LOOK LIKE FRIENDLY PEOPLE.
LIKE THEY KNOW WHAT IT'S LIKE TO BE HATED.
OR VULNERABLE.
--around the ORLANDO gay community, and in COMMUNITIES across this country--
ANOTHER ROUND, FREDDY?
I REALLY HOPE NOT.

Written by Joe Harris • Art by Pete Woods • Lettered by Deron Bennett

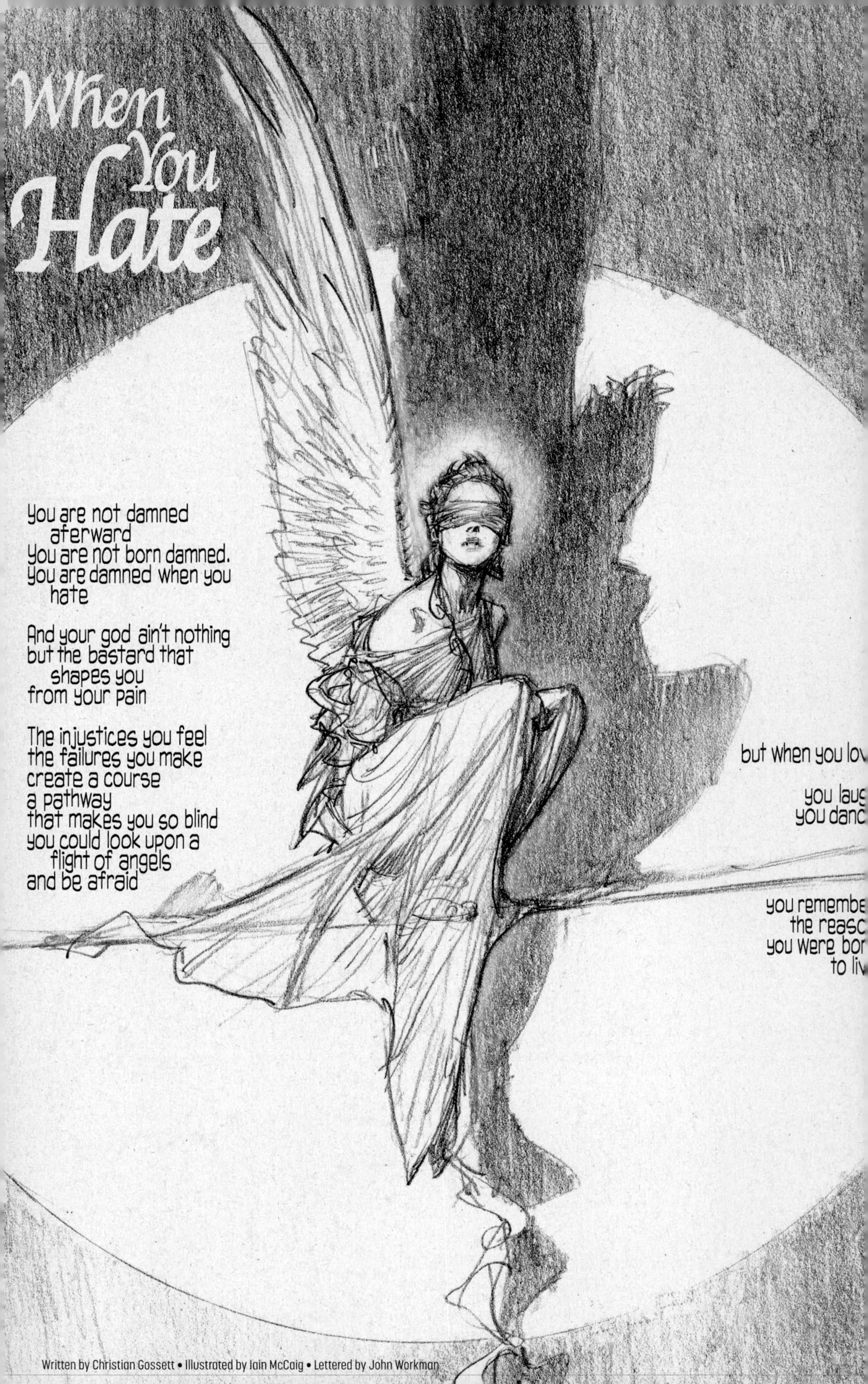
When You Hate
You are not damned
afterward
You are not born damned.
You are damned when you
hate
And your god ain't nothing
but the bastard that
shapes you
from your pain
The injustices you feel
the failures you make
create a course
a pathway
that makes you so blind
you could look upon a
flight of angels
and be afraid
but when you lo
you laug
you danc
you remembe
the reas
you were bor
to li


Written by Christian Gossett • Illustrated by Iain McCaig • Lettered by John Workman

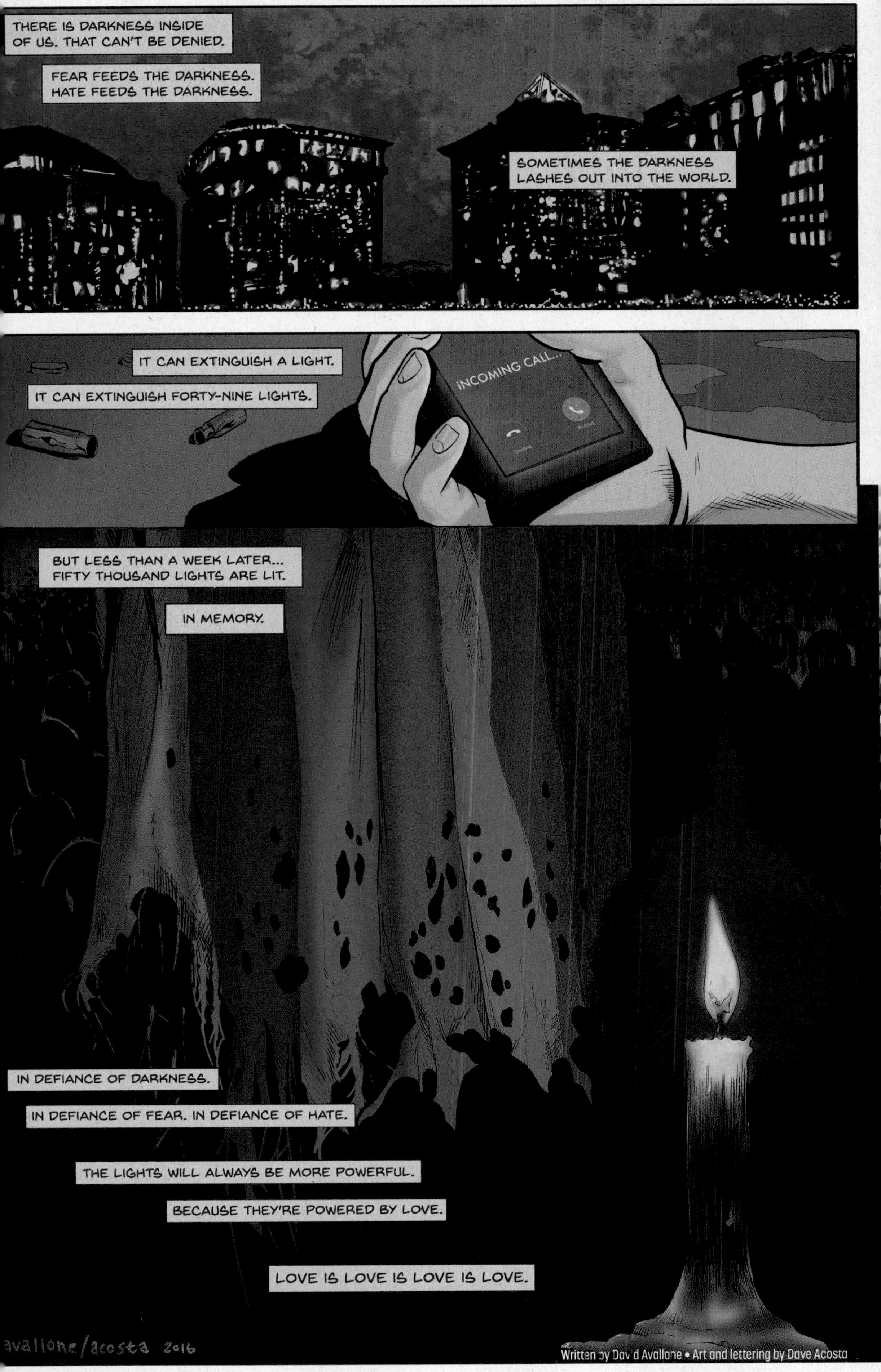
THERE IS DARKNESS INSIDE OF US. THAT CAN'T BE DENIED.
FEAR FEEDS THE DARKNESS. HATE FEEDS THE DARKNESS.
SOMETIMES THE DARKNESS LASHES OUT INTO THE WORLD.
IT CAN EXTINGUISH A LIGHT.
IT CAN EXTINGUISH FORTY-NINE LIGHTS.
INCOMING CALL...
BUT LESS THAN A WEEK LATER... FIFTY THOUSAND LIGHTS ARE LIT.
IN MEMORY.
IN DEFIANCE OF DARKNESS.
IN DEFIANCE OF FEAR. IN DEFIANCE OF HATE.
THE LIGHTS WILL ALWAYS BE MORE POWERFUL.
BECAUSE THEY'RE POWERED BY LOVE.
LOVE IS LOVE IS LOVE IS LOVE.
avallone/acosta 2016
Written by David Avallone • Art and lettering by Dave Acosta

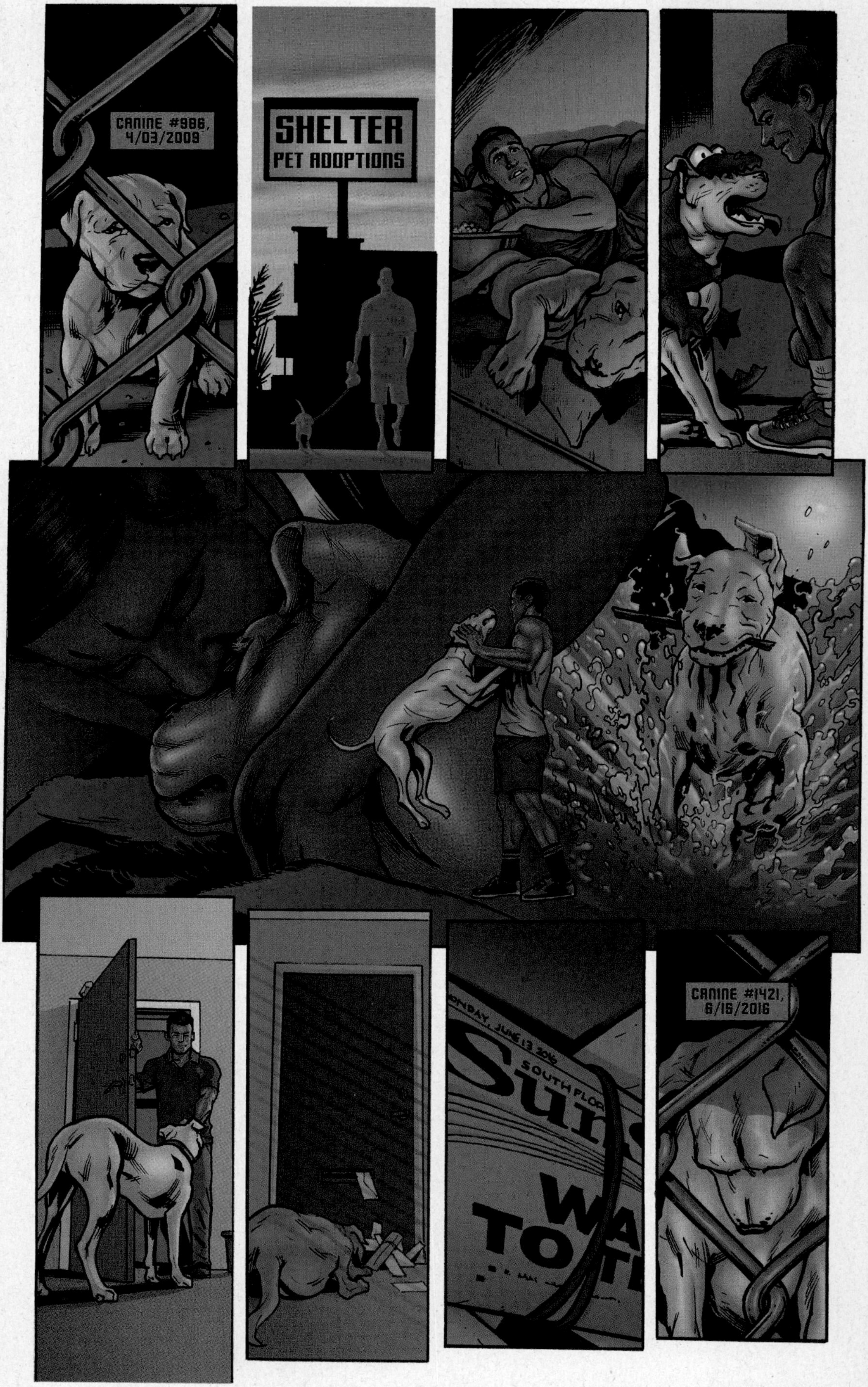
CANINE #986,
4/03/2009
SHELTER
PET ADOPTIONS
CANINE #1421,
6/15/2016

Written by Scott Lope • Illustrated by Stephen Sadowski • Colored by Dan Shadian • Lettered by Joshua Cozine

ANOTHER TRAGIC SHOOTING HAS OCCURRED, THIS TIME RIGHT HERE IN OUR OWN BACK YARD...

>CLICK<

OUR SECOND AMENDMENT RIGHTS HAVE TO BE PROTECTED! IF MORE PEOPLE IN THAT CLUB WERE ARMED, THERE'D BE MORE PEOPLE ALIVE TODAY!

NRA SPOKESMAN JO

>CLICK<

THESE MASS SHOOTINGS ARE JUST ONE PROBLEM...

LIVE WITH KEN VER

>CLICK<

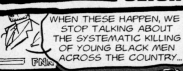

WHEN THESE HAPPEN, WE STOP TALKING ABOUT THE SYSTEMATIC KILLING OF YOUNG BLACK MEN ACROSS THE COUNTRY...

>CLICK<

IT'S ONLY A MATTER OF TIME BEFORE THINGS GET REALLY OUT OF CONTROL...AND WHAT WILL WE DO THEN?

>CLICK<

I DON'T KNOW ABOUT YOU, BUT IF IT SOMEONE COMES FOR MY GUNS, THEY'RE GONNA GET MORE THAN THEY BARGAINED FOR--

>CLICK<

© 2016 SPURLOCK/DWYER

Written by Morgan Spurlock - Art and lettering by Kieron Dwyer

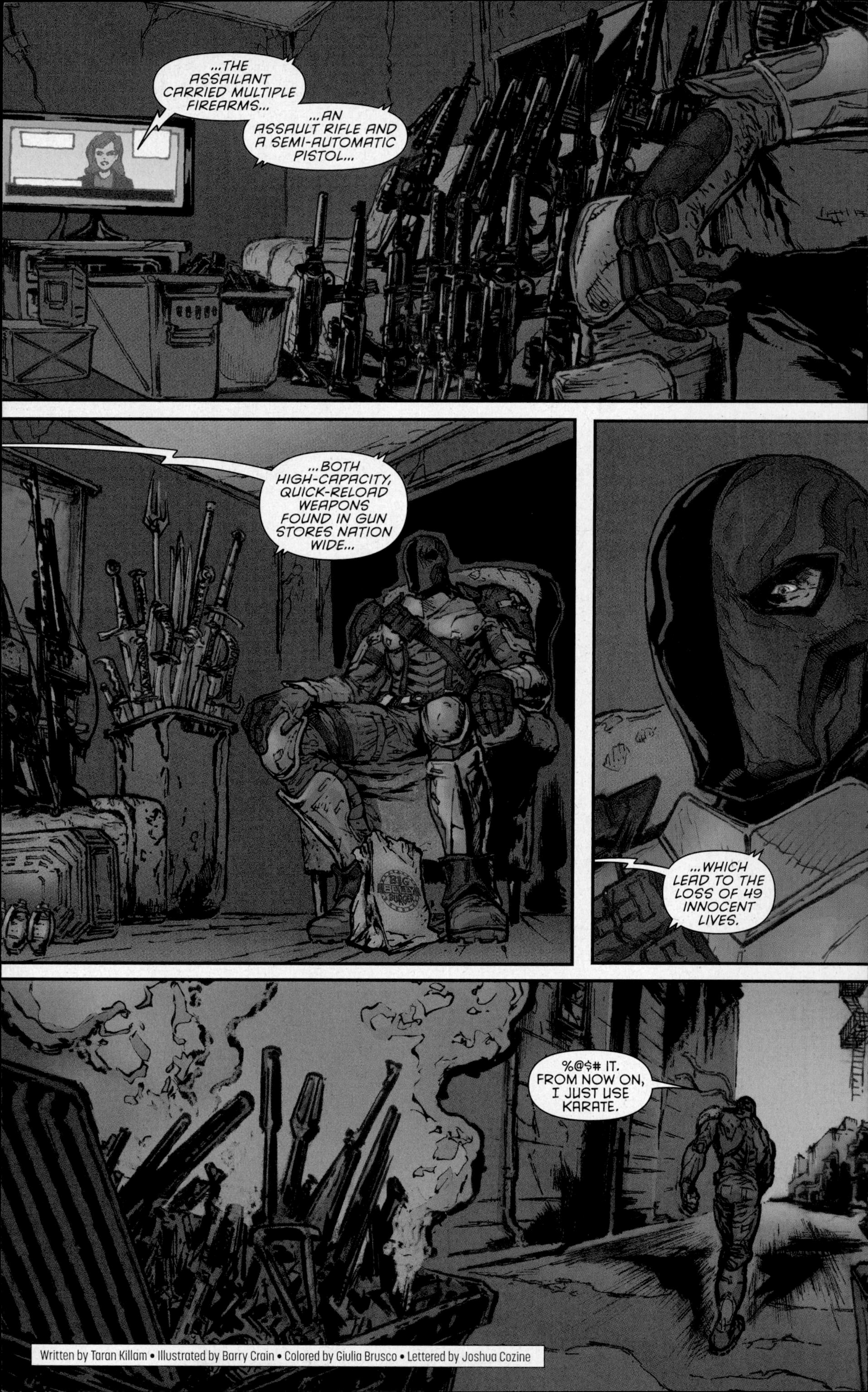
...THE ASSAILANT CARRIED MULTIPLE FIREARMS...
...AN ASSAULT RIFLE AND A SEMI-AUTOMATIC PISTOL...
...BOTH HIGH-CAPACITY, QUICK-RELOAD WEAPONS FOUND IN GUN STORES NATION WIDE...
...WHICH LEAD TO THE LOSS OF 49 INNOCENT LIVES.
%@$# IT. FROM NOW ON, I JUST USE KARATE.

Written by Taran Killam • Illustrated by Barry Crain • Colored by Giulia Brusco • Lettered by Joshua Cozine

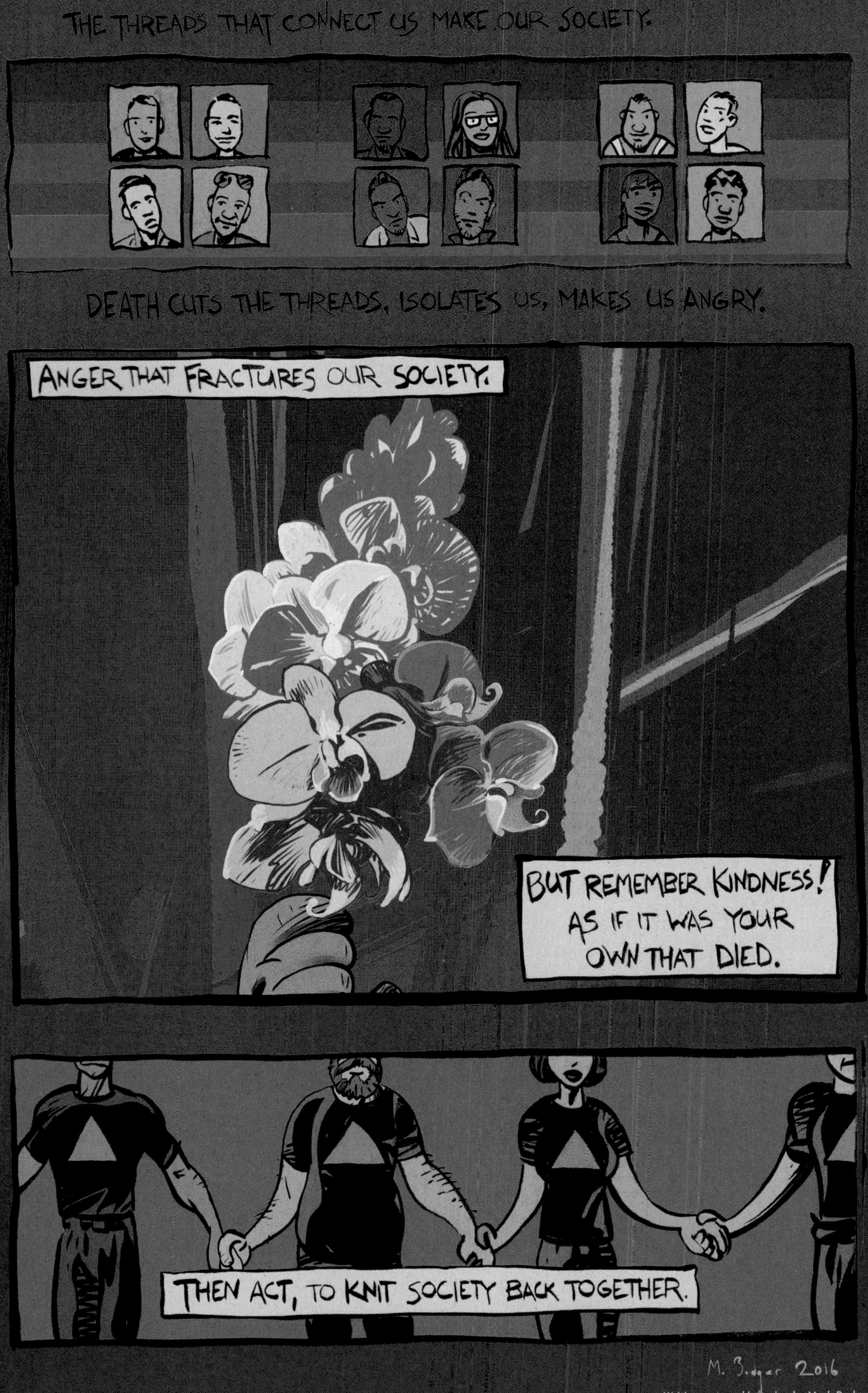
THE THREADS THAT CONNECT US MAKE OUR SOCIETY.
DEATH CUTS THE THREADS, ISOLATES US, MAKES US ANGRY.
ANGER THAT FRACTURES OUR SOCIETY.
BUT REMEMBER KINDNESS! AS IF IT WAS YOUR OWN THAT DIED.
THEN ACT, TO KNIT SOCIETY BACK TOGETHER.
M. Badger 2016

Writing, art, and lettering by Mark Badger

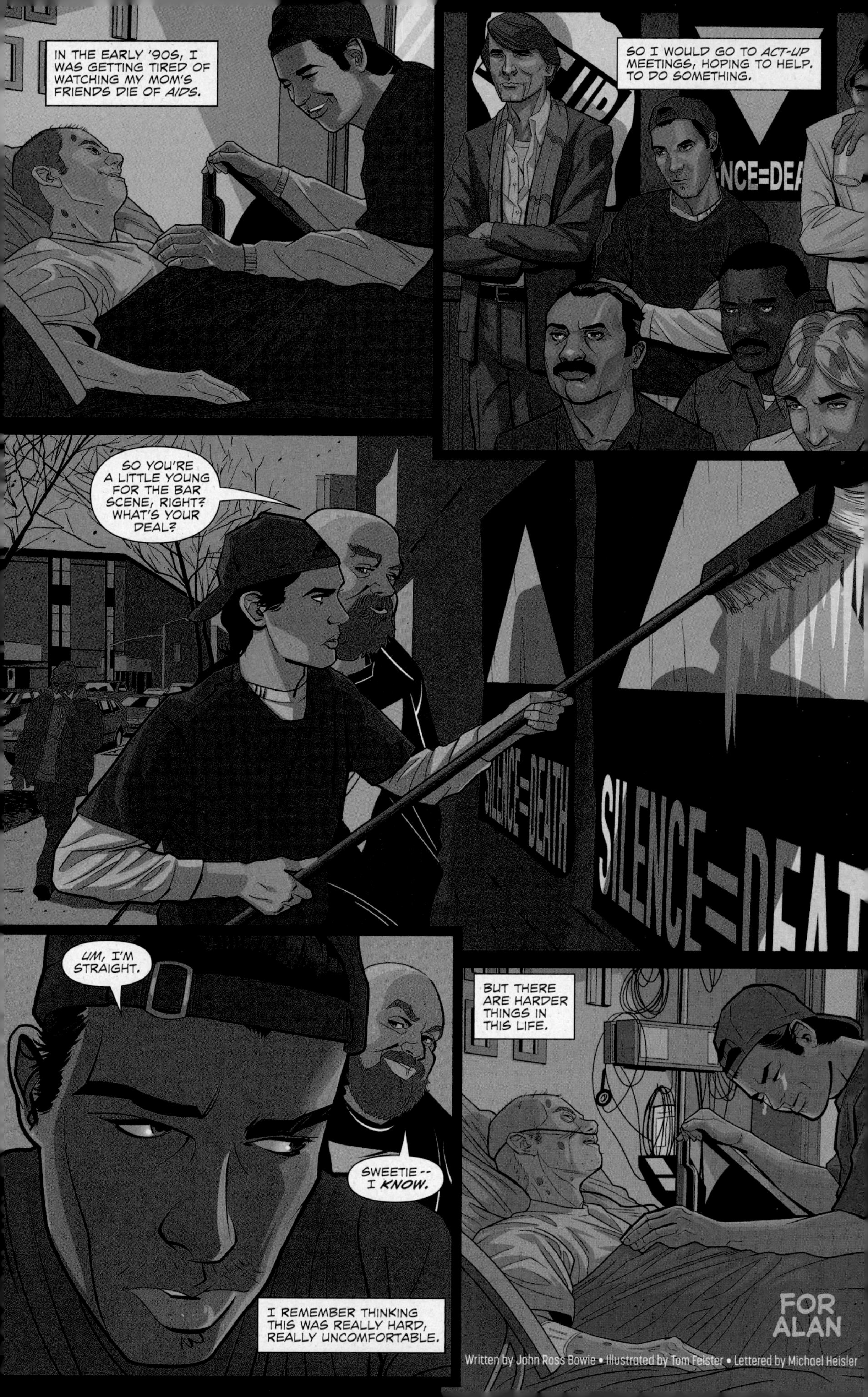

IN THE EARLY '90S, I WAS GETTING TIRED OF WATCHING MY MOM'S FRIENDS DIE OF *AIDS*.
SO I WOULD GO TO *ACT-UP* MEETINGS, HOPING TO HELP. TO DO SOMETHING.
NCE=DEA
SO YOU'RE A LITTLE YOUNG FOR THE BAR SCENE, RIGHT? WHAT'S YOUR DEAL?
SILENCE=DEATH
SILENCE=DEAT
UM, I'M STRAIGHT.
SWEETIE -- I ***KNOW***.
I REMEMBER THINKING THIS WAS REALLY HARD, REALLY UNCOMFORTABLE.
BUT THERE ARE HARDER THINGS IN THIS LIFE.
FOR ALAN
Written by John Ross Bowie • Illustrated by Tom Feister • Lettered by Michael Heisler

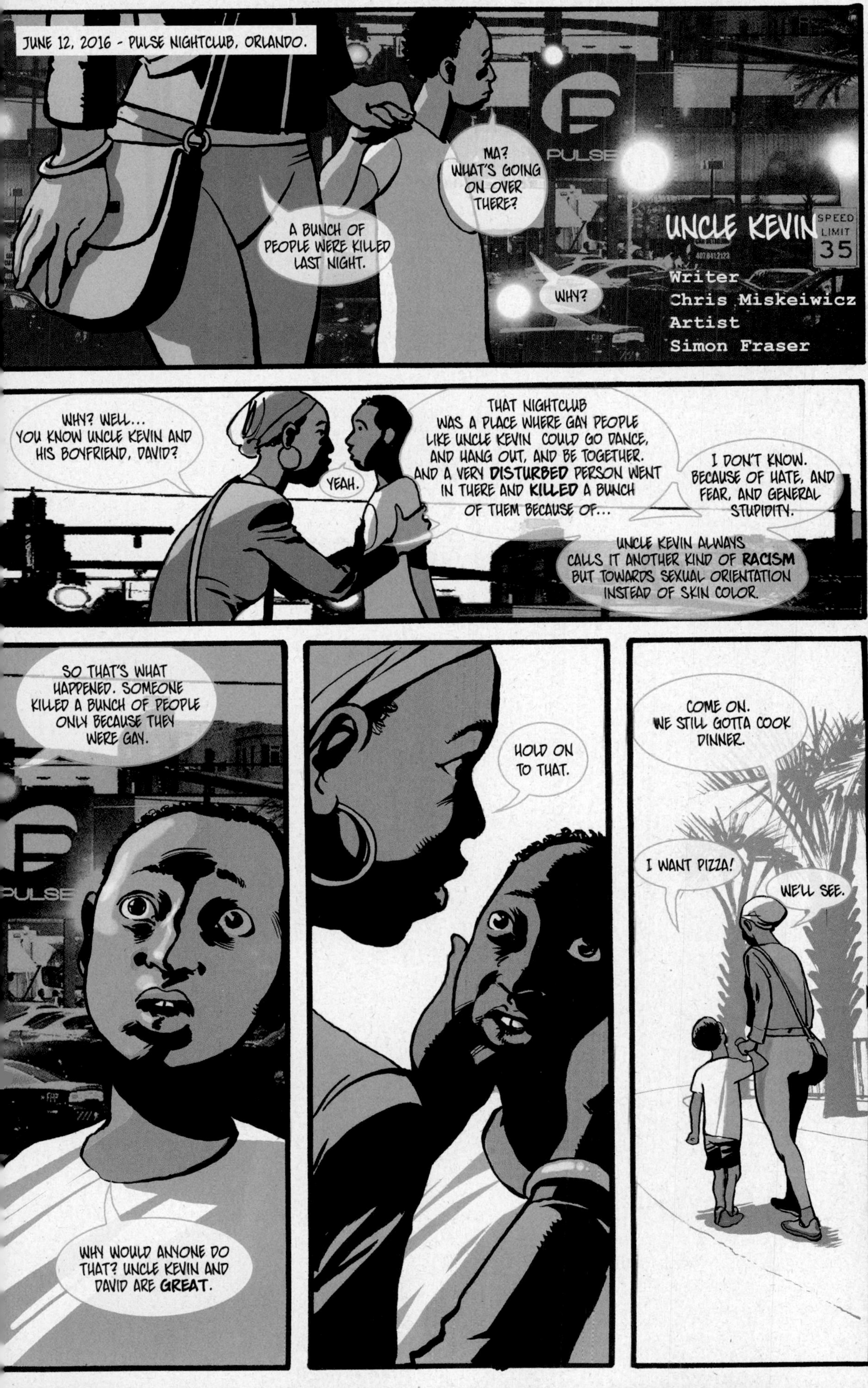
JUNE 12, 2016 - PULSE NIGHTCLUB, ORLANDO.
MA? WHAT'S GOING ON OVER THERE?
A BUNCH OF PEOPLE WERE KILLED LAST NIGHT.
UNCLE KEVIN
Writer
Chris Miskeiwicz
Artist
Simon Fraser
WHY?
WHY? WELL... YOU KNOW UNCLE KEVIN AND HIS BOYFRIEND, DAVID?
YEAH.
THAT NIGHTCLUB WAS A PLACE WHERE GAY PEOPLE LIKE UNCLE KEVIN COULD GO DANCE, AND HANG OUT, AND BE TOGETHER. AND A VERY **DISTURBED** PERSON WENT IN THERE AND **KILLED** A BUNCH OF THEM BECAUSE OF...
I DON'T KNOW. BECAUSE OF HATE, AND FEAR, AND GENERAL STUPIDITY.
UNCLE KEVIN ALWAYS CALLS IT ANOTHER KIND OF **RACISM** BUT TOWARDS SEXUAL ORIENTATION INSTEAD OF SKIN COLOR.
SO THAT'S WHAT HAPPENED. SOMEONE KILLED A BUNCH OF PEOPLE ONLY BECAUSE THEY WERE GAY.
WHY WOULD ANYONE DO THAT? UNCLE KEVIN AND DAVID ARE **GREAT**.
HOLD ON TO THAT.
COME ON. WE STILL GOTTA COOK DINNER.
I WANT PIZZA!
WE'LL SEE.

## 2,000 Characters

There is so much to me that 2,000 characters cannot begin to explain, so I'll try to be plain.

**I - have - a brain.**

Two eyes. Muscular thighs to walk in the park before dark and connect through the windows of the soul sharing our deepest thoughts and ultimate goal: "I want to be somebody when I grow up." Somebody with grown-up dreams & screams for these dreams to be crossover dreams into reality. My reality are dreams put into action.
I'm into grown-up fractions.

**YOU** divided by **ME** equals **WE**.

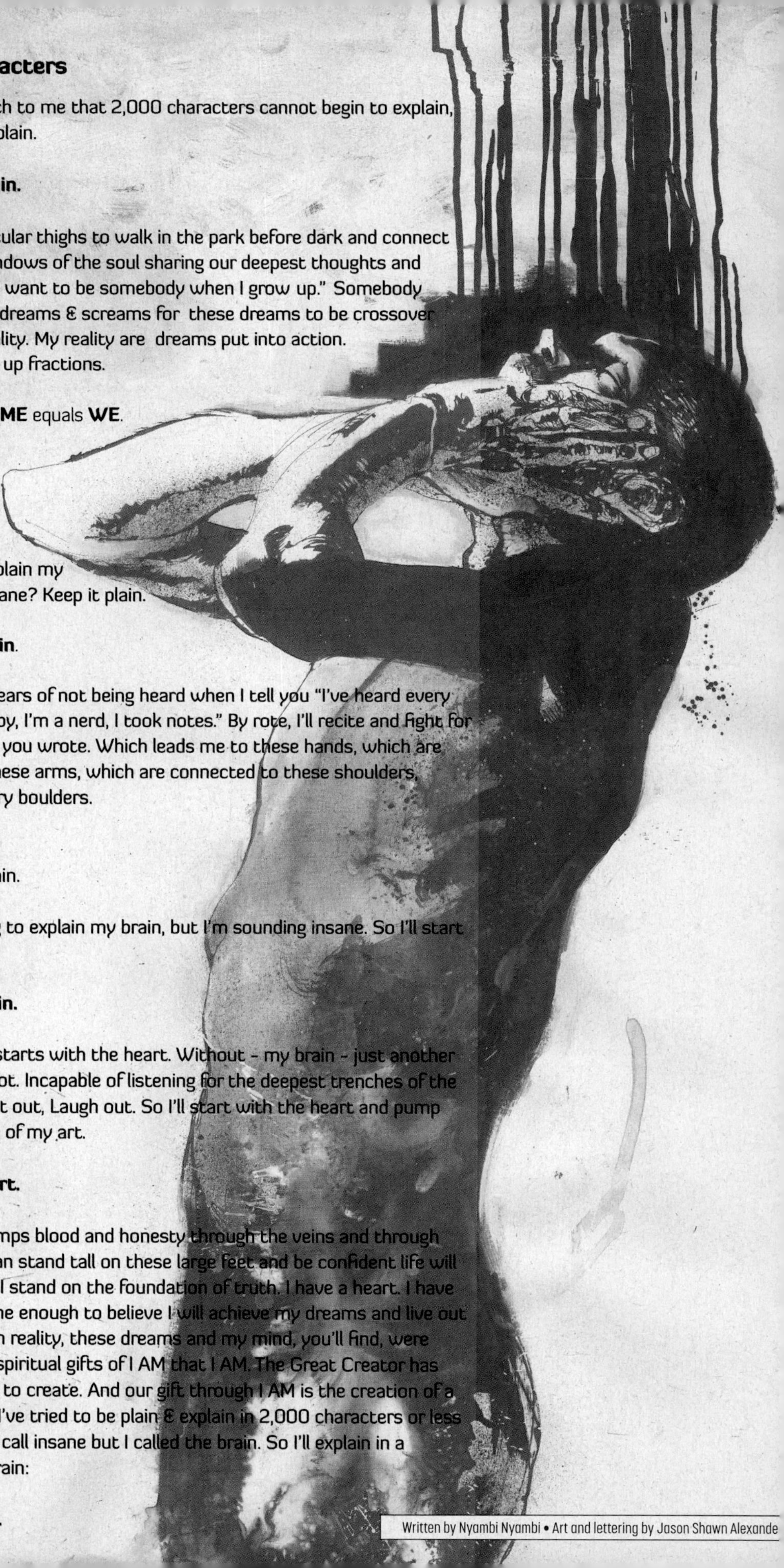

I'm trying to explain my
brain, sound insane? Keep it plain.

**I - have - a brain**.

Two ears. And fears of not being heard when I tell you "I've heard every word, c'mon baby, I'm a nerd, I took notes." By rote, I'll recite and fight for every note that you wrote. Which leads me to these hands, which are connected to these arms, which are connected to these shoulders, equipped to carry boulders.

Of doubt.
Frustration & pain.

Again, I'm trying to explain my brain, but I'm sounding insane. So I'll start again.

**I - have - a brain.**

But everything starts with the heart. Without - my brain - just another part, on auto pilot. Incapable of listening for the deepest trenches of the soul Cry out, Act out, Laugh out. So I'll start with the heart and pump from the source of my art.

**I - have - a heart.**

A heart that pumps blood and honesty through the veins and through these lips so I can stand tall on these large feet and be confident life will be sweet cause I stand on the foundation of truth. I have a heart. I have a brain. I'm insane enough to believe I will achieve my dreams and live out my reality. But in reality, these dreams and my mind, you'll find, were founded by the spiritual gifts of I AM that I AM. The Great Creator has given us the gift to create. And our gift through I AM is the creation of a new beginning. I've tried to be plain & explain in 2,000 characters or less what you might call insane but I called the brain. So I'll explain in a complicated refrain:

**I - am - human.**

Written by Nyambi Nyambi • Art and lettering by Jason Shawn Alexande

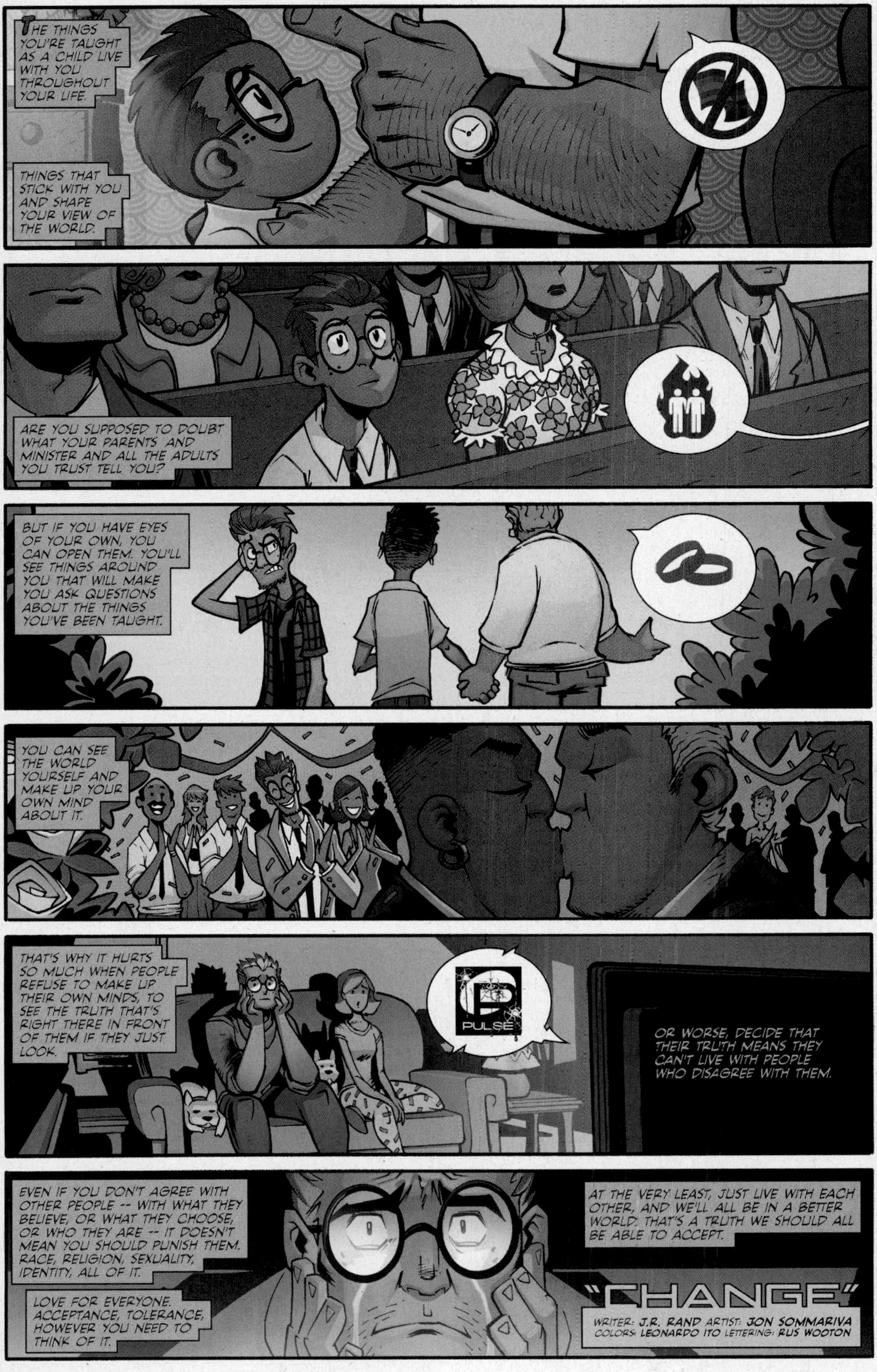
THE THINGS YOU'RE TAUGHT AS A CHILD LIVE WITH YOU THROUGHOUT YOUR LIFE.
THINGS THAT STICK WITH YOU AND SHAPE YOUR VIEW OF THE WORLD.
ARE YOU SUPPOSED TO DOUBT WHAT YOUR PARENTS AND MINISTER AND ALL THE ADULTS YOU TRUST TELL YOU?
BUT IF YOU HAVE EYES OF YOUR OWN, YOU CAN OPEN THEM. YOU'LL SEE THINGS AROUND YOU THAT WILL MAKE YOU ASK QUESTIONS ABOUT THE THINGS YOU'VE BEEN TAUGHT.
YOU CAN SEE THE WORLD YOURSELF AND MAKE UP YOUR OWN MIND ABOUT IT.
THAT'S WHY IT HURTS SO MUCH WHEN PEOPLE REFUSE TO MAKE UP THEIR OWN MINDS, TO SEE THE TRUTH THAT'S RIGHT THERE IN FRONT OF THEM IF THEY JUST LOOK.
PULSE
OR WORSE, DECIDE THAT THEIR TRUTH MEANS THEY CAN'T LIVE WITH PEOPLE WHO DISAGREE WITH THEM.
EVEN IF YOU DON'T AGREE WITH OTHER PEOPLE -- WITH WHAT THEY BELIEVE, OR WHAT THEY CHOOSE, OR WHO THEY ARE -- IT DOESN'T MEAN YOU SHOULD PUNISH THEM. RACE, RELIGION, SEXUALITY, IDENTITY, ALL OF IT.
LOVE FOR EVERYONE. ACCEPTANCE, TOLERANCE, HOWEVER YOU NEED TO THINK OF IT.
AT THE VERY LEAST, JUST LIVE WITH EACH OTHER, AND WE'LL ALL BE IN A BETTER WORLD. THAT'S A TRUTH WE SHOULD ALL BE ABLE TO ACCEPT.
"CHANGE"
WRITER: J.R. RAND ARTIST: JON SOMMARIVA
COLORS: LEONARDO ITO LETTERING: RUS WOOTON

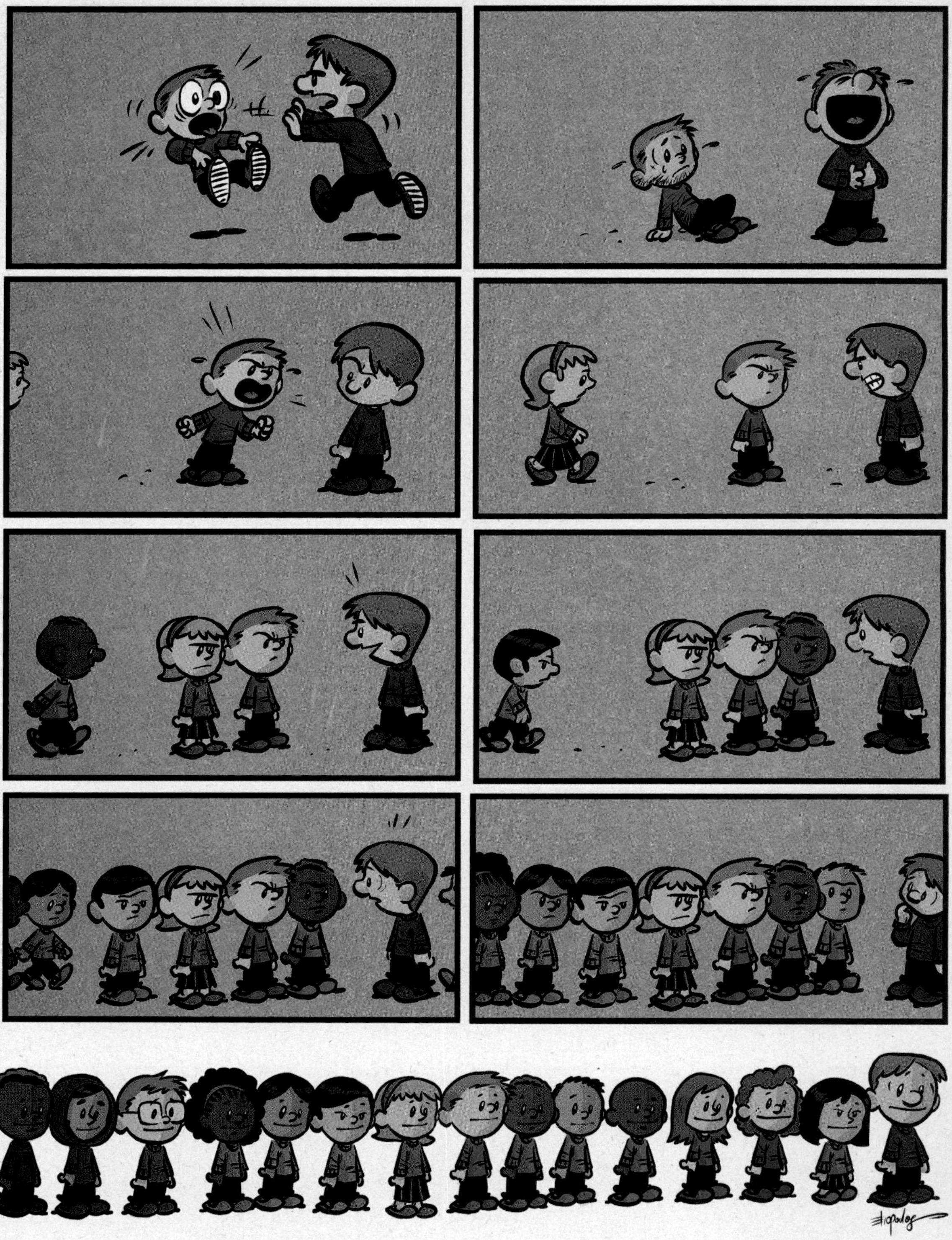

WHEN YOU BELIEVE IN SOMETHING, FIGHT FOR IT.
AND WHEN YOU SEE INJUSTICE, FIGHT HARDER THAN YOU'VE EVER FOUGHT BEFORE.

~BRAD MELTZER

Art and lettering by Chris Eliopoulos

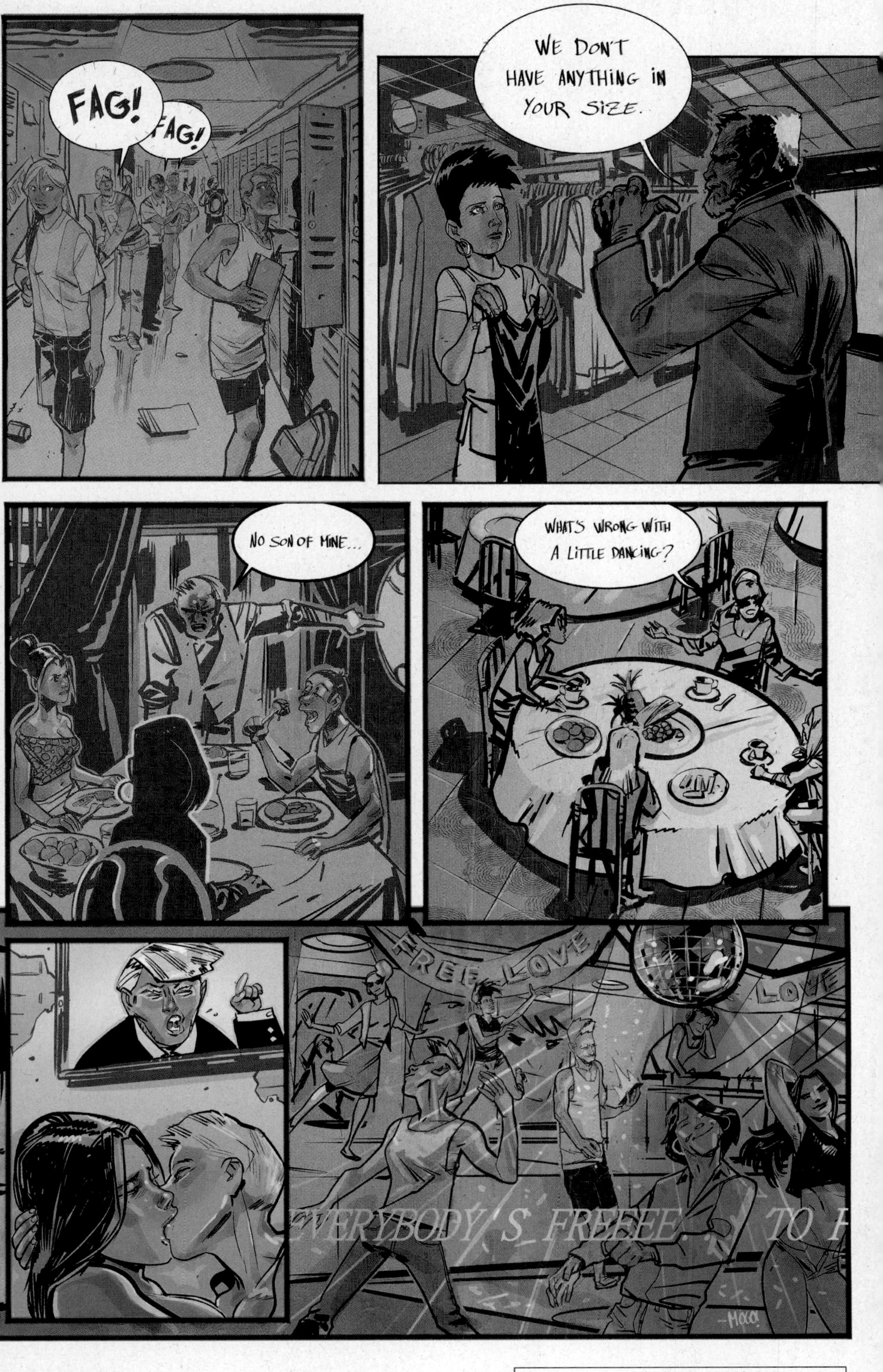
FAG!
FAG!
WE DON'T HAVE ANYTHING IN YOUR SIZE.
NO SON OF MINE...
WHAT'S WRONG WITH A LITTLE DANCING?
FREE LOVE
LOVE
EVERYBODY'S FREEEE... TO F
MOGO

Written by Drew Droege • Art and lettering by Guillermo Mogorron

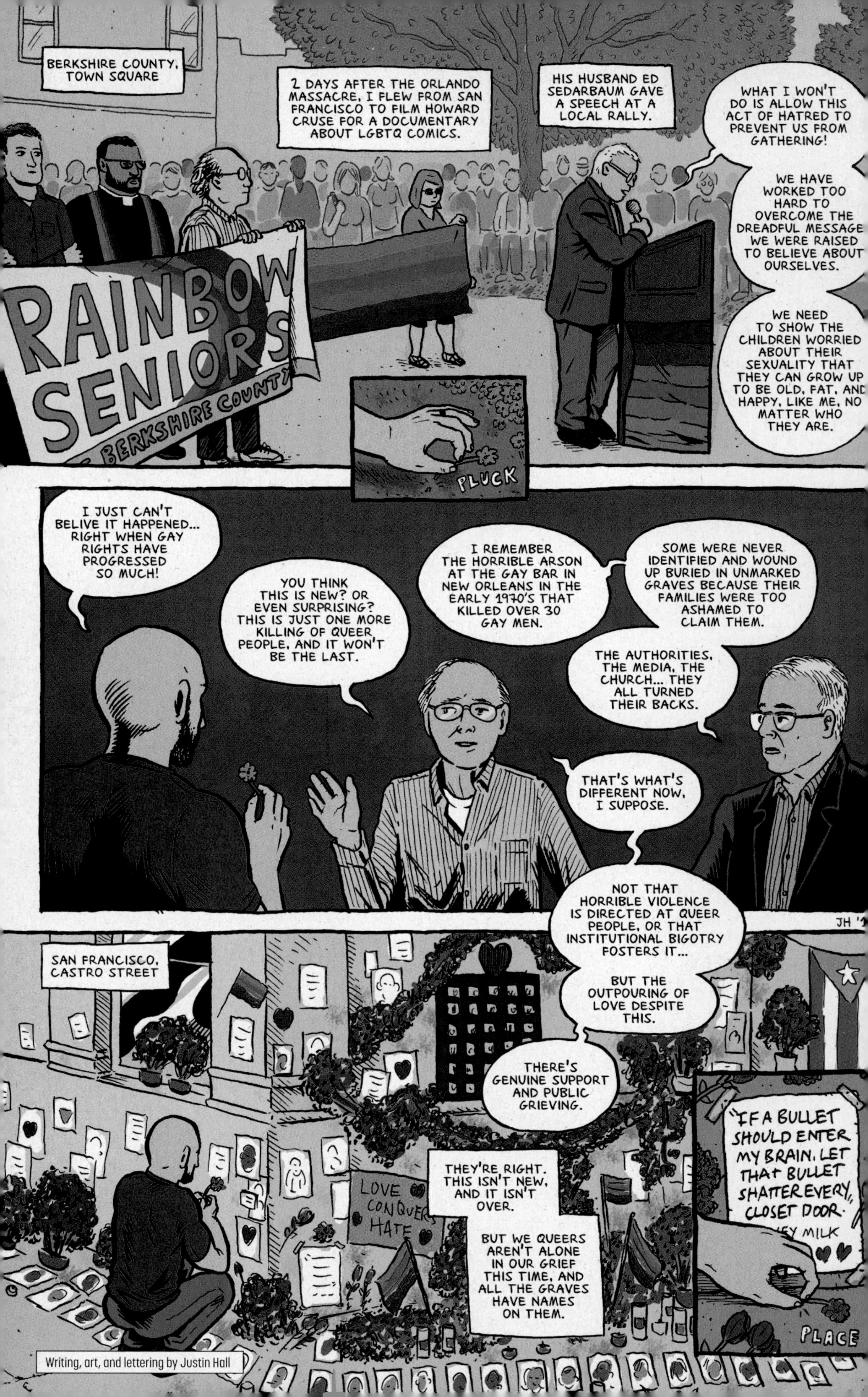
BERKSHIRE COUNTY, TOWN SQUARE
2 DAYS AFTER THE ORLANDO MASSACRE, I FLEW FROM SAN FRANCISCO TO FILM HOWARD CRUSE FOR A DOCUMENTARY ABOUT LGBTQ COMICS.
RAINBOW SENIORS BERKSHIRE COUNTY
HIS HUSBAND ED SEDARBAUM GAVE A SPEECH AT A LOCAL RALLY.
WHAT I WON'T DO IS ALLOW THIS ACT OF HATRED TO PREVENT US FROM GATHERING!
WE HAVE WORKED TOO HARD TO OVERCOME THE DREADFUL MESSAGE WE WERE RAISED TO BELIEVE ABOUT OURSELVES.
WE NEED TO SHOW THE CHILDREN WORRIED ABOUT THEIR SEXUALITY THAT THEY CAN GROW UP TO BE OLD, FAT, AND HAPPY, LIKE ME, NO MATTER WHO THEY ARE.
PLUCK
I JUST CAN'T BELIVE IT HAPPENED... RIGHT WHEN GAY RIGHTS HAVE PROGRESSED SO MUCH!
YOU THINK THIS IS NEW? OR EVEN SURPRISING? THIS IS JUST ONE MORE KILLING OF QUEER PEOPLE, AND IT WON'T BE THE LAST.
I REMEMBER THE HORRIBLE ARSON AT THE GAY BAR IN NEW ORLEANS IN THE EARLY 1970'S THAT KILLED OVER 30 GAY MEN.
SOME WERE NEVER IDENTIFIED AND WOUND UP BURIED IN UNMARKED GRAVES BECAUSE THEIR FAMILIES WERE TOO ASHAMED TO CLAIM THEM.
THE AUTHORITIES, THE MEDIA, THE CHURCH... THEY ALL TURNED THEIR BACKS.
THAT'S WHAT'S DIFFERENT NOW, I SUPPOSE.
NOT THAT HORRIBLE VIOLENCE IS DIRECTED AT QUEER PEOPLE, OR THAT INSTITUTIONAL BIGOTRY FOSTERS IT...
BUT THE OUTPOURING OF LOVE DESPITE THIS.
SAN FRANCISCO, CASTRO STREET
THERE'S GENUINE SUPPORT AND PUBLIC GRIEVING.
LOVE CONQUERS HATE
THEY'RE RIGHT. THIS ISN'T NEW, AND IT ISN'T OVER.
BUT WE QUEERS AREN'T ALONE IN OUR GRIEF THIS TIME, AND ALL THE GRAVES HAVE NAMES ON THEM.
"IF A BULLET SHOULD ENTER MY BRAIN, LET THAT BULLET SHATTER EVERY CLOSET DOOR."
PLACE
Writing, art, and lettering by Justin Hall

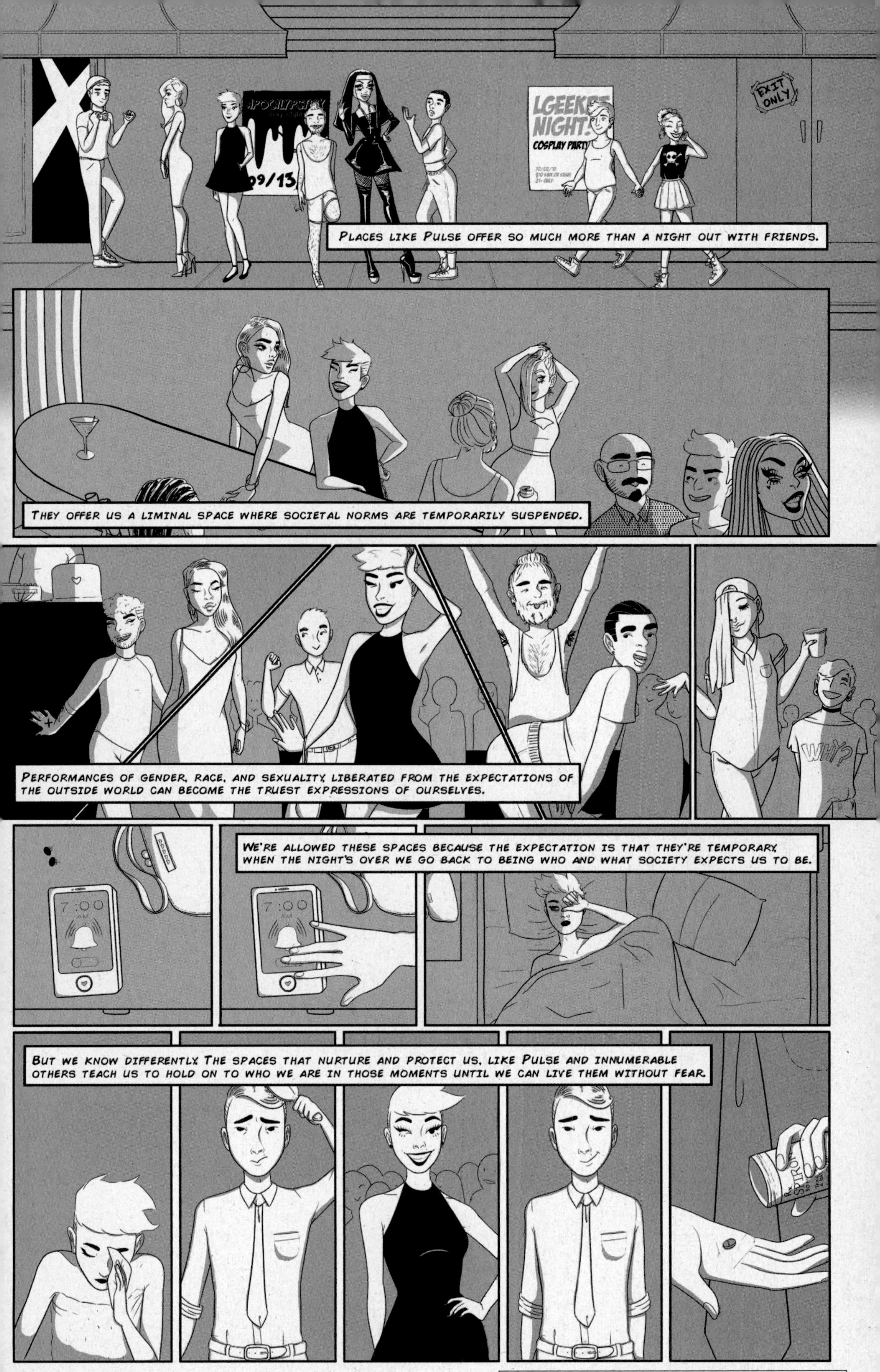
EXIT ONLY
09/13
PLACES LIKE PULSE OFFER SO MUCH MORE THAN A NIGHT OUT WITH FRIENDS.
THEY OFFER US A LIMINAL SPACE WHERE SOCIETAL NORMS ARE TEMPORARILY SUSPENDED.
PERFORMANCES OF GENDER, RACE, AND SEXUALITY, LIBERATED FROM THE EXPECTATIONS OF THE OUTSIDE WORLD CAN BECOME THE TRUEST EXPRESSIONS OF OURSELVES.
WHY?
7:00 AM
WE'RE ALLOWED THESE SPACES BECAUSE THE EXPECTATION IS THAT THEY'RE TEMPORARY, WHEN THE NIGHT'S OVER WE GO BACK TO BEING WHO AND WHAT SOCIETY EXPECTS US TO BE.
BUT WE KNOW DIFFERENTLY. THE SPACES THAT NURTURE AND PROTECT US, LIKE PULSE AND INNUMERABLE OTHERS TEACH US TO HOLD ON TO WHO WE ARE IN THOSE MOMENTS UNTIL WE CAN LIVE THEM WITHOUT FEAR.

Written by Emma Houxbois • Art and lettering by Alejandra Gutierrez

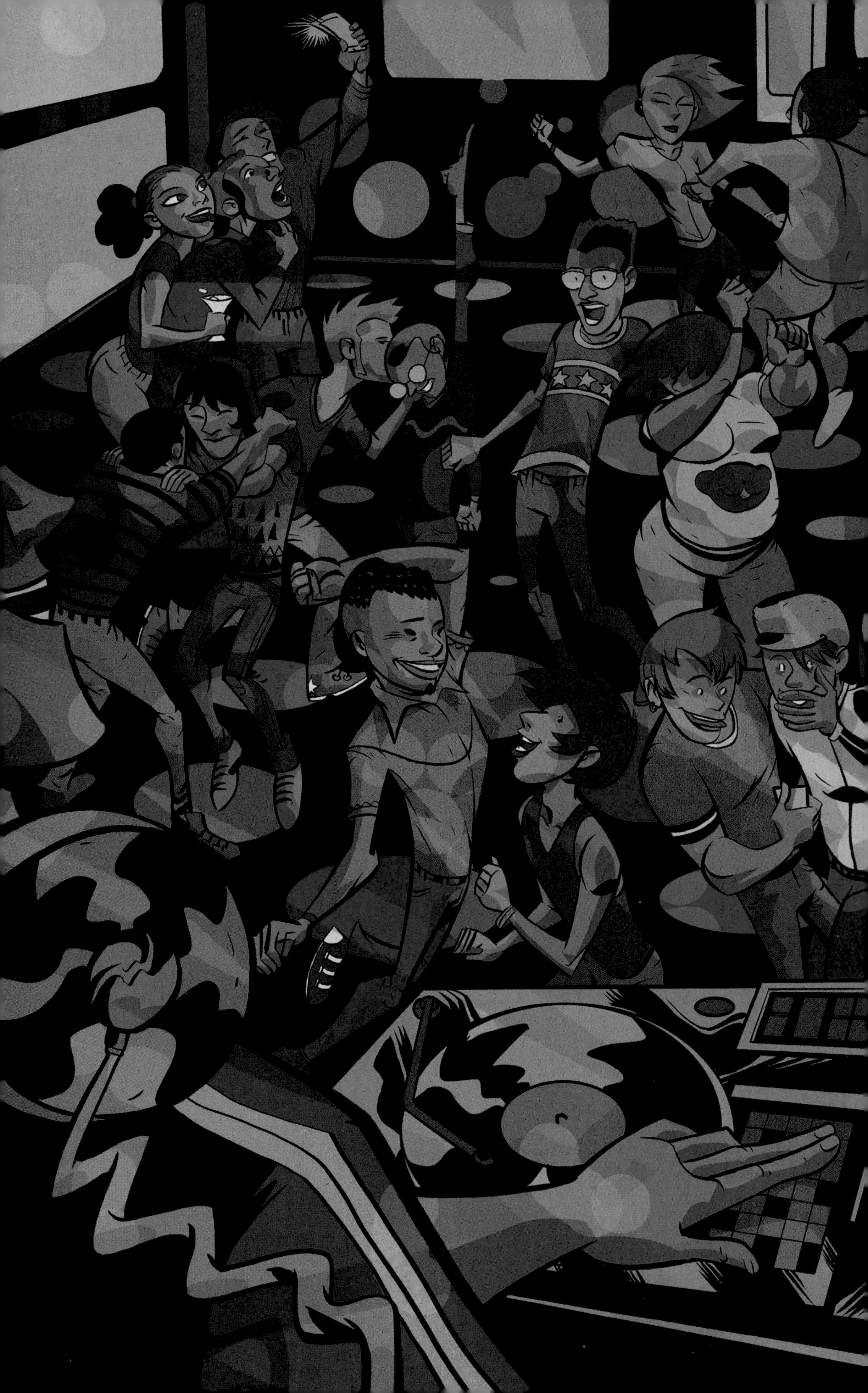

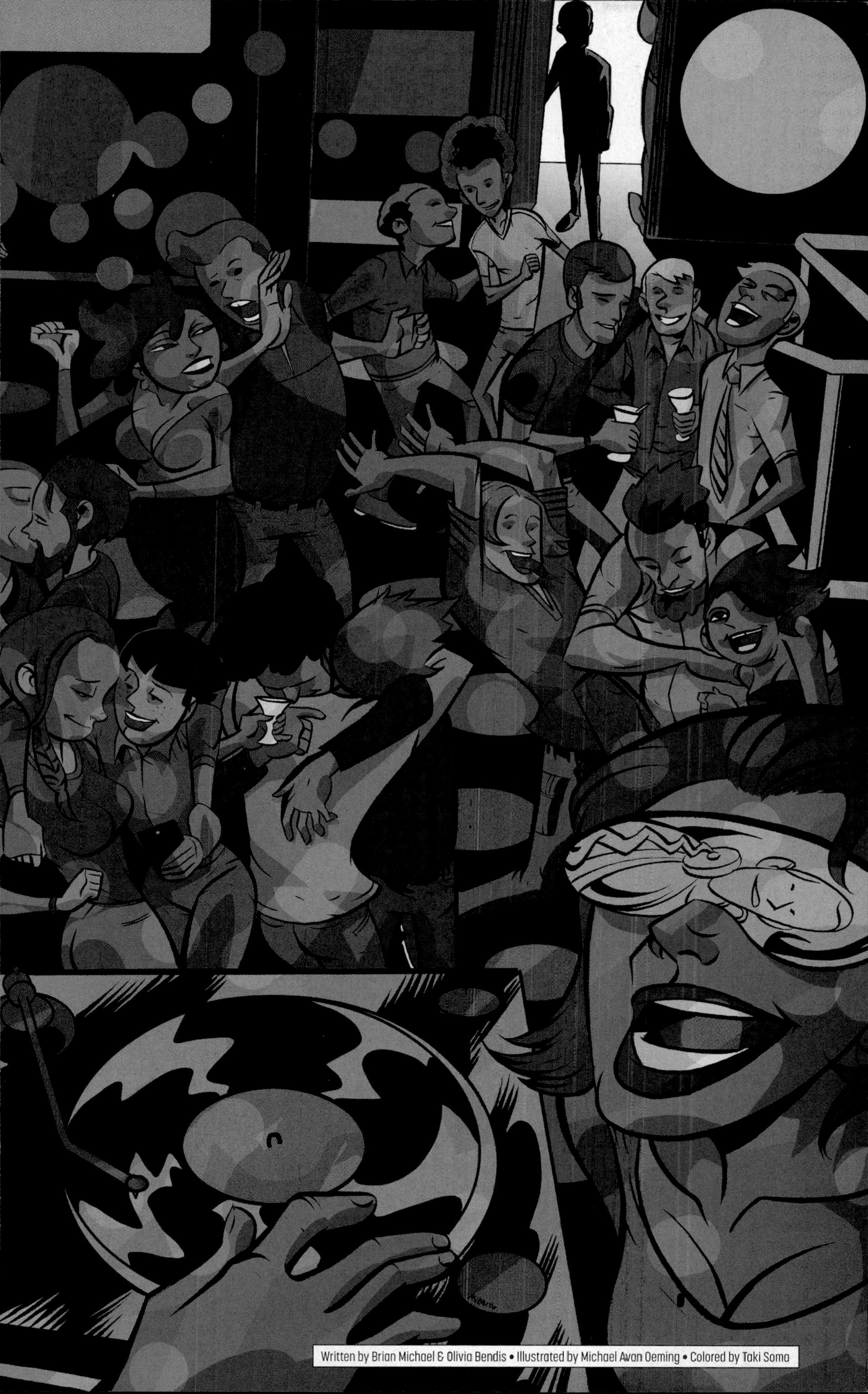

Written by Brian Michael & Olivia Bendis • Illustrated by Michael Avon Oeming • Colored by Taki Soma

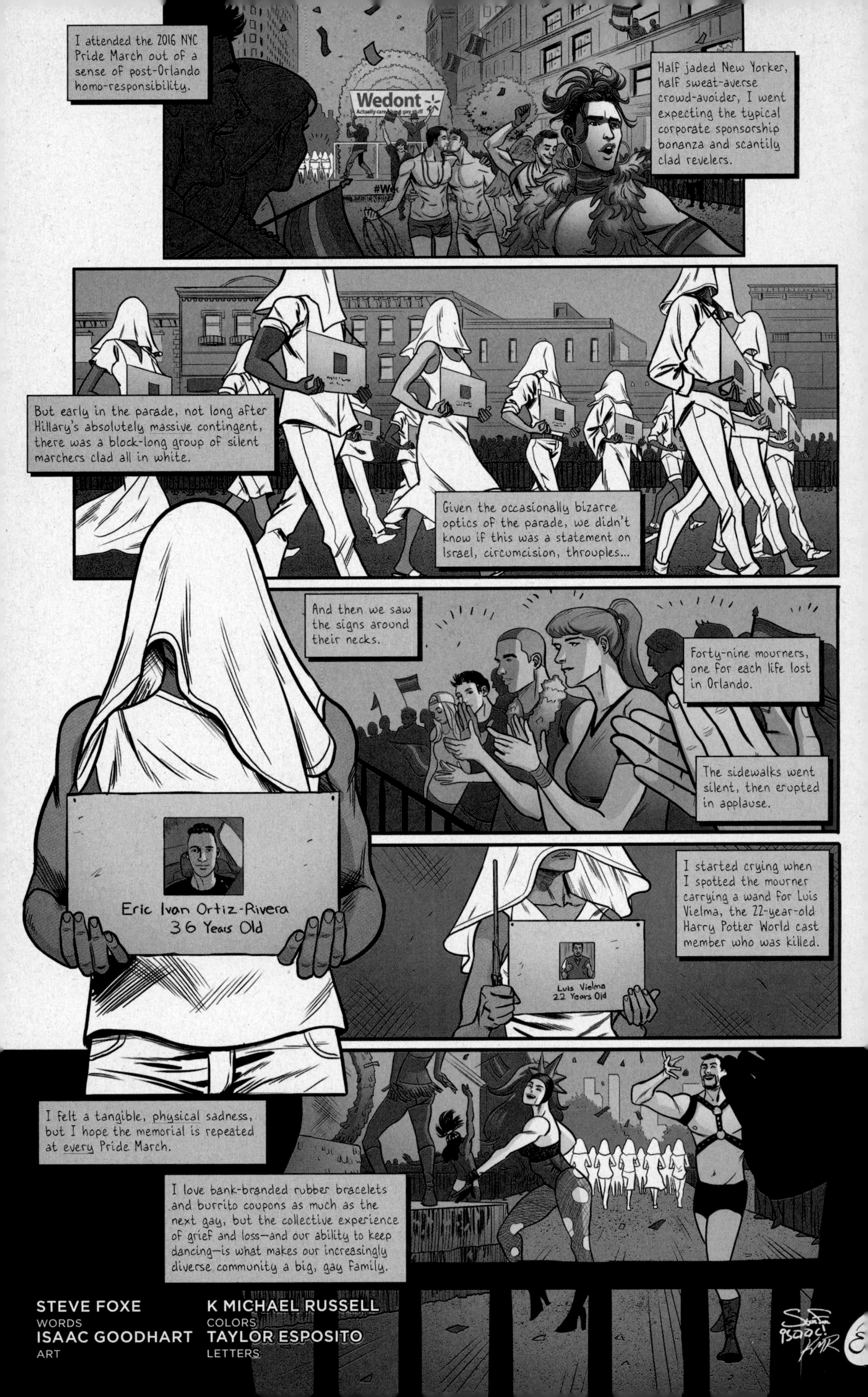
I attended the 2016 NYC Pride March out of a sense of post-Orlando homo-responsibility.
Wedont
Half jaded New Yorker, half sweat-averse crowd-avoider, I went expecting the typical corporate sponsorship bonanza and scantily clad revelers.
But early in the parade, not long after Hillary's absolutely massive contingent, there was a block-long group of silent marchers clad all in white.
Given the occasionally bizarre optics of the parade, we didn't know if this was a statement on Israel, circumcision, throuples...
Eric Ivan Ortiz-Rivera
36 Years Old
And then we saw the signs around their necks.
Forty-nine mourners, one for each life lost in Orlando.
The sidewalks went silent, then erupted in applause.
I started crying when I spotted the mourner carrying a wand for Luis Vielma, the 22-year-old Harry Potter World cast member who was killed.
Luis Vielma
22 Years Old
I felt a tangible, physical sadness, but I hope the memorial is repeated at every Pride March.
I love bank-branded rubber bracelets and burrito coupons as much as the next gay, but the collective experience of grief and loss—and our ability to keep dancing—is what makes our increasingly diverse community a big, gay family.
STEVE FOXE
WORDS
ISAAC GOODHART
ART
K MICHAEL RUSSELL
COLORS
TAYLOR ESPOSITO
LETTERS

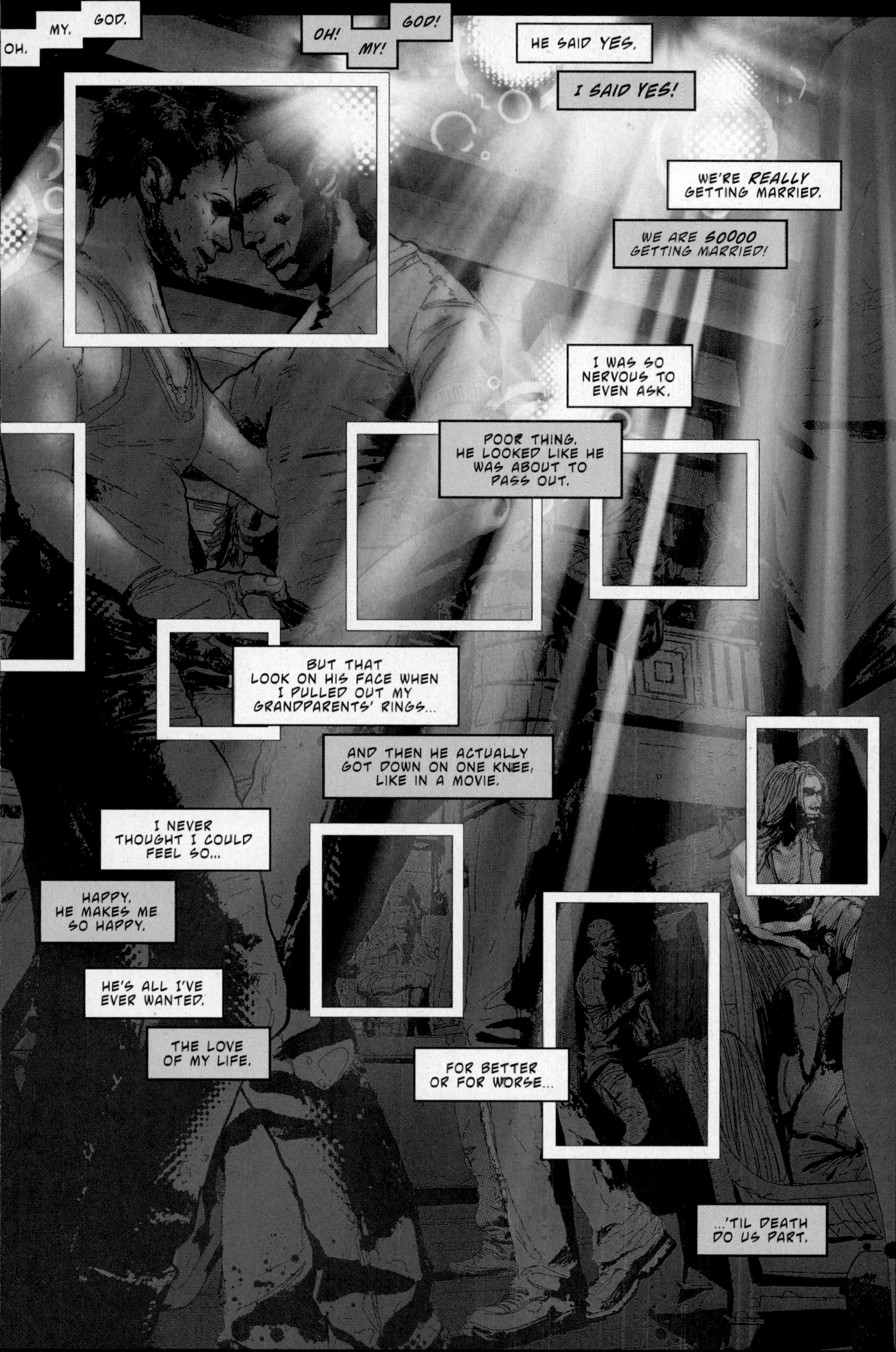
OH. MY. GOD.
OH! MY! GOD!
HE SAID YES.
I SAID YES!
WE'RE REALLY GETTING MARRIED.
WE ARE SOOOO GETTING MARRIED!
I WAS SO NERVOUS TO EVEN ASK.
POOR THING. HE LOOKED LIKE HE WAS ABOUT TO PASS OUT.
BUT THAT LOOK ON HIS FACE WHEN I PULLED OUT MY GRANDPARENTS' RINGS...
AND THEN HE ACTUALLY GOT DOWN ON ONE KNEE, LIKE IN A MOVIE.
I NEVER THOUGHT I COULD FEEL SO...
HAPPY. HE MAKES ME SO HAPPY.
HE'S ALL I'VE EVER WANTED.
THE LOVE OF MY LIFE.
FOR BETTER OR FOR WORSE...
...'TIL DEATH DO US PART.

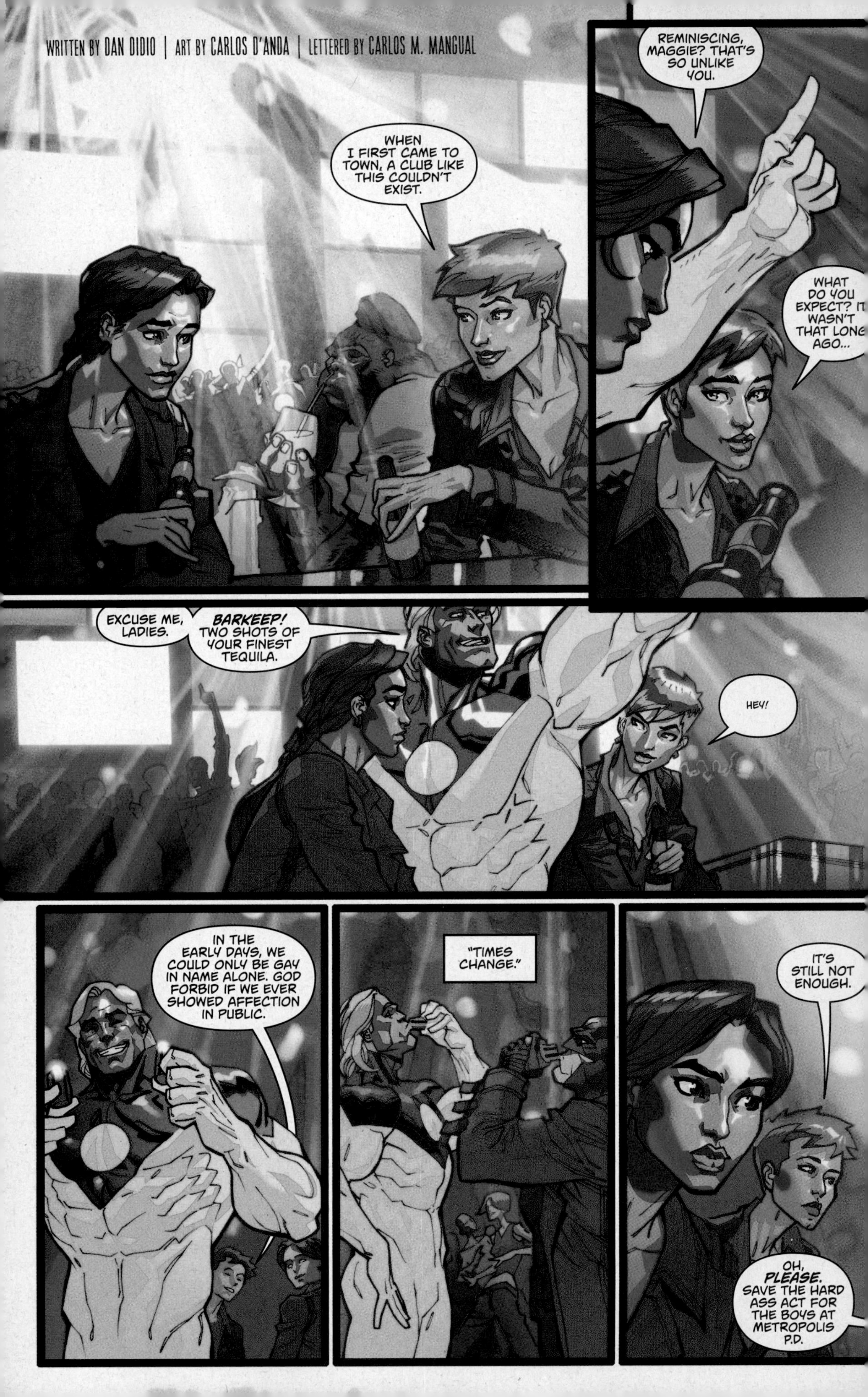
WRITTEN BY DAN DIDIO | ART BY CARLOS D'ANDA | LETTERED BY CARLOS M. MANGUAL
WHEN I FIRST CAME TO TOWN, A CLUB LIKE THIS COULDN'T EXIST.
REMINISCING, MAGGIE? THAT'S SO UNLIKE YOU.
WHAT DO YOU EXPECT? IT WASN'T THAT LONG AGO...
EXCUSE ME, LADIES.
*BARKEEP!* TWO SHOTS OF YOUR FINEST TEQUILA.
HEY!
IN THE EARLY DAYS, WE COULD ONLY BE GAY IN NAME ALONE. GOD FORBID IF WE EVER SHOWED AFFECTION IN PUBLIC.
"TIMES CHANGE."
IT'S STILL NOT ENOUGH.
OH, *PLEASE.* SAVE THE HARD ASS ACT FOR THE BOYS AT METROPOLIS P.D.

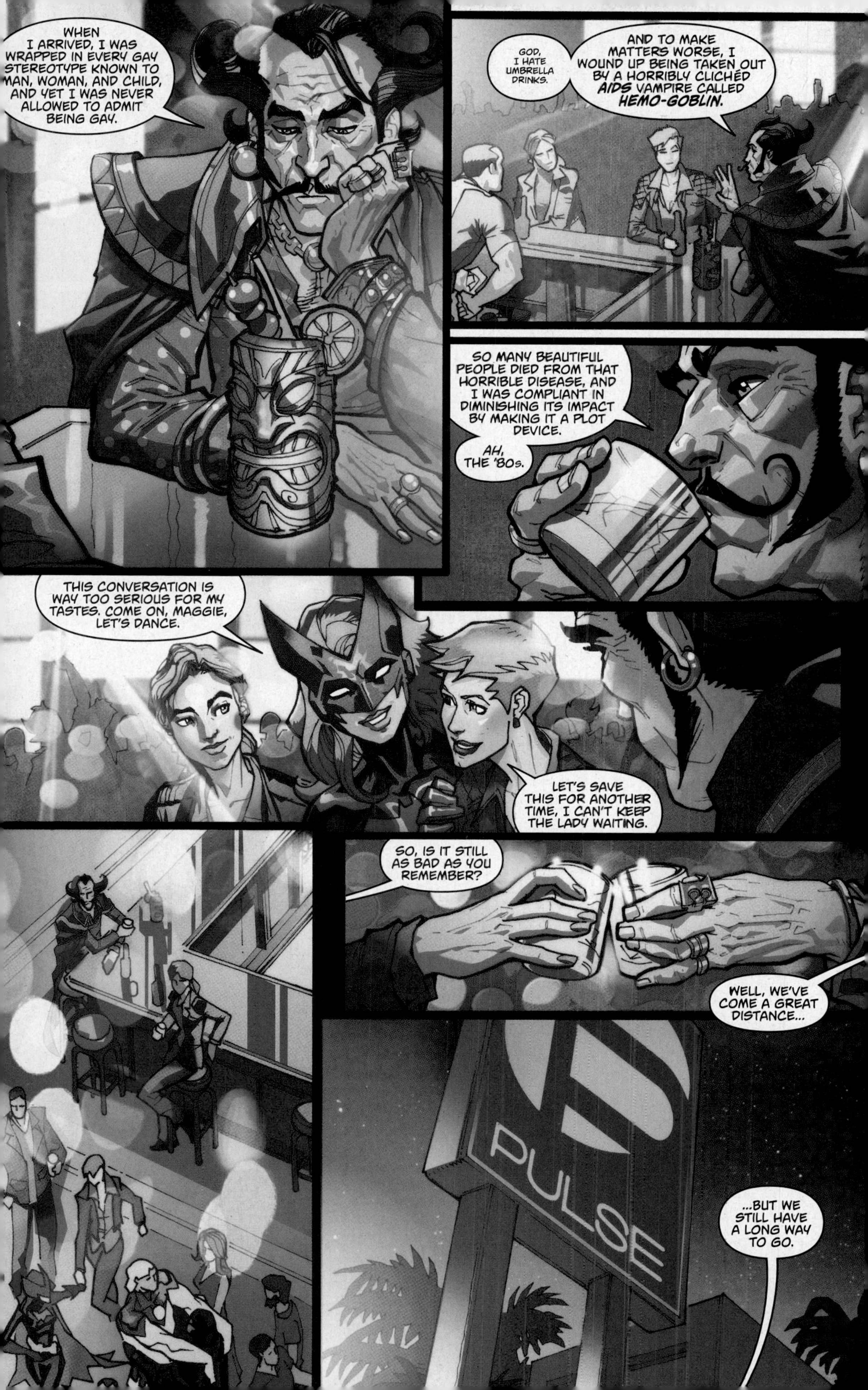
WHEN I ARRIVED, I WAS WRAPPED IN EVERY GAY STEREOTYPE KNOWN TO MAN, WOMAN, AND CHILD, AND YET I WAS NEVER ALLOWED TO ADMIT BEING GAY.
GOD, I HATE UMBRELLA DRINKS.
AND TO MAKE MATTERS WORSE, I WOUND UP BEING TAKEN OUT BY A HORRIBLY CLICHÉD AIDS VAMPIRE CALLED HEMO-GOBLIN.
SO MANY BEAUTIFUL PEOPLE DIED FROM THAT HORRIBLE DISEASE, AND I WAS COMPLIANT IN DIMINISHING ITS IMPACT BY MAKING IT A PLOT DEVICE.
AH, THE '80s.
THIS CONVERSATION IS WAY TOO SERIOUS FOR MY TASTES. COME ON, MAGGIE, LET'S DANCE.
LET'S SAVE THIS FOR ANOTHER TIME, I CAN'T KEEP THE LADY WAITING.
SO, IS IT STILL AS BAD AS YOU REMEMBER?
WELL, WE'VE COME A GREAT DISTANCE...
PULSE
...BUT WE STILL HAVE A LONG WAY TO GO.

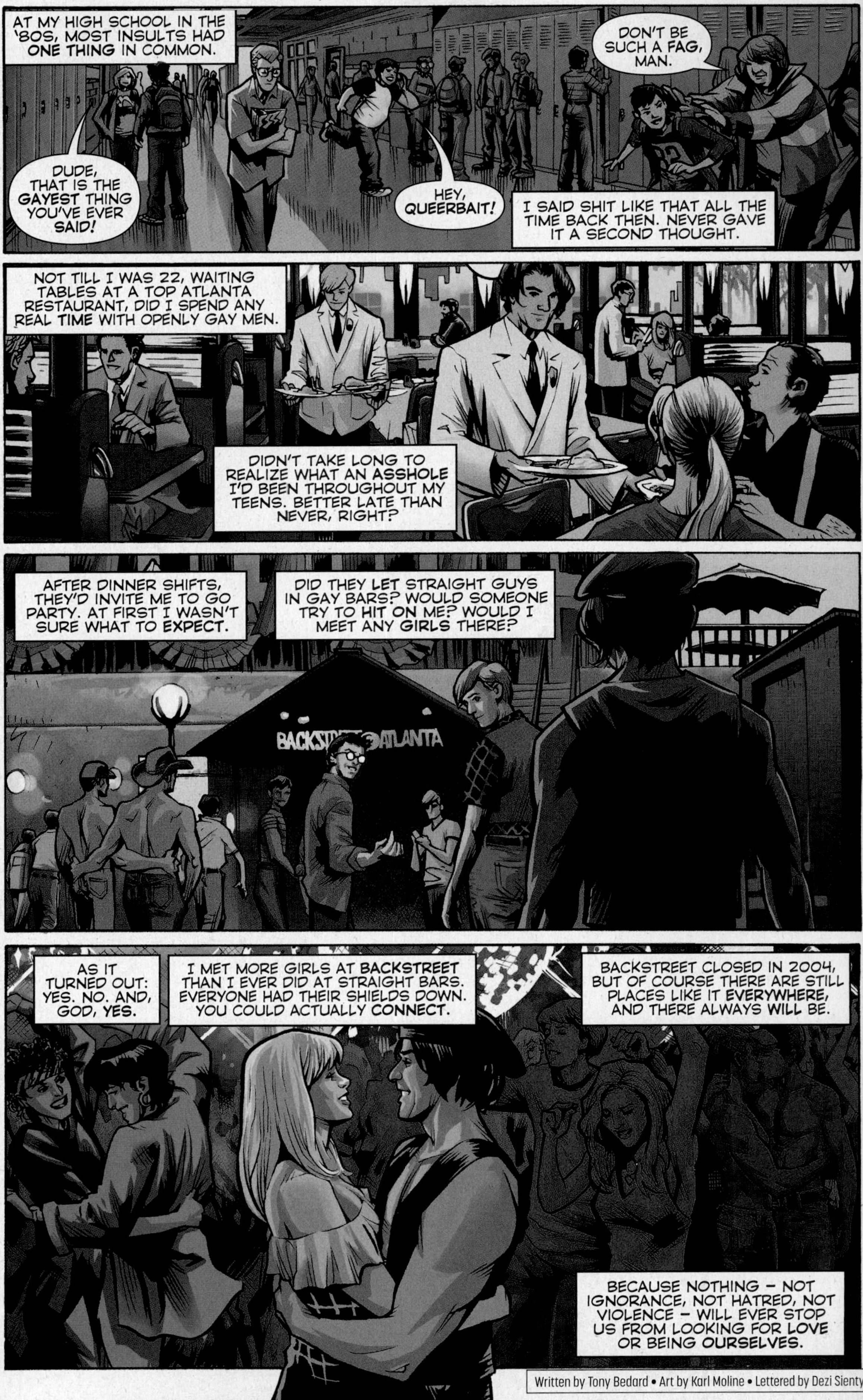
AT MY HIGH SCHOOL IN THE '80S, MOST INSULTS HAD ONE THING IN COMMON.
DUDE, THAT IS THE GAYEST THING YOU'VE EVER SAID!
HEY, QUEERBAIT!
DON'T BE SUCH A FAG, MAN.
I SAID SHIT LIKE THAT ALL THE TIME BACK THEN. NEVER GAVE IT A SECOND THOUGHT.
NOT TILL I WAS 22, WAITING TABLES AT A TOP ATLANTA RESTAURANT, DID I SPEND ANY REAL TIME WITH OPENLY GAY MEN.
DIDN'T TAKE LONG TO REALIZE WHAT AN ASSHOLE I'D BEEN THROUGHOUT MY TEENS. BETTER LATE THAN NEVER, RIGHT?
AFTER DINNER SHIFTS, THEY'D INVITE ME TO GO PARTY. AT FIRST I WASN'T SURE WHAT TO EXPECT.
DID THEY LET STRAIGHT GUYS IN GAY BARS? WOULD SOMEONE TRY TO HIT ON ME? WOULD I MEET ANY GIRLS THERE?
BACKSTREET ATLANTA
AS IT TURNED OUT: YES. NO. AND, GOD, YES.
I MET MORE GIRLS AT BACKSTREET THAN I EVER DID AT STRAIGHT BARS. EVERYONE HAD THEIR SHIELDS DOWN. YOU COULD ACTUALLY CONNECT.
BACKSTREET CLOSED IN 2004, BUT OF COURSE THERE ARE STILL PLACES LIKE IT EVERYWHERE, AND THERE ALWAYS WILL BE.
BECAUSE NOTHING – NOT IGNORANCE, NOT HATRED, NOT VIOLENCE – WILL EVER STOP US FROM LOOKING FOR LOVE OR BEING OURSELVES.

Written by Tony Bedard • Art by Karl Moline • Lettered by Dezi Sienty

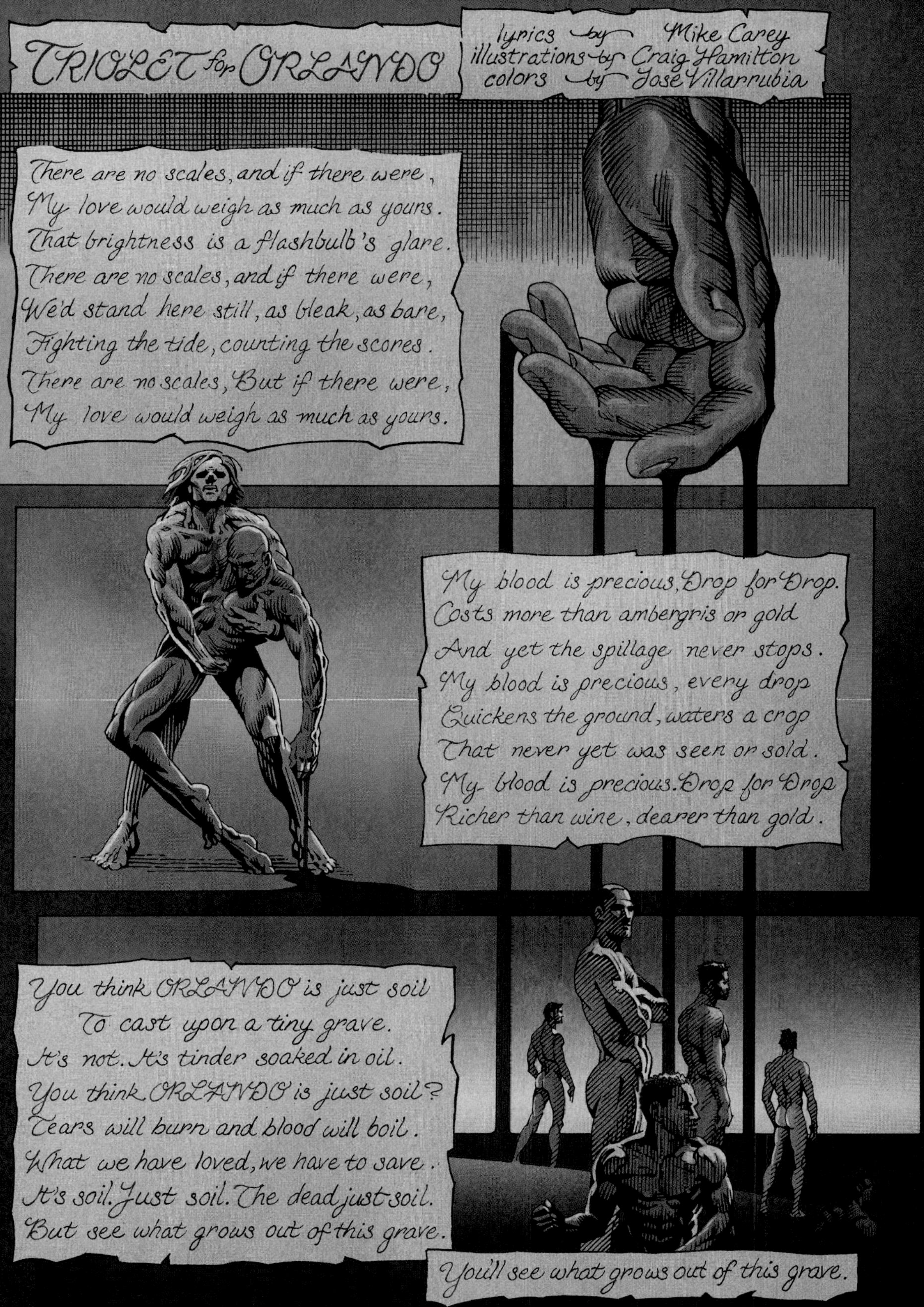
TRIOLET for ORLANDO
lyrics by Mike Carey
illustrations by Craig Hamilton
colors by Jose Villarrubia
There are no scales, and if there were,
My love would weigh as much as yours.
That brightness is a flashbulb's glare.
There are no scales, and if there were,
We'd stand here still, as bleak, as bare,
Fighting the tide, counting the scores.
There are no scales, But if there were,
My love would weigh as much as yours.
My blood is precious, Drop for Drop.
Costs more than ambergris or gold
And yet the spillage never stops.
My blood is precious, every drop
Quickens the ground, waters a crop
That never yet was seen or sold.
My blood is precious. Drop for Drop
Richer than wine, dearer than gold.
You think ORLANDO is just soil
To cast upon a tiny grave.
It's not. It's tinder soaked in oil.
You think ORLANDO is just soil?
Tears will burn and blood will boil.
What we have loved, we have to save.
It's soil. Just soil. The dead just soil.
But see what grows out of this grave.
You'll see what grows out of this grave.

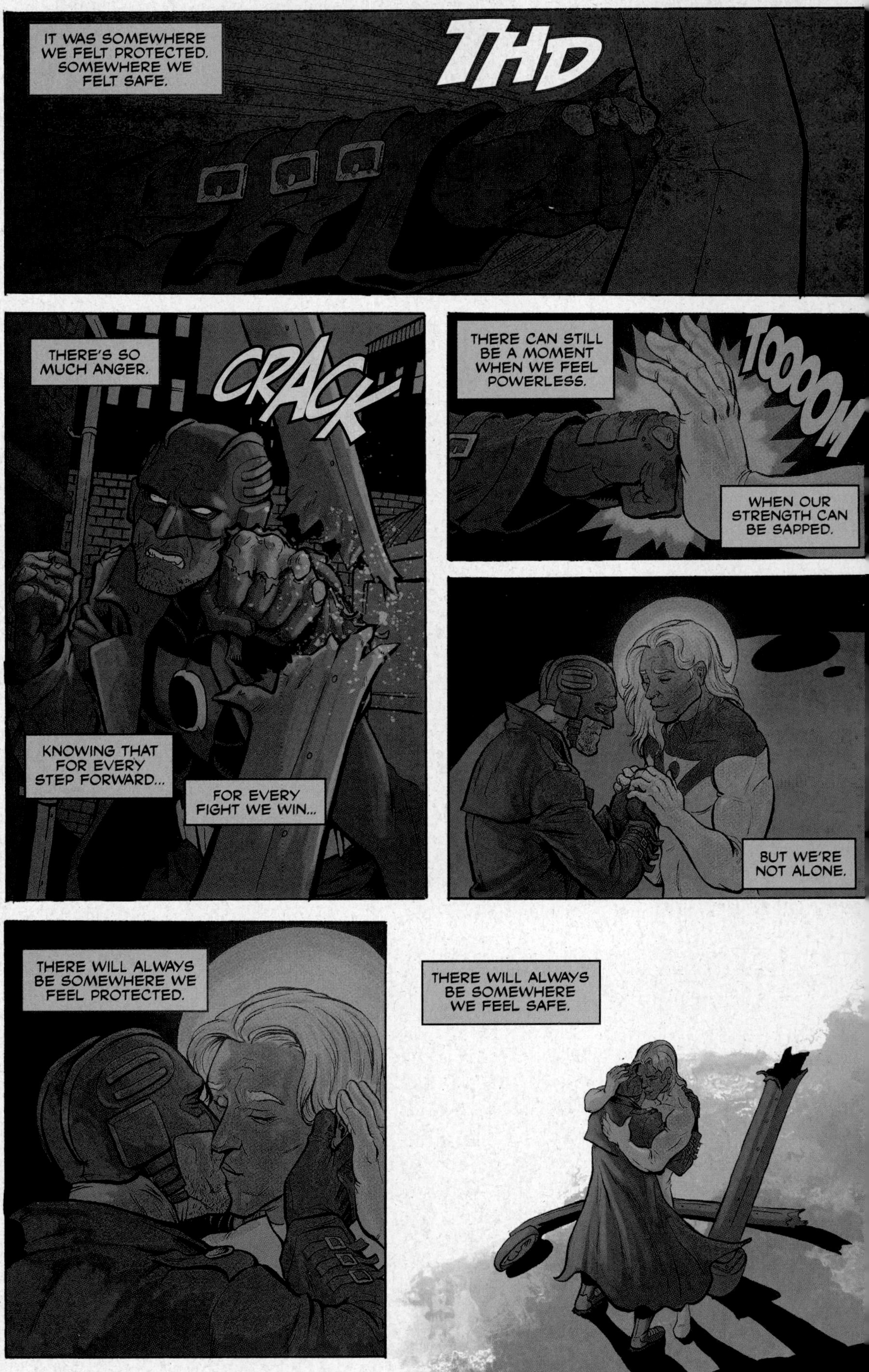
IT WAS SOMEWHERE WE FELT PROTECTED. SOMEWHERE WE FELT SAFE.
THD
THERE'S SO MUCH ANGER.
CRACK
KNOWING THAT FOR EVERY STEP FORWARD...
FOR EVERY FIGHT WE WIN...
THERE CAN STILL BE A MOMENT WHEN WE FEEL POWERLESS.
TOOOOM
WHEN OUR STRENGTH CAN BE SAPPED.
BUT WE'RE NOT ALONE.
THERE WILL ALWAYS BE SOMEWHERE WE FEEL PROTECTED.
THERE WILL ALWAYS BE SOMEWHERE WE FEEL SAFE.

Written by Tom Taylor • Illustrated by Emily Smith • Colored by Michael Garland • Lettered by Deron Bennett

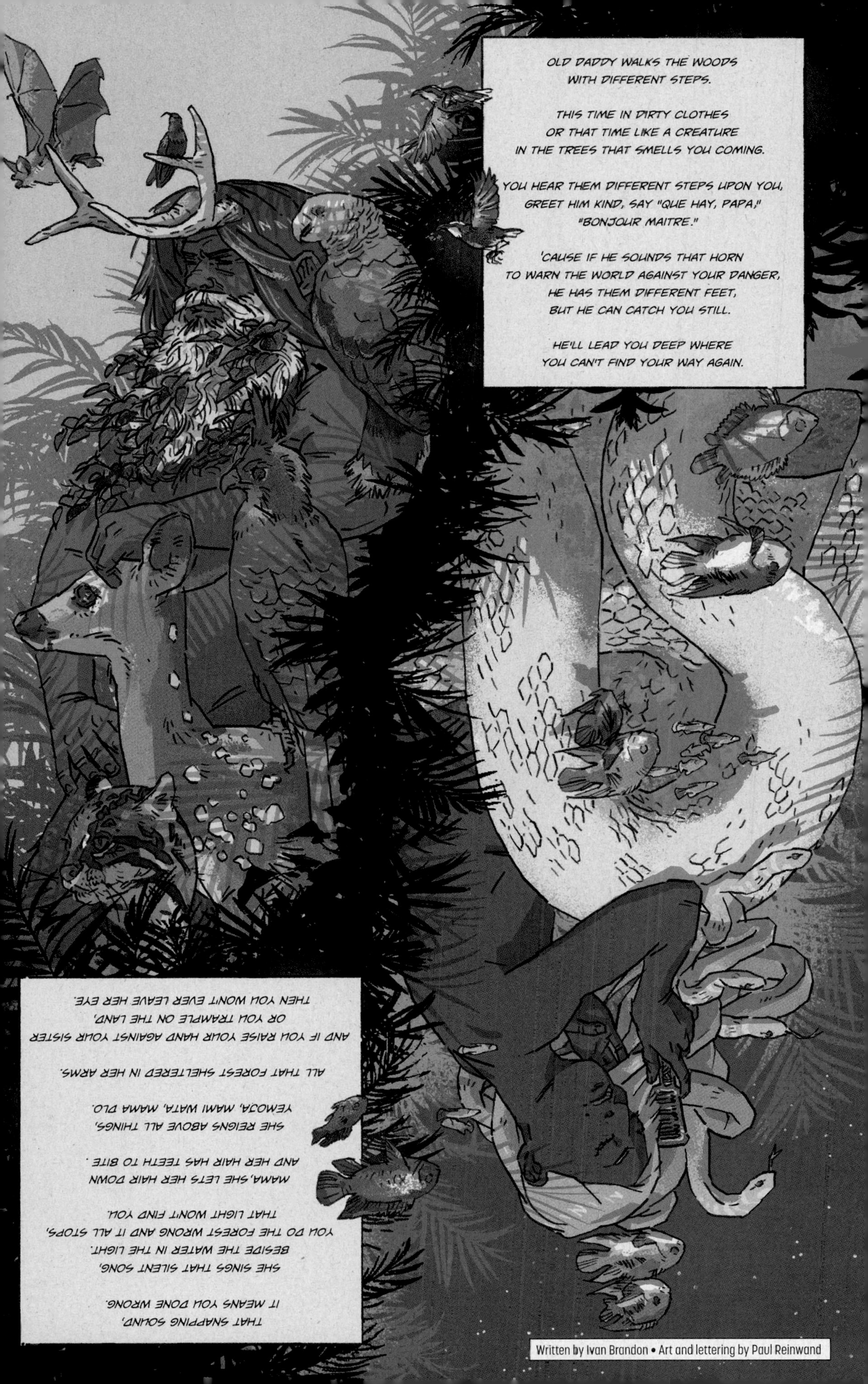
OLD DADDY WALKS THE WOODS
WITH DIFFERENT STEPS.

THIS TIME IN DIRTY CLOTHES
OR THAT TIME LIKE A CREATURE
IN THE TREES THAT SMELLS YOU COMING.

YOU HEAR THEM DIFFERENT STEPS UPON YOU,
GREET HIM KIND, SAY "QUE HAY, PAPA,"
"BONJOUR MAITRE."

'CAUSE IF HE SOUNDS THAT HORN
TO WARN THE WORLD AGAINST YOUR DANGER,
HE HAS THEM DIFFERENT FEET,
BUT HE CAN CATCH YOU STILL.

HE'LL LEAD YOU DEEP WHERE
YOU CAN'T FIND YOUR WAY AGAIN.

THAT SNAPPING SOUND,
IT MEANS YOU DONE WRONG.

SHE SINGS THAT SILENT SONG,
BESIDE THE WATER IN THE LIGHT.
YOU DO THE FOREST WRONG AND IT ALL STOPS,
THAT LIGHT WON'T FIND YOU.

MAMA, SHE LETS HER HAIR DOWN
AND HER HAIR HAS TEETH TO BITE.

SHE REIGNS ABOVE ALL THINGS,
YEMOJA, MAMI WATA, MAMA DLO.

ALL THAT FOREST SHELTERED IN HER ARMS.

AND IF YOU RAISE YOUR HAND AGAINST YOUR SISTER
OR YOU TRAMPLE ON THE LAND,
THEN YOU WON'T EVER LEAVE HER EYE.

Written by Ivan Brandon • Art and lettering by Paul Reinwand

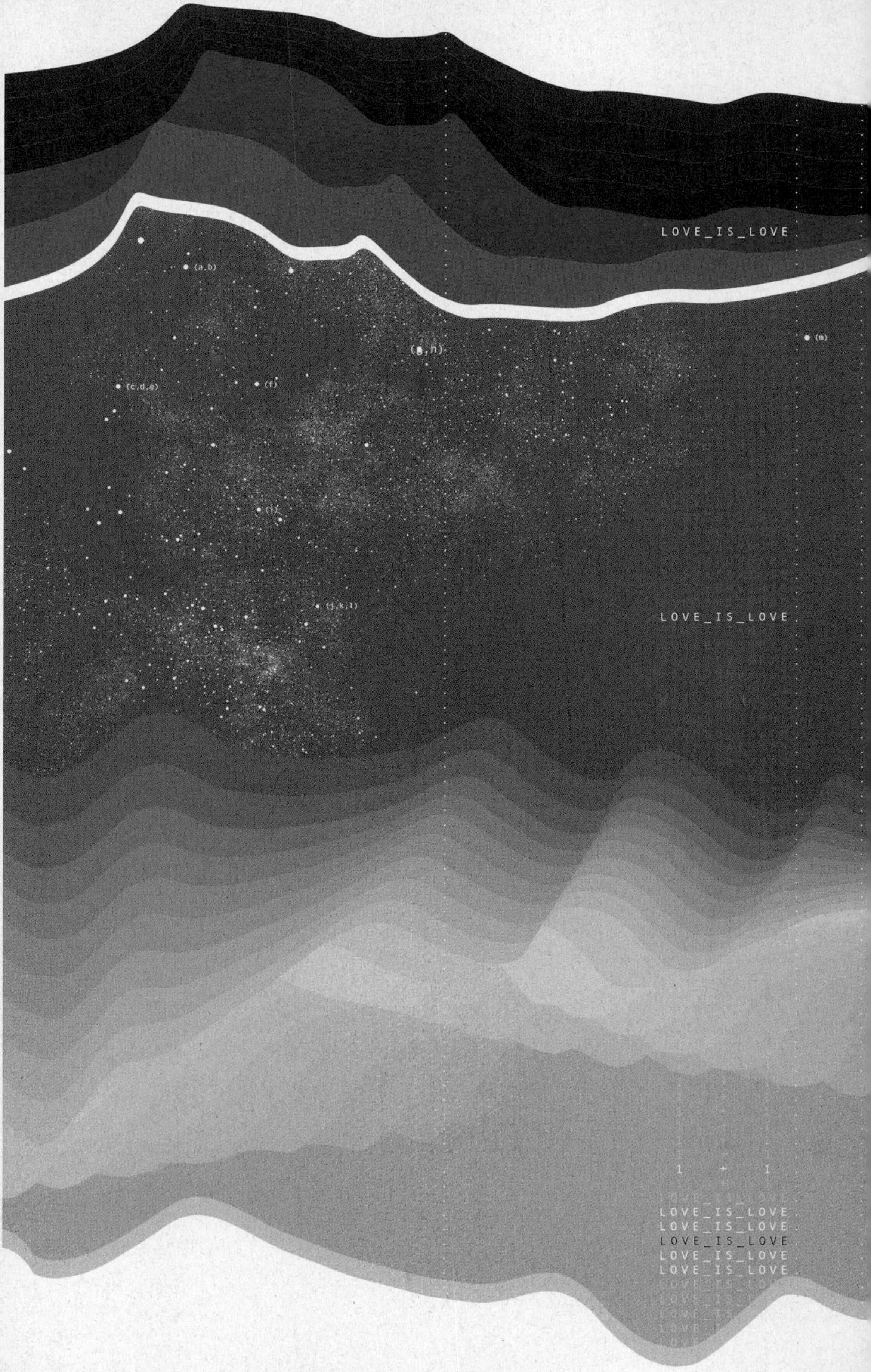
LOVE_IS_LOVE
(a,b)
(g,h)
(m)
(c,d,e)
(f)
(i)
(j,k,l)
LOVE_IS_LOVE
1 + 1
LOVE_IS_LOVE
LOVE_IS_LOVE
LOVE_IS_LOVE
LOVE_IS_LOVE
LOVE_IS_LOVE

Art by Jonathan Hickman

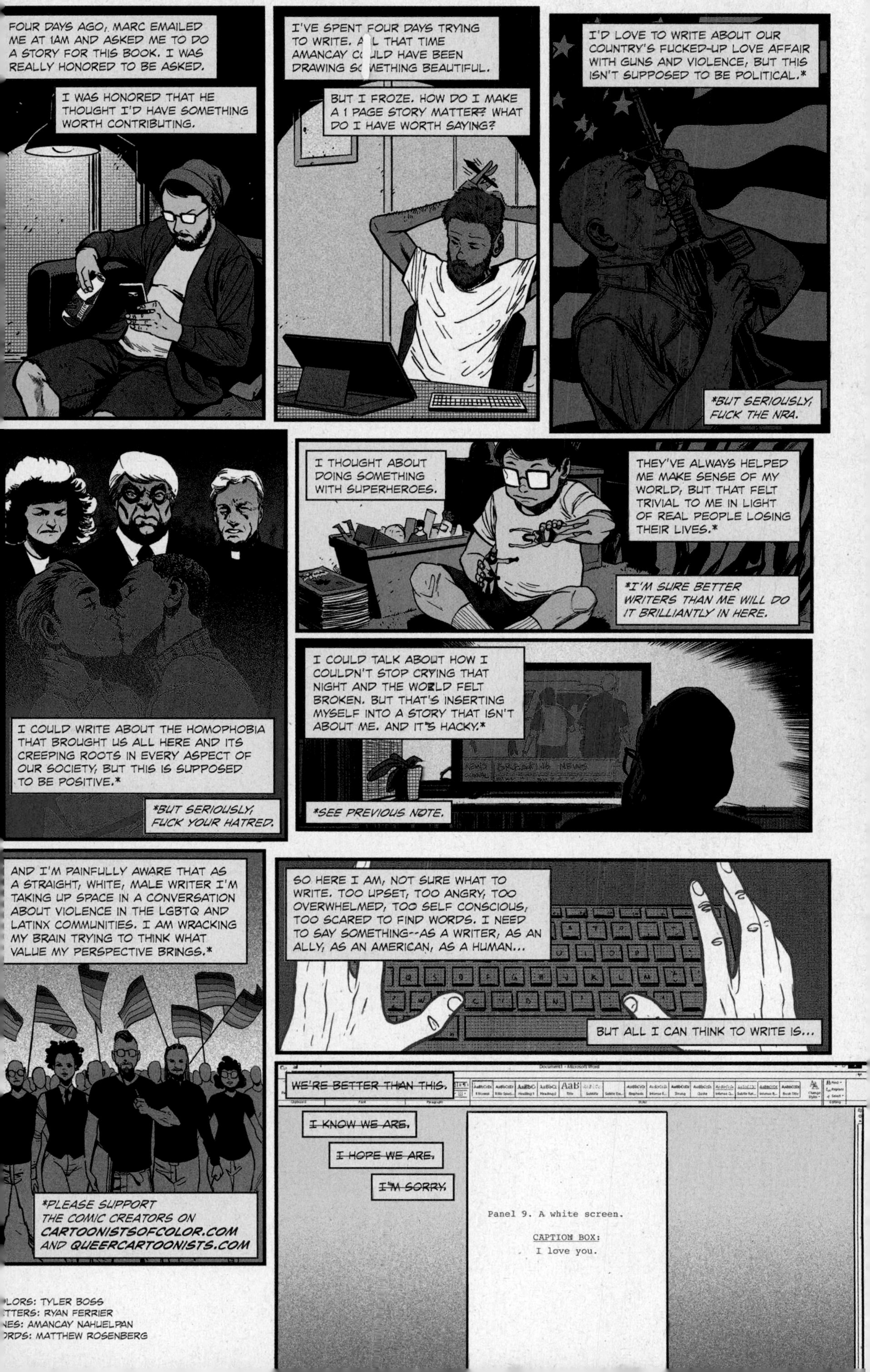
FOUR DAYS AGO, MARC EMAILED ME AT 1AM AND ASKED ME TO DO A STORY FOR THIS BOOK. I WAS REALLY HONORED TO BE ASKED.
I WAS HONORED THAT HE THOUGHT I'D HAVE SOMETHING WORTH CONTRIBUTING.
I'VE SPENT FOUR DAYS TRYING TO WRITE. ALL THAT TIME AMANCAY COULD HAVE BEEN DRAWING SOMETHING BEAUTIFUL.
BUT I FROZE. HOW DO I MAKE A 1 PAGE STORY MATTER? WHAT DO I HAVE WORTH SAYING?
I'D LOVE TO WRITE ABOUT OUR COUNTRY'S FUCKED-UP LOVE AFFAIR WITH GUNS AND VIOLENCE, BUT THIS ISN'T SUPPOSED TO BE POLITICAL.*
*BUT SERIOUSLY, FUCK THE NRA.
I COULD WRITE ABOUT THE HOMOPHOBIA THAT BROUGHT US ALL HERE AND ITS CREEPING ROOTS IN EVERY ASPECT OF OUR SOCIETY, BUT THIS IS SUPPOSED TO BE POSITIVE.*
*BUT SERIOUSLY, FUCK YOUR HATRED.
I THOUGHT ABOUT DOING SOMETHING WITH SUPERHEROES.
THEY'VE ALWAYS HELPED ME MAKE SENSE OF MY WORLD, BUT THAT FELT TRIVIAL TO ME IN LIGHT OF REAL PEOPLE LOSING THEIR LIVES.*
*I'M SURE BETTER WRITERS THAN ME WILL DO IT BRILLIANTLY IN HERE.
I COULD TALK ABOUT HOW I COULDN'T STOP CRYING THAT NIGHT AND THE WORLD FELT BROKEN. BUT THAT'S INSERTING MYSELF INTO A STORY THAT ISN'T ABOUT ME. AND IT'S HACKY.*
BREAKING NEWS
*SEE PREVIOUS NOTE.
AND I'M PAINFULLY AWARE THAT AS A STRAIGHT, WHITE, MALE WRITER I'M TAKING UP SPACE IN A CONVERSATION ABOUT VIOLENCE IN THE LGBTQ AND LATINX COMMUNITIES. I AM WRACKING MY BRAIN TRYING TO THINK WHAT VALUE MY PERSPECTIVE BRINGS.*
*PLEASE SUPPORT THE COMIC CREATORS ON CARTOONISTSOFCOLOR.COM AND QUEERCARTOONISTS.COM
SO HERE I AM, NOT SURE WHAT TO WRITE. TOO UPSET, TOO ANGRY, TOO OVERWHELMED, TOO SELF CONSCIOUS, TOO SCARED TO FIND WORDS. I NEED TO SAY SOMETHING--AS A WRITER, AS AN ALLY, AS AN AMERICAN, AS A HUMAN...
BUT ALL I CAN THINK TO WRITE IS...
Document1 - Microsoft Word
~~WE'RE BETTER THAN THIS.~~
~~I KNOW WE ARE.~~
~~I HOPE WE ARE.~~
~~I'M SORRY.~~
Panel 9. A white screen.
CAPTION BOX:
I love you.
LORS: TYLER BOSS
TTERS: RYAN FERRIER
NES: AMANCAY NAHUELPAN
RDS: MATTHEW ROSENBERG

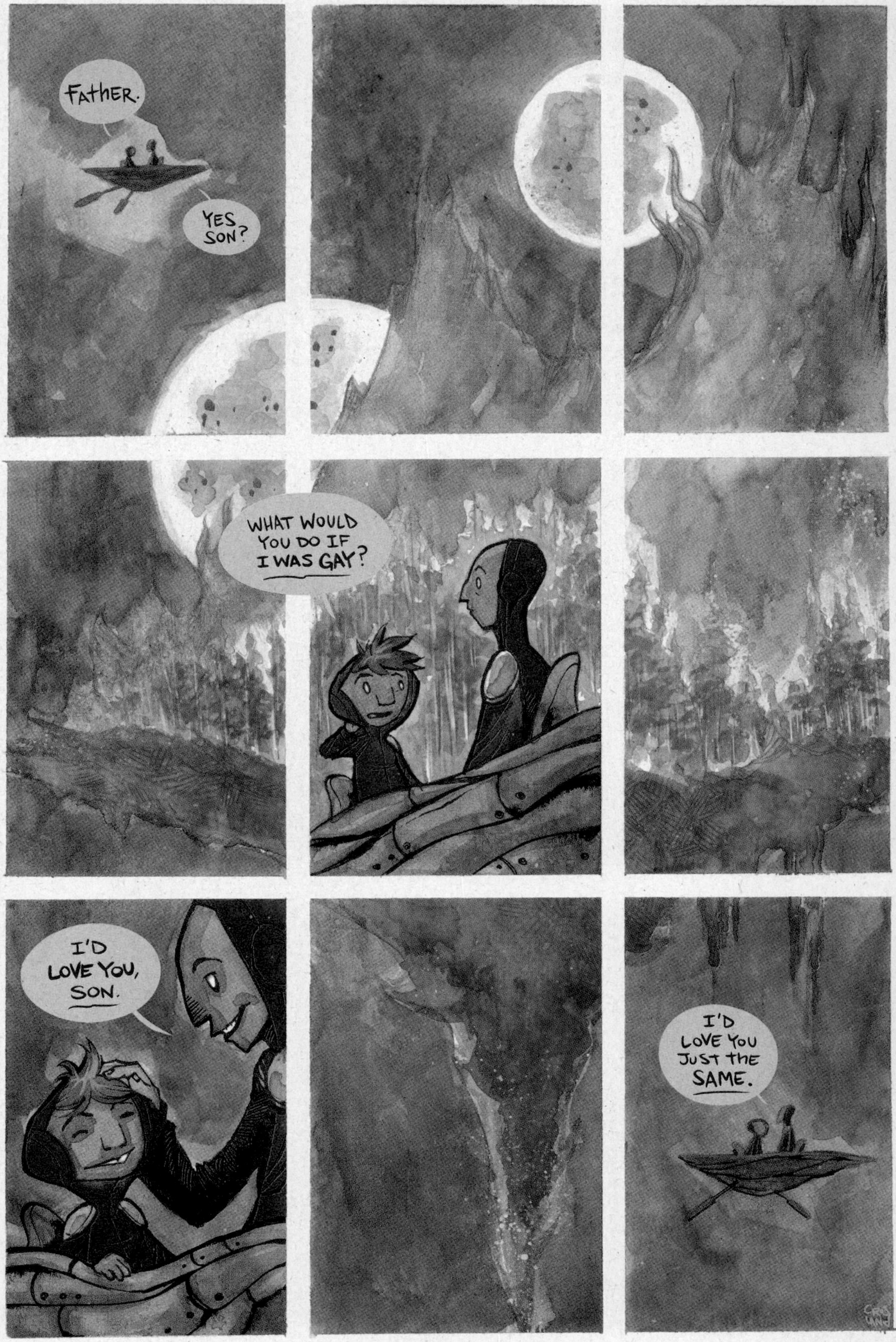
FATHER.
YES SON?
WHAT WOULD YOU DO IF I WAS GAY?
I'D LOVE YOU, SON.
I'D LOVE YOU JUST THE SAME.

Writing, art, and lettering by Dave Crosland

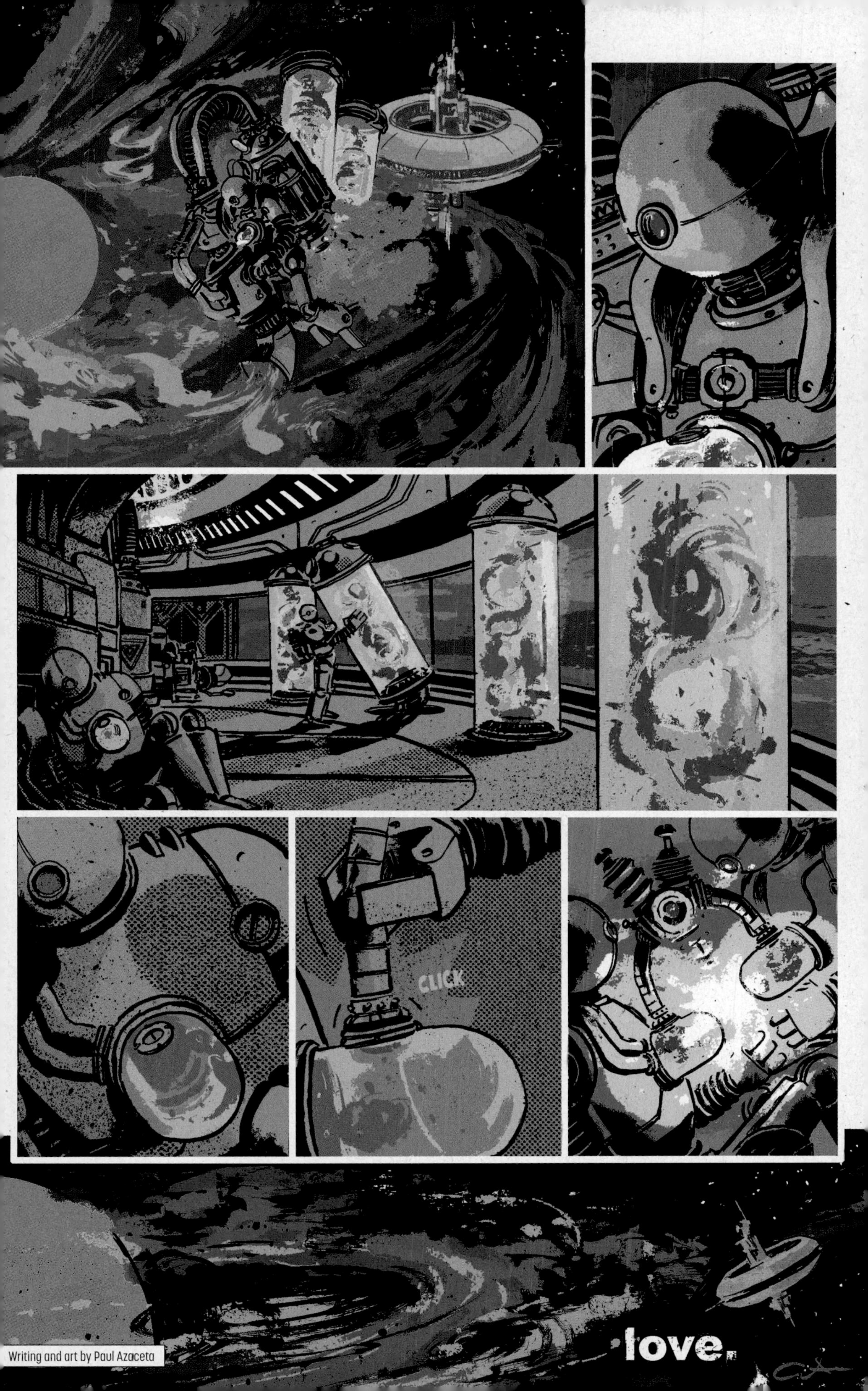
CLICK
love.
Writing and art by Paul Azaceta

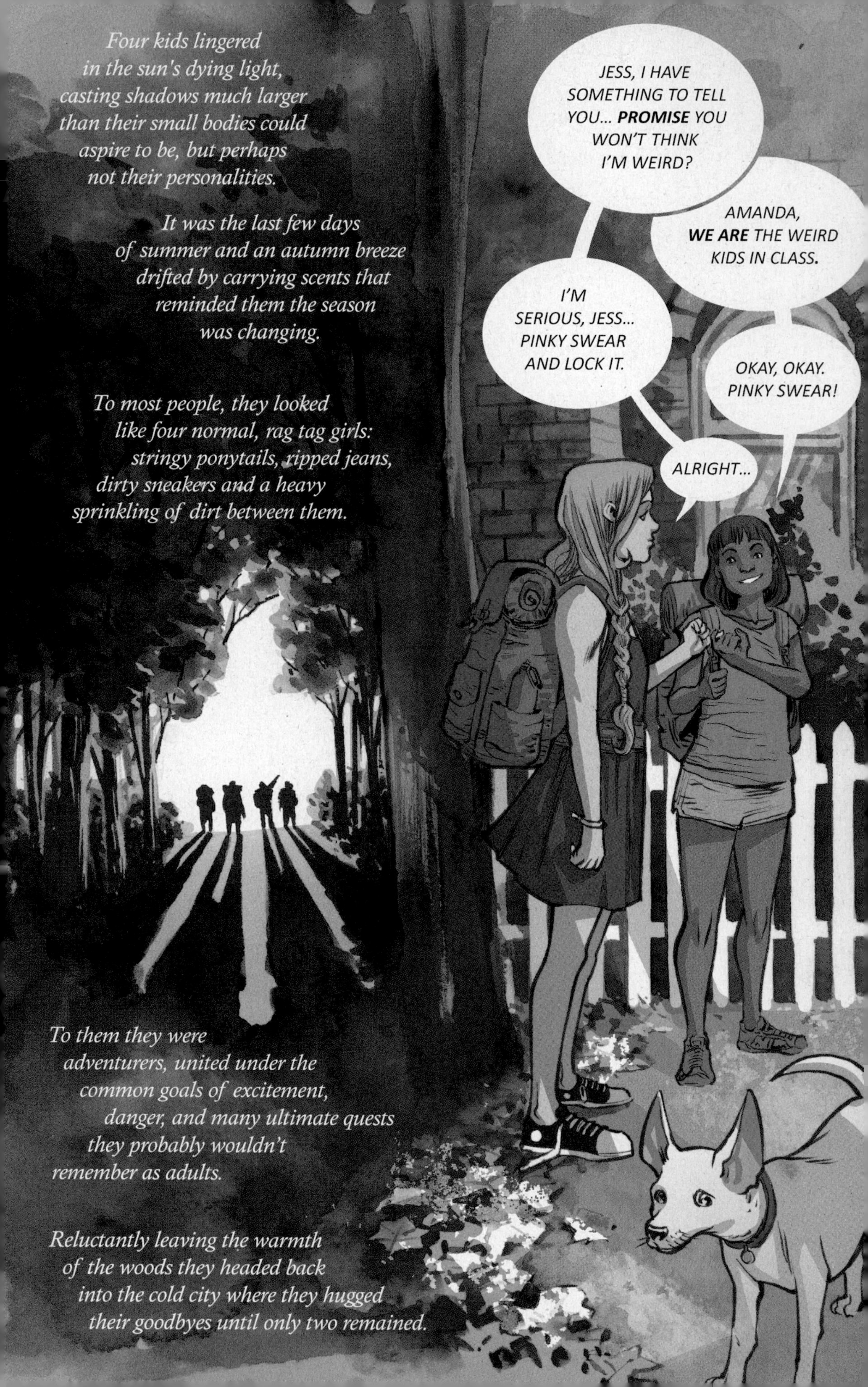
Four kids lingered in the sun's dying light, casting shadows much larger than their small bodies could aspire to be, but perhaps not their personalities.
It was the last few days of summer and an autumn breeze drifted by carrying scents that reminded them the season was changing.
To most people, they looked like four normal, rag tag girls: stringy ponytails, ripped jeans, dirty sneakers and a heavy sprinkling of dirt between them.
To them they were adventurers, united under the common goals of excitement, danger, and many ultimate quests they probably wouldn't remember as adults.
Reluctantly leaving the warmth of the woods they headed back into the cold city where they hugged their goodbyes until only two remained.
JESS, I HAVE SOMETHING TO TELL YOU... **PROMISE** YOU WON'T THINK I'M WEIRD?
AMANDA, **WE ARE** THE WEIRD KIDS IN CLASS.
I'M SERIOUS, JESS... PINKY SWEAR AND LOCK IT.
OKAY, OKAY. PINKY SWEAR!
ALRIGHT...

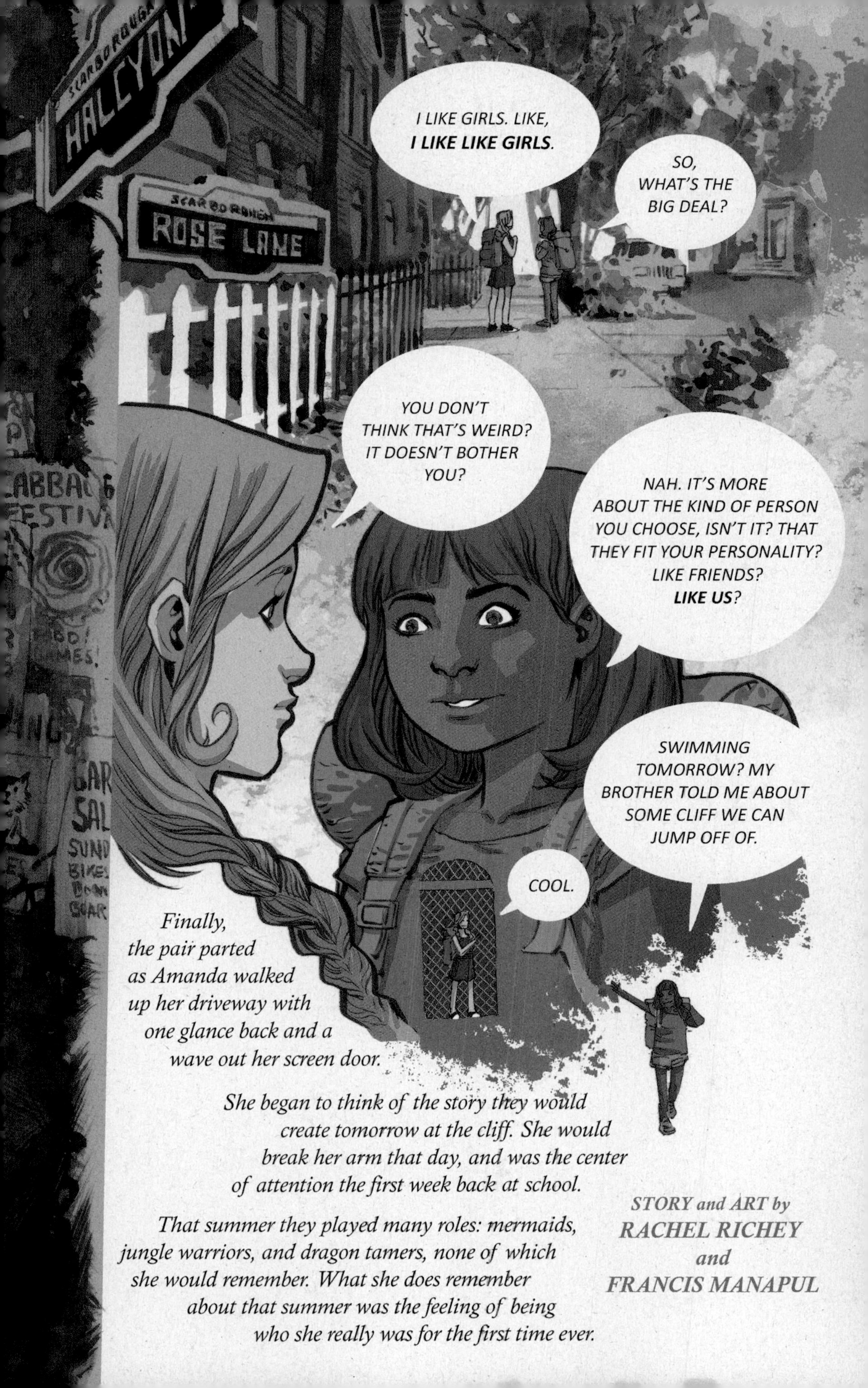
HALCYON
SCARBOROUGH
ROSE LANE
I LIKE GIRLS. LIKE, **I LIKE LIKE GIRLS**.
SO, WHAT'S THE BIG DEAL?
YOU DON'T THINK THAT'S WEIRD? IT DOESN'T BOTHER YOU?
NAH. IT'S MORE ABOUT THE KIND OF PERSON YOU CHOOSE, ISN'T IT? THAT THEY FIT YOUR PERSONALITY? LIKE FRIENDS? **LIKE US**?
SWIMMING TOMORROW? MY BROTHER TOLD ME ABOUT SOME CLIFF WE CAN JUMP OFF OF.
COOL.
*Finally, the pair parted as Amanda walked up her driveway with one glance back and a wave out her screen door.*
*She began to think of the story they would create tomorrow at the cliff. She would break her arm that day, and was the center of attention the first week back at school.*
*That summer they played many roles: mermaids, jungle warriors, and dragon tamers, none of which she would remember. What she does remember about that summer was the feeling of being who she really was for the first time ever.*
STORY and ART by RACHEL RICHEY and FRANCIS MANAPUL

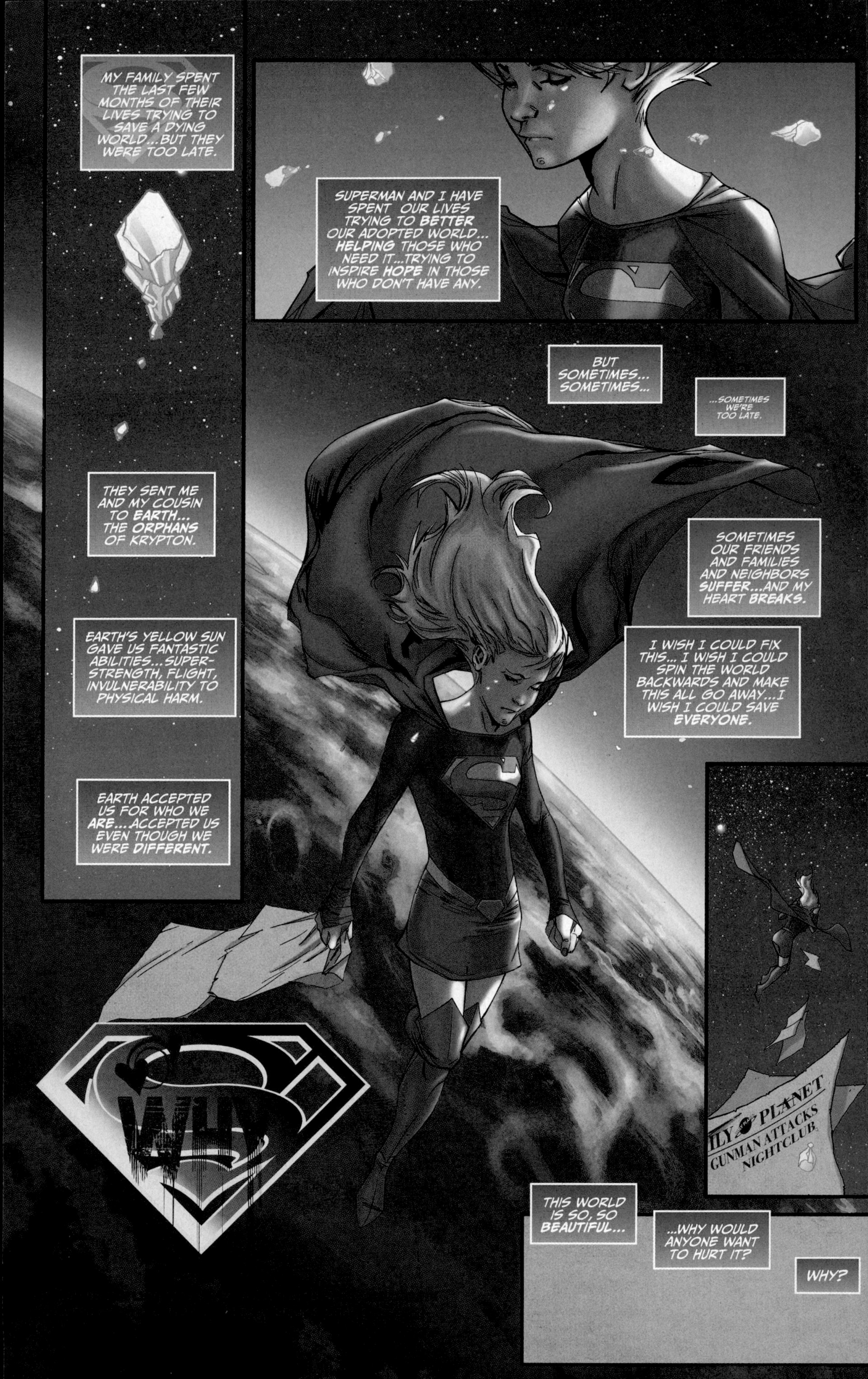
MY FAMILY SPENT THE LAST FEW MONTHS OF THEIR LIVES TRYING TO SAVE A DYING WORLD...BUT THEY WERE TOO LATE.
THEY SENT ME AND MY COUSIN TO EARTH... THE ORPHANS OF KRYPTON.
EARTH'S YELLOW SUN GAVE US FANTASTIC ABILITIES...SUPER-STRENGTH, FLIGHT, INVULNERABILITY TO PHYSICAL HARM.
EARTH ACCEPTED US FOR WHO WE ARE...ACCEPTED US EVEN THOUGH WE WERE DIFFERENT.
SUPERMAN AND I HAVE SPENT OUR LIVES TRYING TO BETTER OUR ADOPTED WORLD... HELPING THOSE WHO NEED IT...TRYING TO INSPIRE HOPE IN THOSE WHO DON'T HAVE ANY.
BUT SOMETIMES... SOMETIMES...
...SOMETIMES WE'RE TOO LATE.
SOMETIMES OUR FRIENDS AND FAMILIES AND NEIGHBORS SUFFER...AND MY HEART BREAKS.
I WISH I COULD FIX THIS... I WISH I COULD SPIN THE WORLD BACKWARDS AND MAKE THIS ALL GO AWAY...I WISH I COULD SAVE EVERYONE.
WHY
ILY PLANET
GUNMAN ATTACKS NIGHTCLUB.
THIS WORLD IS SO, SO BEAUTIFUL...
...WHY WOULD ANYONE WANT TO HURT IT?
WHY?

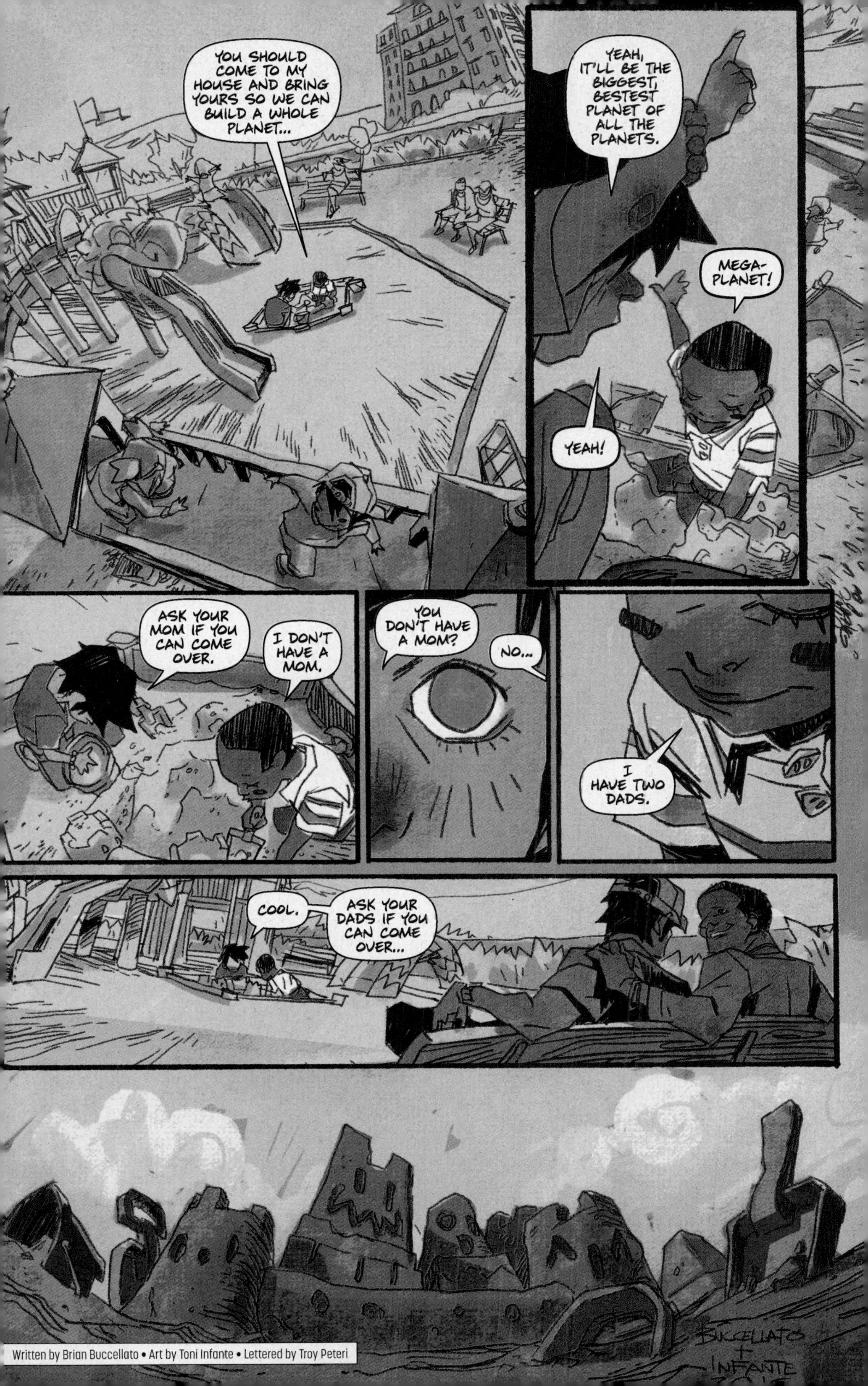
YOU SHOULD COME TO MY HOUSE AND BRING YOURS SO WE CAN BUILD A WHOLE PLANET...
YEAH, IT'LL BE THE BIGGEST, BESTEST PLANET OF ALL THE PLANETS.
MEGA-PLANET!
YEAH!
ASK YOUR MOM IF YOU CAN COME OVER.
I DON'T HAVE A MOM.
YOU DON'T HAVE A MOM?
NO...
I HAVE TWO DADS.
COOL.
ASK YOUR DADS IF YOU CAN COME OVER...
BUCCELLATO + INFANTE

Written by Brian Buccellato • Art by Toni Infante • Lettered by Troy Peteri

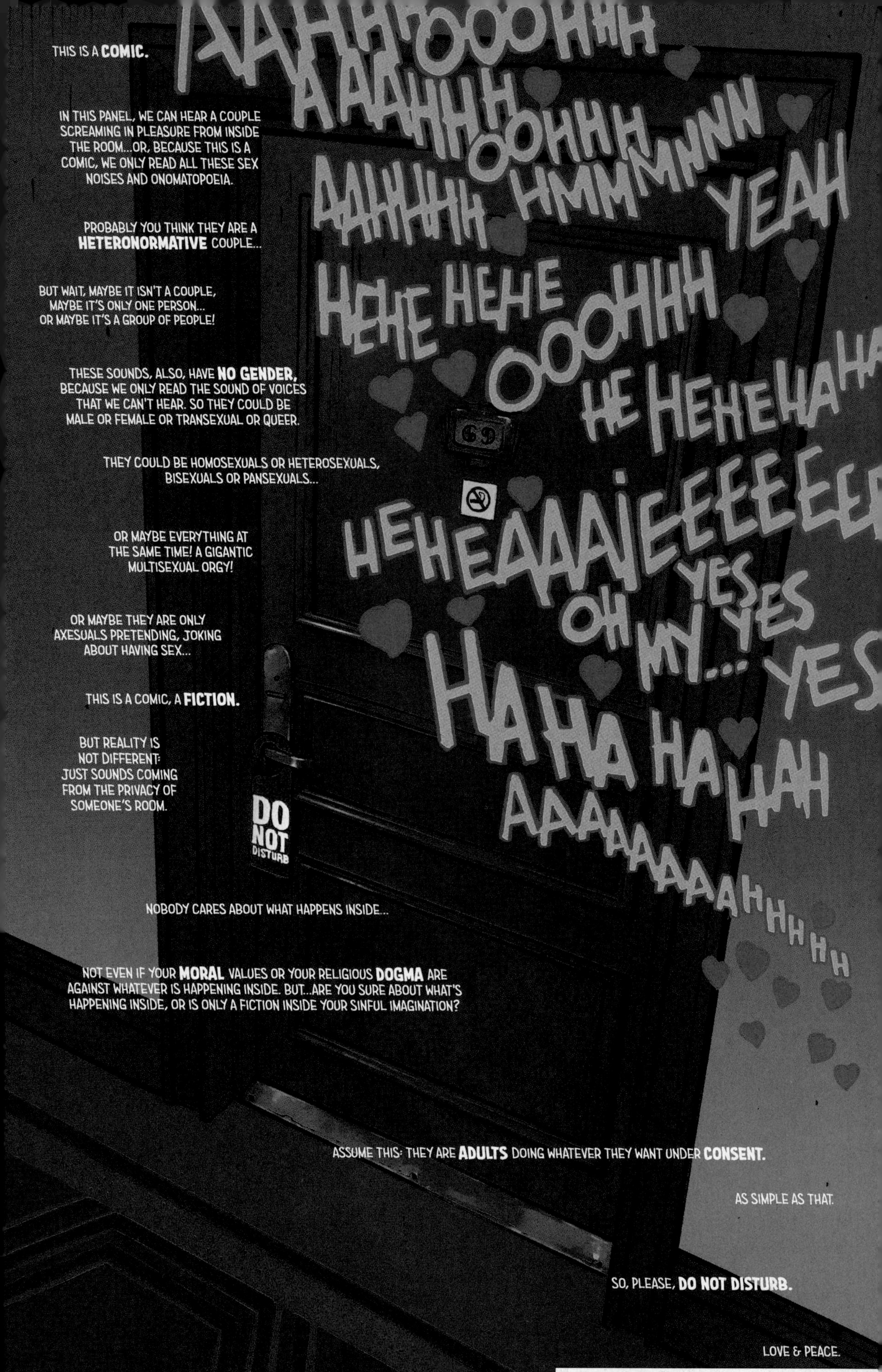
THIS IS A **COMIC.**
AAHHOOOHHH
AAAHHH
IN THIS PANEL, WE CAN HEAR A COUPLE SCREAMING IN PLEASURE FROM INSIDE THE ROOM...OR, BECAUSE THIS IS A COMIC, WE ONLY READ ALL THESE SEX NOISES AND ONOMATOPOEIA.
OOHHH
AAHHHHH HMMMMNN
YEAH
PROBABLY YOU THINK THEY ARE A **HETERONORMATIVE** COUPLE...
HEHE HEHE
OOOHHH
BUT WAIT, MAYBE IT ISN'T A COUPLE, MAYBE IT'S ONLY ONE PERSON... OR MAYBE IT'S A GROUP OF PEOPLE!
THESE SOUNDS, ALSO, HAVE **NO GENDER,** BECAUSE WE ONLY READ THE SOUND OF VOICES THAT WE CAN'T HEAR. SO THEY COULD BE MALE OR FEMALE OR TRANSEXUAL OR QUEER.
HE HEHEHAHA
69
THEY COULD BE HOMOSEXUALS OR HETEROSEXUALS, BISEXUALS OR PANSEXUALS...
HEHEAAAIEEEEEE
OR MAYBE EVERYTHING AT THE SAME TIME! A GIGANTIC MULTISEXUAL ORGY!
OH MY... YES YES YES
OR MAYBE THEY ARE ONLY AXESUALS PRETENDING, JOKING ABOUT HAVING SEX...
THIS IS A COMIC, A **FICTION.**
HA HA HA HAH
BUT REALITY IS NOT DIFFERENT: JUST SOUNDS COMING FROM THE PRIVACY OF SOMEONE'S ROOM.
DO NOT DISTURB
AAAAAAAAHHHHH
NOBODY CARES ABOUT WHAT HAPPENS INSIDE...
NOT EVEN IF YOUR **MORAL** VALUES OR YOUR RELIGIOUS **DOGMA** ARE AGAINST WHATEVER IS HAPPENING INSIDE. BUT...ARE YOU SURE ABOUT WHAT'S HAPPENING INSIDE, OR IS ONLY A FICTION INSIDE YOUR SINFUL IMAGINATION?
ASSUME THIS: THEY ARE **ADULTS** DOING WHATEVER THEY WANT UNDER **CONSENT.**
AS SIMPLE AS THAT.
SO, PLEASE, **DO NOT DISTURB.**
LOVE & PEACE.

Writting & Art by Fernando Blanco • Lettered by Jared K. Fletcher

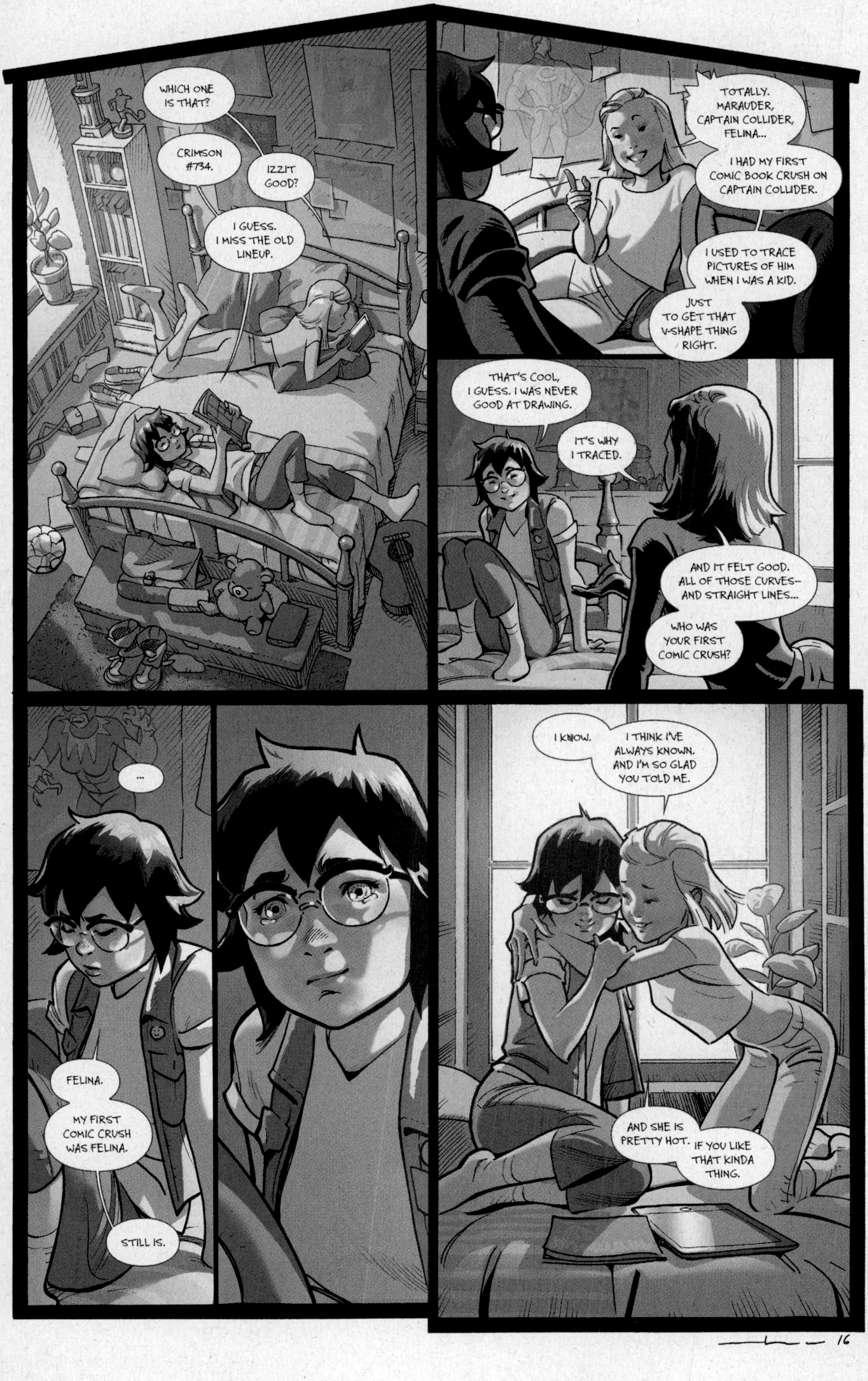
WHICH ONE IS THAT?
CRIMSON #734.
IZZIT GOOD?
I GUESS. I MISS THE OLD LINEUP.
TOTALLY. MARAUDER, CAPTAIN COLLIDER, FELINA...
I HAD MY FIRST COMIC BOOK CRUSH ON CAPTAIN COLLIDER.
I USED TO TRACE PICTURES OF HIM WHEN I WAS A KID.
JUST TO GET THAT V-SHAPE THING RIGHT.
THAT'S COOL, I GUESS. I WAS NEVER GOOD AT DRAWING.
IT'S WHY I TRACED.
AND IT FELT GOOD. ALL OF THOSE CURVES— AND STRAIGHT LINES...
WHO WAS YOUR FIRST COMIC CRUSH?
...
FELINA.
MY FIRST COMIC CRUSH WAS FELINA.
STILL IS.
I KNOW.
I THINK I'VE ALWAYS KNOWN. AND I'M SO GLAD YOU TOLD ME.
AND SHE IS PRETTY HOT.
IF YOU LIKE THAT KINDA THING.
16

Written by Marc Bernardin • Art and lettering by Marcial Toledano

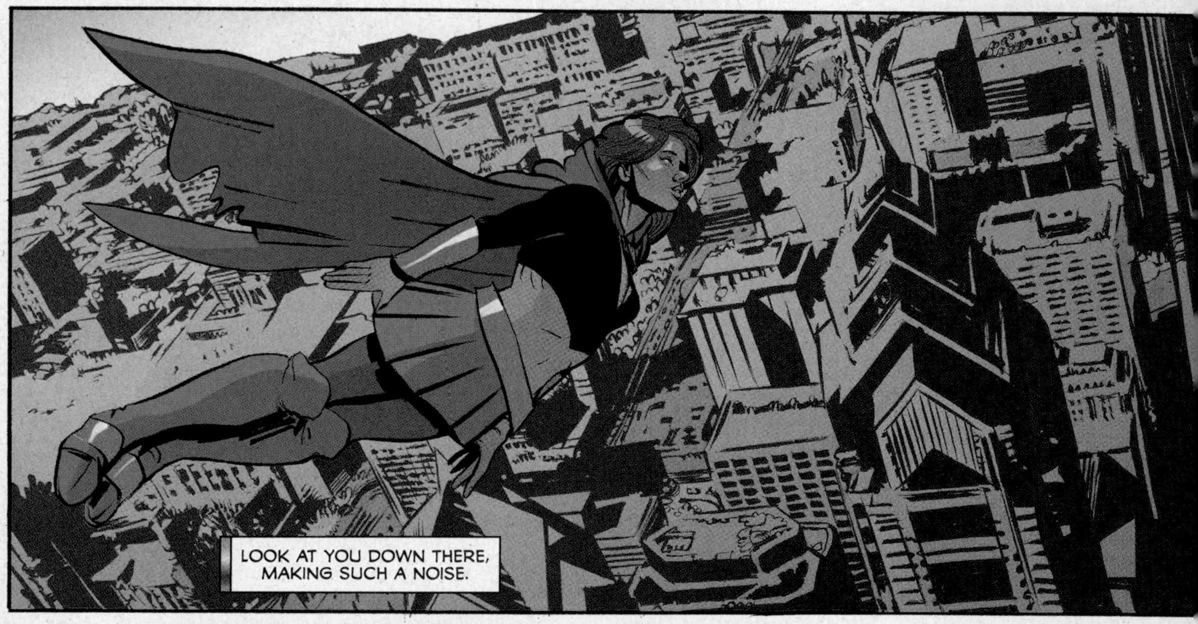
LOOK AT YOU DOWN THERE, MAKING SUCH A NOISE.

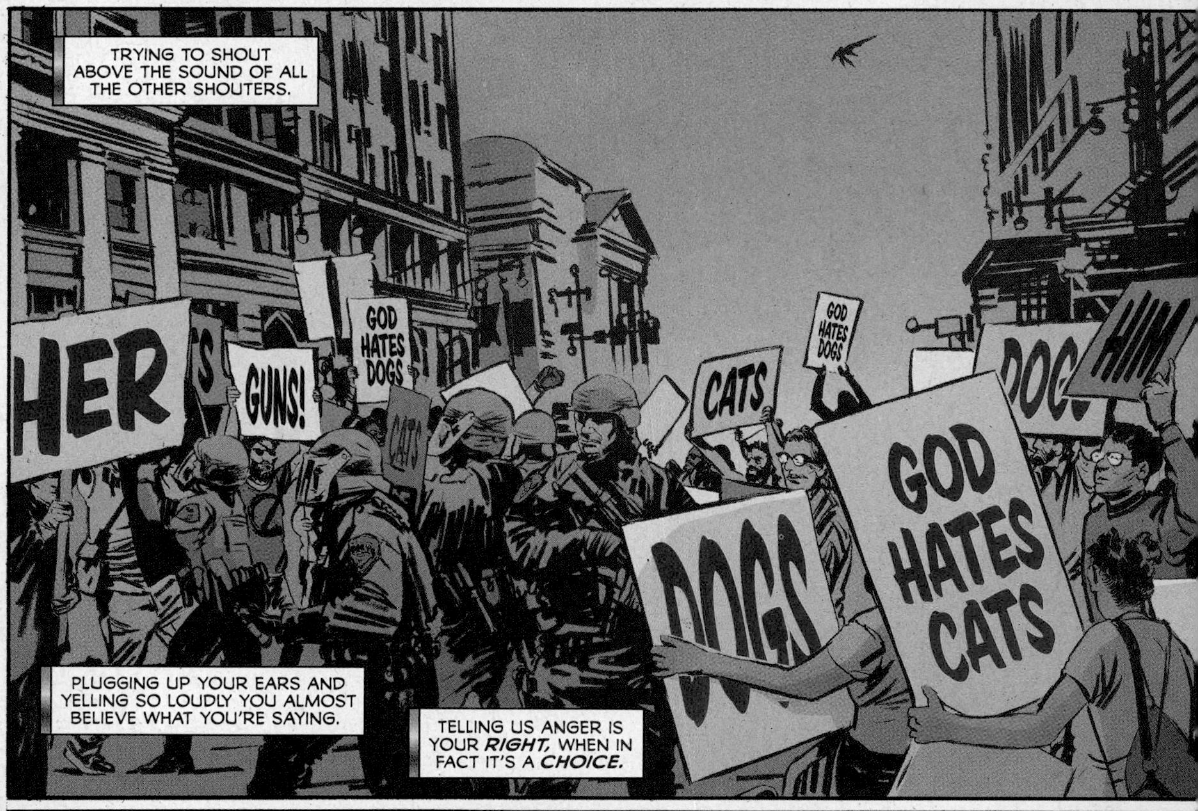
TRYING TO SHOUT ABOVE THE SOUND OF ALL THE OTHER SHOUTERS.
HER
GUNS!
GOD HATES DOGS
CATS
GOD HATES DOGS
HIM
GOD HATES CATS
DOGS
PLUGGING UP YOUR EARS AND YELLING SO LOUDLY YOU ALMOST BELIEVE WHAT YOU'RE SAYING.
TELLING US ANGER IS YOUR ***RIGHT,*** WHEN IN FACT IT'S A ***CHOICE.***

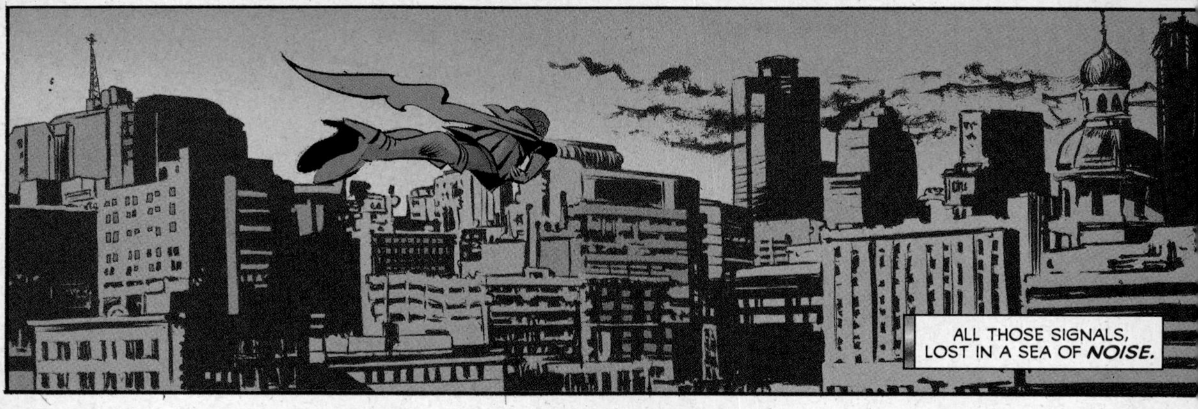
ALL THOSE SIGNALS, LOST IN A SEA OF ***NOISE.***

Written by Paul Jenkins • Illustrated by Robert Hack • Colored by Tamra Bonvillain • Lettered by Sal Cipriano

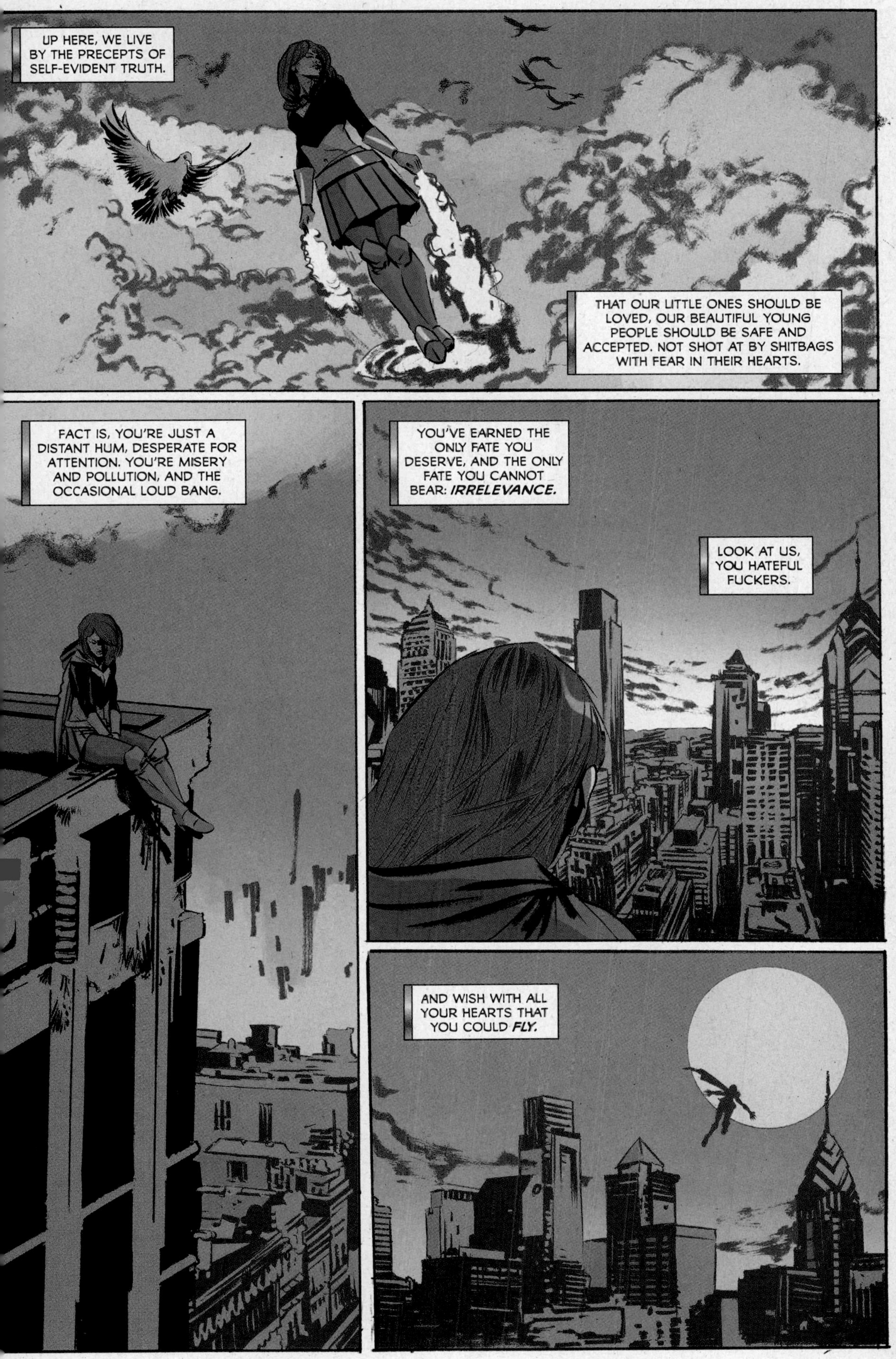
UP HERE, WE LIVE BY THE PRECEPTS OF SELF-EVIDENT TRUTH.
THAT OUR LITTLE ONES SHOULD BE LOVED, OUR BEAUTIFUL YOUNG PEOPLE SHOULD BE SAFE AND ACCEPTED. NOT SHOT AT BY SHITBAGS WITH FEAR IN THEIR HEARTS.
FACT IS, YOU'RE JUST A DISTANT HUM, DESPERATE FOR ATTENTION. YOU'RE MISERY AND POLLUTION, AND THE OCCASIONAL LOUD BANG.
YOU'VE EARNED THE ONLY FATE YOU DESERVE, AND THE ONLY FATE YOU CANNOT BEAR: *IRRELEVANCE.*
LOOK AT US, YOU HATEFUL FUCKERS.
AND WISH WITH ALL YOUR HEARTS THAT YOU COULD *FLY.*

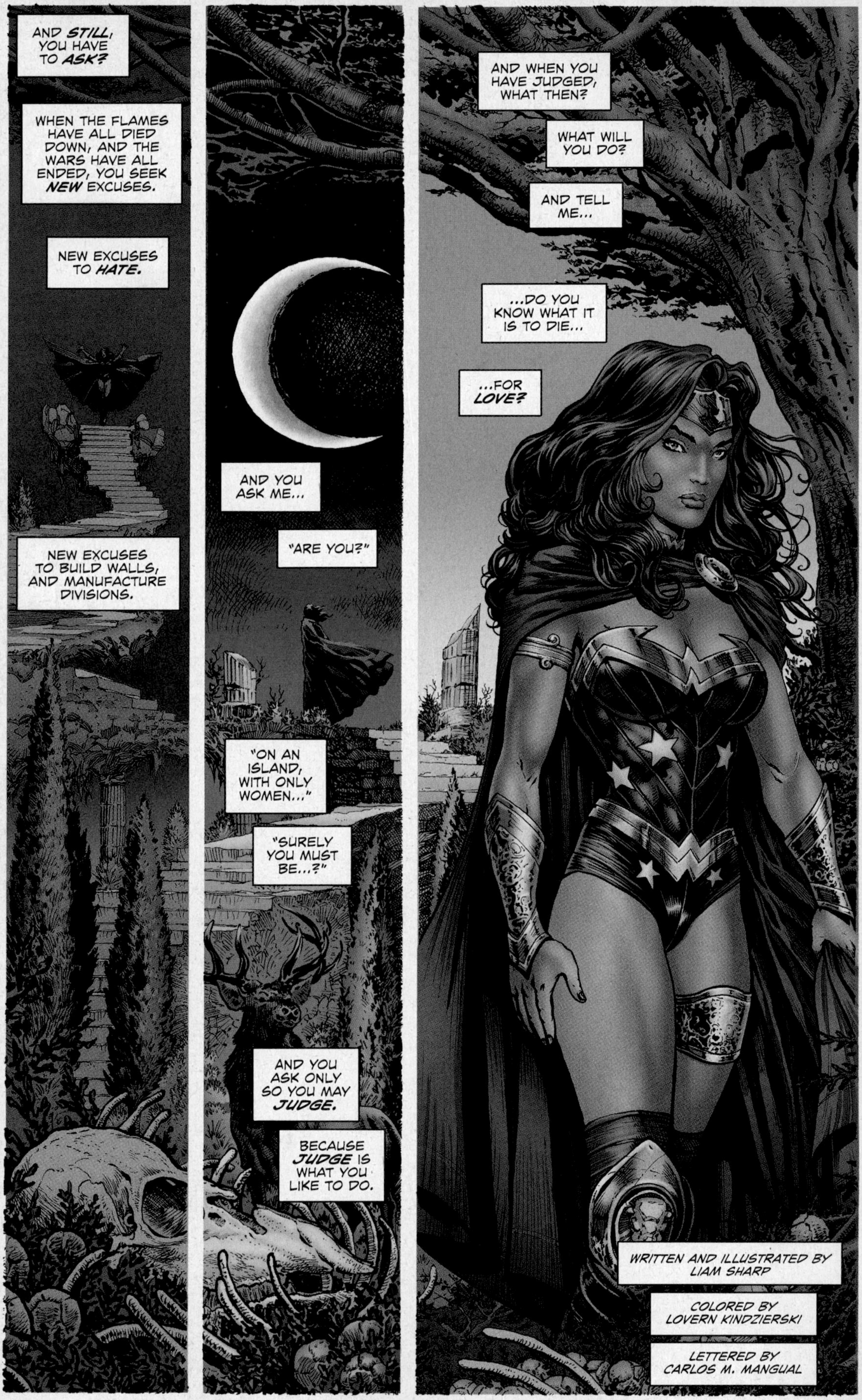
AND STILL, YOU HAVE TO ASK?
WHEN THE FLAMES HAVE ALL DIED DOWN, AND THE WARS HAVE ALL ENDED, YOU SEEK NEW EXCUSES.
NEW EXCUSES TO HATE.
NEW EXCUSES TO BUILD WALLS, AND MANUFACTURE DIVISIONS.
AND YOU ASK ME...
"ARE YOU?"
"ON AN ISLAND, WITH ONLY WOMEN..."
"SURELY YOU MUST BE...?"
AND YOU ASK ONLY SO YOU MAY JUDGE.
BECAUSE JUDGE IS WHAT YOU LIKE TO DO.
AND WHEN YOU HAVE JUDGED, WHAT THEN?
WHAT WILL YOU DO?
AND TELL ME...
...DO YOU KNOW WHAT IT IS TO DIE...
...FOR LOVE?
WRITTEN AND ILLUSTRATED BY LIAM SHARP
COLORED BY LOVERN KINDZIERSKI
LETTERED BY CARLOS M. MANGUAL

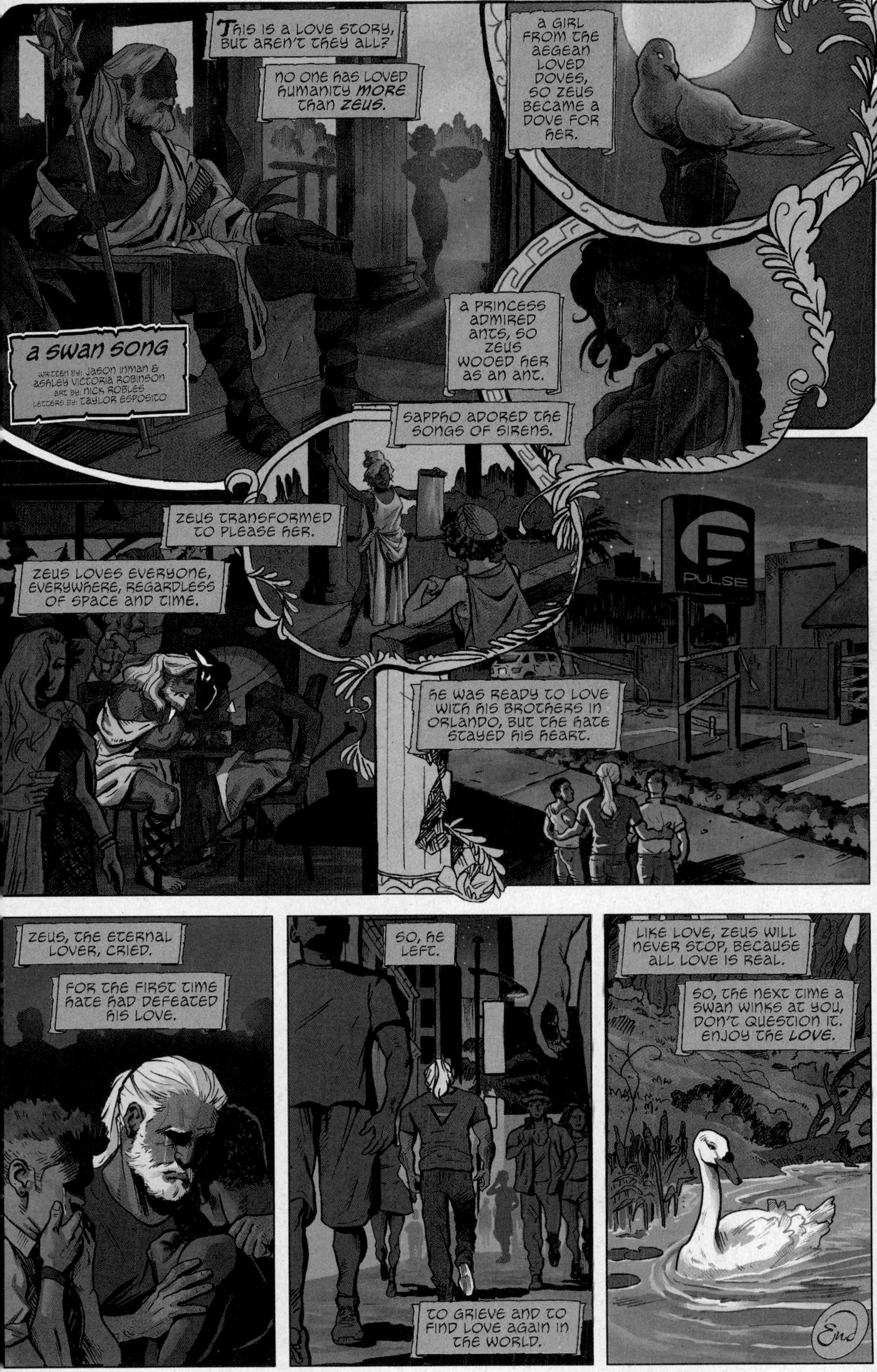
This is a love story, but aren't they all?
no one has loved humanity MORE than ZEUS.
a girl from the aegean loved doves, so zeus became a dove for her.
a swan song
written by: Jason Inman & Ashley Victoria Robinson
art by: Nick Robles
letters by: Taylor Esposito
a princess admired ants, so zeus wooed her as an ant.
Sappho adored the songs of sirens.
Zeus transformed to please her.
Zeus loves everyone, everywhere, regardless of space and time.
PULSE
He was ready to love with his brothers in Orlando, but the hate stayed his heart.
Zeus, the eternal lover, cried.
For the first time hate had defeated his love.
So, he left.
To grieve and to find love again in the world.
Like love, Zeus will never stop, because all love is real.
So, the next time a swan winks at you, don't question it. Enjoy the LOVE.
End

# GET UP

SCRIPT: JOSHUA YEHL ART: AUSTIN JAMES

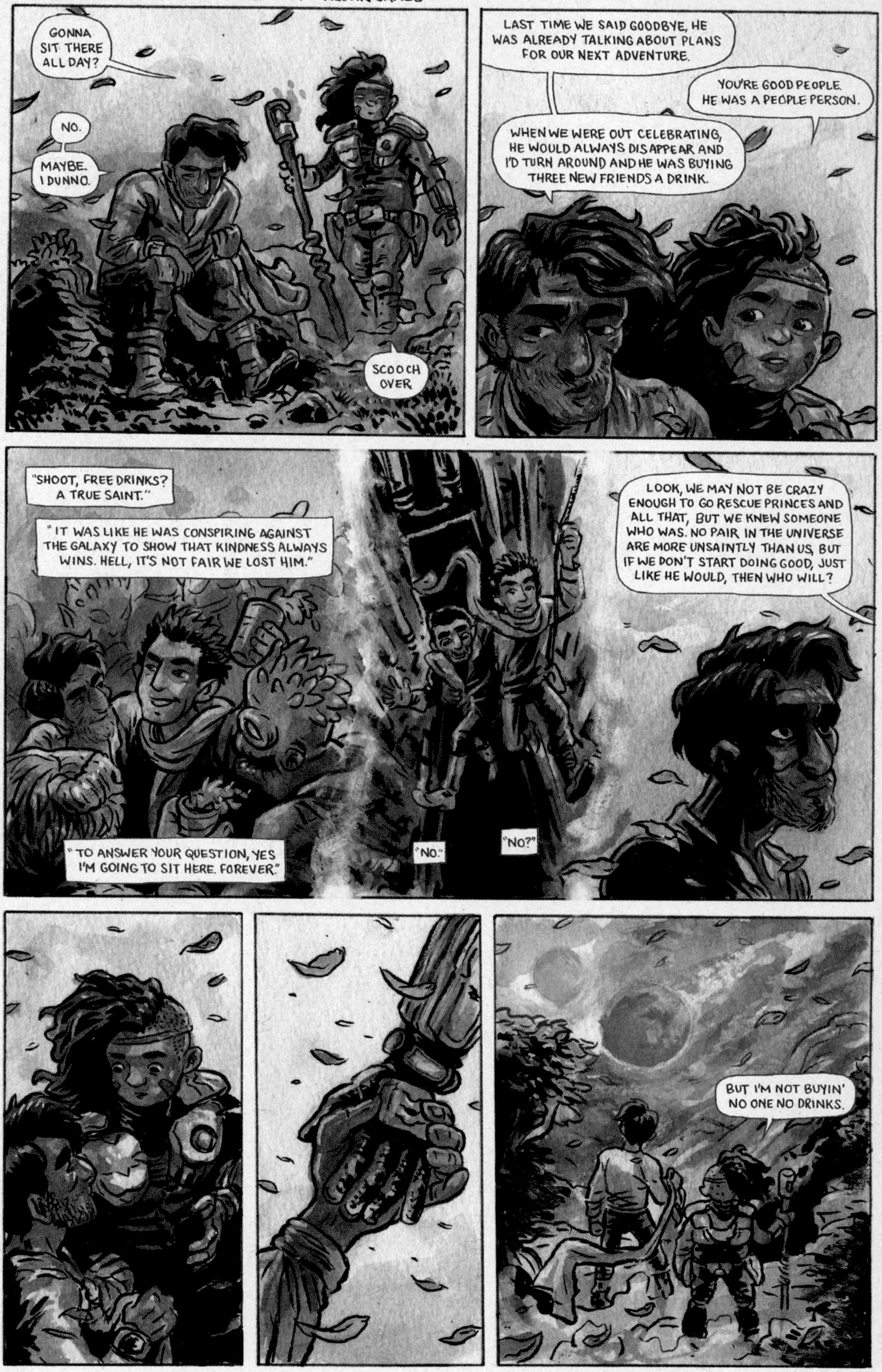
GONNA SIT THERE ALL DAY?
NO.
MAYBE. I DUNNO.
SCOOCH OVER
LAST TIME WE SAID GOODBYE, HE WAS ALREADY TALKING ABOUT PLANS FOR OUR NEXT ADVENTURE.
WHEN WE WERE OUT CELEBRATING, HE WOULD ALWAYS DISAPPEAR AND I'D TURN AROUND AND HE WAS BUYING THREE NEW FRIENDS A DRINK.
YOU'RE GOOD PEOPLE. HE WAS A PEOPLE PERSON.
"SHOOT, FREE DRINKS? A TRUE SAINT."
"IT WAS LIKE HE WAS CONSPIRING AGAINST THE GALAXY TO SHOW THAT KINDNESS ALWAYS WINS. HELL, IT'S NOT FAIR WE LOST HIM."
"TO ANSWER YOUR QUESTION, YES I'M GOING TO SIT HERE. FOREVER."
"NO."
"NO?"
LOOK, WE MAY NOT BE CRAZY ENOUGH TO GO RESCUE PRINCES AND ALL THAT, BUT WE KNEW SOMEONE WHO WAS. NO PAIR IN THE UNIVERSE ARE MORE UNSAINTLY THAN US, BUT IF WE DON'T START DOING GOOD, JUST LIKE HE WOULD, THEN WHO WILL?
BUT I'M NOT BUYIN' NO ONE NO DRINKS.

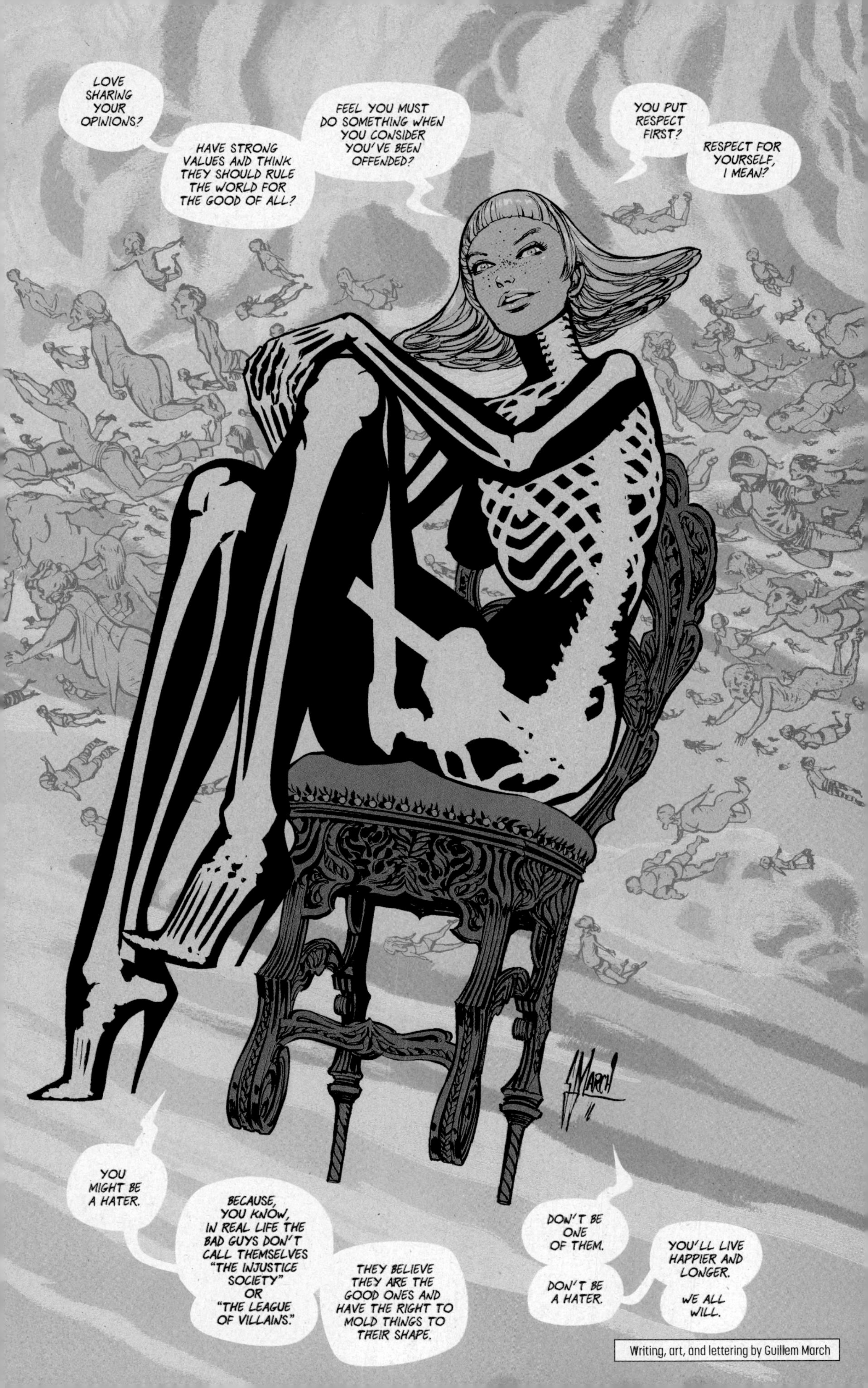
LOVE SHARING YOUR OPINIONS?
HAVE STRONG VALUES AND THINK THEY SHOULD RULE THE WORLD FOR THE GOOD OF ALL?
FEEL YOU MUST DO SOMETHING WHEN YOU CONSIDER YOU'VE BEEN OFFENDED?
YOU PUT RESPECT FIRST?
RESPECT FOR YOURSELF, I MEAN?
G. MARCH '16
YOU MIGHT BE A HATER.
BECAUSE, YOU KNOW, IN REAL LIFE THE BAD GUYS DON'T CALL THEMSELVES "THE INJUSTICE SOCIETY" OR "THE LEAGUE OF VILLAINS."
THEY BELIEVE THEY ARE THE GOOD ONES AND HAVE THE RIGHT TO MOLD THINGS TO THEIR SHAPE.
DON'T BE ONE OF THEM.
DON'T BE A HATER.
YOU'LL LIVE HAPPIER AND LONGER.
WE ALL WILL.

Writing, art, and lettering by Guillem March

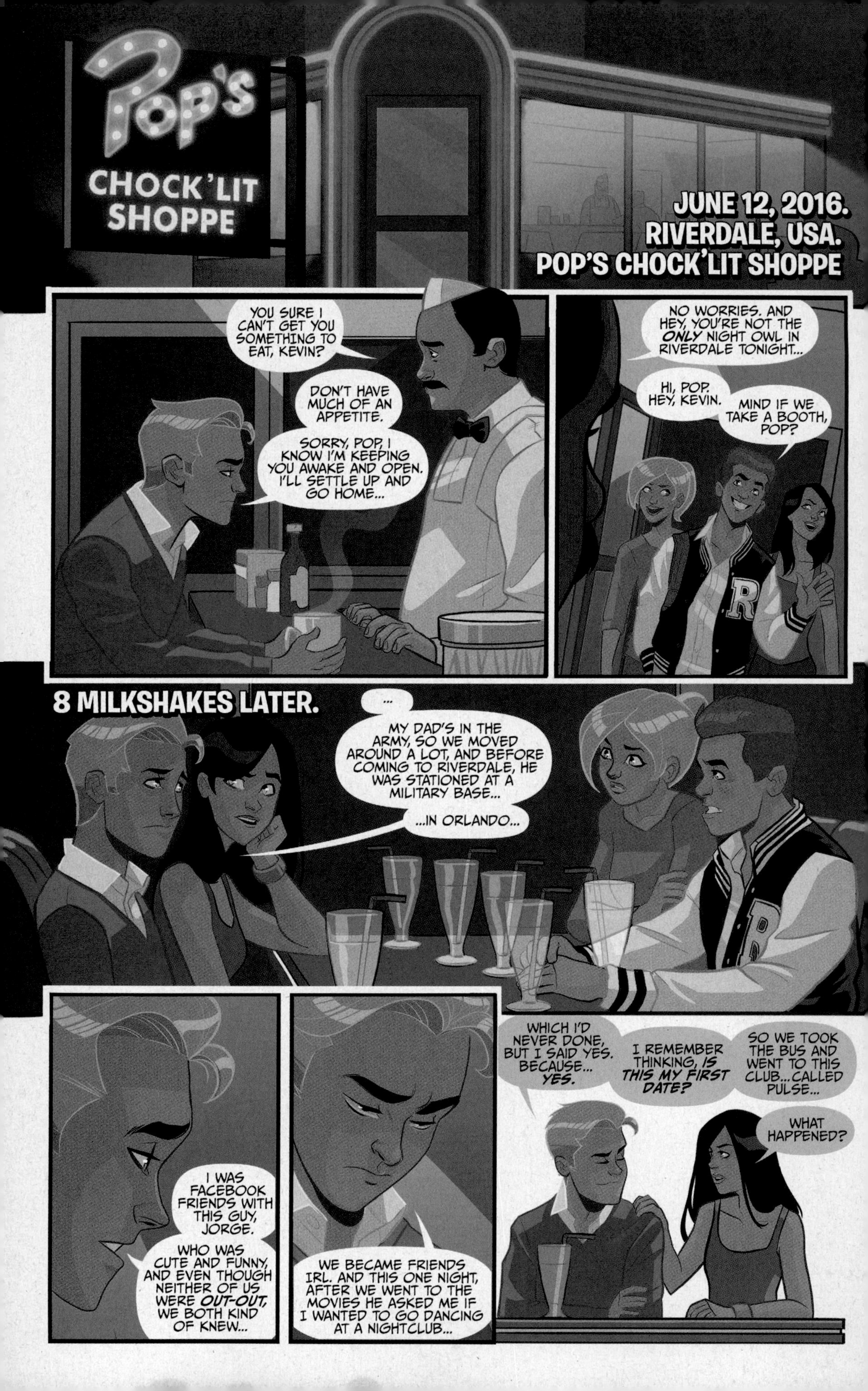
POP'S
CHOCK'LIT SHOPPE
JUNE 12, 2016. RIVERDALE, USA. POP'S CHOCK'LIT SHOPPE
YOU SURE I CAN'T GET YOU SOMETHING TO EAT, KEVIN?
DON'T HAVE MUCH OF AN APPETITE.
SORRY, POP, I KNOW I'M KEEPING YOU AWAKE AND OPEN. I'LL SETTLE UP AND GO HOME...
NO WORRIES. AND HEY, YOU'RE NOT THE ONLY NIGHT OWL IN RIVERDALE TONIGHT...
HI, POP. HEY, KEVIN.
MIND IF WE TAKE A BOOTH, POP?
8 MILKSHAKES LATER.
...
MY DAD'S IN THE ARMY, SO WE MOVED AROUND A LOT, AND BEFORE COMING TO RIVERDALE, HE WAS STATIONED AT A MILITARY BASE...
...IN ORLANDO...
I WAS FACEBOOK FRIENDS WITH THIS GUY, JORGE.
WHO WAS CUTE AND FUNNY, AND EVEN THOUGH NEITHER OF US WERE OUT-OUT, WE BOTH KIND OF KNEW...
WE BECAME FRIENDS IRL. AND THIS ONE NIGHT, AFTER WE WENT TO THE MOVIES HE ASKED ME IF I WANTED TO GO DANCING AT A NIGHTCLUB...
WHICH I'D NEVER DONE, BUT I SAID YES. BECAUSE... YES.
I REMEMBER THINKING, IS THIS MY FIRST DATE?
SO WE TOOK THE BUS AND WENT TO THIS CLUB...CALLED PULSE...
WHAT HAPPENED?

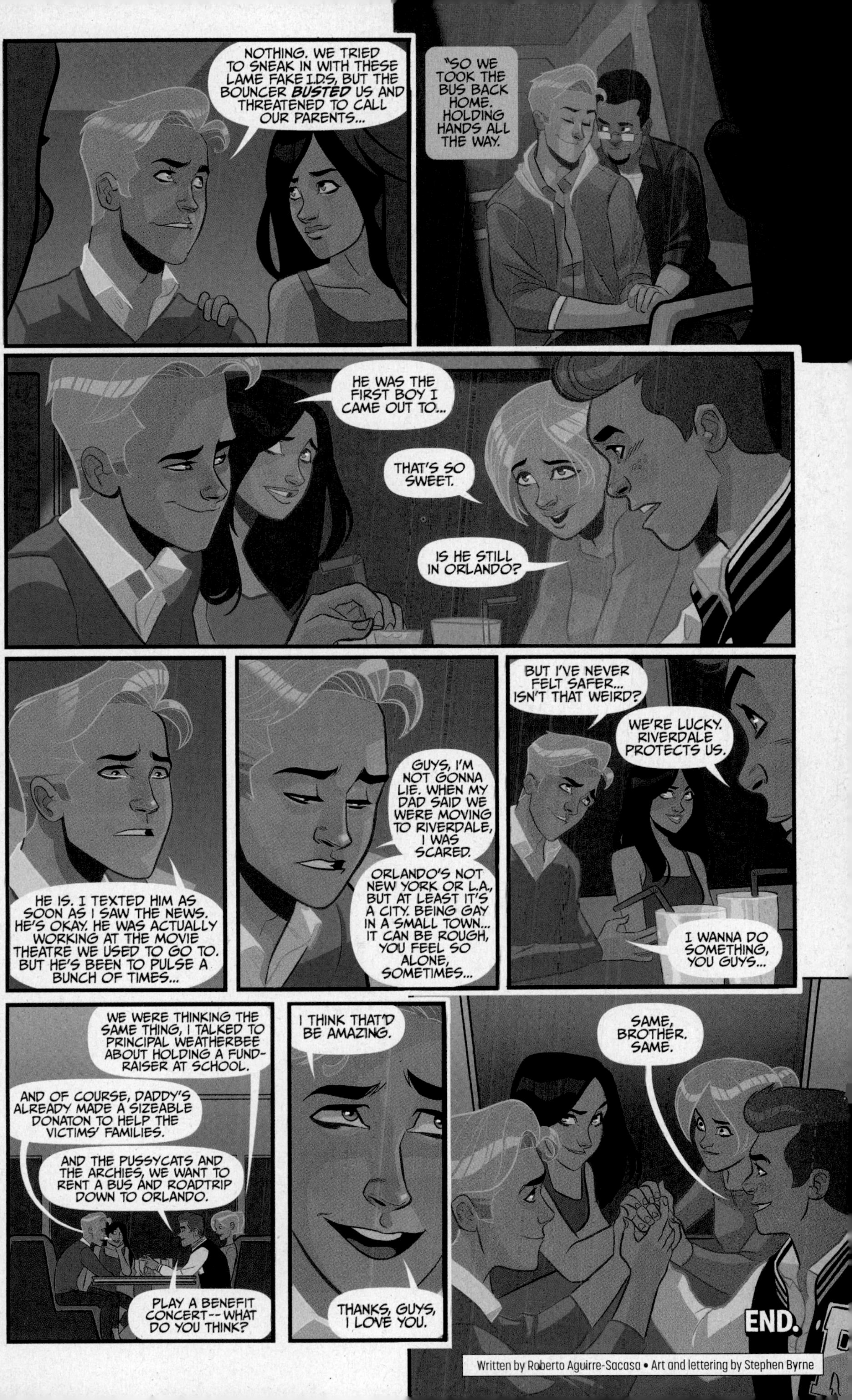
NOTHING. WE TRIED TO SNEAK IN WITH THESE LAME FAKE I.D.S, BUT THE BOUNCER BUSTED US AND THREATENED TO CALL OUR PARENTS...
"SO WE TOOK THE BUS BACK HOME. HOLDING HANDS ALL THE WAY.
HE WAS THE FIRST BOY I CAME OUT TO...
THAT'S SO SWEET.
IS HE STILL IN ORLANDO?
HE IS. I TEXTED HIM AS SOON AS I SAW THE NEWS. HE'S OKAY. HE WAS ACTUALLY WORKING AT THE MOVIE THEATRE WE USED TO GO TO. BUT HE'S BEEN TO PULSE A BUNCH OF TIMES...
GUYS, I'M NOT GONNA LIE. WHEN MY DAD SAID WE WERE MOVING TO RIVERDALE, I WAS SCARED.
ORLANDO'S NOT NEW YORK OR L.A., BUT AT LEAST IT'S A CITY. BEING GAY IN A SMALL TOWN... IT CAN BE ROUGH, YOU FEEL SO ALONE, SOMETIMES...
BUT I'VE NEVER FELT SAFER... ISN'T THAT WEIRD?
WE'RE LUCKY. RIVERDALE PROTECTS US.
I WANNA DO SOMETHING, YOU GUYS...
WE WERE THINKING THE SAME THING, I TALKED TO PRINCIPAL WEATHERBEE ABOUT HOLDING A FUND-RAISER AT SCHOOL.
AND OF COURSE, DADDY'S ALREADY MADE A SIZEABLE DONATON TO HELP THE VICTIMS' FAMILIES.
AND THE PUSSYCATS AND THE ARCHIES, WE WANT TO RENT A BUS AND ROADTRIP DOWN TO ORLANDO.
PLAY A BENEFIT CONCERT--WHAT DO YOU THINK?
I THINK THAT'D BE AMAZING.
THANKS, GUYS, I LOVE YOU.
SAME, BROTHER. SAME.
END.
Written by Roberto Aguirre-Sacasa • Art and lettering by Stephen Byrne

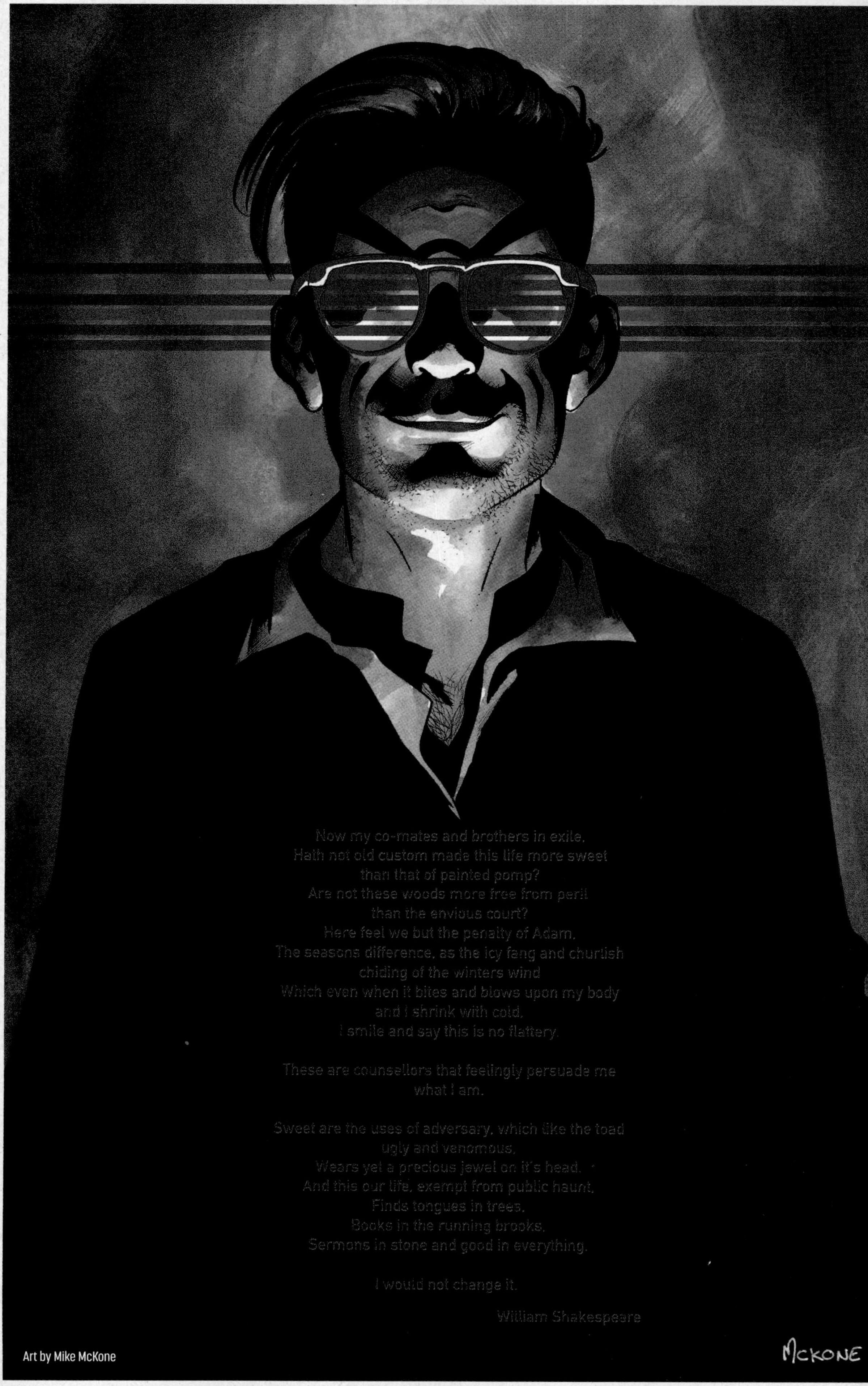
Now my co-mates and brothers in exile,
Hath not old custom made this life more sweet
than that of painted pomp?
Are not these woods more free from peril
than the envious court?
Here feel we but the penalty of Adam,
The seasons difference, as the icy fang and churlish
chiding of the winters wind
Which even when it bites and blows upon my body
and I shrink with cold,
I smile and say this is no flattery.
These are counsellors that feelingly persuade me
what I am.
Sweet are the uses of adversary, which like the toad
ugly and venomous,
Wears yet a precious jewel on it's head.
And this our life, exempt from public haunt,
Finds tongues in trees,
Books in the running brooks,
Sermons in stone and good in everything.
I would not change it.
William Shakespeare
MCKONE
Art by Mike McKone

*"Love? What is it?
Most natural painkiller
what there is.
LOVE."*

*Last words of William S. Burroughs*

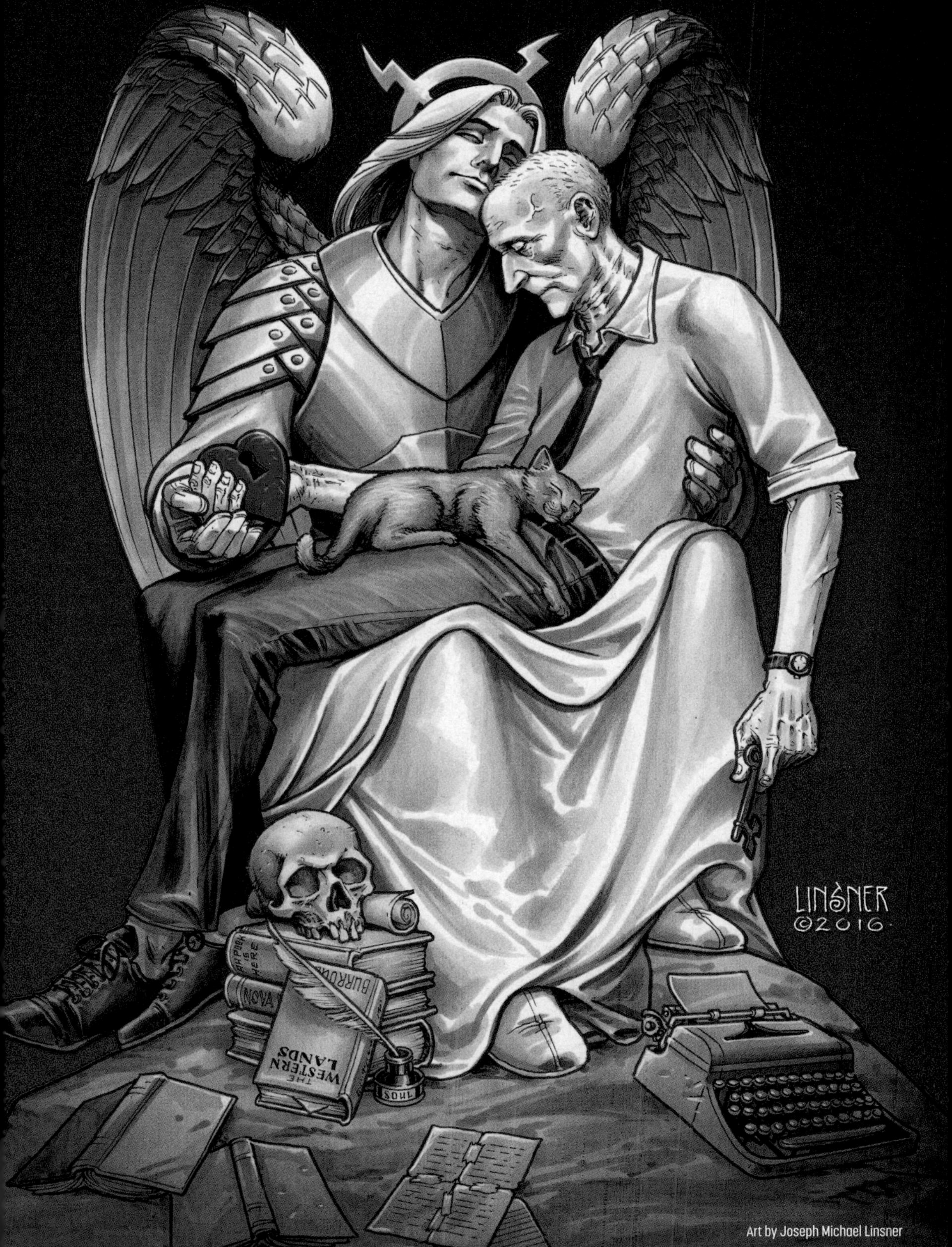
LINSNER
©2016
THE WESTERN LANDS
NOVA
SOUL

Art by Joseph Michael Linsner

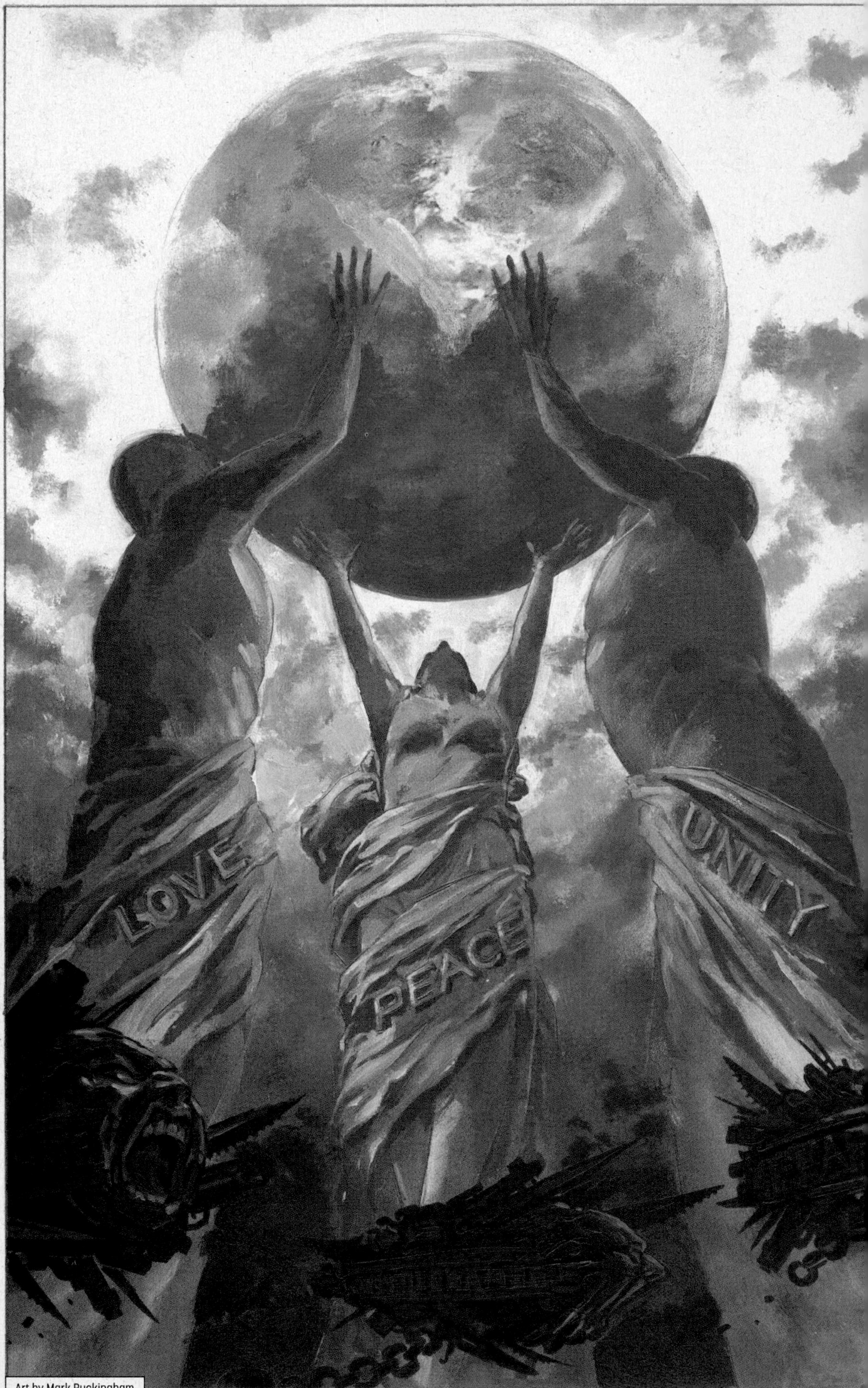
LOVE
PEACE
UNITY
Art by Mark Buckingham

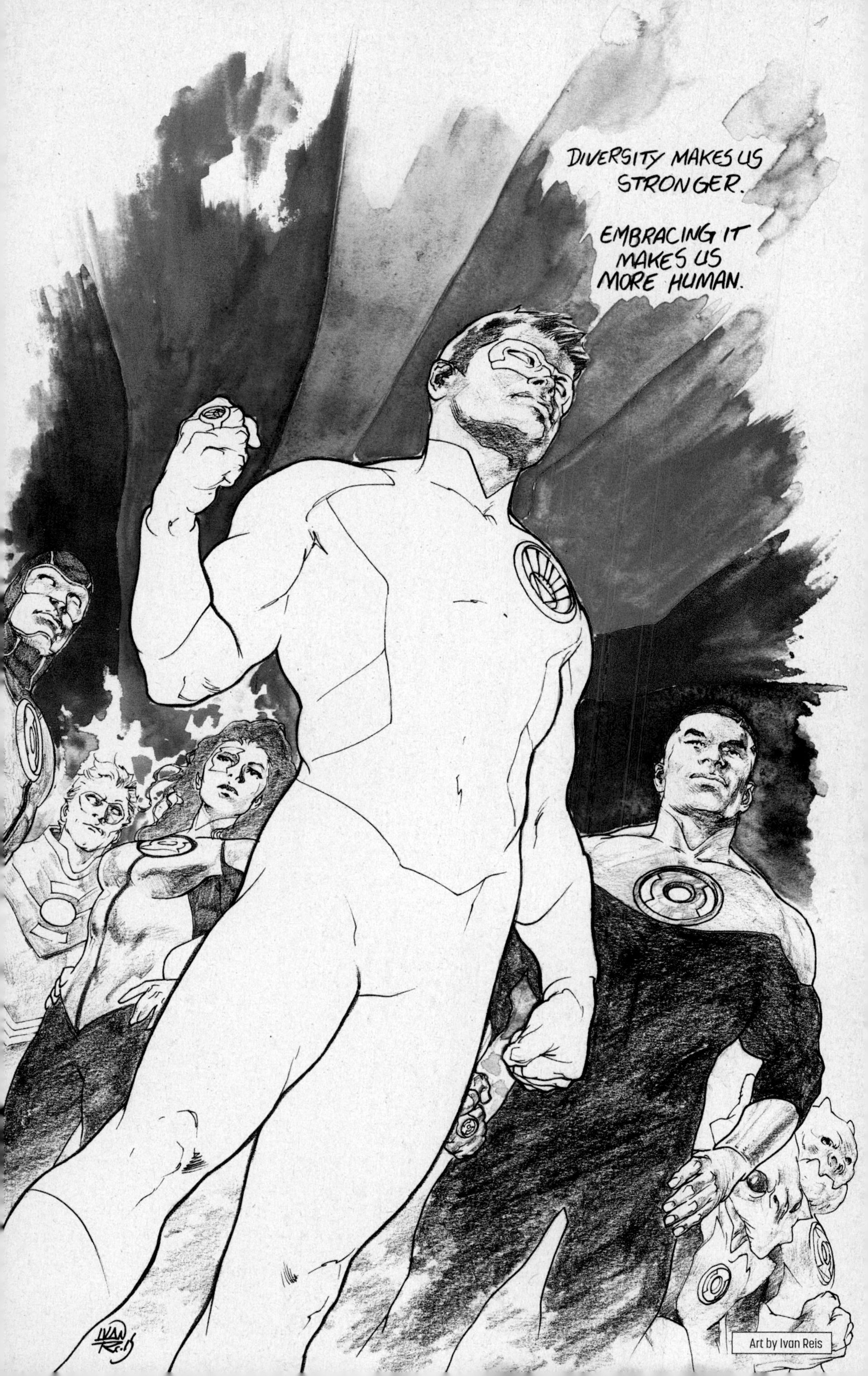
DIVERSITY MAKES US STRONGER.
EMBRACING IT MAKES US MORE HUMAN.
IVAN REIS

Art by Ivan Reis

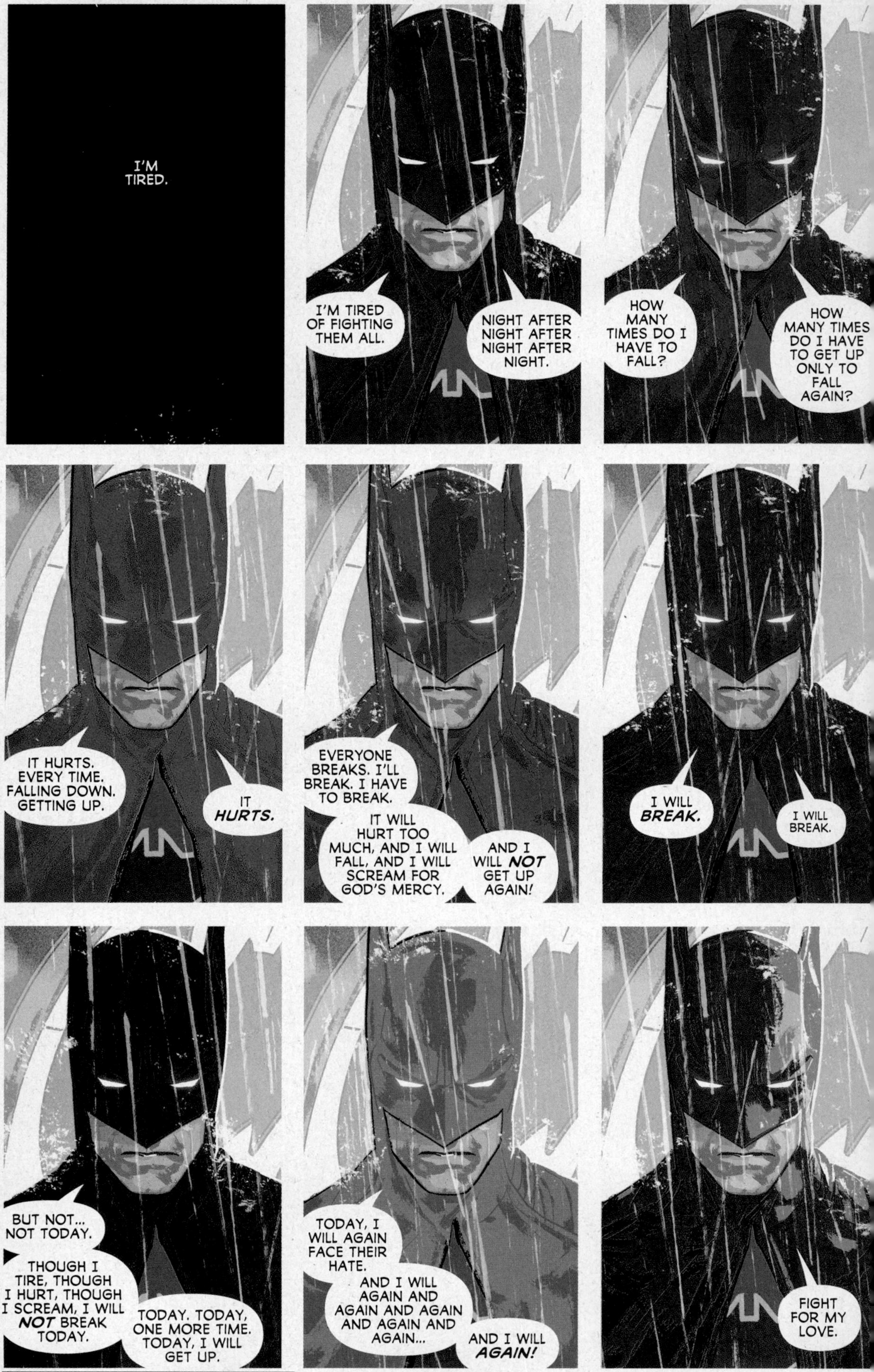
I'M TIRED.
I'M TIRED OF FIGHTING THEM ALL.
NIGHT AFTER NIGHT AFTER NIGHT AFTER NIGHT.
HOW MANY TIMES DO I HAVE TO FALL?
HOW MANY TIMES DO I HAVE TO GET UP ONLY TO FALL AGAIN?
IT HURTS. EVERY TIME. FALLING DOWN. GETTING UP.
IT ***HURTS.***
EVERYONE BREAKS. I'LL BREAK. I HAVE TO BREAK.
IT WILL HURT TOO MUCH, AND I WILL FALL, AND I WILL SCREAM FOR GOD'S MERCY.
AND I WILL ***NOT*** GET UP AGAIN!
I WILL ***BREAK.***
I WILL BREAK.
BUT NOT... NOT TODAY.
THOUGH I TIRE, THOUGH I HURT, THOUGH I SCREAM, I WILL ***NOT*** BREAK TODAY.
TODAY. TODAY, ONE MORE TIME. TODAY, I WILL GET UP.
TODAY, I WILL AGAIN FACE THEIR HATE.
AND I WILL AGAIN AND AGAIN AND AGAIN AND AGAIN AND AGAIN...
AND I WILL ***AGAIN!***
FIGHT FOR MY LOVE.

By Mitch Gerads & Tom King • lettered by Travis Lanham

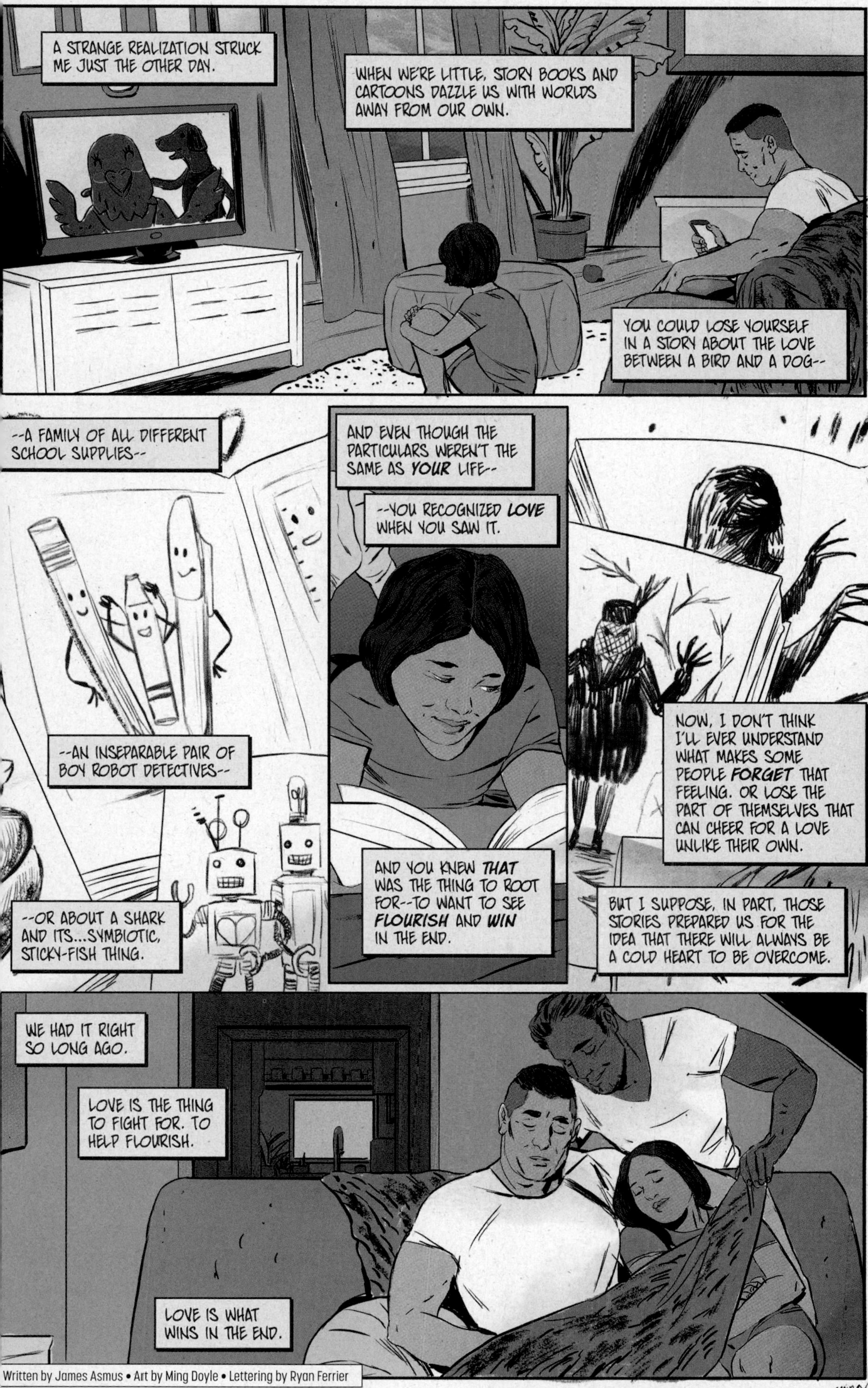
A STRANGE REALIZATION STRUCK ME JUST THE OTHER DAY.
WHEN WE'RE LITTLE, STORY BOOKS AND CARTOONS DAZZLE US WITH WORLDS AWAY FROM OUR OWN.
YOU COULD LOSE YOURSELF IN A STORY ABOUT THE LOVE BETWEEN A BIRD AND A DOG--
--A FAMILY OF ALL DIFFERENT SCHOOL SUPPLIES--
--AN INSEPARABLE PAIR OF BOY ROBOT DETECTIVES--
--OR ABOUT A SHARK AND ITS...SYMBIOTIC, STICKY-FISH THING.
AND EVEN THOUGH THE PARTICULARS WEREN'T THE SAME AS ***YOUR*** LIFE--
--YOU RECOGNIZED ***LOVE*** WHEN YOU SAW IT.
AND YOU KNEW ***THAT*** WAS THE THING TO ROOT FOR--TO WANT TO SEE ***FLOURISH*** AND ***WIN*** IN THE END.
NOW, I DON'T THINK I'LL EVER UNDERSTAND WHAT MAKES SOME PEOPLE ***FORGET*** THAT FEELING. OR LOSE THE PART OF THEMSELVES THAT CAN CHEER FOR A LOVE UNLIKE THEIR OWN.
BUT I SUPPOSE, IN PART, THOSE STORIES PREPARED US FOR THE IDEA THAT THERE WILL ALWAYS BE A COLD HEART TO BE OVERCOME.
WE HAD IT RIGHT SO LONG AGO.
LOVE IS THE THING TO FIGHT FOR. TO HELP FLOURISH.
LOVE IS WHAT WINS IN THE END.

Written by James Asmus • Art by Ming Doyle • Lettering by Ryan Ferrier

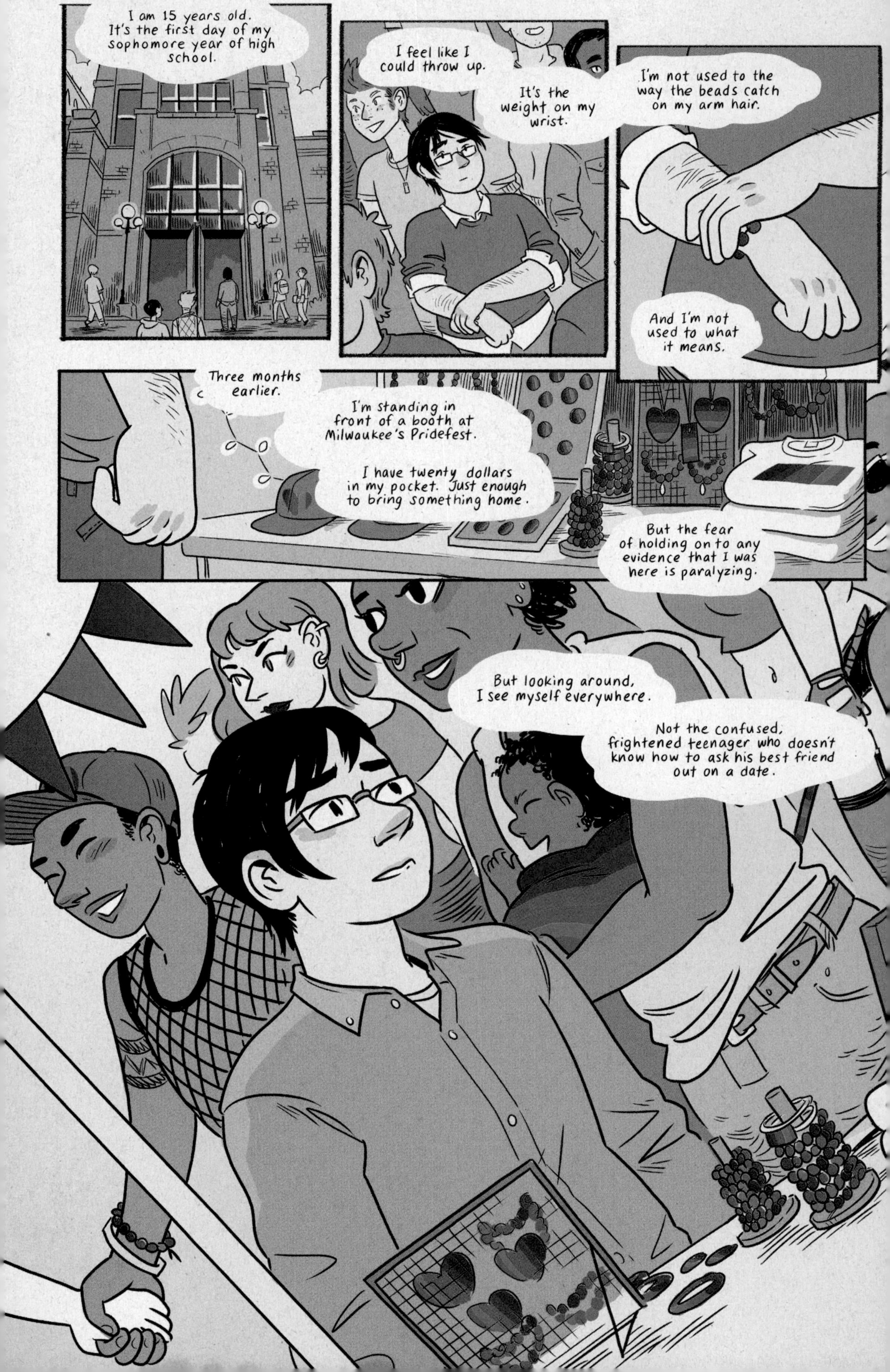
I am 15 years old. It's the first day of my sophomore year of high school.
I feel like I could throw up.
It's the weight on my wrist.
I'm not used to the way the beads catch on my arm hair.
And I'm not used to what it means.
Three months earlier.
I'm standing in front of a booth at Milwaukee's Pridefest.
I have twenty dollars in my pocket. Just enough to bring something home.
But the fear of holding on to any evidence that I was here is paralyzing.
But looking around, I see myself everywhere.
Not the confused, frightened teenager who doesn't know how to ask his best friend out on a date.

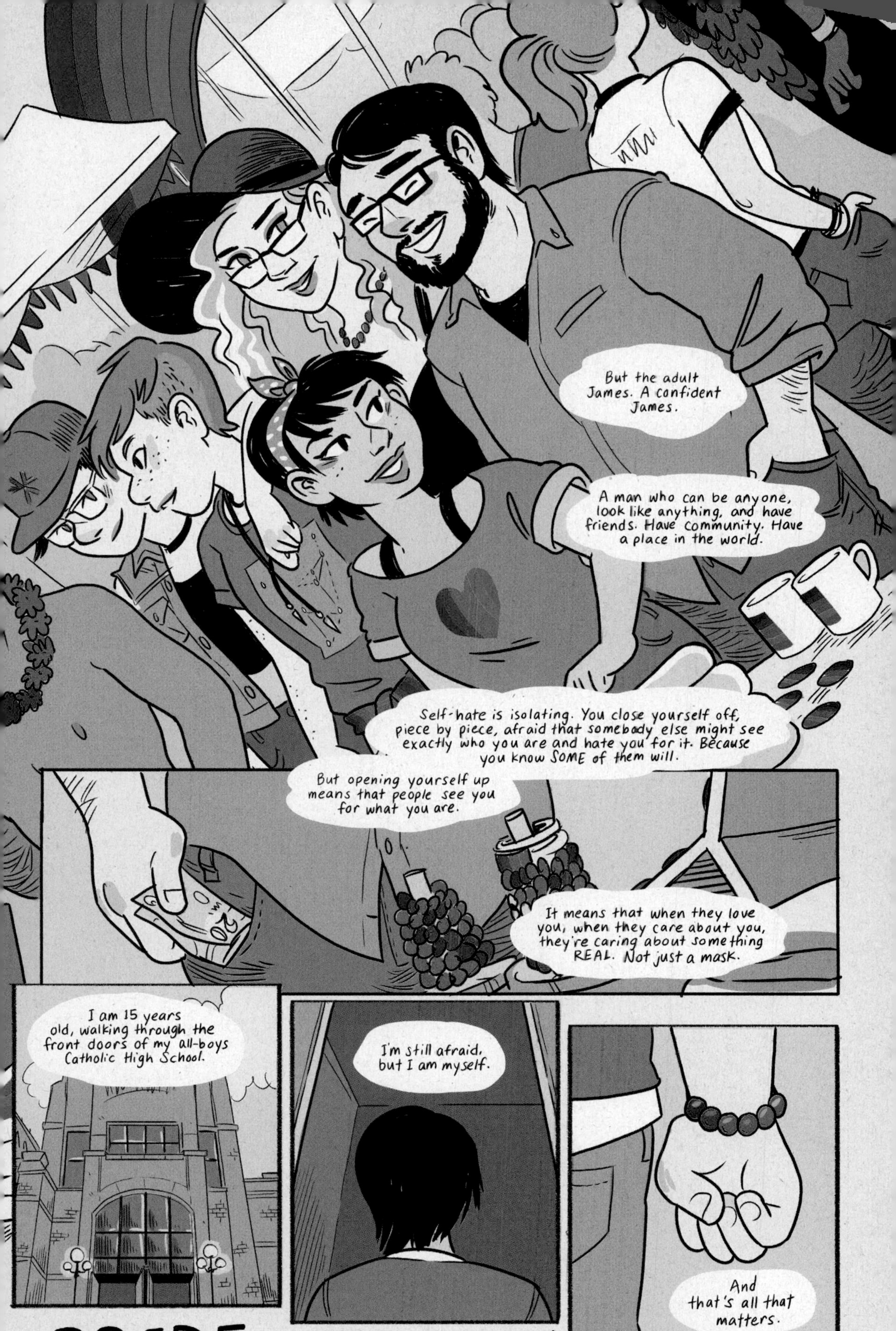
But the adult James. A confident James.
A man who can be anyone, look like anything, and have friends. Have community. Have a place in the world.
Self-hate is isolating. You close yourself off, piece by piece, afraid that somebody else might see exactly who you are and hate you for it. Because you know SOME of them will.
But opening yourself up means that people see you for what you are.
It means that when they love you, when they care about you, they're caring about something REAL. Not just a mask.
I am 15 years old, walking through the front doors of my all-boys Catholic High School.
I'm still afraid, but I am myself.
And that's all that matters.

# PRIDE

by James Tynion IV & Molly Knox Ostertag

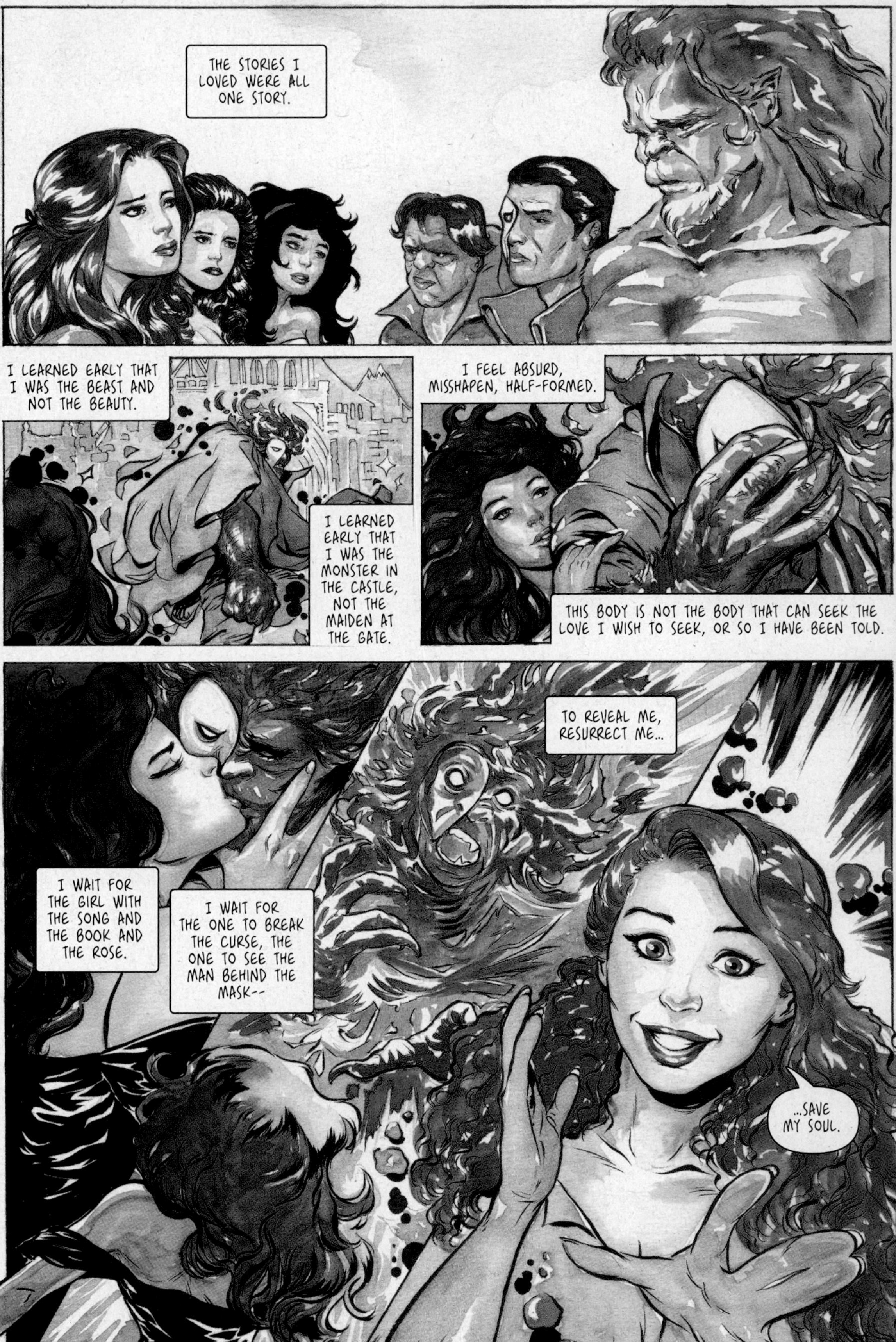
THE STORIES I LOVED WERE ALL ONE STORY.
I LEARNED EARLY THAT I WAS THE BEAST AND NOT THE BEAUTY.
I LEARNED EARLY THAT I WAS THE MONSTER IN THE CASTLE, NOT THE MAIDEN AT THE GATE.
I FEEL ABSURD, MISSHAPEN, HALF-FORMED.
THIS BODY IS NOT THE BODY THAT CAN SEEK THE LOVE I WISH TO SEEK, OR SO I HAVE BEEN TOLD.
I WAIT FOR THE GIRL WITH THE SONG AND THE BOOK AND THE ROSE.
I WAIT FOR THE ONE TO BREAK THE CURSE, THE ONE TO SEE THE MAN BEHIND THE MASK--
TO REVEAL ME, RESURRECT ME...
...SAVE MY SOUL.

Written by Marguerite Bennett • Art by Aneke • Lettered by Travis Lanham

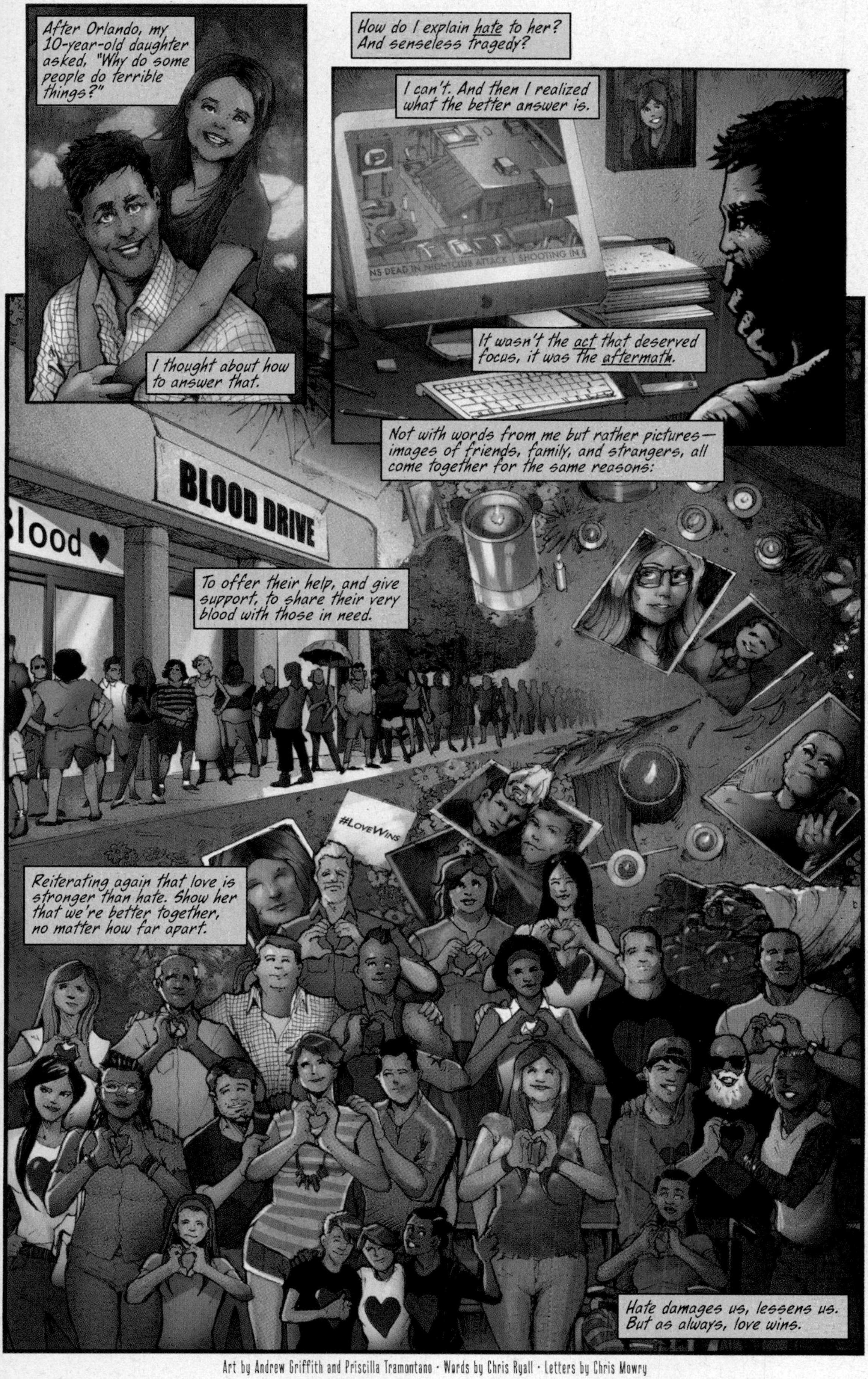
After Orlando, my 10-year-old daughter asked, "Why do some people do terrible things?"
I thought about how to answer that.
How do I explain hate to her? And senseless tragedy?
I can't. And then I realized what the better answer is.
It wasn't the act that deserved focus, it was the aftermath.
Not with words from me but rather pictures—images of friends, family, and strangers, all come together for the same reasons:
BLOOD DRIVE
To offer their help, and give support, to share their very blood with those in need.
#LoveWins
Reiterating again that love is stronger than hate. Show her that we're better together, no matter how far apart.
Hate damages us, lessens us. But as always, love wins.

Art by Andrew Griffith and Priscilla Tramontano • Words by Chris Ryall • Letters by Chris Mowry

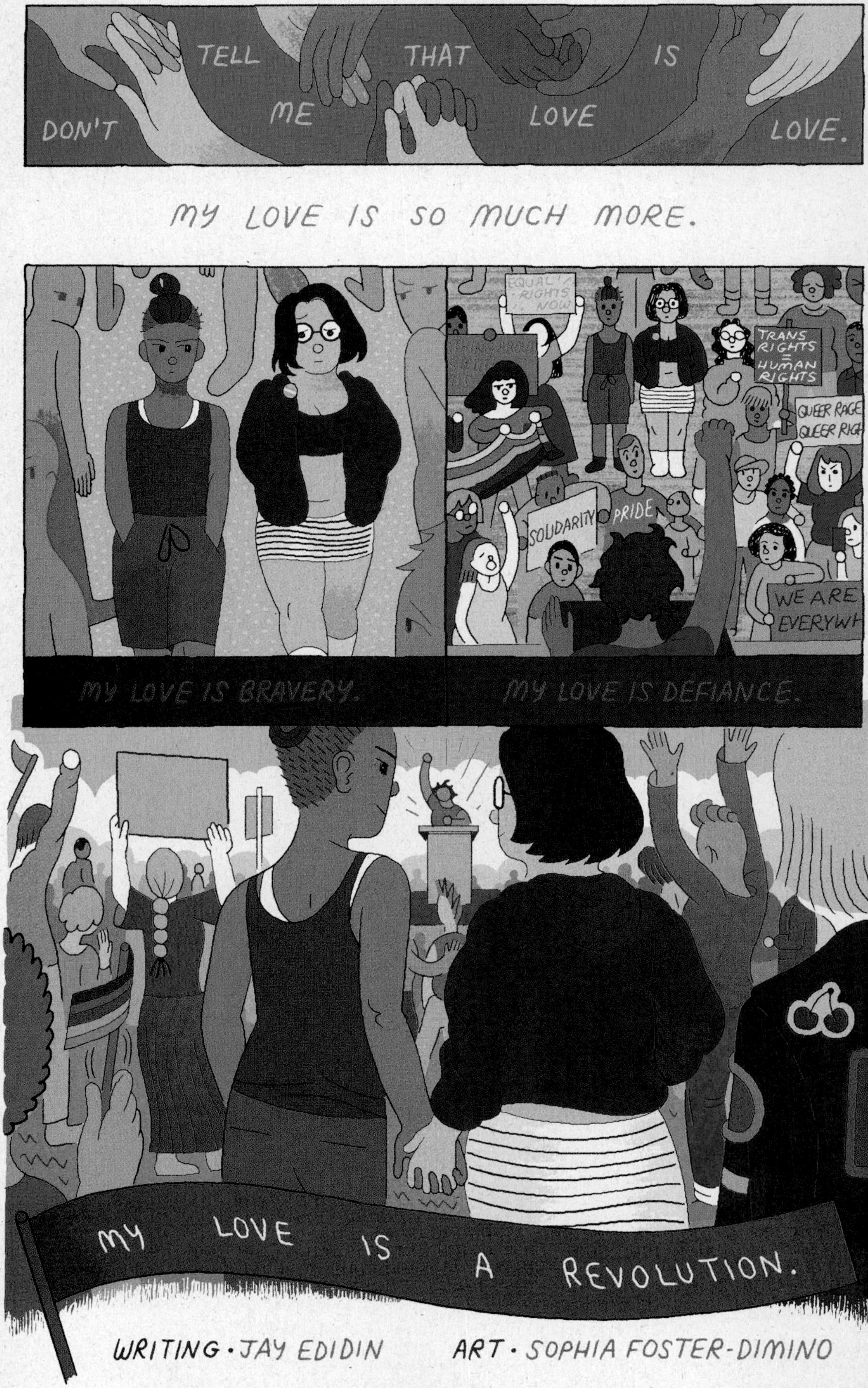
DON'T TELL ME THAT LOVE IS LOVE.
MY LOVE IS SO MUCH MORE.
EQUAL RIGHTS NOW
TRANS RIGHTS = HUMAN RIGHTS
QUEER RAGE
QUEER RIGH
SOLIDARITY
PRIDE
WE ARE EVERYWH
MY LOVE IS BRAVERY.
MY LOVE IS DEFIANCE.
MY LOVE IS A REVOLUTION.

WRITING · JAY EDIDIN ART · SOPHIA FOSTER-DIMINO

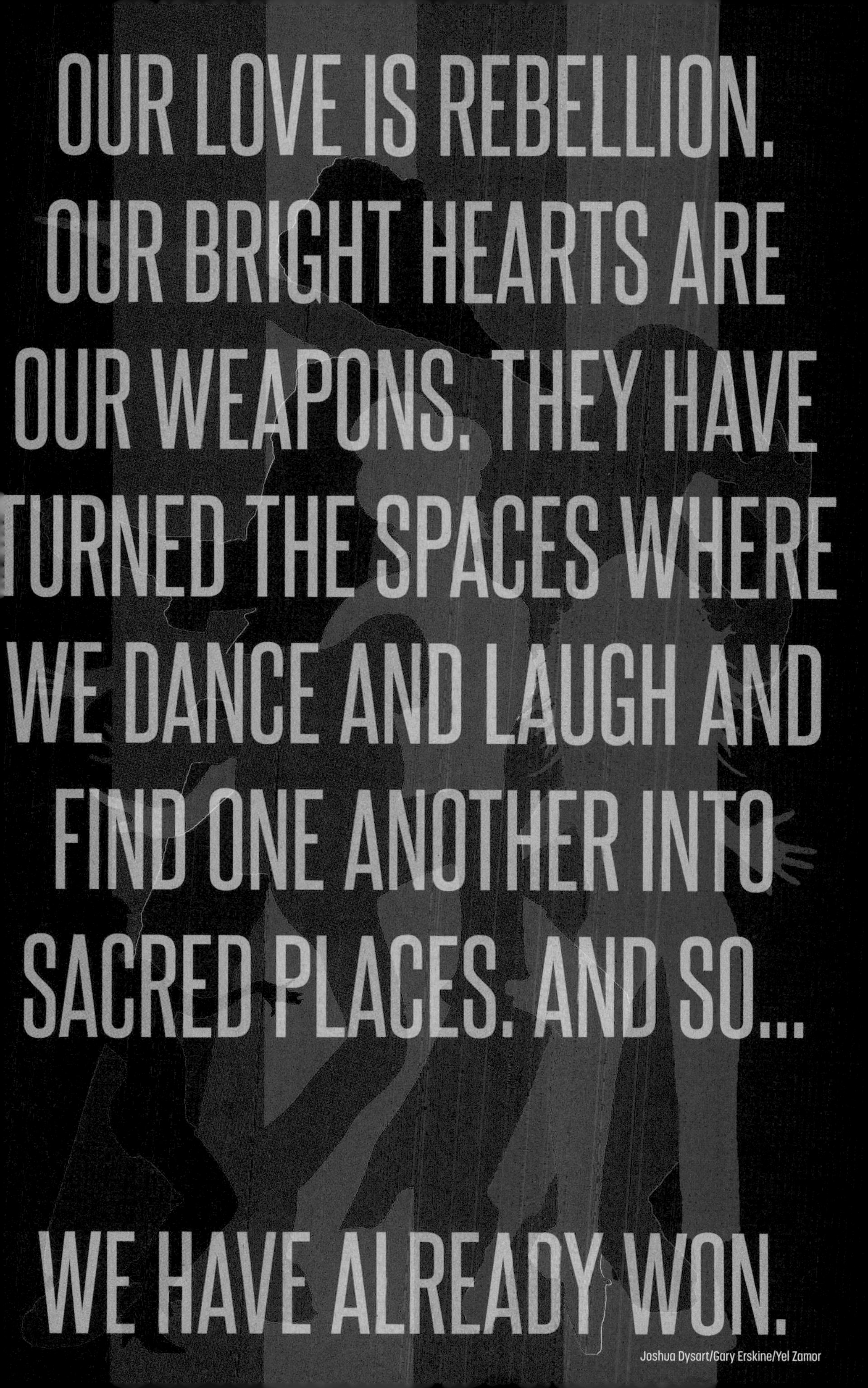
OUR LOVE IS REBELLION. OUR BRIGHT HEARTS ARE OUR WEAPONS. THEY HAVE TURNED THE SPACES WHERE WE DANCE AND LAUGH AND FIND ONE ANOTHER INTO SACRED PLACES. AND SO...
WE HAVE ALREADY WON.

Joshua Dysart/Gary Erskine/Yel Zamor

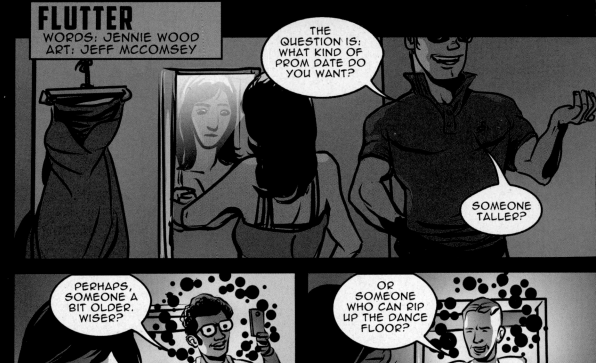

FLUTTER
WORDS: JENNIE WOOD
ART: JEFF McCOMSEY

THE QUESTION IS: WHAT KIND OF PROM DATE DO YOU WANT?

SOMEONE TALLER?

PERHAPS, SOMEONE A BIT OLDER, WISER?

OR SOMEONE WHO CAN RIP UP THE DANCE FLOOR?

I WANT TO GO WITH YOU, LILY.

BUT OUR CLASSMATES... THEY MIGHT...

THEY MIGHT NOT EVEN CARE. THERE'S ONLY ONE WAY TO FIND OUT.

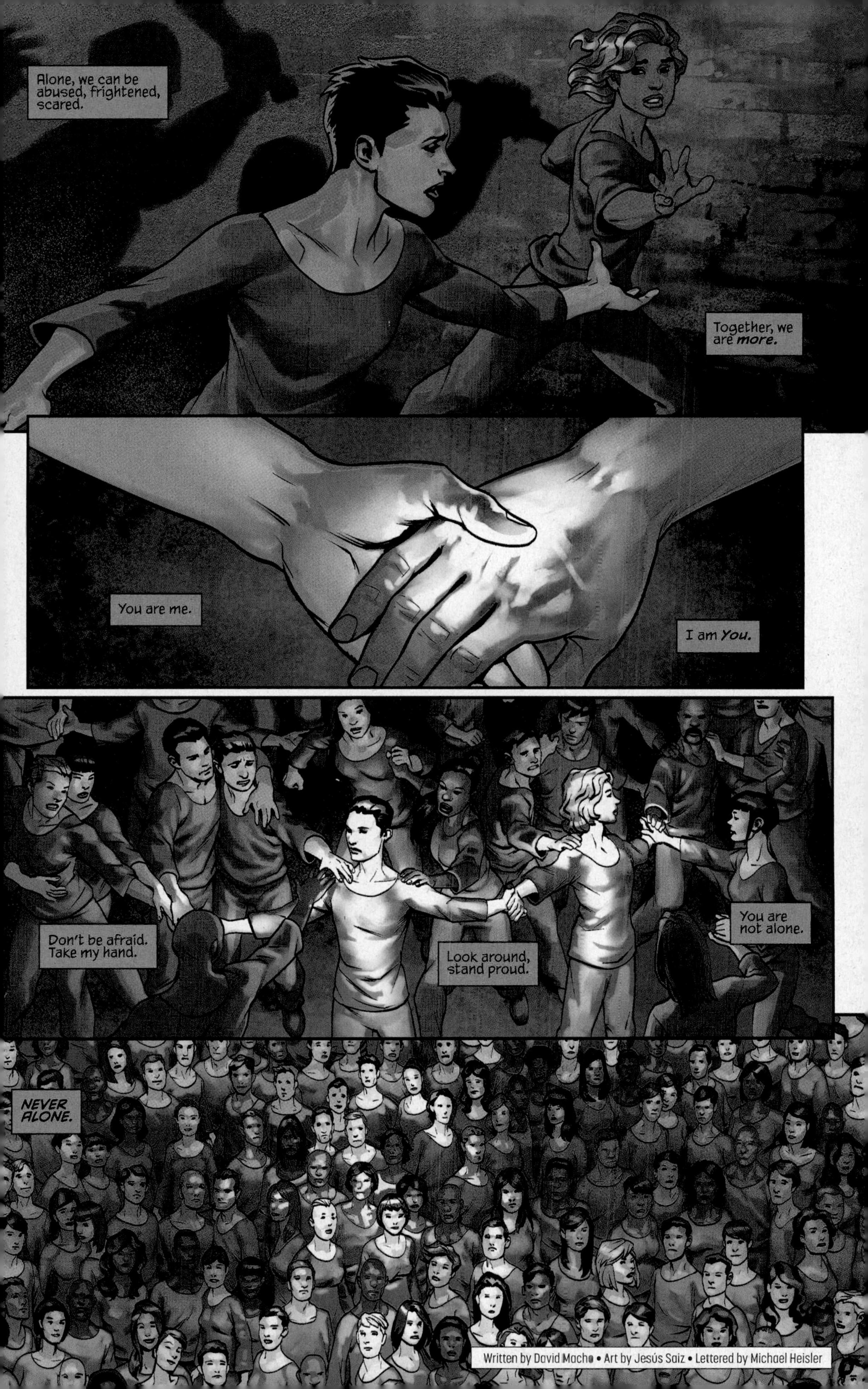
Alone, we can be abused, frightened, scared.
Together, we are *more.*
You are me.
I am *You.*
Don't be afraid. Take my hand.
Look around, stand proud.
You are not alone.
*NEVER ALONE.*
Written by David Macho • Art by Jesús Saiz • Lettered by Michael Heisler

# Jayson™ PINUP

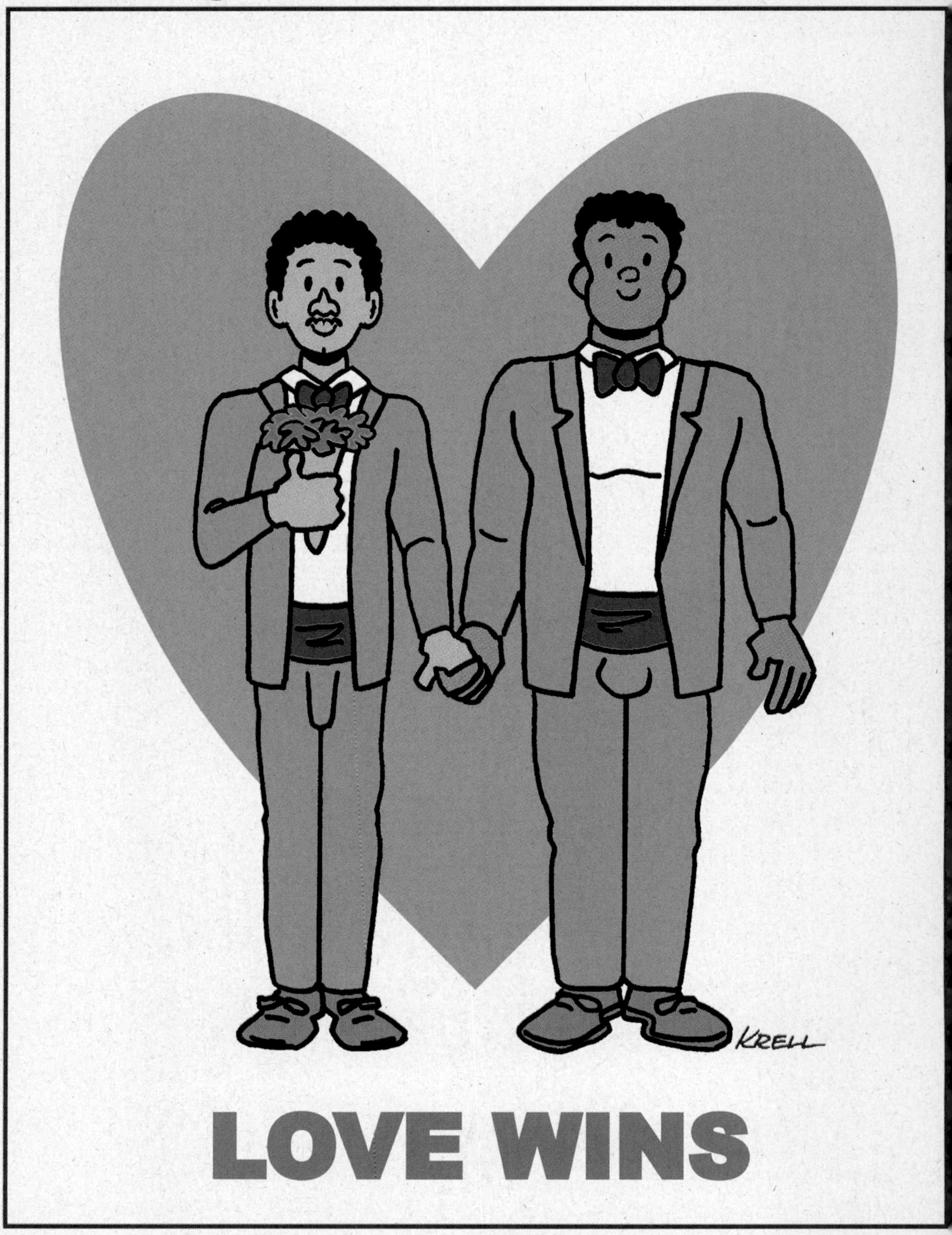
KRELL
LOVE WINS

Art by Jeff Krell

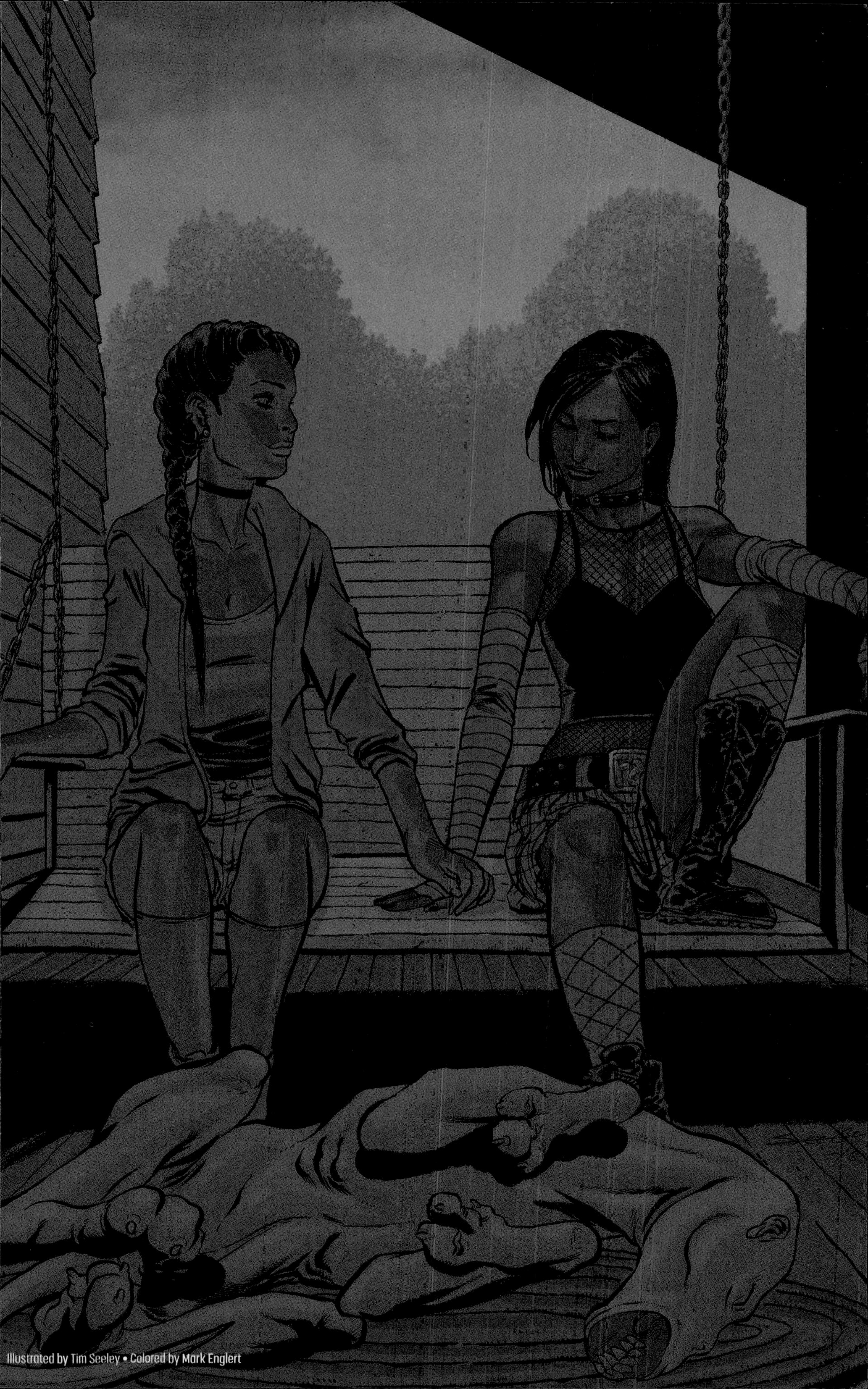

Illustrated by Tim Seeley • Colored by Mark Englert

# CENTURION

writer// Van Jensen artist // Álvaro Ortiz

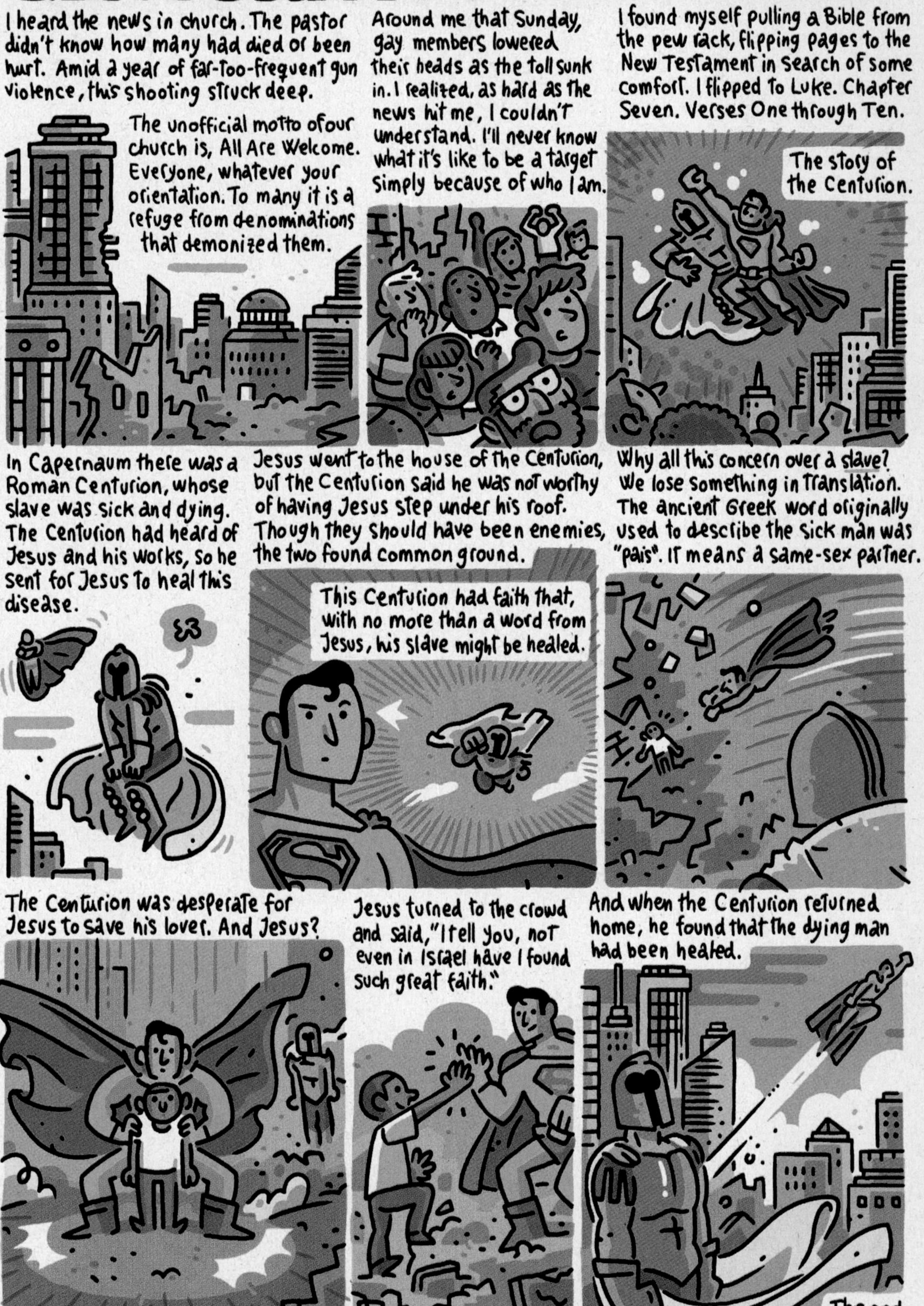
I heard the news in church. The pastor didn't know how many had died or been hurt. Amid a year of far-too-frequent gun violence, this shooting struck deep.
The unofficial motto of our church is, All Are Welcome. Everyone, whatever your orientation. To many it is a refuge from denominations that demonized them.
Around me that Sunday, gay members lowered their heads as the toll sunk in. I realized, as hard as the news hit me, I couldn't understand. I'll never know what it's like to be a target simply because of who I am.
I found myself pulling a Bible from the pew rack, flipping pages to the New Testament in search of some comfort. I flipped to Luke. Chapter Seven. Verses One through Ten.
The story of the Centurion.
In Capernaum there was a Roman Centurion, whose slave was sick and dying. The Centurion had heard of Jesus and his works, so he sent for Jesus to heal this disease.
Jesus went to the house of the Centurion, but the Centurion said he was not worthy of having Jesus step under his roof. Though they should have been enemies, the two found common ground.
This Centurion had faith that, with no more than a word from Jesus, his slave might be healed.
Why all this concern over a slave? We lose something in translation. The ancient Greek word originally used to describe the sick man was "pais". It means a same-sex partner.
The Centurion was desperate for Jesus to save his lover. And Jesus?
Jesus turned to the crowd and said, "I tell you, not even in Israel have I found such great faith."
And when the Centurion returned home, he found that the dying man had been healed.
The end

tory by B. Alex Thompson, Art by Kevin Richardson & Letters by Elisa M. Coletti

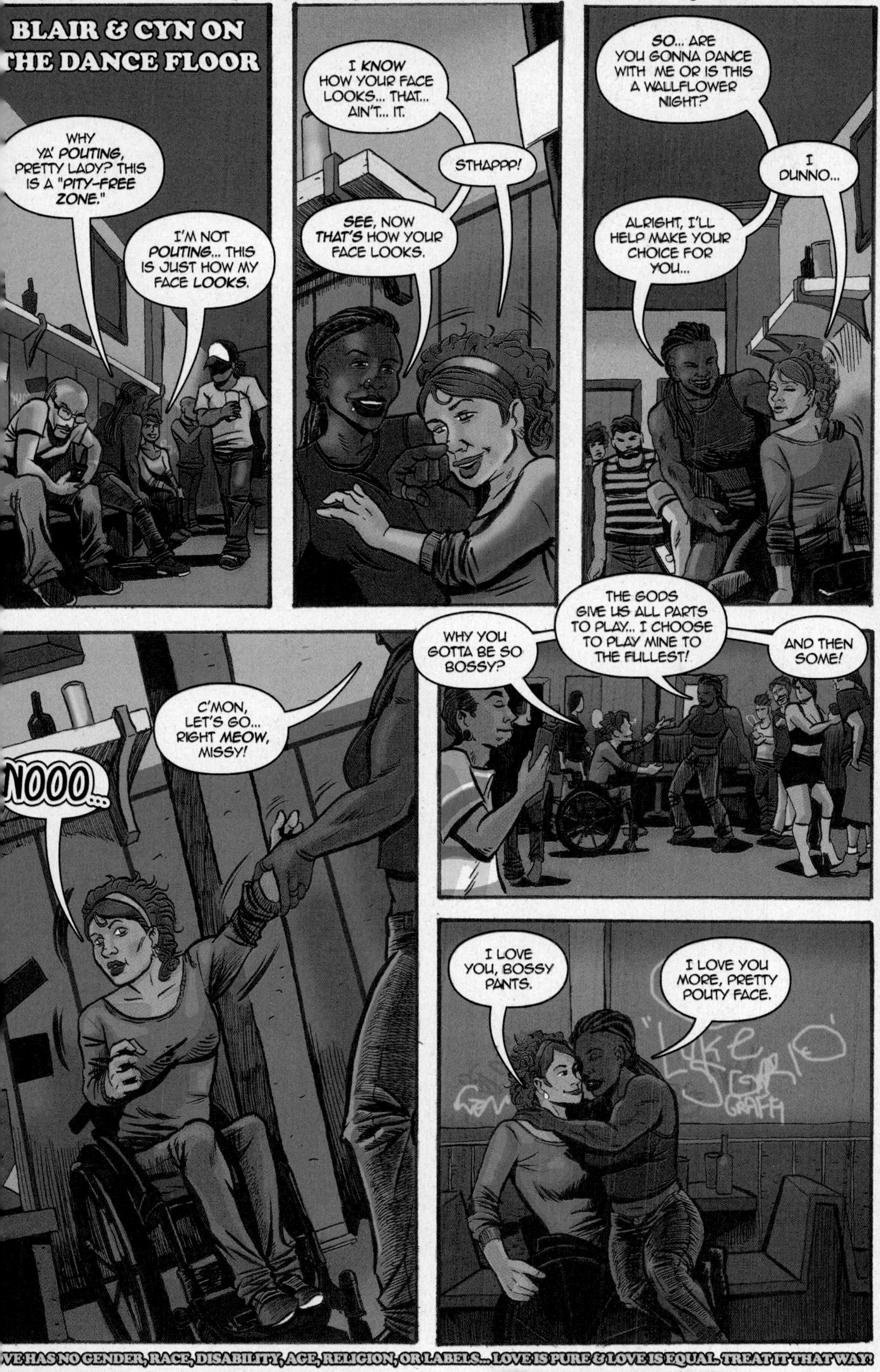
BLAIR & CYN ON
THE DANCE FLOOR
WHY YA' POUTING, PRETTY LADY? THIS IS A "PITY-FREE ZONE."
I'M NOT POUTING... THIS IS JUST HOW MY FACE LOOKS.
I KNOW HOW YOUR FACE LOOKS... THAT... AIN'T... IT.
STHAPPP!
SEE, NOW THAT'S HOW YOUR FACE LOOKS.
SO... ARE YOU GONNA DANCE WITH ME OR IS THIS A WALLFLOWER NIGHT?
I DUNNO...
ALRIGHT, I'LL HELP MAKE YOUR CHOICE FOR YOU...
C'MON, LET'S GO... RIGHT MEOW, MISSY!
NOOO...
WHY YOU GOTTA BE SO BOSSY?
THE GODS GIVE US ALL PARTS TO PLAY... I CHOOSE TO PLAY MINE TO THE FULLEST!
AND THEN SOME!
I LOVE YOU, BOSSY PANTS.
I LOVE YOU MORE, PRETTY POUTY FACE.

VE HAS NO GENDER, RACE, DISABILITY, AGE, RELIGION, OR LABELS... LOVE IS PURE & LOVE IS EQUAL. TREAT IT THAT WAY!

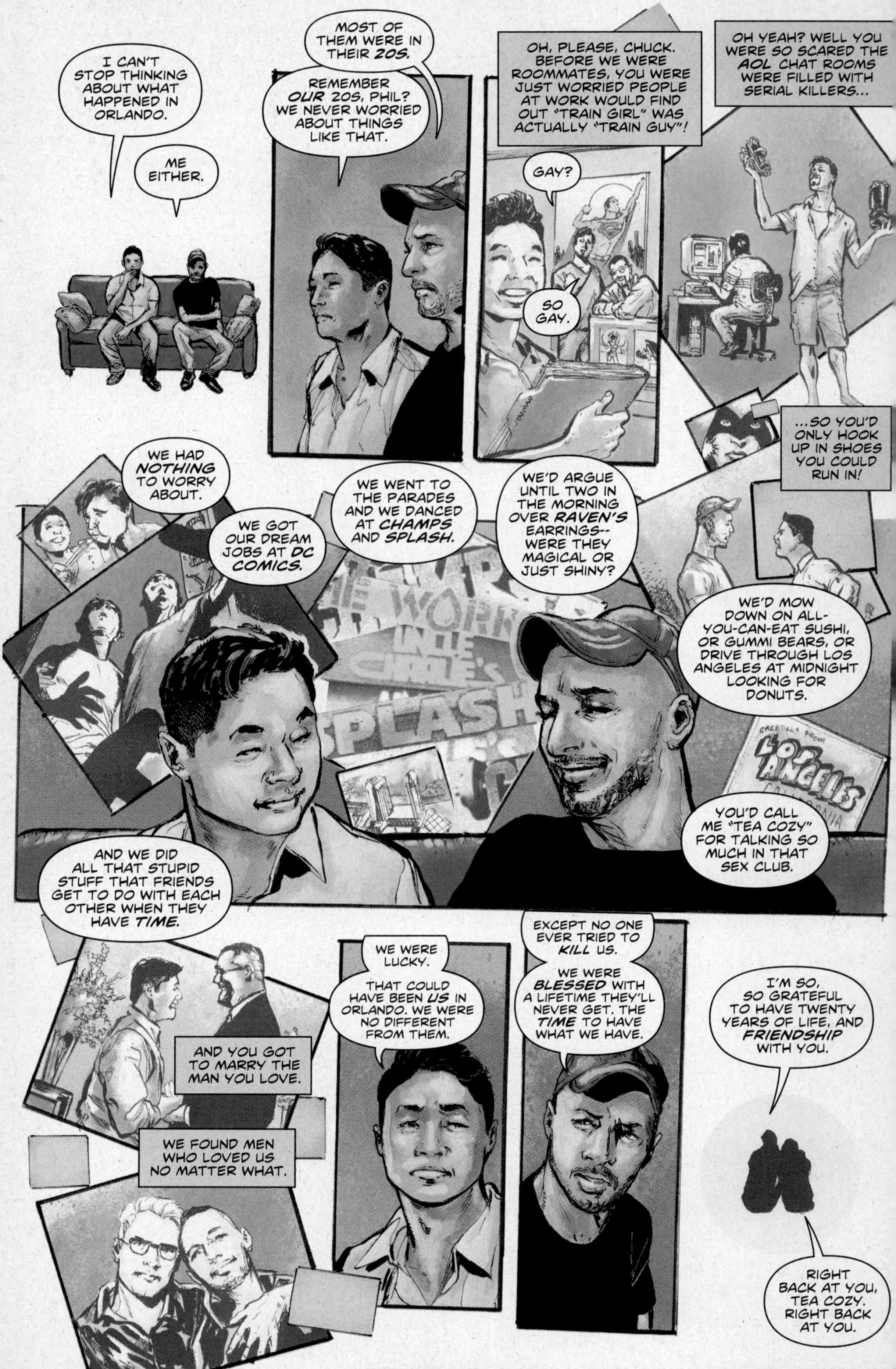
I CAN'T STOP THINKING ABOUT WHAT HAPPENED IN ORLANDO.
ME EITHER.
MOST OF THEM WERE IN THEIR 20S.
REMEMBER OUR 20S, PHIL? WE NEVER WORRIED ABOUT THINGS LIKE THAT.
OH, PLEASE, CHUCK. BEFORE WE WERE ROOMMATES, YOU WERE JUST WORRIED PEOPLE AT WORK WOULD FIND OUT "TRAIN GIRL" WAS ACTUALLY "TRAIN GUY"!
GAY?
SO GAY.
OH YEAH? WELL YOU WERE SO SCARED THE AOL CHAT ROOMS WERE FILLED WITH SERIAL KILLERS...
...SO YOU'D ONLY HOOK UP IN SHOES YOU COULD RUN IN!
WE HAD NOTHING TO WORRY ABOUT.
WE GOT OUR DREAM JOBS AT DC COMICS.
WE WENT TO THE PARADES AND WE DANCED AT CHAMPS AND SPLASH.
WE'D ARGUE UNTIL TWO IN THE MORNING OVER RAVEN'S EARRINGS-- WERE THEY MAGICAL OR JUST SHINY?
WE'D MOW DOWN ON ALL-YOU-CAN-EAT SUSHI, OR GUMMI BEARS, OR DRIVE THROUGH LOS ANGELES AT MIDNIGHT LOOKING FOR DONUTS.
SPLASH
GREETINGS FROM LOS ANGELES CALIFORNIA
YOU'D CALL ME "TEA COZY" FOR TALKING SO MUCH IN THAT SEX CLUB.
AND WE DID ALL THAT STUPID STUFF THAT FRIENDS GET TO DO WITH EACH OTHER WHEN THEY HAVE TIME.
AND YOU GOT TO MARRY THE MAN YOU LOVE.
WE FOUND MEN WHO LOVED US NO MATTER WHAT.
WE WERE LUCKY.
THAT COULD HAVE BEEN US IN ORLANDO. WE WERE NO DIFFERENT FROM THEM.
EXCEPT NO ONE EVER TRIED TO KILL US.
WE WERE BLESSED WITH A LIFETIME THEY'LL NEVER GET. THE TIME TO HAVE WHAT WE HAVE.
I'M SO, SO GRATEFUL TO HAVE TWENTY YEARS OF LIFE, AND FRIENDSHIP WITH YOU.
RIGHT BACK AT YOU, TEA COZY. RIGHT BACK AT YOU.

Written by Chuck Kim • Illustrated by Phil Jimenez • Colored by Jordan Boyd • Lettered by Jared K. Fletcher

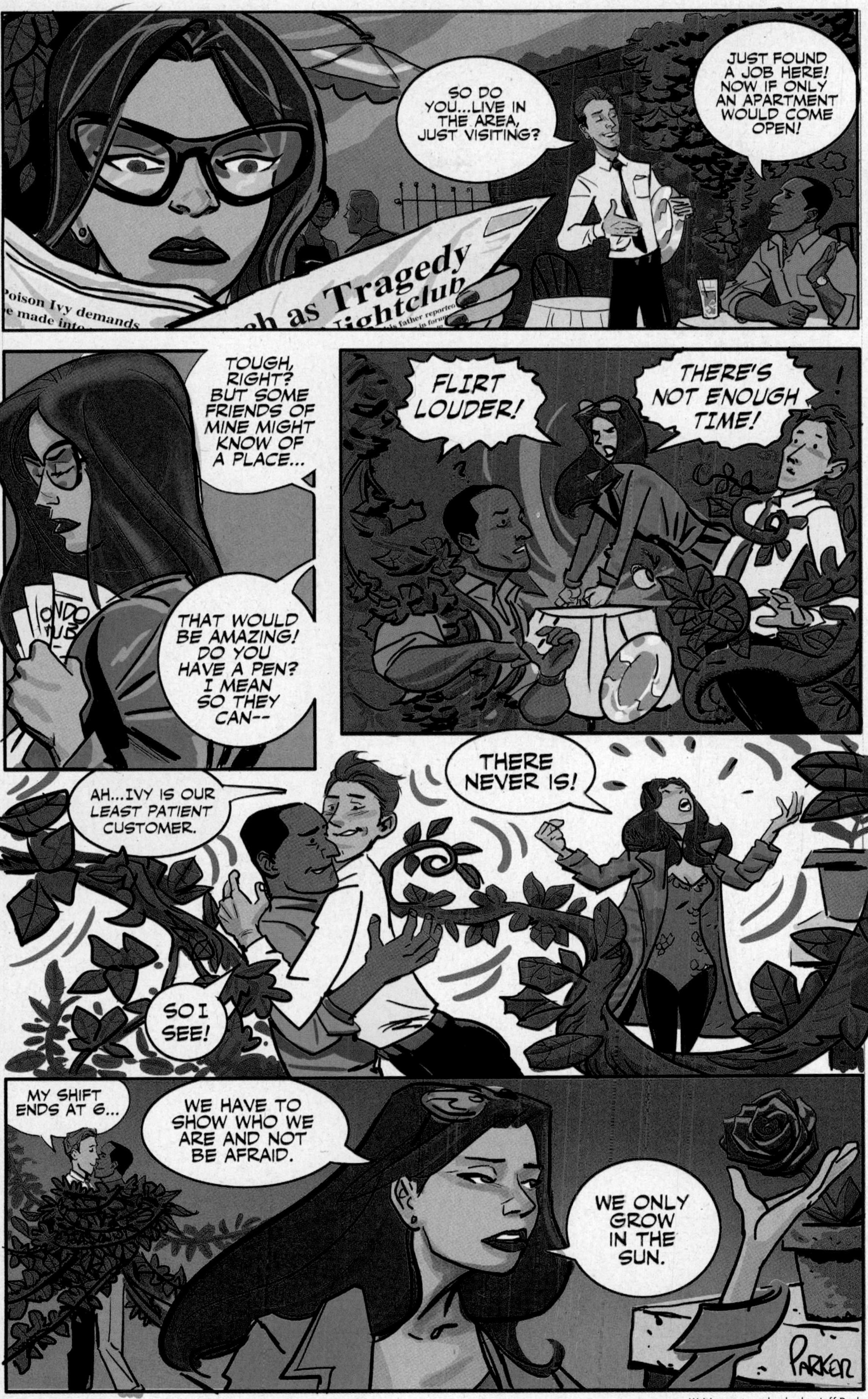
SO DO YOU...LIVE IN THE AREA, JUST VISITING?
JUST FOUND A JOB HERE! NOW IF ONLY AN APARTMENT WOULD COME OPEN!
Poison Ivy demands
TOUGH, RIGHT? BUT SOME FRIENDS OF MINE MIGHT KNOW OF A PLACE...
THAT WOULD BE AMAZING! DO YOU HAVE A PEN? I MEAN SO THEY CAN--
FLIRT LOUDER!
THERE'S NOT ENOUGH TIME!
AH...IVY IS OUR LEAST PATIENT CUSTOMER.
THERE NEVER IS!
SO I SEE!
MY SHIFT ENDS AT 6...
WE HAVE TO SHOW WHO WE ARE AND NOT BE AFRAID.
WE ONLY GROW IN THE SUN.
PARKER

Writing, art, and color by Jeff Parker

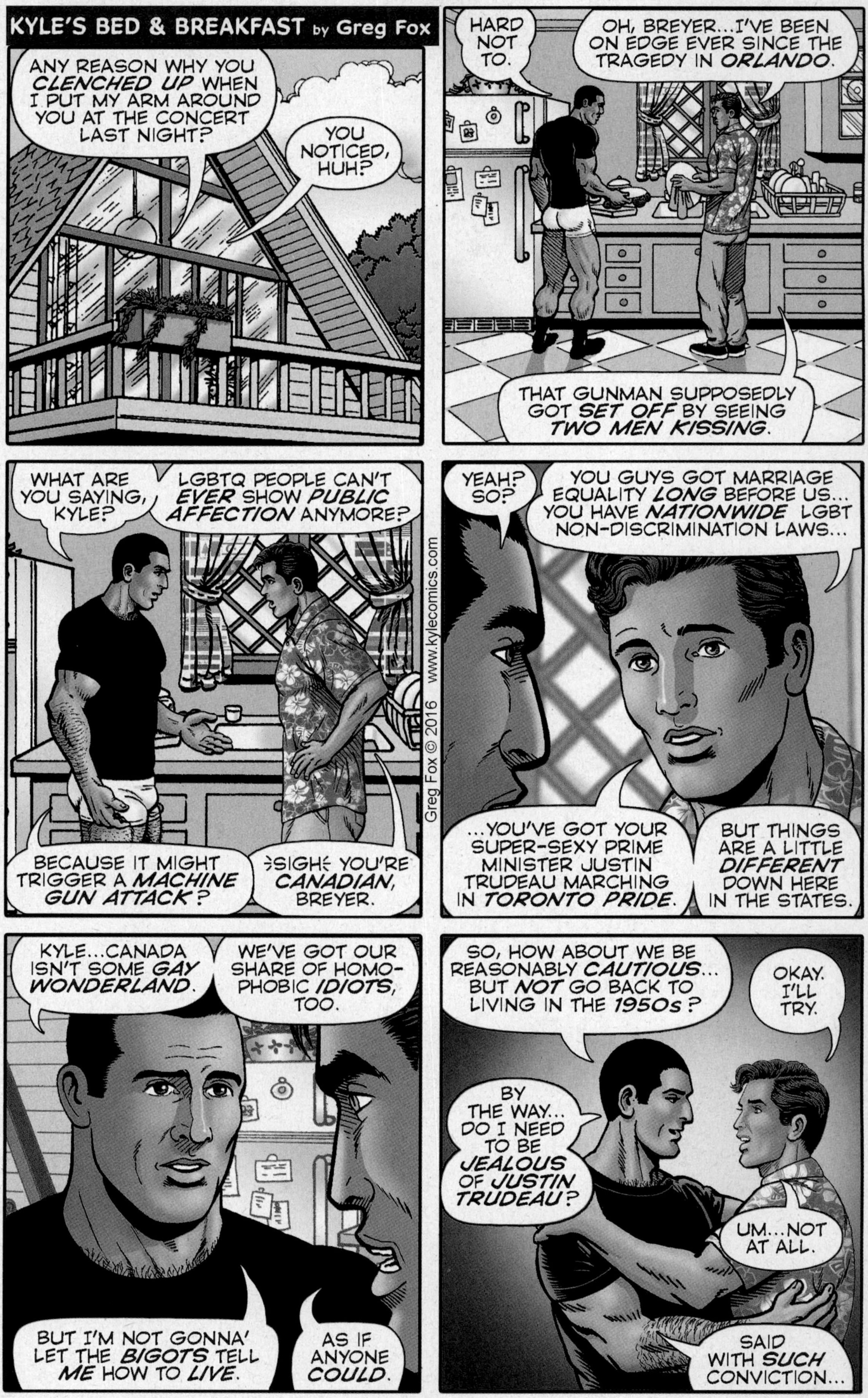
KYLE'S BED & BREAKFAST by Greg Fox
ANY REASON WHY YOU CLENCHED UP WHEN I PUT MY ARM AROUND YOU AT THE CONCERT LAST NIGHT?
YOU NOTICED, HUH?
HARD NOT TO.
OH, BREYER...I'VE BEEN ON EDGE EVER SINCE THE TRAGEDY IN ORLANDO.
THAT GUNMAN SUPPOSEDLY GOT SET OFF BY SEEING TWO MEN KISSING.
WHAT ARE YOU SAYING, KYLE?
LGBTQ PEOPLE CAN'T EVER SHOW PUBLIC AFFECTION ANYMORE?
BECAUSE IT MIGHT TRIGGER A MACHINE GUN ATTACK?
⦚SIGH⦚ YOU'RE CANADIAN, BREYER.
Greg Fox © 2016 www.kylecomics.com
YEAH? SO?
YOU GUYS GOT MARRIAGE EQUALITY LONG BEFORE US... YOU HAVE NATIONWIDE LGBT NON-DISCRIMINATION LAWS...
...YOU'VE GOT YOUR SUPER-SEXY PRIME MINISTER JUSTIN TRUDEAU MARCHING IN TORONTO PRIDE.
BUT THINGS ARE A LITTLE DIFFERENT DOWN HERE IN THE STATES.
KYLE...CANADA ISN'T SOME GAY WONDERLAND.
WE'VE GOT OUR SHARE OF HOMO-PHOBIC IDIOTS, TOO.
BUT I'M NOT GONNA' LET THE BIGOTS TELL ME HOW TO LIVE.
AS IF ANYONE COULD.
SO, HOW ABOUT WE BE REASONABLY CAUTIOUS... BUT NOT GO BACK TO LIVING IN THE 1950s?
OKAY. I'LL TRY.
BY THE WAY... DO I NEED TO BE JEALOUS OF JUSTIN TRUDEAU?
UM...NOT AT ALL.
SAID WITH SUCH CONVICTION...

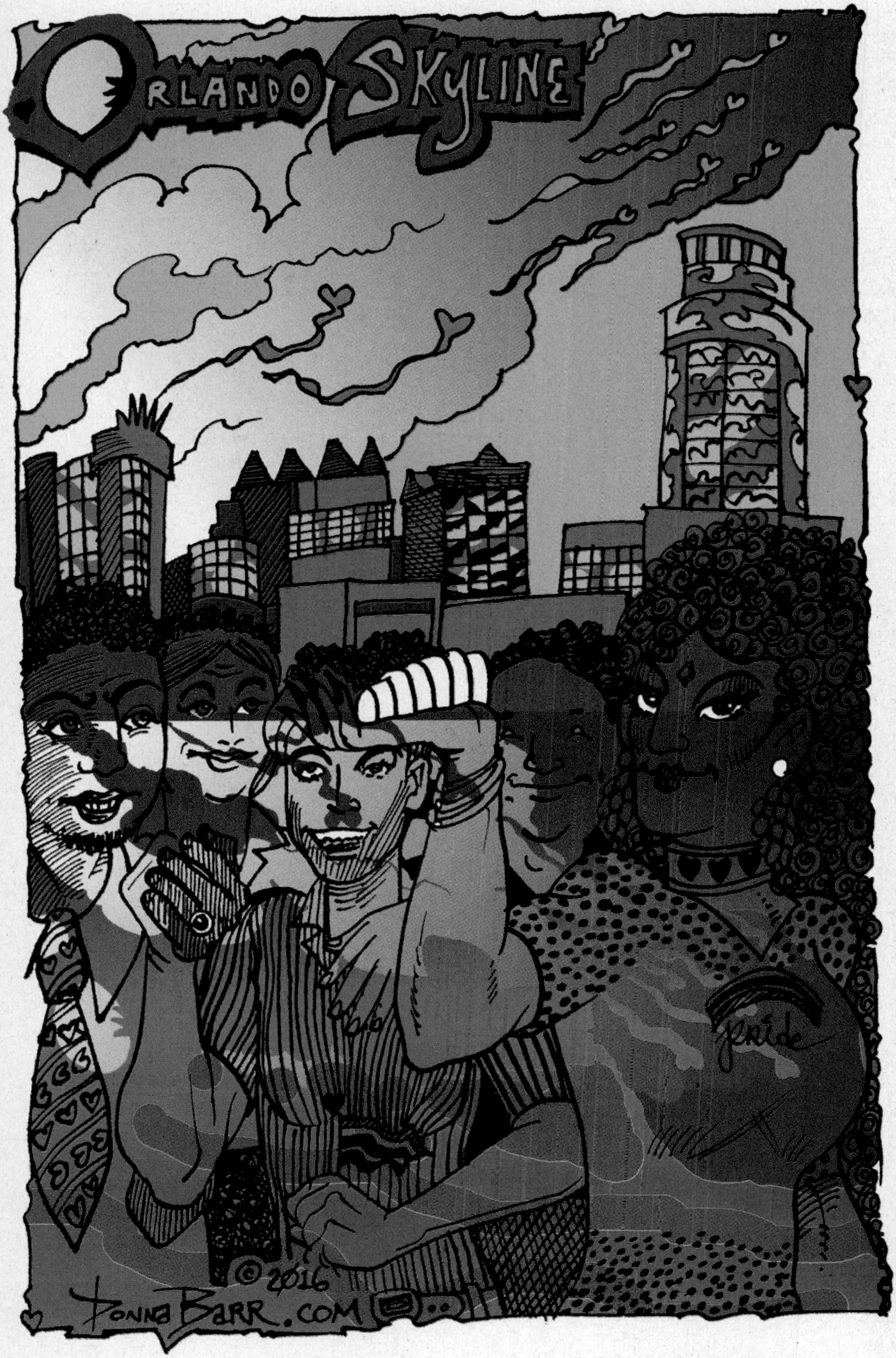
ORLANDO SKYLINE
PRIDE
© 2016
DONNABARR.COM

Art by Donna Barr

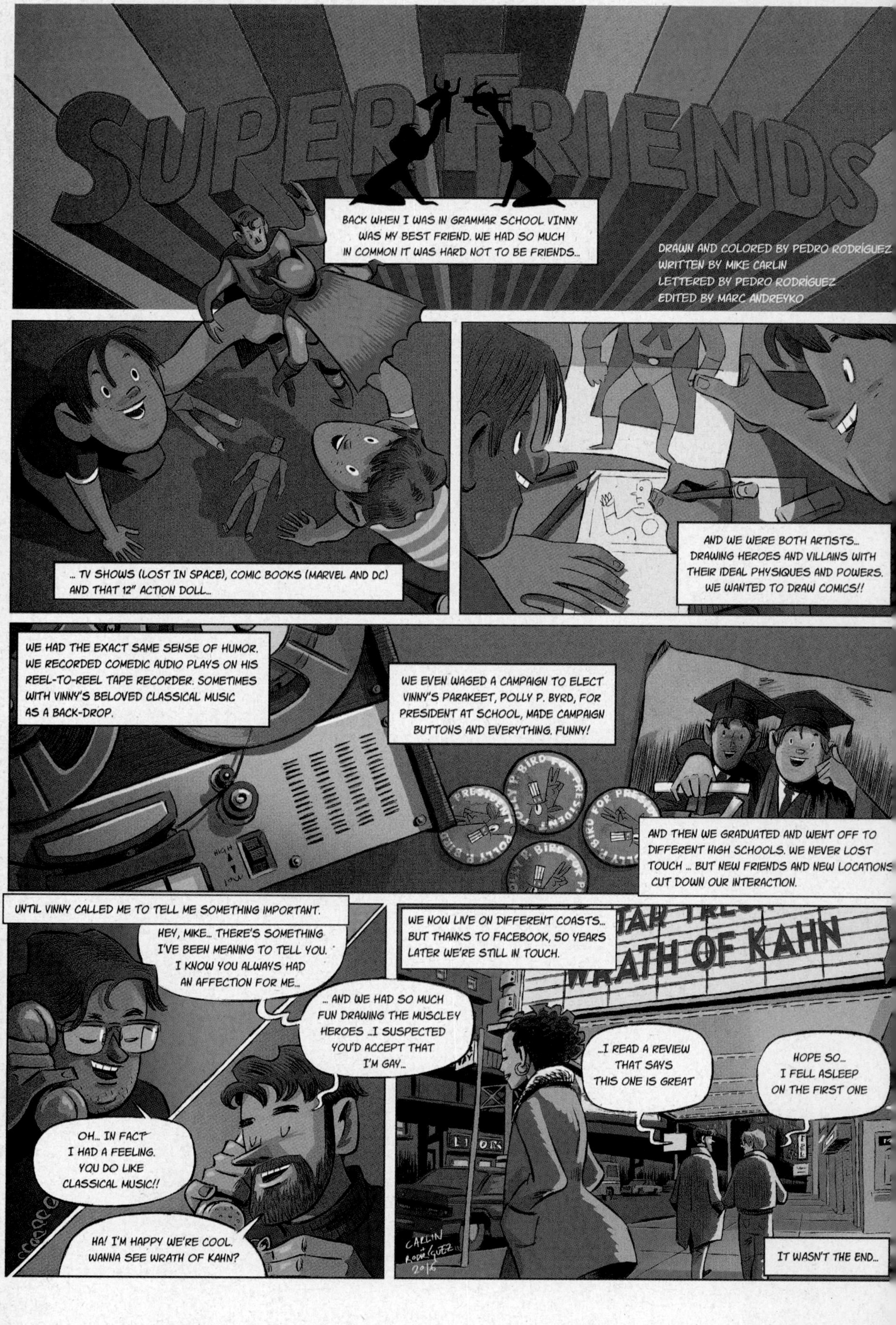
SUPER FRIENDS
BACK WHEN I WAS IN GRAMMAR SCHOOL VINNY WAS MY BEST FRIEND. WE HAD SO MUCH IN COMMON IT WAS HARD NOT TO BE FRIENDS...
DRAWN AND COLORED BY PEDRO RODRÍGUEZ
WRITTEN BY MIKE CARLIN
LETTERED BY PEDRO RODRÍGUEZ
EDITED BY MARC ANDREYKO
... TV SHOWS (LOST IN SPACE), COMIC BOOKS (MARVEL AND DC) AND THAT 12" ACTION DOLL...
AND WE WERE BOTH ARTISTS... DRAWING HEROES AND VILLAINS WITH THEIR IDEAL PHYSIQUES AND POWERS. WE WANTED TO DRAW COMICS!!
WE HAD THE EXACT SAME SENSE OF HUMOR. WE RECORDED COMEDIC AUDIO PLAYS ON HIS REEL-TO-REEL TAPE RECORDER. SOMETIMES WITH VINNY'S BELOVED CLASSICAL MUSIC AS A BACK-DROP.
WE EVEN WAGED A CAMPAIGN TO ELECT VINNY'S PARAKEET, POLLY P. BYRD, FOR PRESIDENT AT SCHOOL, MADE CAMPAIGN BUTTONS AND EVERYTHING. FUNNY!
POLLY P. BIRD FOR PRESIDENT
AND THEN WE GRADUATED AND WENT OFF TO DIFFERENT HIGH SCHOOLS. WE NEVER LOST TOUCH ... BUT NEW FRIENDS AND NEW LOCATIONS CUT DOWN OUR INTERACTION.
UNTIL VINNY CALLED ME TO TELL ME SOMETHING IMPORTANT.
HEY, MIKE... THERE'S SOMETHING I'VE BEEN MEANING TO TELL YOU. I KNOW YOU ALWAYS HAD AN AFFECTION FOR ME...
... AND WE HAD SO MUCH FUN DRAWING THE MUSCLEY HEROES ...I SUSPECTED YOU'D ACCEPT THAT I'M GAY...
OH... IN FACT I HAD A FEELING. YOU DO LIKE CLASSICAL MUSIC!!
HA! I'M HAPPY WE'RE COOL. WANNA SEE WRATH OF KAHN?
WE NOW LIVE ON DIFFERENT COASTS... BUT THANKS TO FACEBOOK, 50 YEARS LATER WE'RE STILL IN TOUCH.
WRATH OF KAHN
...I READ A REVIEW THAT SAYS THIS ONE IS GREAT
HOPE SO... I FELL ASLEEP ON THE FIRST ONE
CARLIN + RODRÍGUEZ 2016
IT WASN'T THE END...

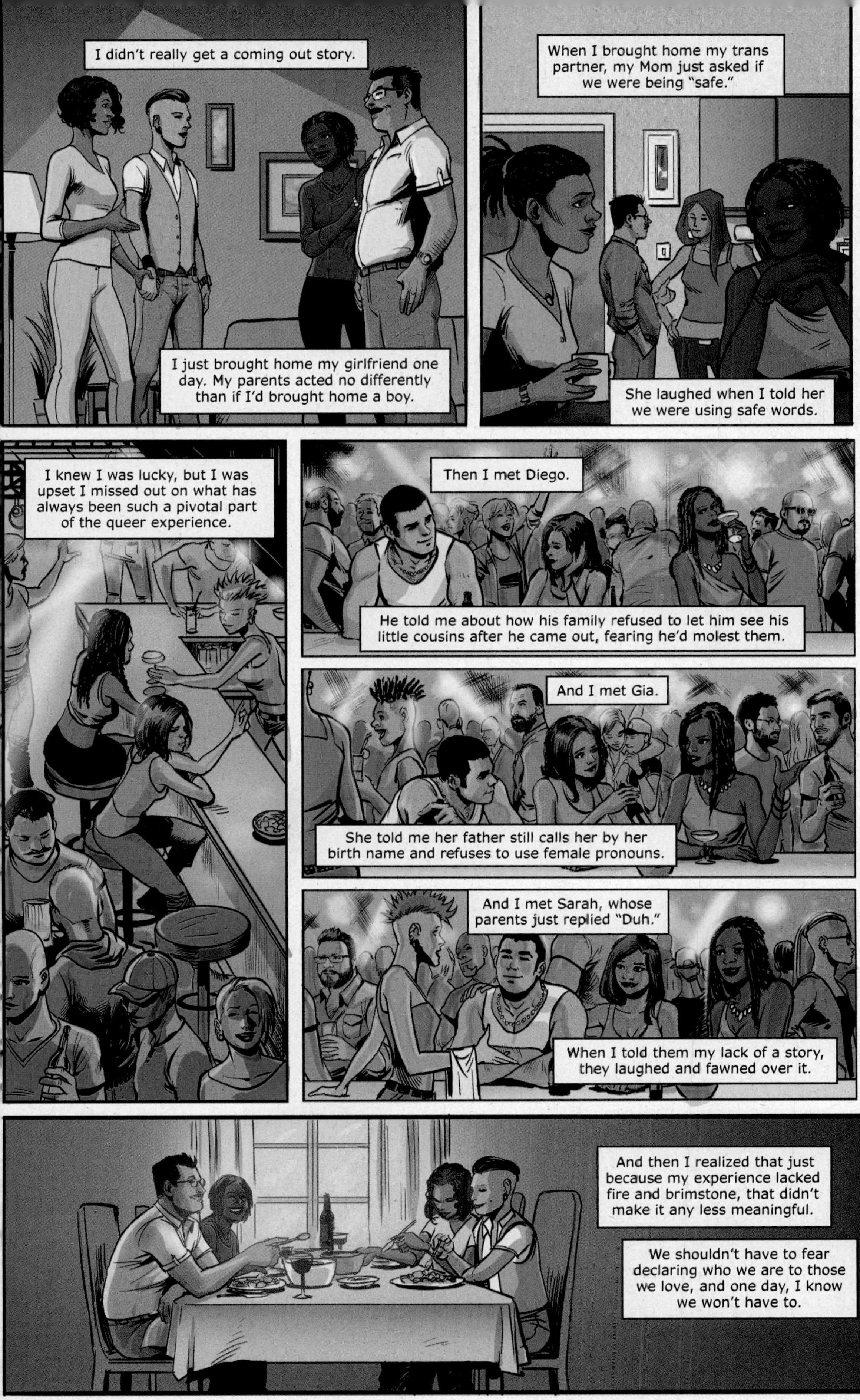
I didn't really get a coming out story.
I just brought home my girlfriend one day. My parents acted no differently than if I'd brought home a boy.
When I brought home my trans partner, my Mom just asked if we were being "safe."
She laughed when I told her we were using safe words.
I knew I was lucky, but I was upset I missed out on what has always been such a pivotal part of the queer experience.
Then I met Diego.
He told me about how his family refused to let him see his little cousins after he came out, fearing he'd molest them.
And I met Gia.
She told me her father still calls her by her birth name and refuses to use female pronouns.
And I met Sarah, whose parents just replied "Duh."
When I told them my lack of a story, they laughed and fawned over it.
And then I realized that just because my experience lacked fire and brimstone, that didn't make it any less meaningful.
We shouldn't have to fear declaring who we are to those we love, and one day, I know we won't have to.

Written by Ross Fisher & Brenna Davis • Art by Yildiray Cinar • Lettered by Deron Bennett

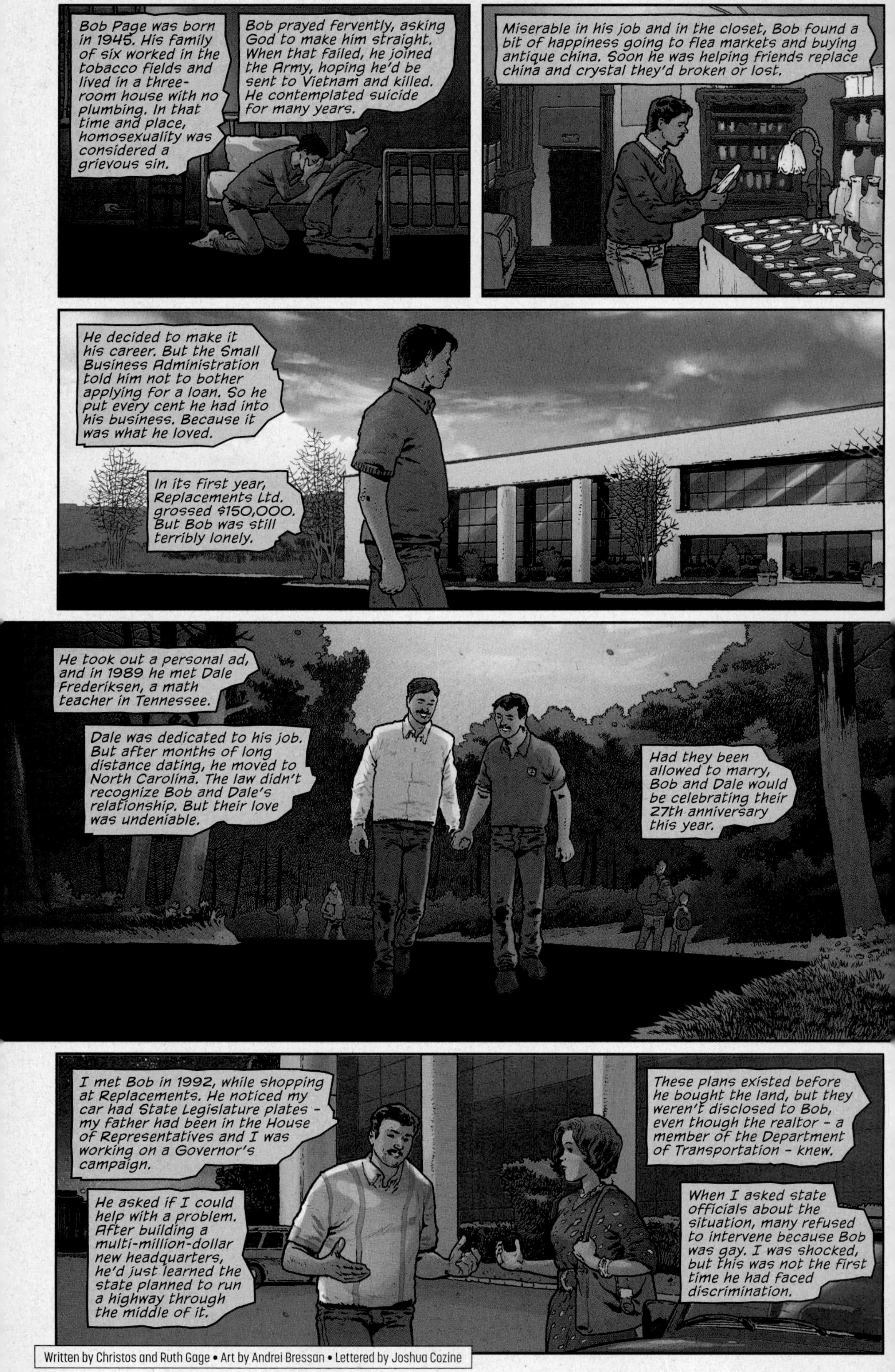
Bob Page was born in 1945. His family of six worked in the tobacco fields and lived in a three-room house with no plumbing. In that time and place, homosexuality was considered a grievous sin.
Bob prayed fervently, asking God to make him straight. When that failed, he joined the Army, hoping he'd be sent to Vietnam and killed. He contemplated suicide for many years.
Miserable in his job and in the closet, Bob found a bit of happiness going to flea markets and buying antique china. Soon he was helping friends replace china and crystal they'd broken or lost.
He decided to make it his career. But the Small Business Administration told him not to bother applying for a loan. So he put every cent he had into his business. Because it was what he loved.
In its first year, Replacements Ltd. grossed $150,000. But Bob was still terribly lonely.
He took out a personal ad, and in 1989 he met Dale Frederiksen, a math teacher in Tennessee.
Dale was dedicated to his job. But after months of long distance dating, he moved to North Carolina. The law didn't recognize Bob and Dale's relationship. But their love was undeniable.
Had they been allowed to marry, Bob and Dale would be celebrating their 27th anniversary this year.
I met Bob in 1992, while shopping at Replacements. He noticed my car had State Legislature plates - my father had been in the House of Representatives and I was working on a Governor's campaign.
He asked if I could help with a problem. After building a multi-million-dollar new headquarters, he'd just learned the state planned to run a highway through the middle of it.
These plans existed before he bought the land, but they weren't disclosed to Bob, even though the realtor - a member of the Department of Transportation - knew.
When I asked state officials about the situation, many refused to intervene because Bob was gay. I was shocked, but this was not the first time he had faced discrimination.

Written by Christos and Ruth Gage • Art by Andrei Bressan • Lettered by Joshua Cozine

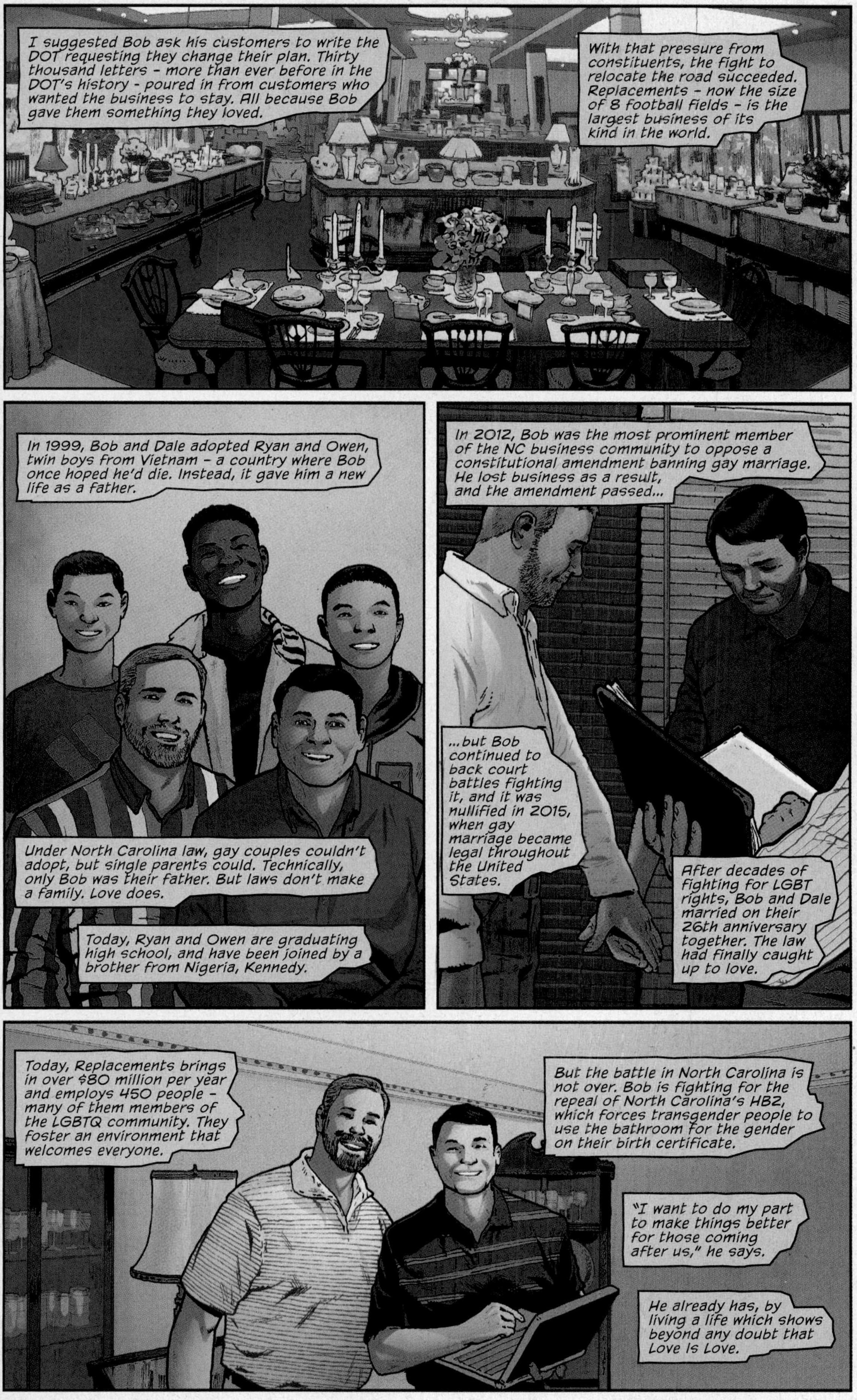
I suggested Bob ask his customers to write the DOT requesting they change their plan. Thirty thousand letters - more than ever before in the DOT's history - poured in from customers who wanted the business to stay. All because Bob gave them something they loved.
With that pressure from constituents, the fight to relocate the road succeeded. Replacements - now the size of 8 football fields - is the largest business of its kind in the world.
In 1999, Bob and Dale adopted Ryan and Owen, twin boys from Vietnam - a country where Bob once hoped he'd die. Instead, it gave him a new life as a father.
Under North Carolina law, gay couples couldn't adopt, but single parents could. Technically, only Bob was their father. But laws don't make a family. Love does.
Today, Ryan and Owen are graduating high school, and have been joined by a brother from Nigeria, Kennedy.
In 2012, Bob was the most prominent member of the NC business community to oppose a constitutional amendment banning gay marriage. He lost business as a result, and the amendment passed...
...but Bob continued to back court battles fighting it, and it was nullified in 2015, when gay marriage became legal throughout the United States.
After decades of fighting for LGBT rights, Bob and Dale married on their 26th anniversary together. The law had finally caught up to love.
Today, Replacements brings in over $80 million per year and employs 450 people - many of them members of the LGBTQ community. They foster an environment that welcomes everyone.
But the battle in North Carolina is not over. Bob is fighting for the repeal of North Carolina's HB2, which forces transgender people to use the bathroom for the gender on their birth certificate.
"I want to do my part to make things better for those coming after us," he says.
He already has, by living a life which shows beyond any doubt that Love Is Love.

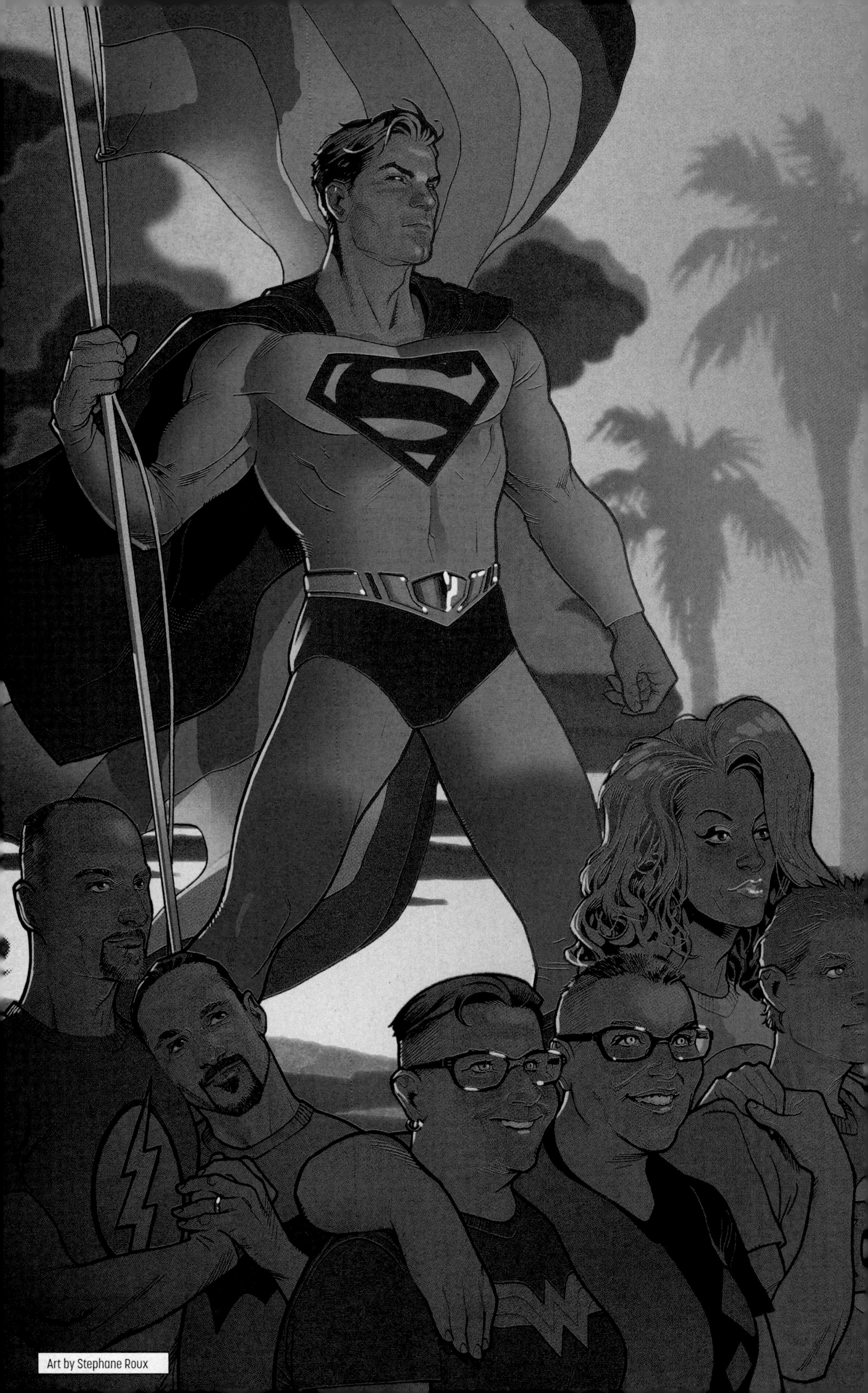

Art by Stephane Roux

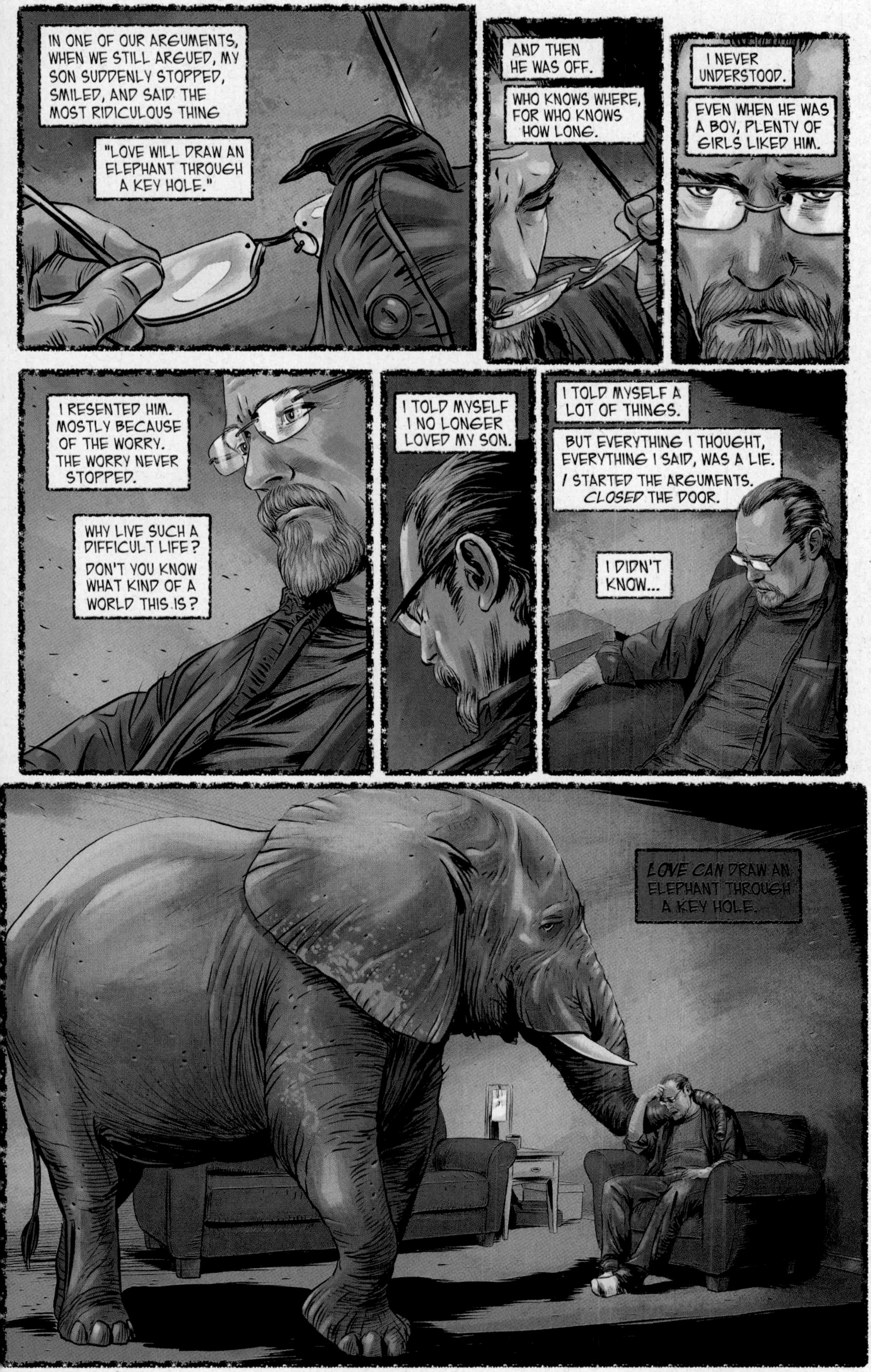
IN ONE OF OUR ARGUMENTS, WHEN WE STILL ARGUED, MY SON SUDDENLY STOPPED, SMILED, AND SAID THE MOST RIDICULOUS THING
"LOVE WILL DRAW AN ELEPHANT THROUGH A KEY HOLE."
AND THEN HE WAS OFF.
WHO KNOWS WHERE, FOR WHO KNOWS HOW LONG.
I NEVER UNDERSTOOD.
EVEN WHEN HE WAS A BOY, PLENTY OF GIRLS LIKED HIM.
I RESENTED HIM. MOSTLY BECAUSE OF THE WORRY. THE WORRY NEVER STOPPED.
WHY LIVE SUCH A DIFFICULT LIFE?
DON'T YOU KNOW WHAT KIND OF A WORLD THIS IS?
I TOLD MYSELF I NO LONGER LOVED MY SON.
I TOLD MYSELF A LOT OF THINGS.
BUT EVERYTHING I THOUGHT, EVERYTHING I SAID, WAS A LIE.
I STARTED THE ARGUMENTS. *CLOSED* THE DOOR.
I DIDN'T KNOW...
*LOVE CAN* DRAW AN ELEPHANT THROUGH A KEY HOLE.

Written, illustrated, and lettered by Patrick Zircher • Colored by Brennan Wagner

MEN KISSING.

MEN LOVING EACH OTHER.

I WAS TAUGHT FROM BIRTH TO FEAR THIS.

QUEERNESS IN GENERAL, BUT THIS ESPECIALLY.

MY GOVERNMENT MADE LAWS AGAINST "THE PROMOTION OF HOMOSEXUALITY," JUST TO MAKE SURE.

THE LESSONS WERE CONSTANT, INSIDIOUS, OSMOTIC. TAUGHT IN SCHOOL, CHURCH, HOME, PLAYGROUND, ON TV.

THE BOXER EMILE GRIFFITH, SPEAKING FROM EXPERIENCE:

"I KILL A MAN AND MOST PEOPLE UNDERSTAND AND FORGIVE ME. HOWEVER, I LOVE A MAN AND TO SO MANY PEOPLE THIS IS AN UNFORGIVABLE SIN."

THIS REMAINS THE DOMINANT CULTURAL PROGRAMMING.

THAT IT'S MORE ACCEPTABLE TO HURT, TO HATE, TO FEAR-- OTHERS, OURSELVES--THAN IT IS TO LOVE.

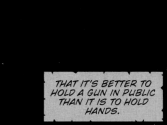

THAT IT'S BETTER TO HOLD A GUN IN PUBLIC THAN IT IS TO HOLD HANDS.

I WAS LUCKY. I WAS EXPOSED TO OTHER LESSONS, OTHER MESSAGES, AND THOSE WERE WHAT STUCK.

WHEN I MOST NEEDED TO SEE IT, LOVE WAS THERE. IN FICTION, IN MUSIC, IN THE CULTURE.

LOVE WAS VISIBLE. VISIBLE AND BEAUTIFUL.

MEN LOVING EACH OTHER.

MEN KISSING.

AL EWING WORDS
LEE GARBETT ART
ANTONIO FABELA COLORS
TAYLOR ESPOSITO LETTERS

End

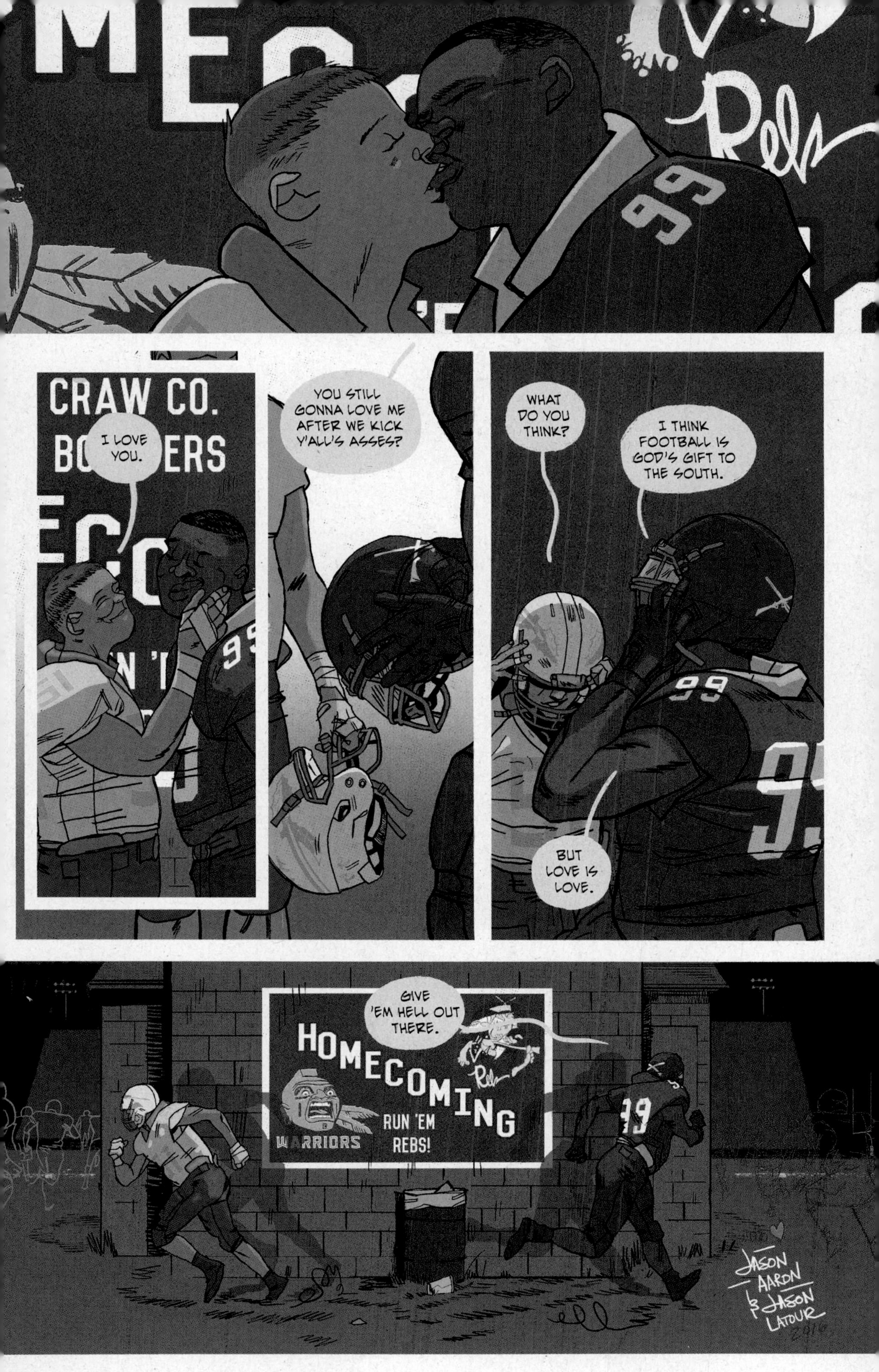
CRAW CO. BO ERS
I LOVE YOU.
YOU STILL GONNA LOVE ME AFTER WE KICK Y'ALL'S ASSES?
WHAT DO YOU THINK?
I THINK FOOTBALL IS GOD'S GIFT TO THE SOUTH.
BUT LOVE IS LOVE.
GIVE 'EM HELL OUT THERE.
HOMECOMING
WARRIORS
RUN 'EM REBS!
JASON AARON & JASON LATOUR

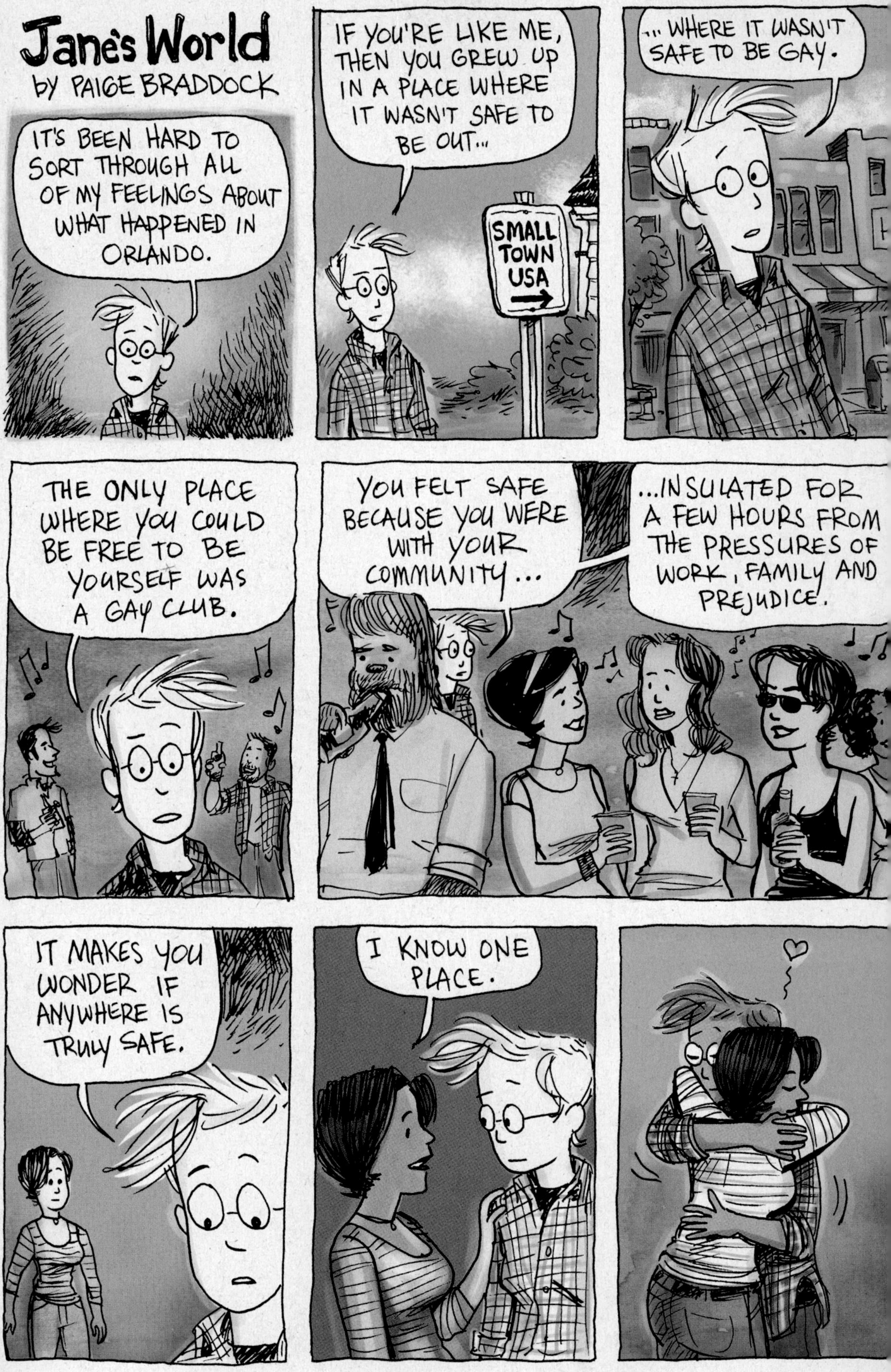
Jane's World
by PAIGE BRADDOCK
IT'S BEEN HARD TO SORT THROUGH ALL OF MY FEELINGS ABOUT WHAT HAPPENED IN ORLANDO.
IF YOU'RE LIKE ME, THEN YOU GREW UP IN A PLACE WHERE IT WASN'T SAFE TO BE OUT...
SMALL TOWN USA
...WHERE IT WASN'T SAFE TO BE GAY.
THE ONLY PLACE WHERE YOU COULD BE FREE TO BE YOURSELF WAS A GAY CLUB.
YOU FELT SAFE BECAUSE YOU WERE WITH YOUR COMMUNITY...
...INSULATED FOR A FEW HOURS FROM THE PRESSURES OF WORK, FAMILY AND PREJUDICE.
IT MAKES YOU WONDER IF ANYWHERE IS TRULY SAFE.
I KNOW ONE PLACE.

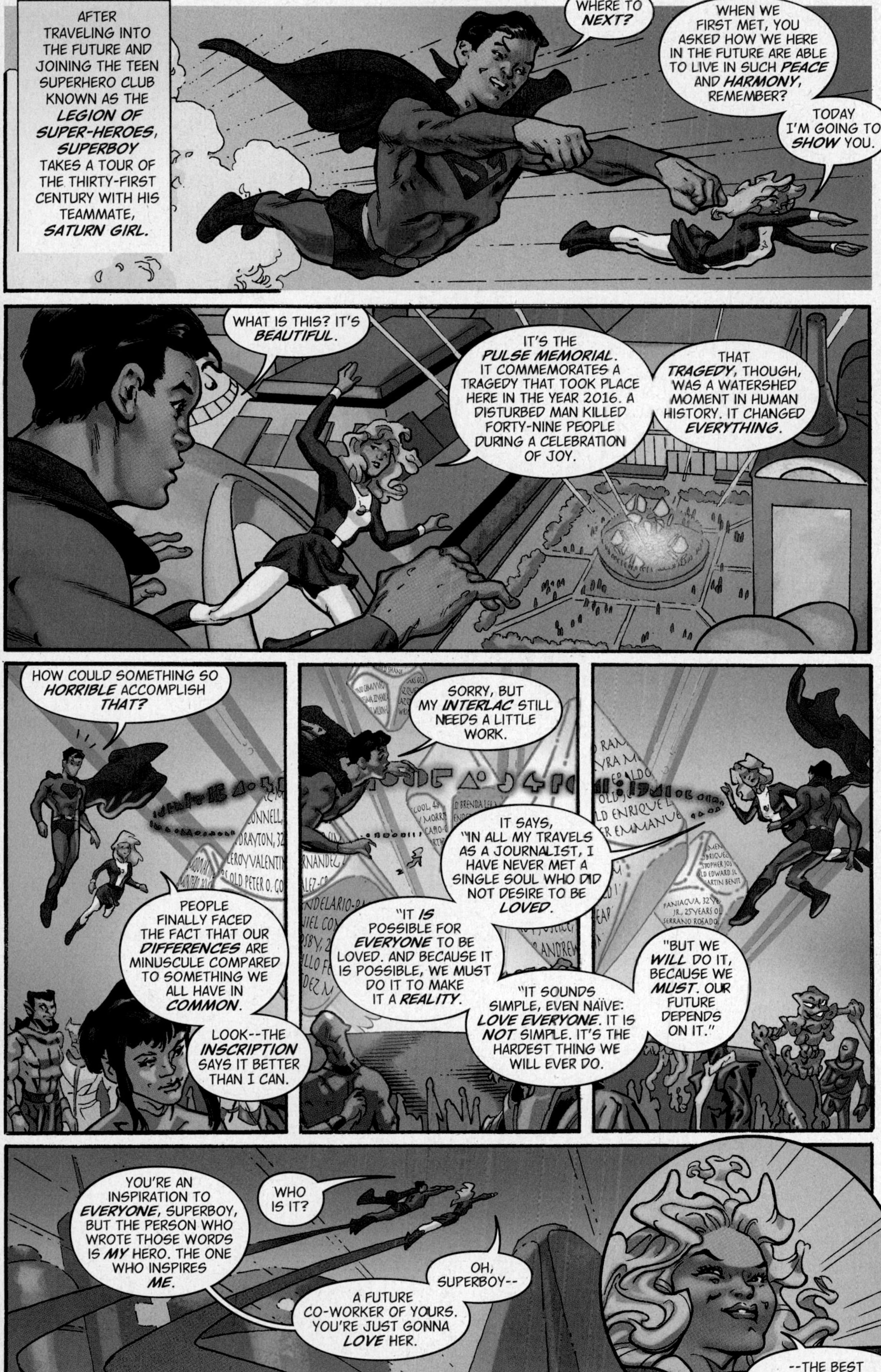
AFTER TRAVELING INTO THE FUTURE AND JOINING THE TEEN SUPERHERO CLUB KNOWN AS THE LEGION OF SUPER-HEROES, SUPERBOY TAKES A TOUR OF THE THIRTY-FIRST CENTURY WITH HIS TEAMMATE, SATURN GIRL.
WHERE TO NEXT?
WHEN WE FIRST MET, YOU ASKED HOW WE HERE IN THE FUTURE ARE ABLE TO LIVE IN SUCH PEACE AND HARMONY, REMEMBER?
TODAY I'M GOING TO SHOW YOU.
WHAT IS THIS? IT'S BEAUTIFUL.
IT'S THE PULSE MEMORIAL. IT COMMEMORATES A TRAGEDY THAT TOOK PLACE HERE IN THE YEAR 2016. A DISTURBED MAN KILLED FORTY-NINE PEOPLE DURING A CELEBRATION OF JOY.
THAT TRAGEDY, THOUGH, WAS A WATERSHED MOMENT IN HUMAN HISTORY. IT CHANGED EVERYTHING.
HOW COULD SOMETHING SO HORRIBLE ACCOMPLISH THAT?
PEOPLE FINALLY FACED THE FACT THAT OUR DIFFERENCES ARE MINUSCULE COMPARED TO SOMETHING WE ALL HAVE IN COMMON.
LOOK--THE INSCRIPTION SAYS IT BETTER THAN I CAN.
SORRY, BUT MY INTERLAC STILL NEEDS A LITTLE WORK.
IT SAYS, "IN ALL MY TRAVELS AS A JOURNALIST, I HAVE NEVER MET A SINGLE SOUL WHO DID NOT DESIRE TO BE LOVED.
"IT IS POSSIBLE FOR EVERYONE TO BE LOVED. AND BECAUSE IT IS POSSIBLE, WE MUST DO IT TO MAKE IT A REALITY.
"IT SOUNDS SIMPLE, EVEN NAÏVE: LOVE EVERYONE. IT IS NOT SIMPLE. IT'S THE HARDEST THING WE WILL EVER DO.
"BUT WE WILL DO IT, BECAUSE WE MUST. OUR FUTURE DEPENDS ON IT."
YOU'RE AN INSPIRATION TO EVERYONE, SUPERBOY, BUT THE PERSON WHO WROTE THOSE WORDS IS MY HERO. THE ONE WHO INSPIRES ME.
WHO IS IT?
OH, SUPERBOY--
A FUTURE CO-WORKER OF YOURS. YOU'RE JUST GONNA LOVE HER.
--THE BEST PART OF YOUR HISTORY IS RIGHT AROUND THE CORNER.

Written by Lilah Sturges • Illustrated by John Lucas • Colored by Michael Wiggam • Lettered by Sal Cipriano

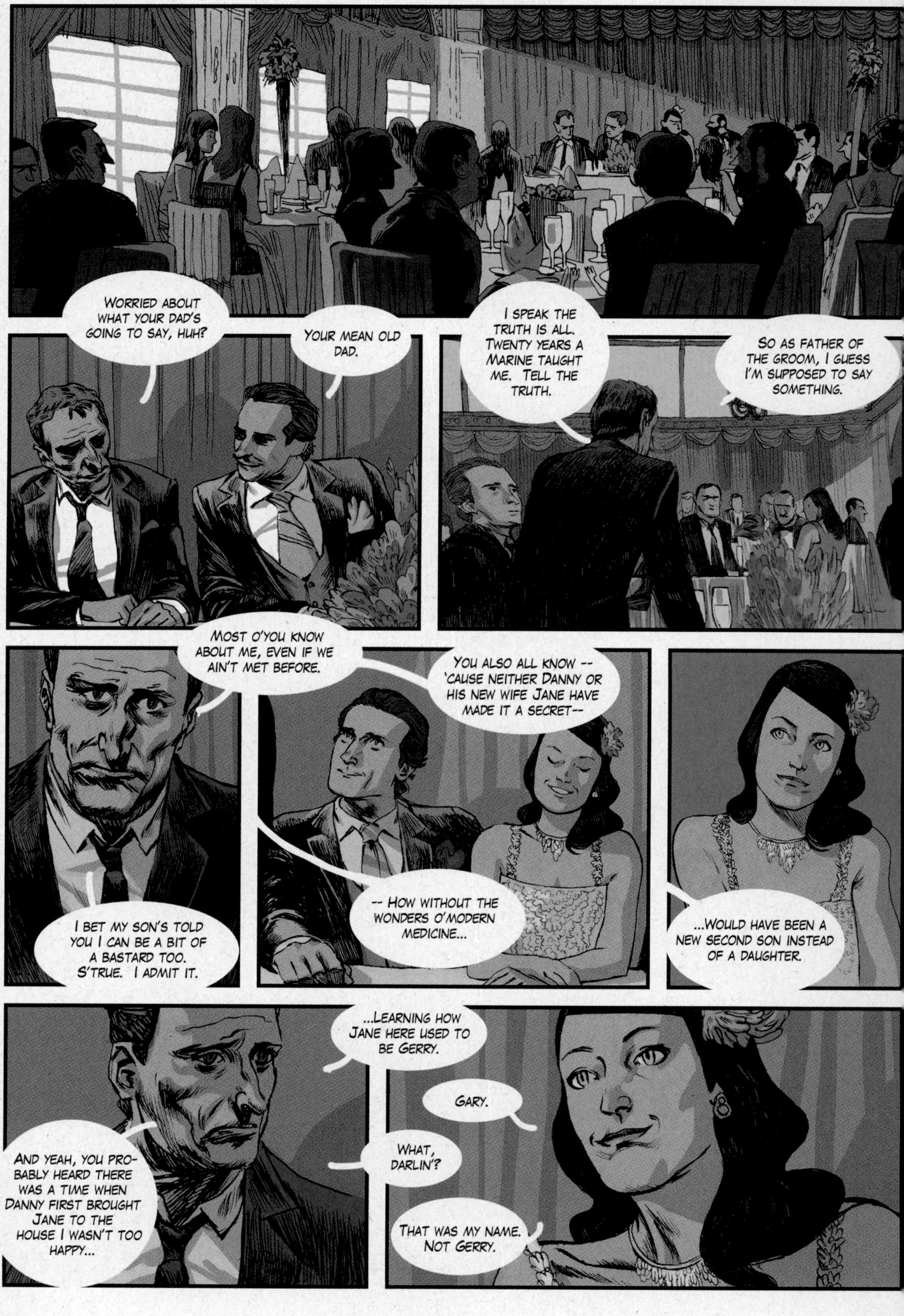

WORRIED ABOUT WHAT YOUR DAD'S GOING TO SAY, HUH?
YOUR MEAN OLD DAD.
I SPEAK THE TRUTH IS ALL. TWENTY YEARS A MARINE TAUGHT ME. TELL THE TRUTH.
SO AS FATHER OF THE GROOM, I GUESS I'M SUPPOSED TO SAY SOMETHING.
MOST O'YOU KNOW ABOUT ME, EVEN IF WE AIN'T MET BEFORE.
I BET MY SON'S TOLD YOU I CAN BE A BIT OF A BASTARD TOO. S'TRUE. I ADMIT IT.
YOU ALSO ALL KNOW -- 'CAUSE NEITHER DANNY OR HIS NEW WIFE JANE HAVE MADE IT A SECRET--
-- HOW WITHOUT THE WONDERS O'MODERN MEDICINE...
...WOULD HAVE BEEN A NEW SECOND SON INSTEAD OF A DAUGHTER.
AND YEAH, YOU PROBABLY HEARD THERE WAS A TIME WHEN DANNY FIRST BROUGHT JANE TO THE HOUSE I WASN'T TOO HAPPY...
...LEARNING HOW JANE HERE USED TO BE GERRY.
GARY.
WHAT, DARLIN'?
THAT WAS MY NAME. NOT GERRY.

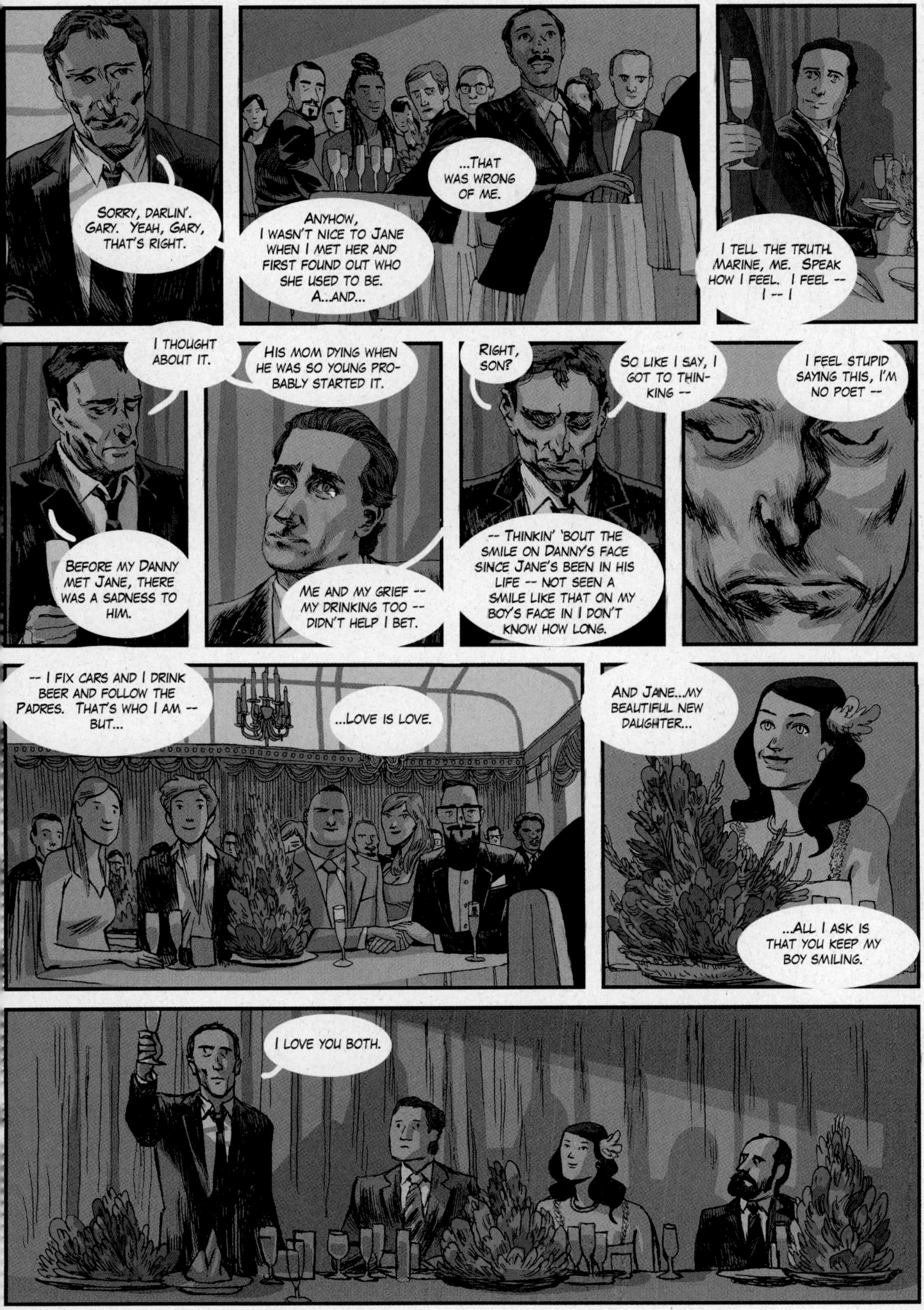
SORRY, DARLIN'. GARY. YEAH, GARY, THAT'S RIGHT.
ANYHOW, I WASN'T NICE TO JANE WHEN I MET HER AND FIRST FOUND OUT WHO SHE USED TO BE. A...AND...
...THAT WAS WRONG OF ME.
I TELL THE TRUTH. MARINE, ME. SPEAK HOW I FEEL. I FEEL -- I -- I
I THOUGHT ABOUT IT.
BEFORE MY DANNY MET JANE, THERE WAS A SADNESS TO HIM.
HIS MOM DYING WHEN HE WAS SO YOUNG PROBABLY STARTED IT.
ME AND MY GRIEF -- MY DRINKING TOO -- DIDN'T HELP I BET.
RIGHT, SON?
SO LIKE I SAY, I GOT TO THINKING --
-- THINKIN' 'BOUT THE SMILE ON DANNY'S FACE SINCE JANE'S BEEN IN HIS LIFE -- NOT SEEN A SMILE LIKE THAT ON MY BOY'S FACE IN I DON'T KNOW HOW LONG.
I FEEL STUPID SAYING THIS, I'M NO POET --
-- I FIX CARS AND I DRINK BEER AND FOLLOW THE PADRES. THAT'S WHO I AM -- BUT...
...LOVE IS LOVE.
AND JANE...MY BEAUTIFUL NEW DAUGHTER...
...ALL I ASK IS THAT YOU KEEP MY BOY SMILING.
I LOVE YOU BOTH.

Written by James Robinson • Art and lettering by Sagar Fornies

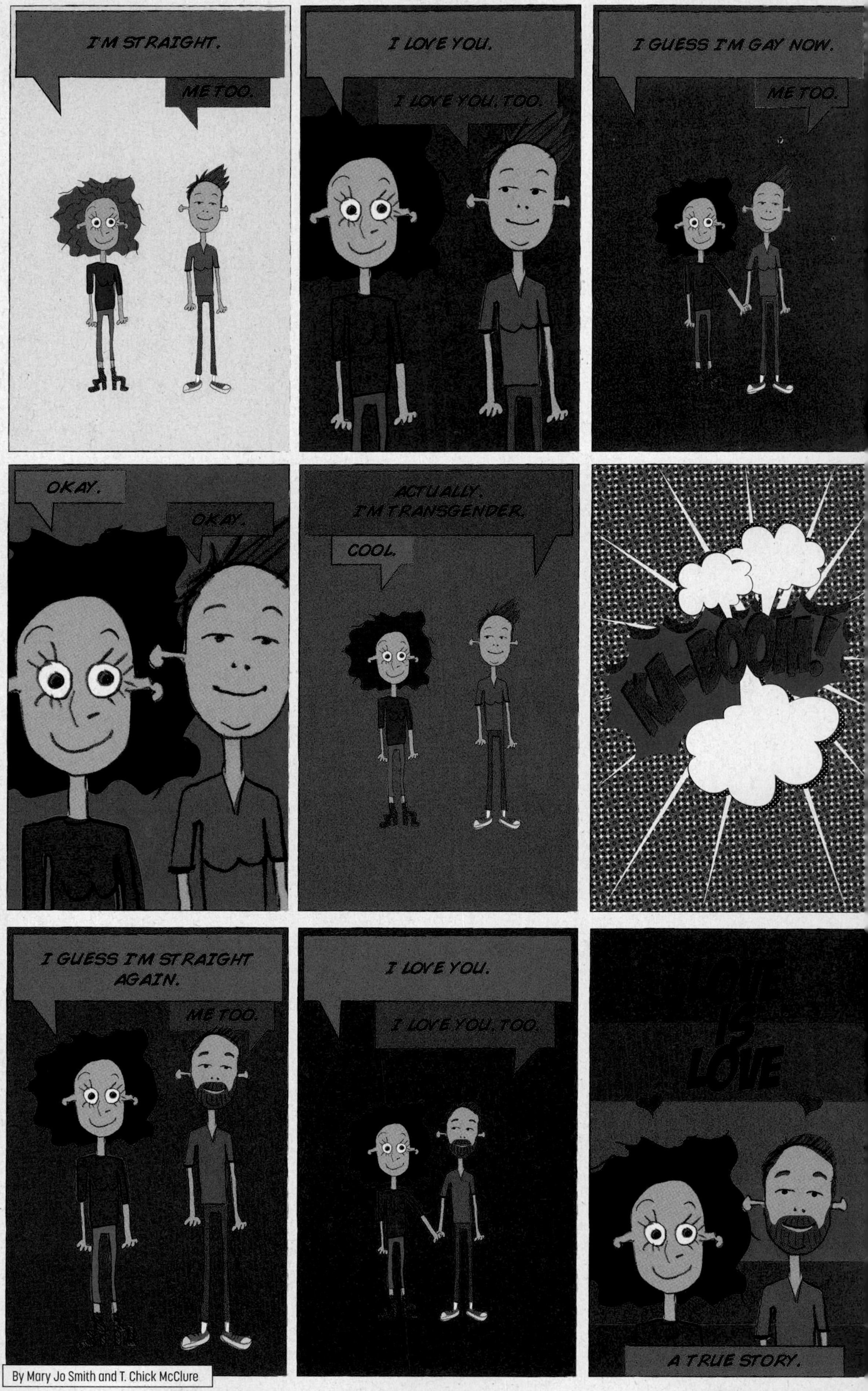
I'M STRAIGHT.
ME TOO.
I LOVE YOU.
I LOVE YOU, TOO.
I GUESS I'M GAY NOW.
ME TOO.
OKAY.
OKAY.
ACTUALLY, I'M TRANSGENDER.
COOL.
KA-BOOM!
I GUESS I'M STRAIGHT AGAIN.
ME TOO.
I LOVE YOU.
I LOVE YOU, TOO.
LOVE IS LOVE
A TRUE STORY.

By Mary Jo Smith and T. Chick McClure

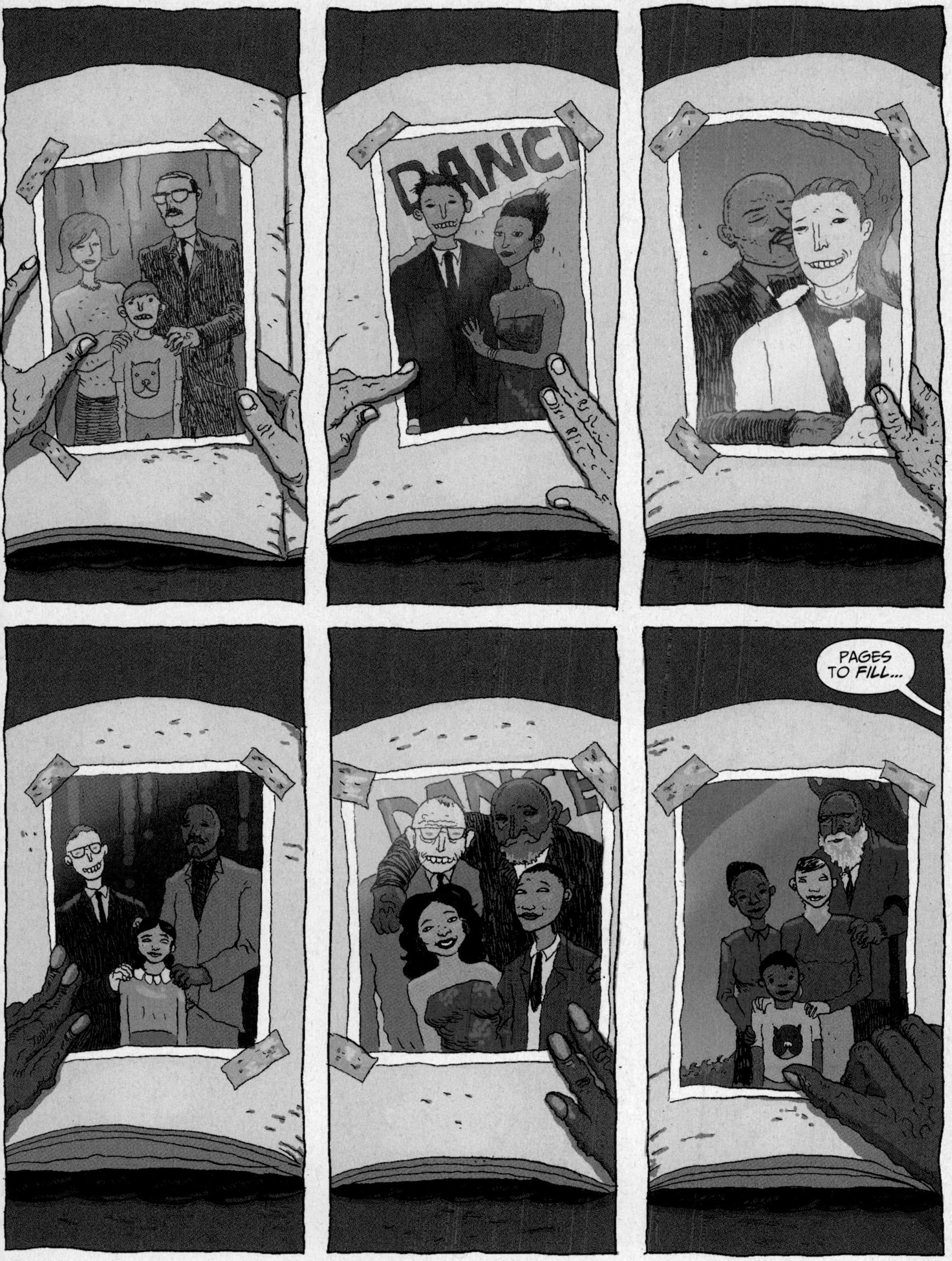
DANC
PAGES TO *FILL*...

# SCRAPBOOK

FROM STEVE ORLANDO, IAIN LAURIE, HARRY SAXON, COREY BREEN

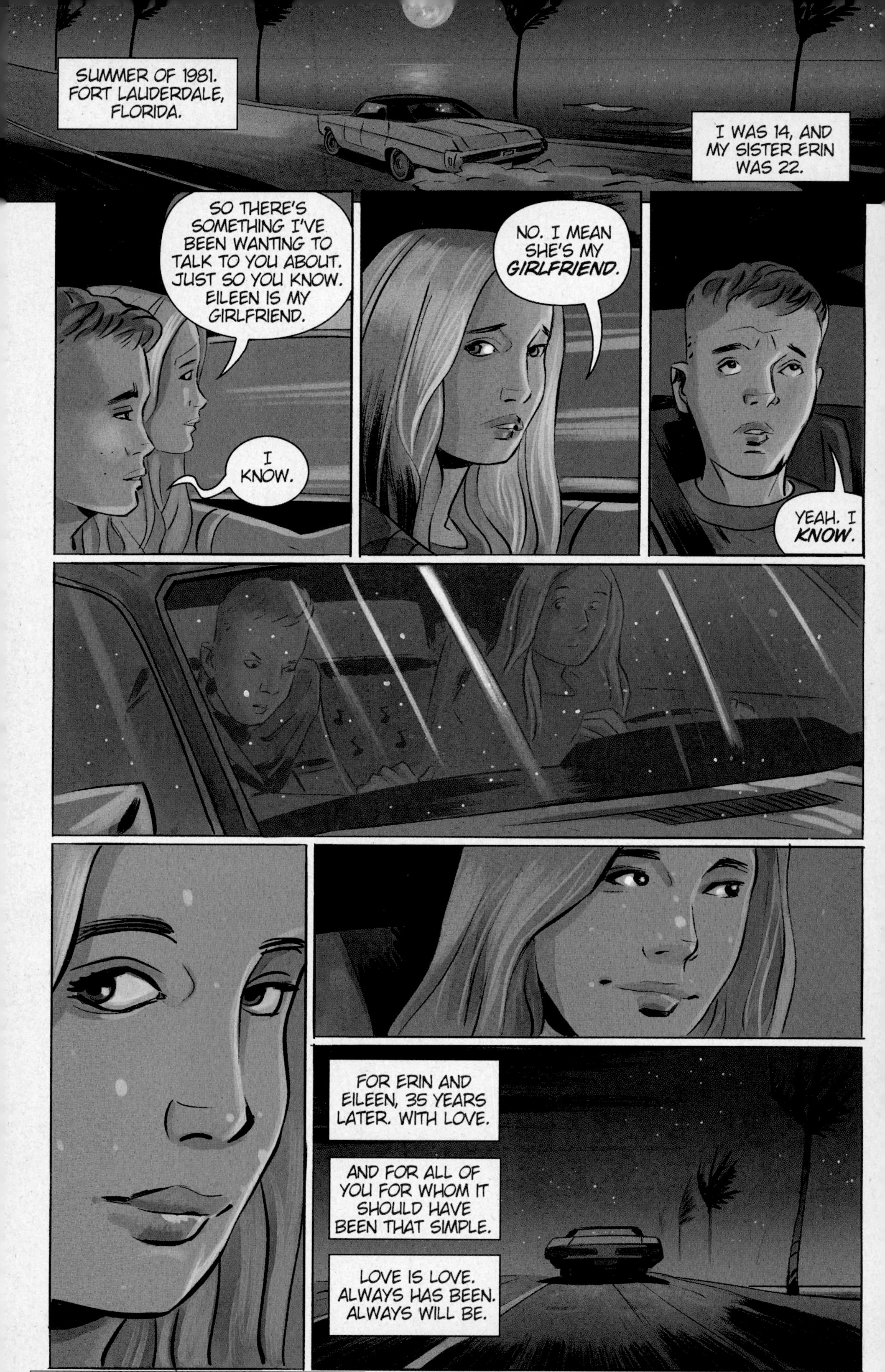
SUMMER OF 1981. FORT LAUDERDALE, FLORIDA.
I WAS 14, AND MY SISTER ERIN WAS 22.
SO THERE'S SOMETHING I'VE BEEN WANTING TO TALK TO YOU ABOUT. JUST SO YOU KNOW. EILEEN IS MY GIRLFRIEND.
I KNOW.
NO. I MEAN SHE'S MY ***GIRLFRIEND***.
YEAH. I ***KNOW***.
FOR ERIN AND EILEEN, 35 YEARS LATER. WITH LOVE.
AND FOR ALL OF YOU FOR WHOM IT SHOULD HAVE BEEN THAT SIMPLE.
LOVE IS LOVE. ALWAYS HAS BEEN. ALWAYS WILL BE.

Written by Christopher Golden • Art and lettering by Peter Bergting

# WE AREN'T BORN WITH HATE IN OUR HEARTS.

# WE TEACH IT.

Written by Dan Jurgens • Illustrated by Alé Garza • Colored by Gabriel Cassata • Lettered by Taylor Esposito

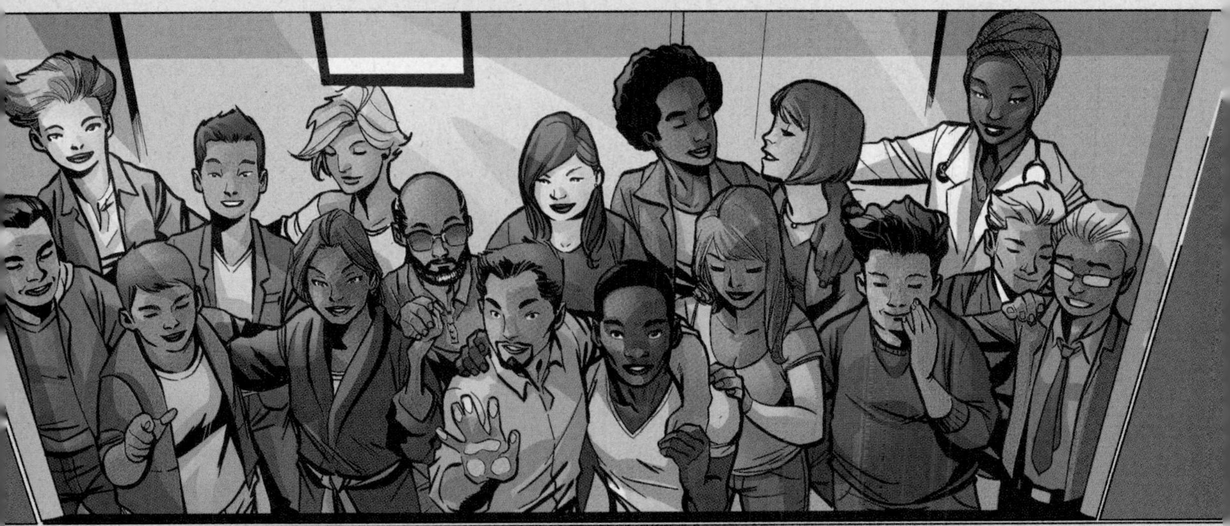

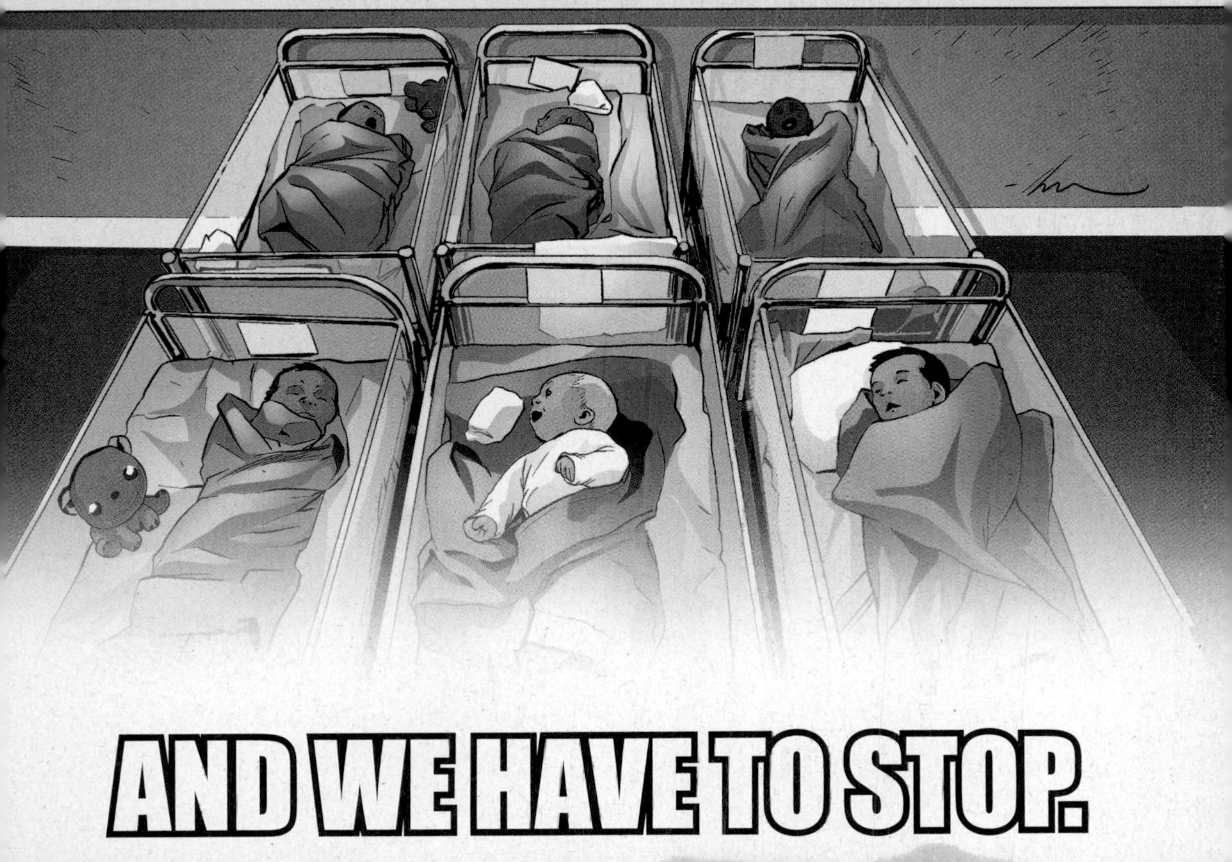
AND WE HAVE TO STOP.

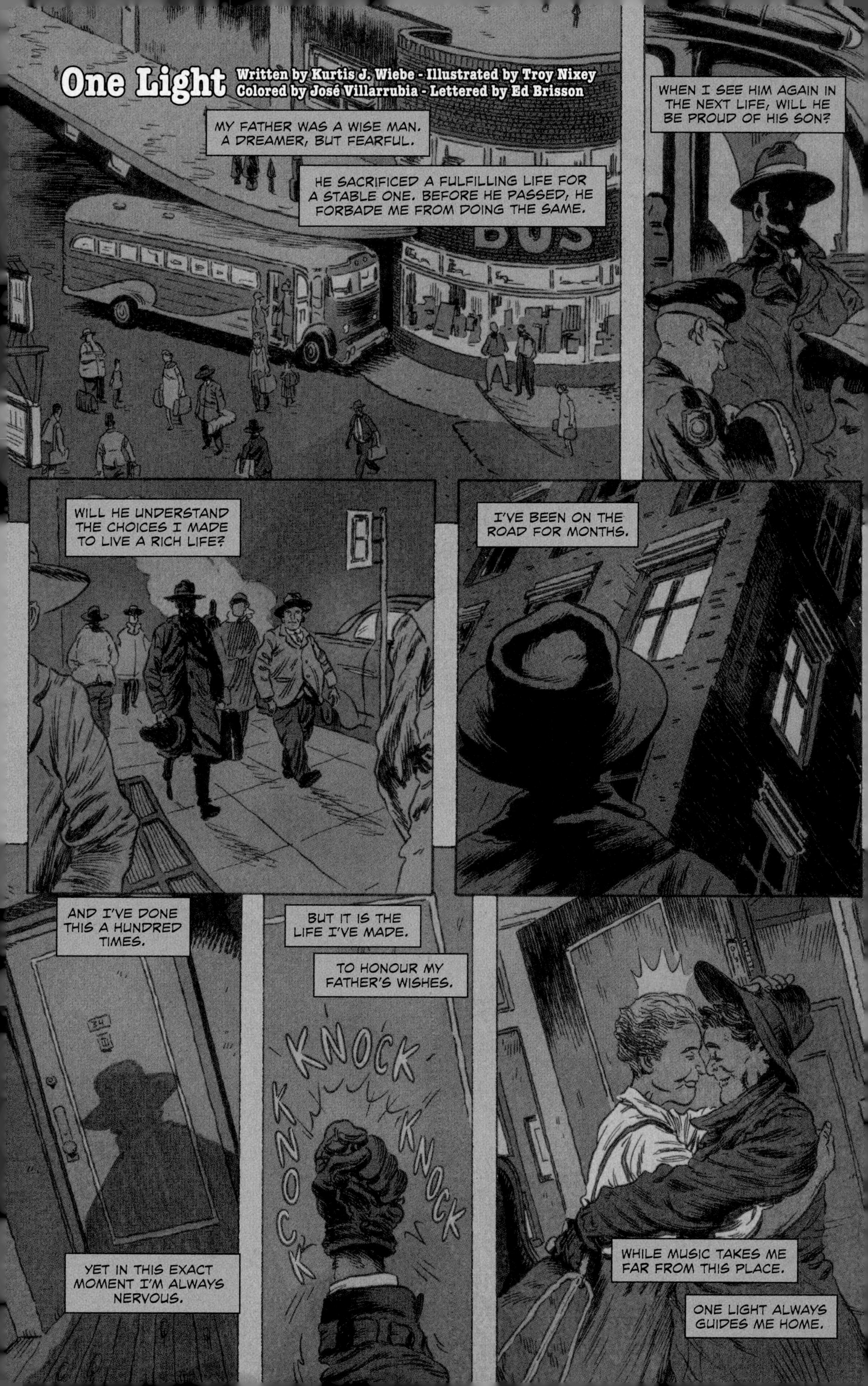
One Light
Written by Kurtis J. Wiebe - Illustrated by Troy Nixey
Colored by José Villarrubia - Lettered by Ed Brisson
MY FATHER WAS A WISE MAN. A DREAMER, BUT FEARFUL.
HE SACRIFICED A FULFILLING LIFE FOR A STABLE ONE. BEFORE HE PASSED, HE FORBADE ME FROM DOING THE SAME.
BUS
WHEN I SEE HIM AGAIN IN THE NEXT LIFE, WILL HE BE PROUD OF HIS SON?
WILL HE UNDERSTAND THE CHOICES I MADE TO LIVE A RICH LIFE?
I'VE BEEN ON THE ROAD FOR MONTHS.
AND I'VE DONE THIS A HUNDRED TIMES.
YET IN THIS EXACT MOMENT I'M ALWAYS NERVOUS.
BUT IT IS THE LIFE I'VE MADE.
TO HONOUR MY FATHER'S WISHES.
KNOCK
KNOCK
KNOCK
WHILE MUSIC TAKES ME FAR FROM THIS PLACE.
ONE LIGHT ALWAYS GUIDES ME HOME.

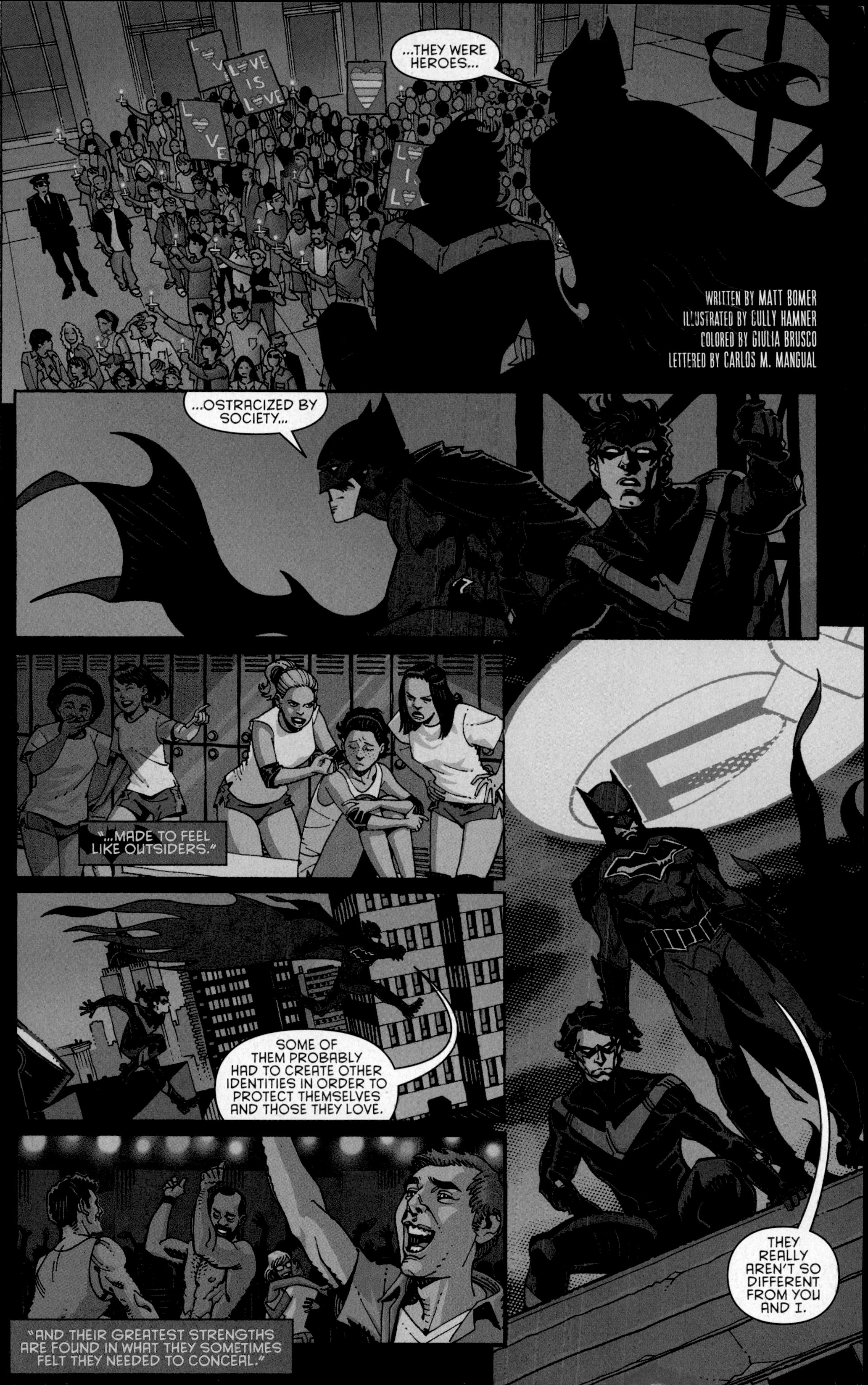
LOVE IS LOVE
LOVE
...THEY WERE HEROES...
WRITTEN BY MATT BOMER
ILLUSTRATED BY CULLY HAMNER
COLORED BY GIULIA BRUSCO
LETTERED BY CARLOS M. MANGUAL
...OSTRACIZED BY SOCIETY...
"...MADE TO FEEL LIKE OUTSIDERS."
SOME OF THEM PROBABLY HAD TO CREATE OTHER IDENTITIES IN ORDER TO PROTECT THEMSELVES AND THOSE THEY LOVE.
"AND THEIR GREATEST STRENGTHS ARE FOUND IN WHAT THEY SOMETIMES FELT THEY NEEDED TO CONCEAL."
THEY REALLY AREN'T SO DIFFERENT FROM YOU AND I.

Born here of parents born here from parents the same, and their parents the same.

I AM LARGE. I CONTAIN MULTITUDES.

SONG OF MYSELF (REMIX)

| ALEJANDRO ARBONA | WILFREDO TORRES | JOSÉ VILLARRUBIA | TODD KLEIN | JAMIE S. RICH |
|---|---|---|---|---|
| writer | artist | colorist | letterer | editor |

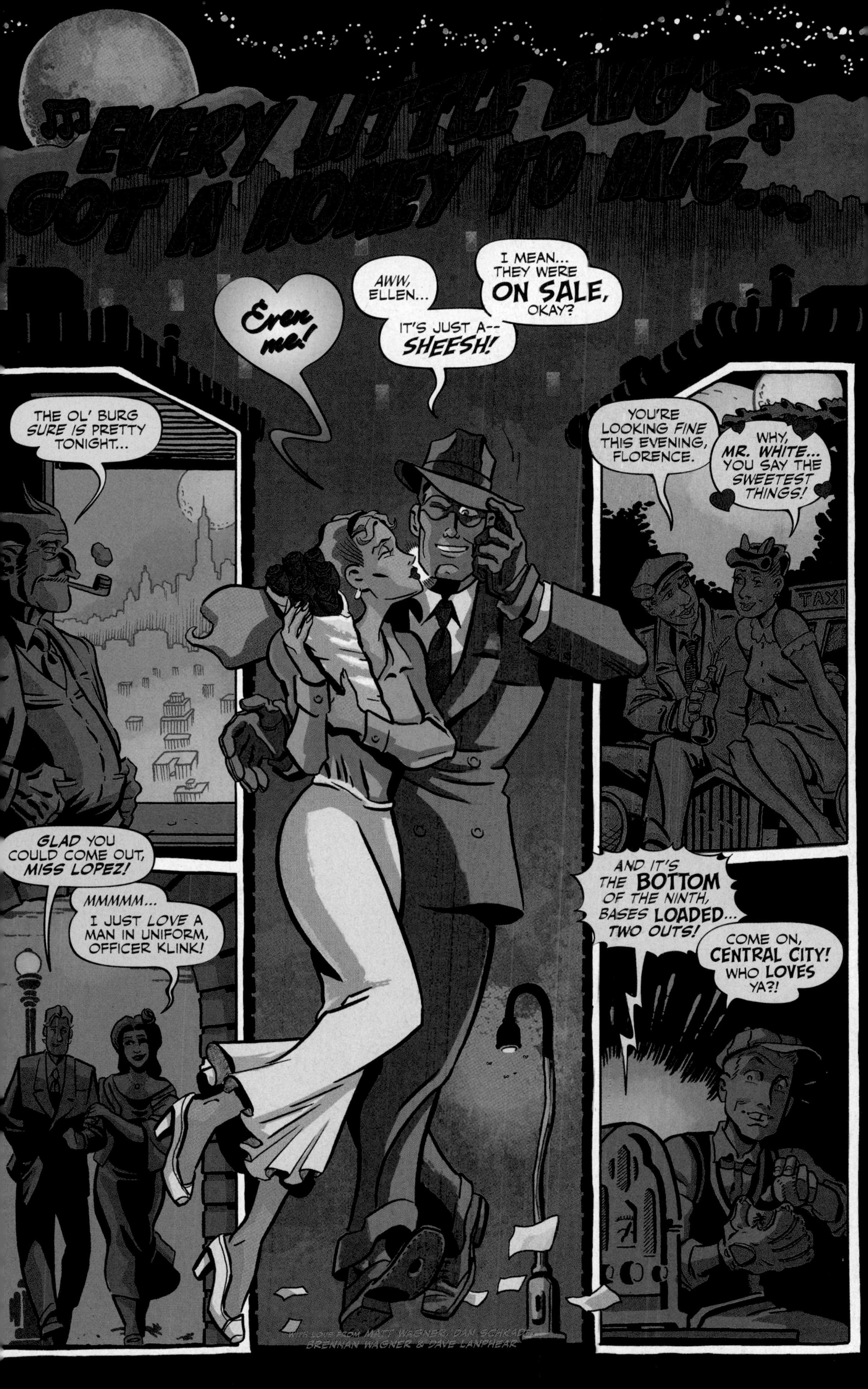
"EVERY LITTLE BUG'S GOT A HONEY TO HUG..."
THE OL' BURG SURE IS PRETTY TONIGHT...
GLAD YOU COULD COME OUT, MISS LOPEZ!
MMMMM... I JUST LOVE A MAN IN UNIFORM, OFFICER KLINK!
Even me!
AWW, ELLEN...
IT'S JUST A-- SHEESH!
I MEAN... THEY WERE ON SALE, OKAY?
YOU'RE LOOKING FINE THIS EVENING, FLORENCE.
WHY, MR. WHITE... YOU SAY THE SWEETEST THINGS!
TAXI
AND IT'S THE BOTTOM OF THE NINTH, BASES LOADED... TWO OUTS!
COME ON, CENTRAL CITY! WHO LOVES YA?!
WITH LOVE FROM MATT WAGNER, DAN SCHRADE, BRENNAN WAGNER & DAVE LANPHEAR

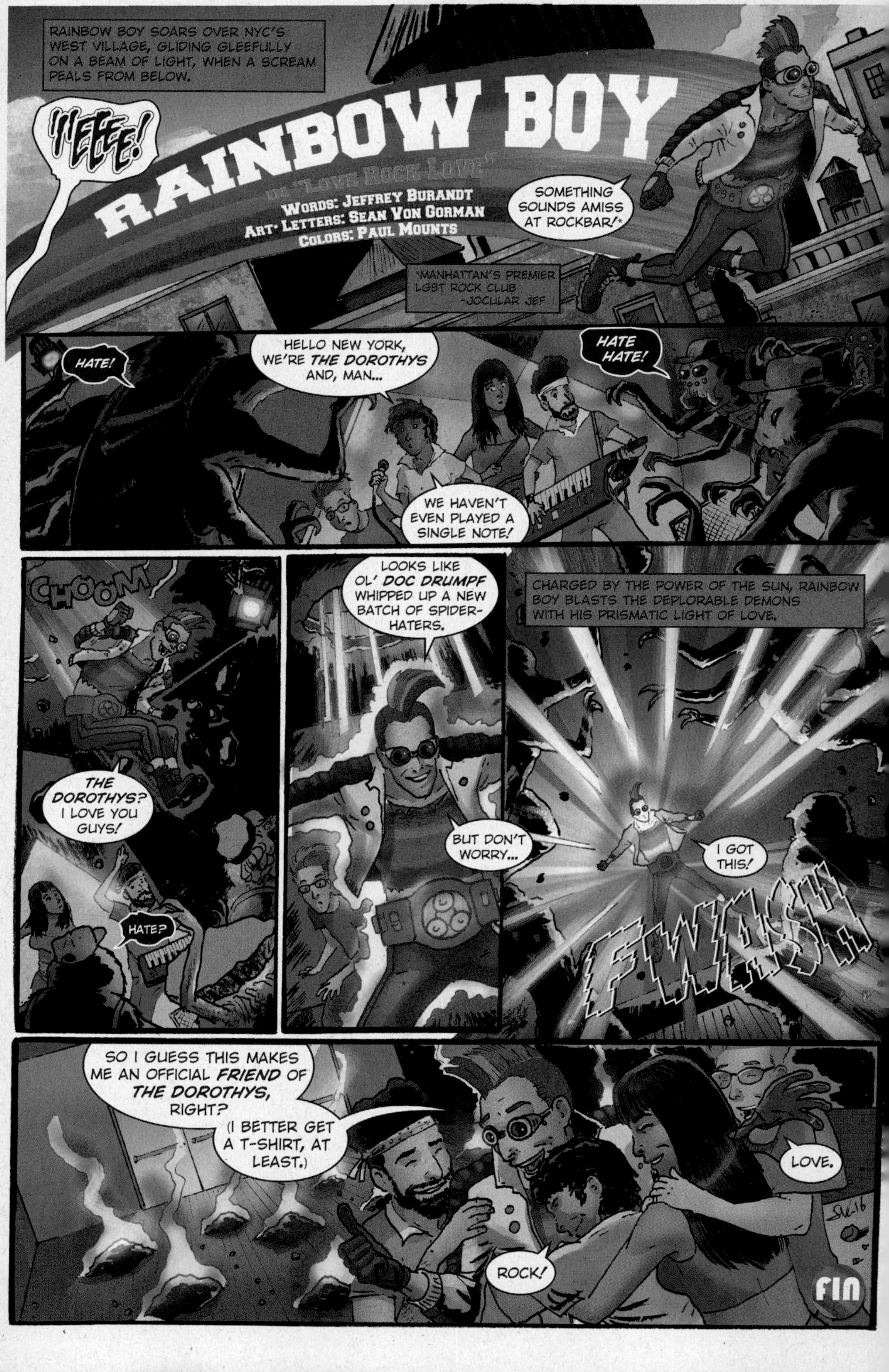
RAINBOW BOY SOARS OVER NYC'S WEST VILLAGE, GLIDING GLEEFULLY ON A BEAM OF LIGHT, WHEN A SCREAM PEALS FROM BELOW.
YEEEE!
RAINBOW BOY
"LOVE ROCK LOVE"
WORDS: JEFFREY BURANDT
ART• LETTERS: SEAN VON GORMAN
COLORS: PAUL MOUNTS
SOMETHING SOUNDS AMISS AT ROCKBAR!*
*MANHATTAN'S PREMIER LGBT ROCK CLUB -JOCULAR JEF
HATE!
HELLO NEW YORK, WE'RE THE DOROTHYS AND, MAN...
HATE HATE!
WE HAVEN'T EVEN PLAYED A SINGLE NOTE!
CHOOM
THE DOROTHYS? I LOVE YOU GUYS!
HATE?
LOOKS LIKE OL' DOC DRUMPF WHIPPED UP A NEW BATCH OF SPIDER-HATERS.
BUT DON'T WORRY...
CHARGED BY THE POWER OF THE SUN, RAINBOW BOY BLASTS THE DEPLORABLE DEMONS WITH HIS PRISMATIC LIGHT OF LOVE.
I GOT THIS!
FWASH!
SO I GUESS THIS MAKES ME AN OFFICIAL FRIEND OF THE DOROTHYS, RIGHT?
(I BETTER GET A T-SHIRT, AT LEAST.)
LOVE.
ROCK!
FIN

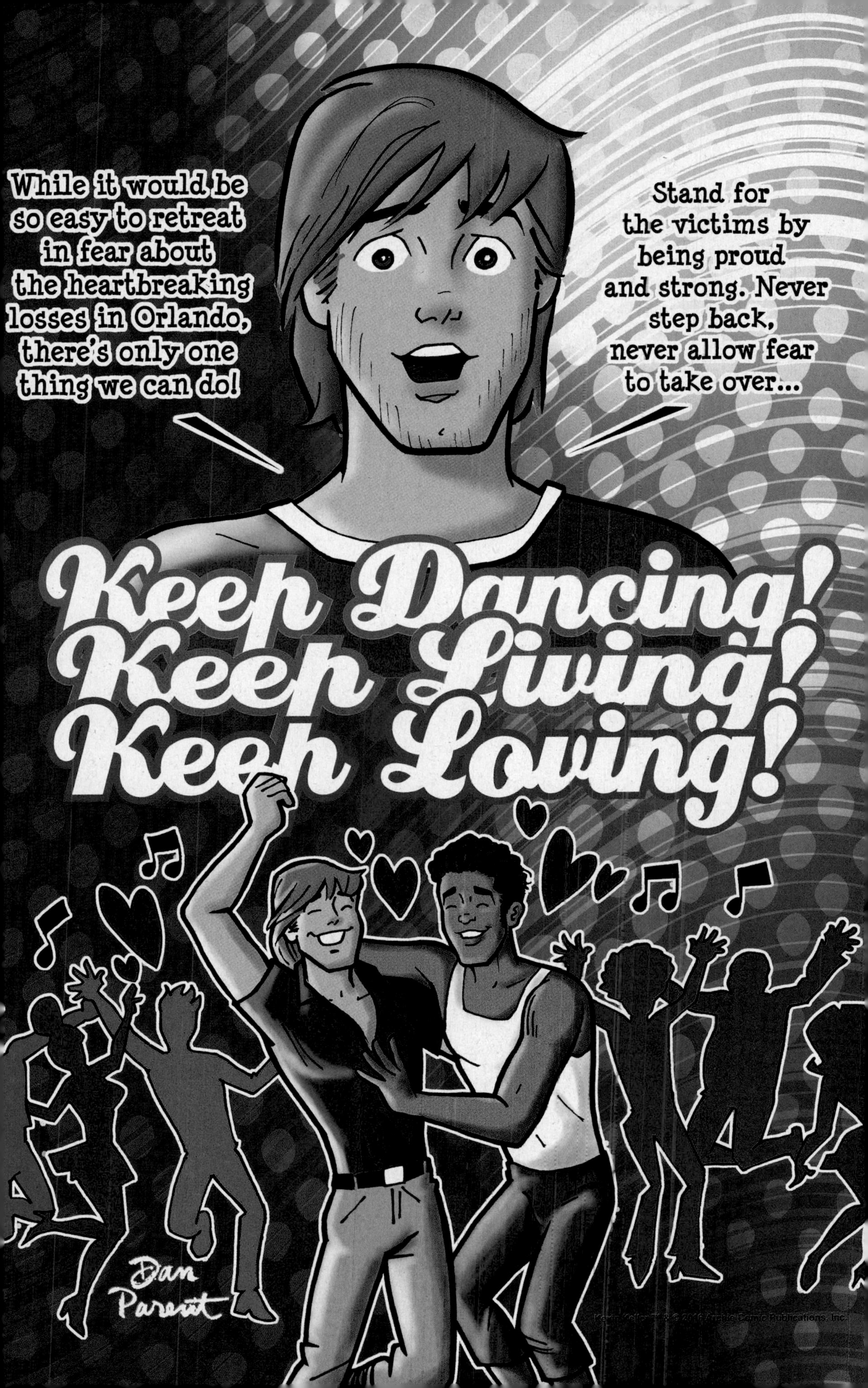
While it would be so easy to retreat in fear about the heartbreaking losses in Orlando, there's only one thing we can do!
Stand for the victims by being proud and strong. Never step back, never allow fear to take over...
Keep Dancing! Keep Living! Keep Loving!
Dan Parent
Kevin Keller TM & © 2016 Archie Comic Publications, Inc.

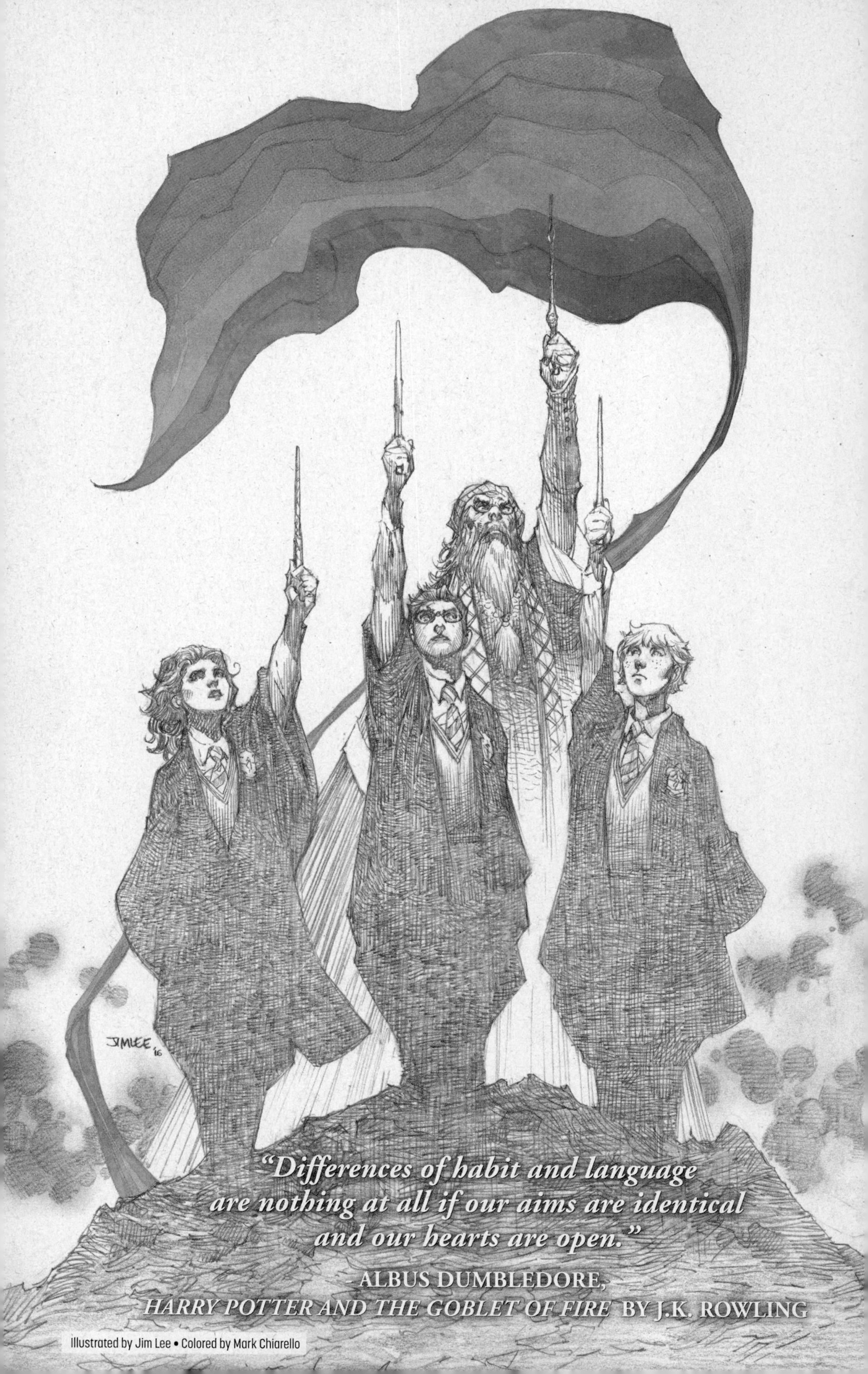
"Differences of habit and language are nothing at all if our aims are identical and our hearts are open."
- ALBUS DUMBLEDORE,
*HARRY POTTER AND THE GOBLET OF FIRE* BY J.K. ROWLING

Illustrated by Jim Lee • Colored by Mark Chiarello

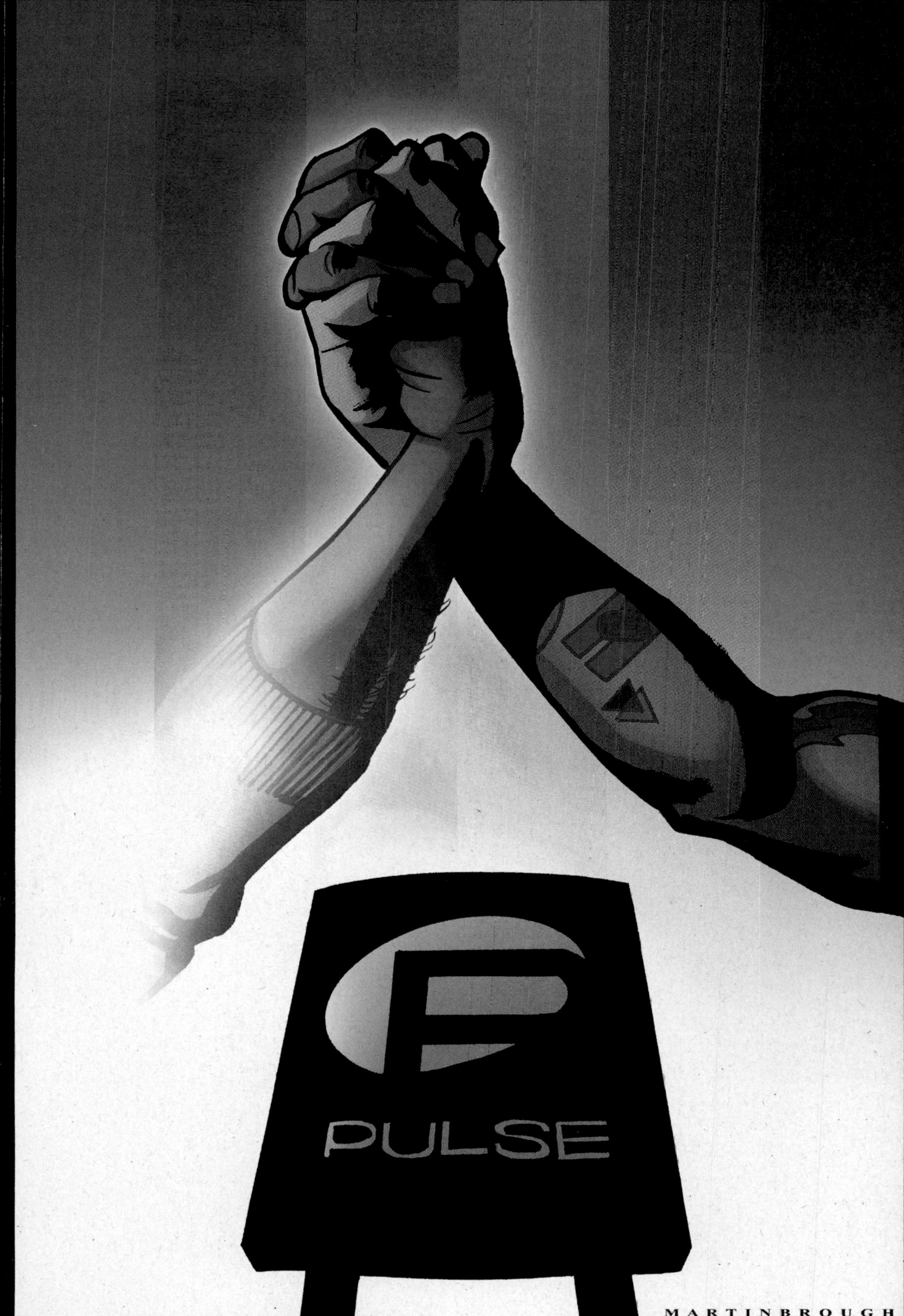
PULSE

MARTINBROUGH
ADR

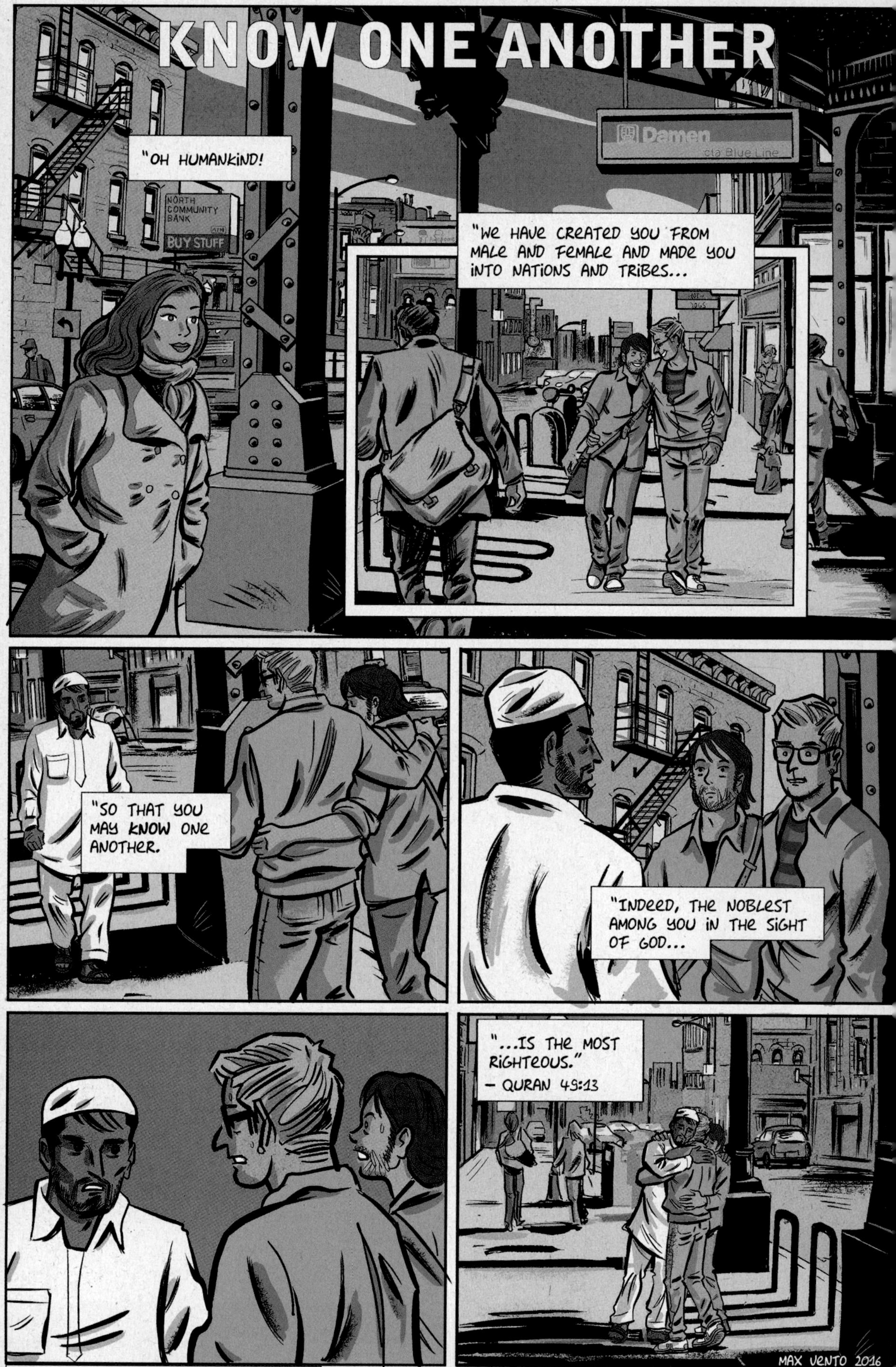
KNOW ONE ANOTHER
"OH HUMANKIND!
NORTH COMMUNITY BANK
BUY STUFF
Damen
cta Blue Line
"WE HAVE CREATED YOU FROM MALE AND FEMALE AND MADE YOU INTO NATIONS AND TRIBES...
"SO THAT YOU MAY KNOW ONE ANOTHER.
"INDEED, THE NOBLEST AMONG YOU IN THE SIGHT OF GOD...
"...IS THE MOST RIGHTEOUS."
– QURAN 49:13
MAX VENTO 2016

Written by G. Willow Wilson • Art and lettering by Max Vento

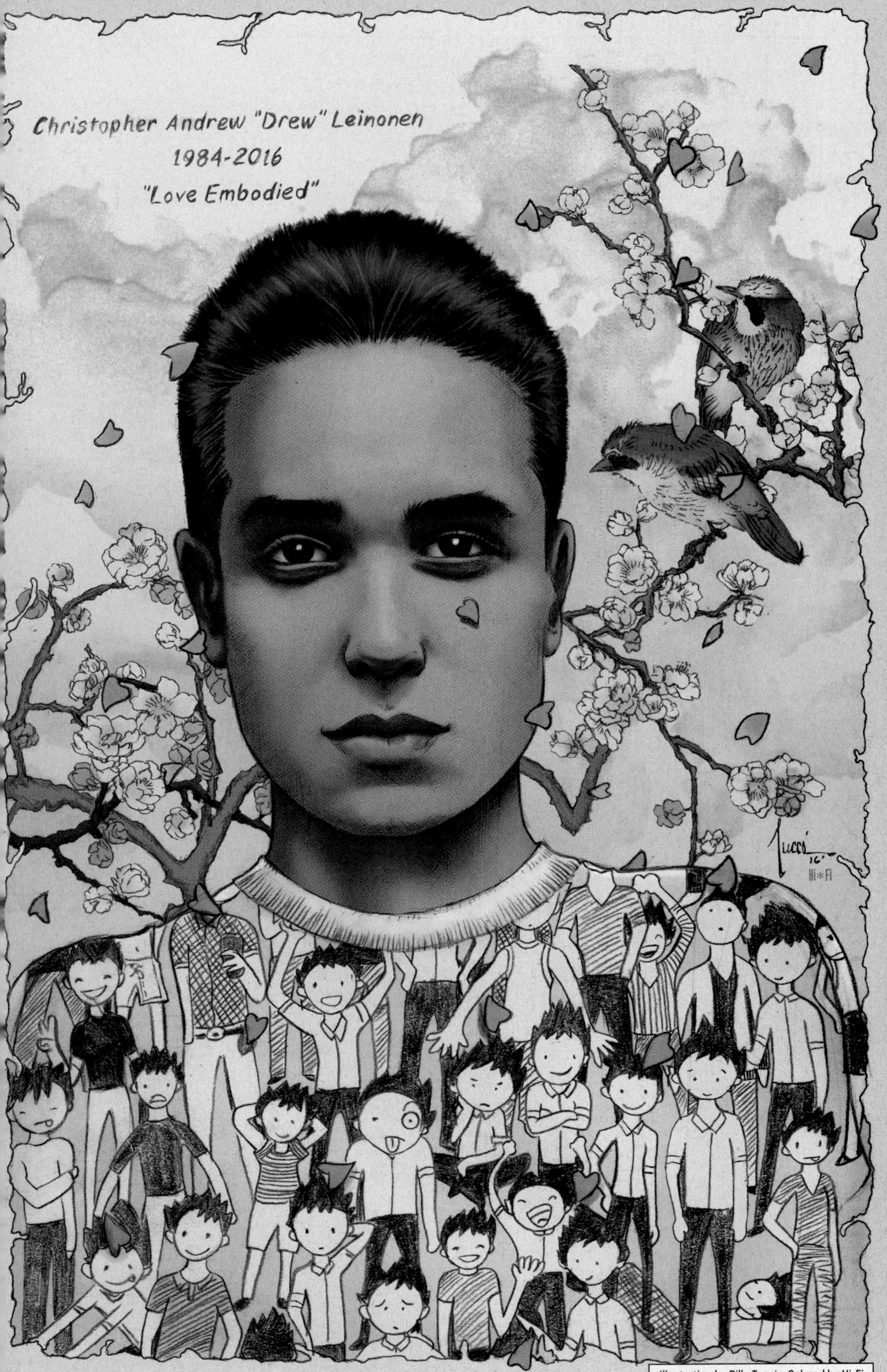
Christopher Andrew "Drew" Leinonen
1984-2016
"Love Embodied"
Tucci '16
Hi*Fi
Illustration by Billy Tucci • Colored by Hi-Fi

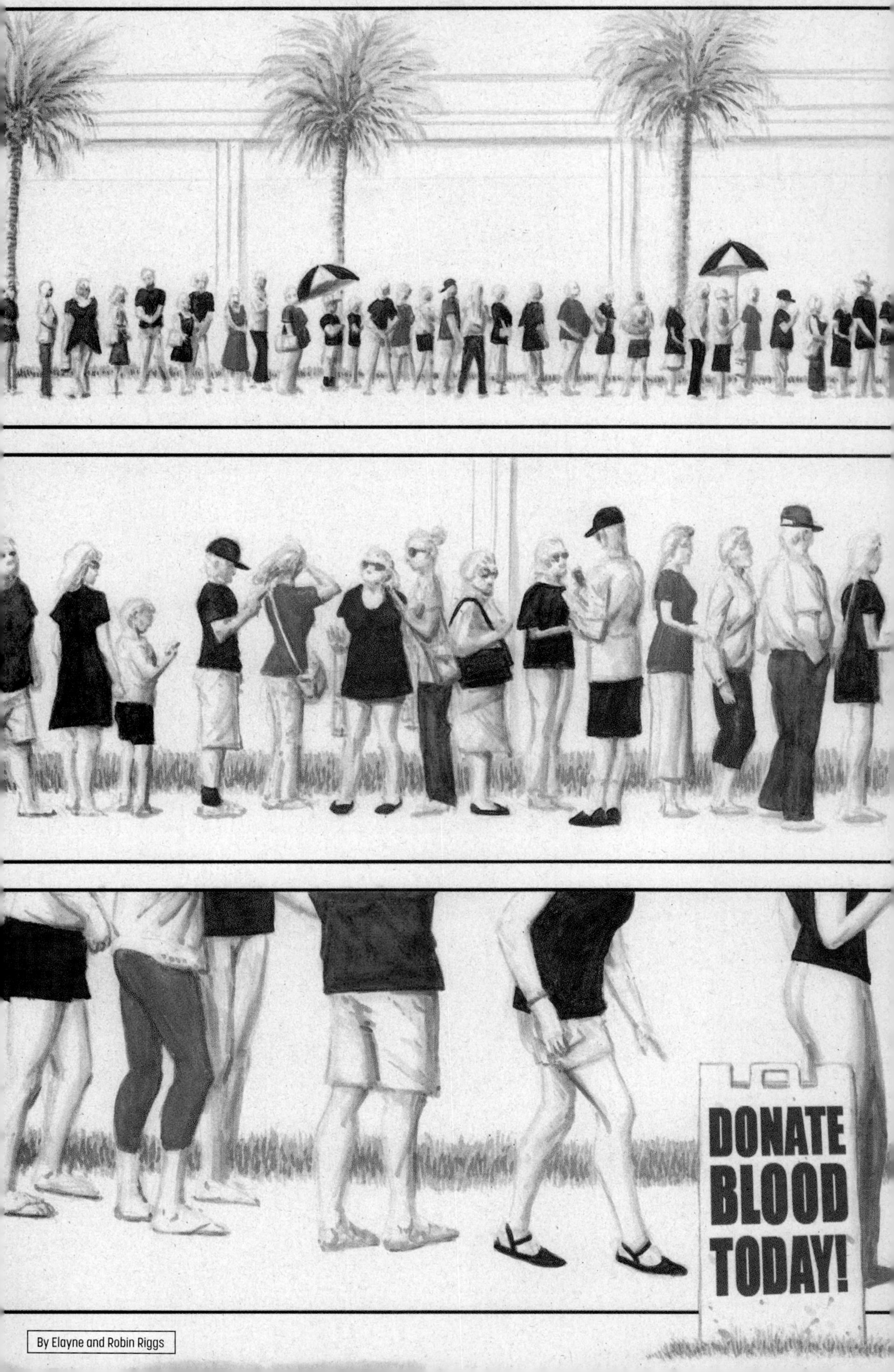
DONATE
BLOOD
TODAY!

By Elayne and Robin Riggs

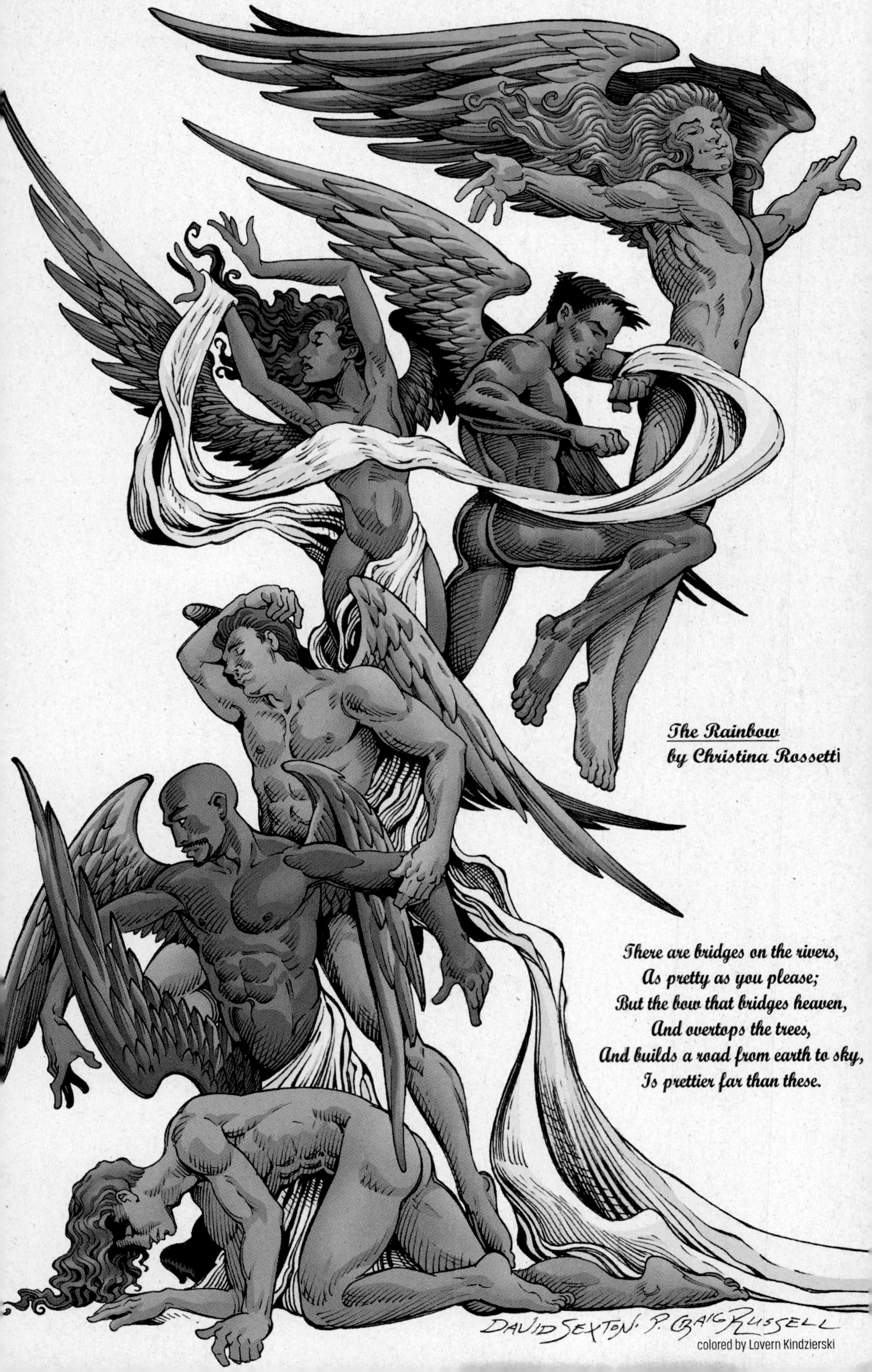
The Rainbow
by Christina Rossetti
There are bridges on the rivers,
As pretty as you please;
But the bow that bridges heaven,
And overtops the trees,
And builds a road from earth to sky,
Is prettier far than these.
DAVID SEXTON · P. CRAIG RUSSELL
colored by Lovern Kindzierski

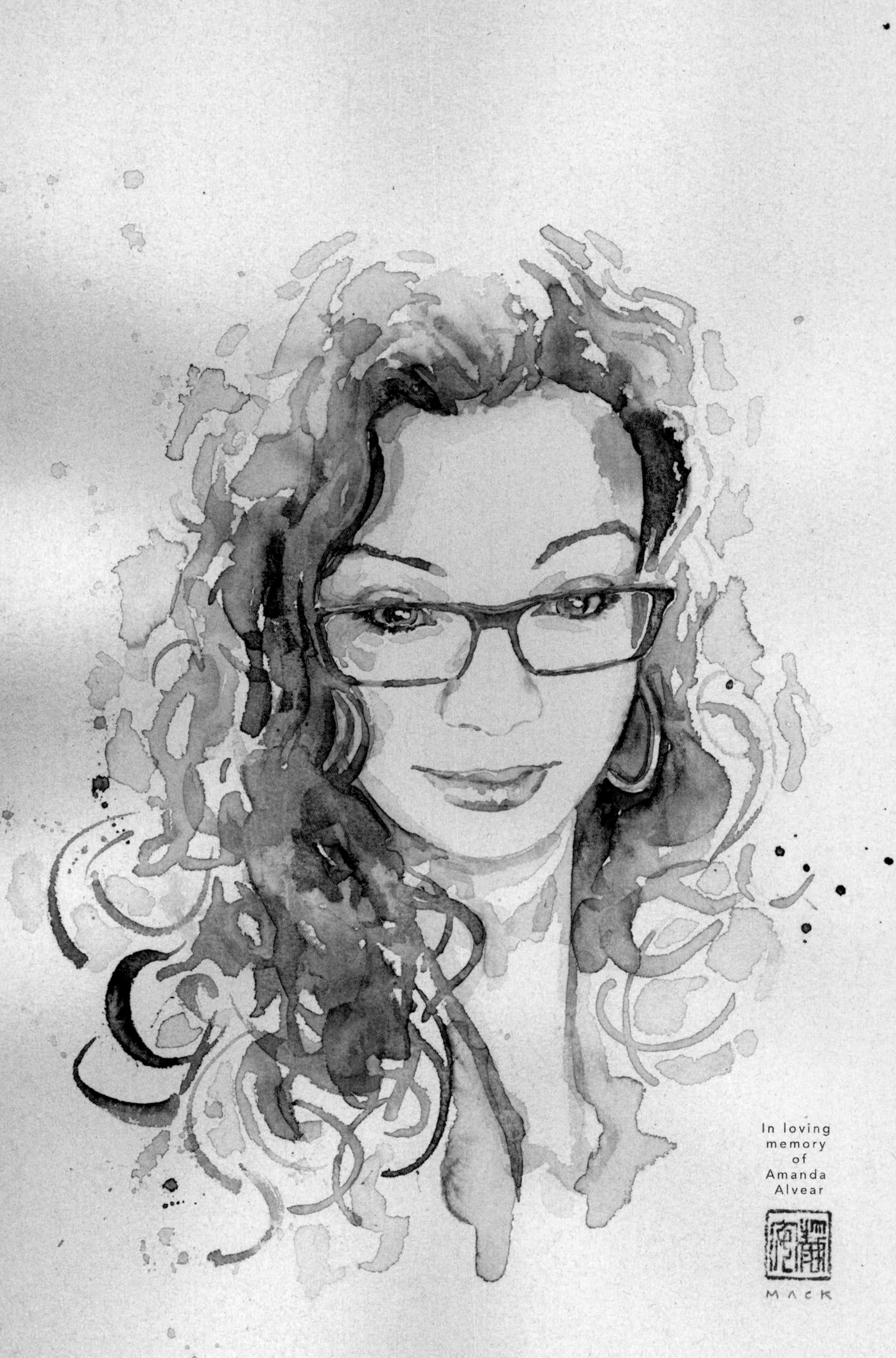
In loving memory of Amanda Alvear
MACK

Art by David Mack

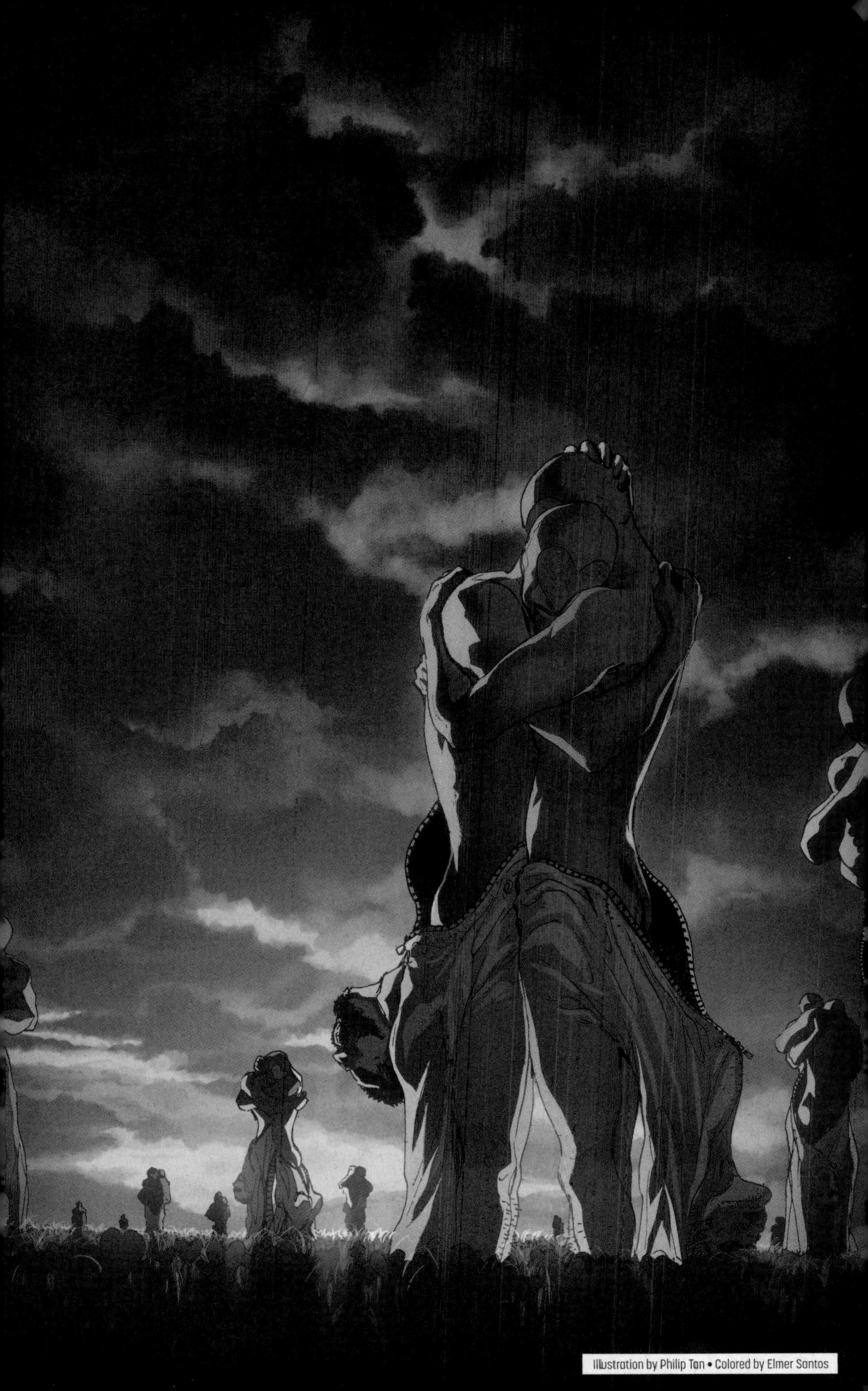

Illustration by Philip Tan • Colored by Elmer Santos

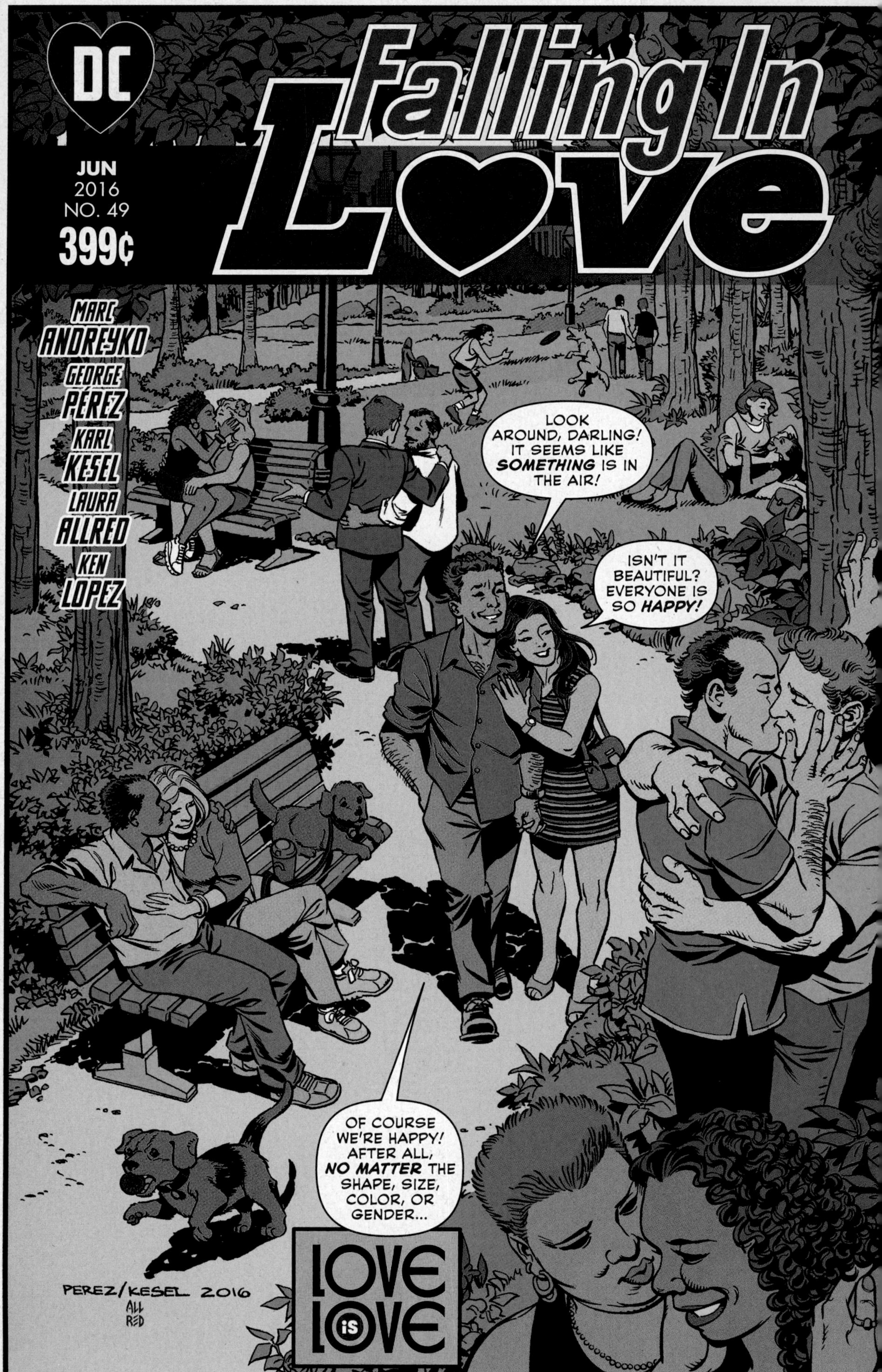
DC
Falling In Love
JUN
2016
NO. 49
399¢
MARC ANDREYKO
GEORGE PÉREZ
KARL KESEL
LAURA ALLRED
KEN LOPEZ
LOOK AROUND, DARLING! IT SEEMS LIKE **SOMETHING** IS IN THE AIR!
ISN'T IT BEAUTIFUL? EVERYONE IS SO **HAPPY!**
OF COURSE WE'RE HAPPY! AFTER ALL, **NO MATTER** THE SHAPE, SIZE, COLOR, OR GENDER...
LOVE is LOVE
PEREZ/KESEL 2016
ALLRED

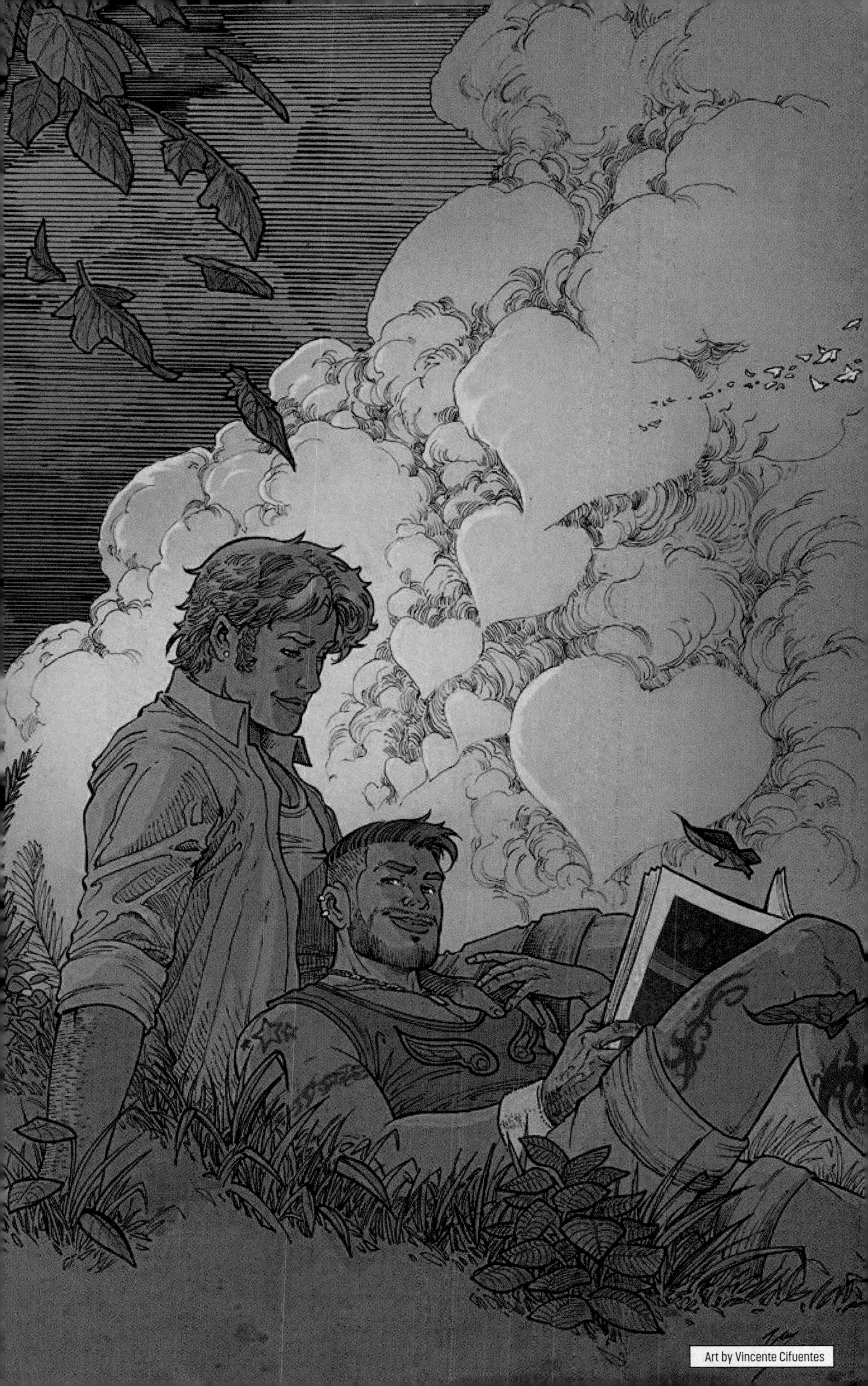

Art by Vincente Cifuentes

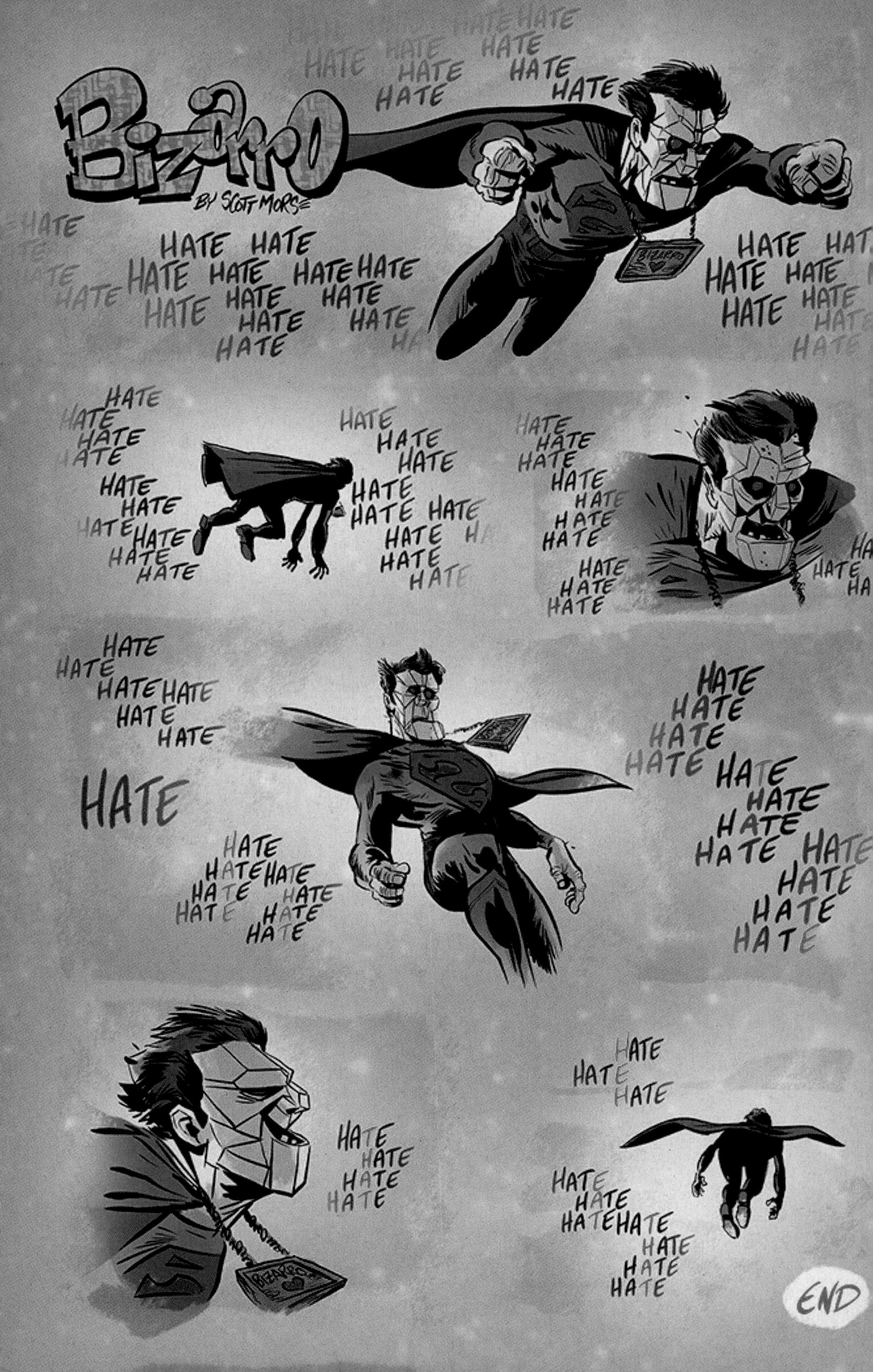

BIZARRO
BY SCOTT MORSE
HATE HATE HATE HATE HATE HATE HATE HATE
HATE HATE HATE HATE HATE HATE HATE HATE HATE HATE
HATE HATE HATE HATE HATE HATE HATE
HATE HATE HATE HATE HATE HATE HATE HATE HATE HATE
HATE HATE HATE HATE HATE HATE HATE HATE HATE HATE HATE
HATE HATE HATE HATE HATE HATE HATE HATE HATE HATE HATE HATE HATE
HATE HATE HATE HATE HATE HATE
HATE
HATE HATE HATE HATE HATE HATE HATE
HATE HATE HATE HATE HATE HATE HATE HATE HATE HATE HATE HATE HATE
HATE HATE HATE HATE
HATE HATE HATE HATE HATE HATE HATE HATE HATE HATE
END

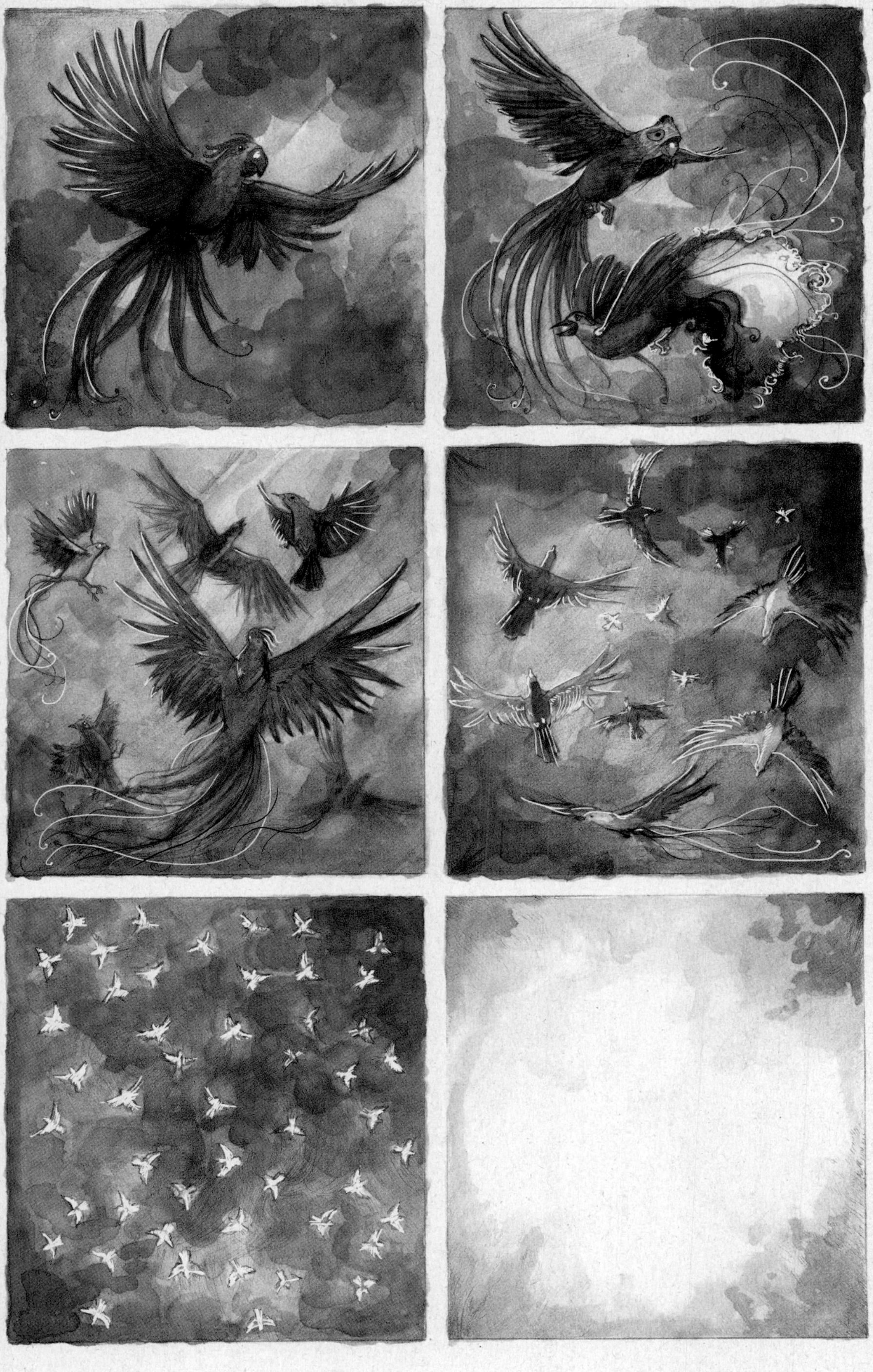

Written by Kieron Gillen • Art by Sarah Gordon

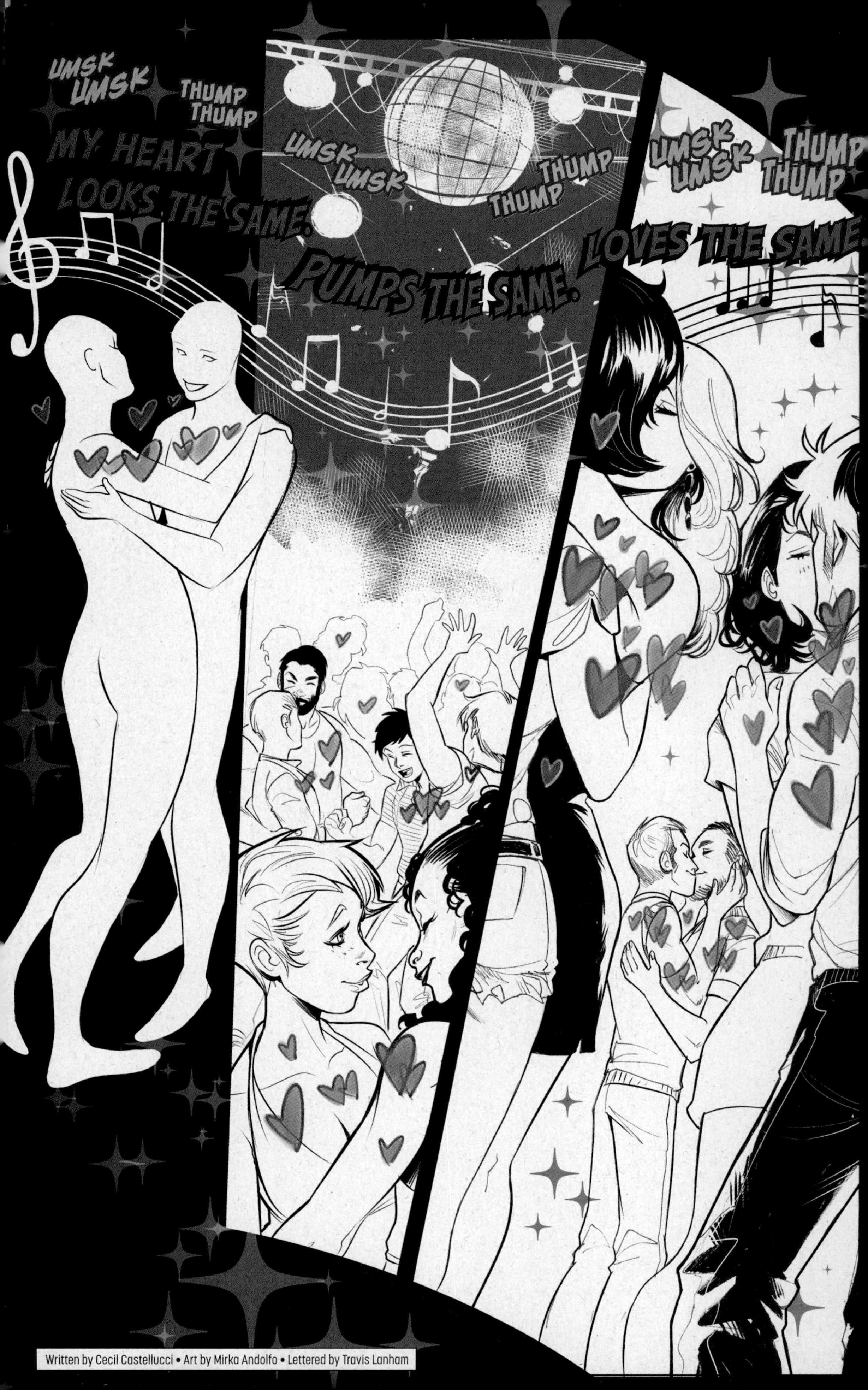
UMSK UMSK
THUMP THUMP
MY HEART LOOKS THE SAME.
UMSK UMSK
THUMP THUMP
PUMPS THE SAME.
UMSK UMSK
THUMP THUMP
LOVES THE SAME.
Written by Cecil Castellucci • Art by Mirka Andolfo • Lettered by Travis Lanham

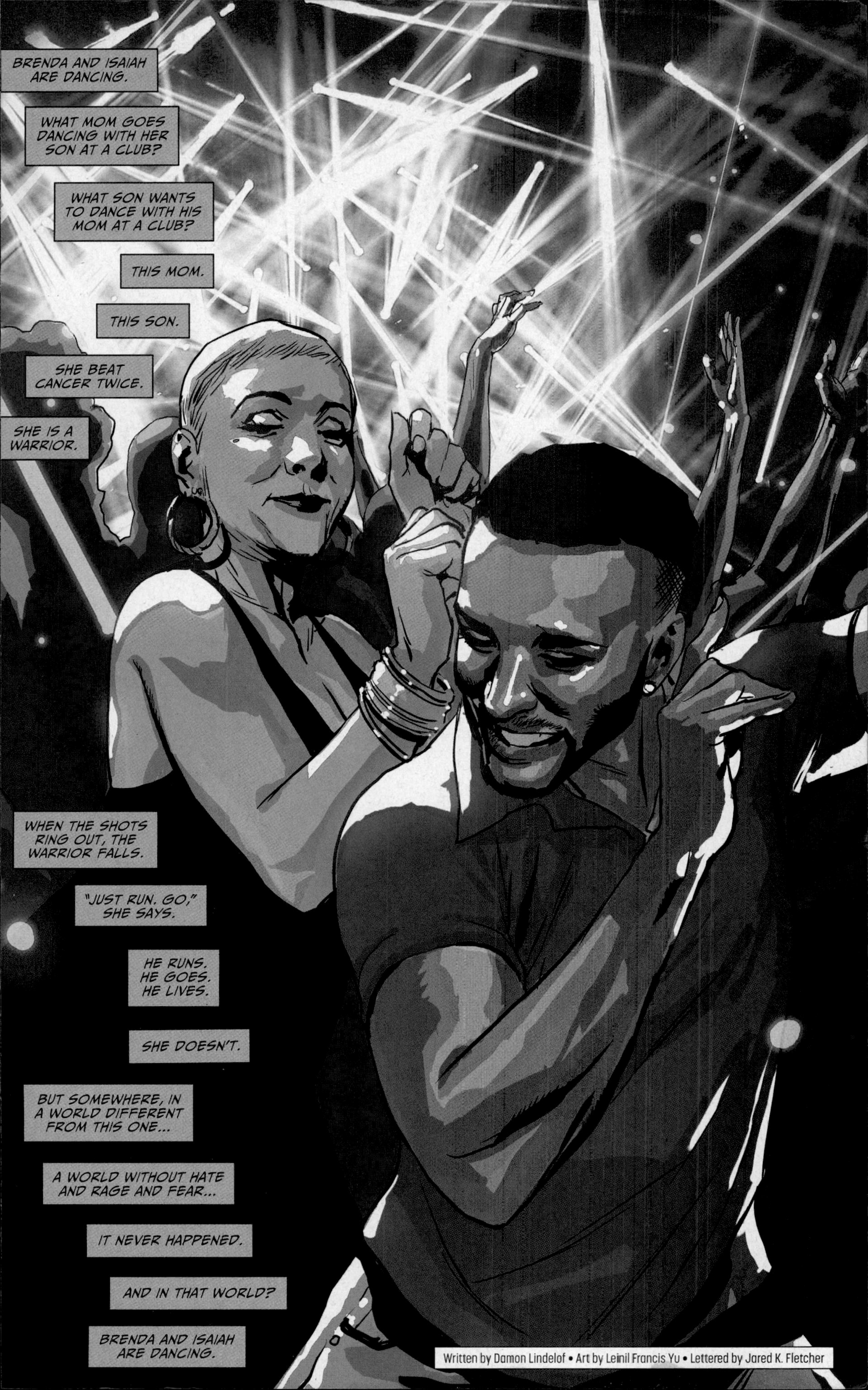
BRENDA AND ISAIAH ARE DANCING.
WHAT MOM GOES DANCING WITH HER SON AT A CLUB?
WHAT SON WANTS TO DANCE WITH HIS MOM AT A CLUB?
THIS MOM.
THIS SON.
SHE BEAT CANCER TWICE.
SHE IS A WARRIOR.
WHEN THE SHOTS RING OUT, THE WARRIOR FALLS.
"JUST RUN. GO," SHE SAYS.
HE RUNS. HE GOES. HE LIVES.
SHE DOESN'T.
BUT SOMEWHERE, IN A WORLD DIFFERENT FROM THIS ONE...
A WORLD WITHOUT HATE AND RAGE AND FEAR...
IT NEVER HAPPENED.
AND IN THAT WORLD?
BRENDA AND ISAIAH ARE DANCING.
Written by Damon Lindelof • Art by Leinil Francis Yu • Lettered by Jared K. Fletcher

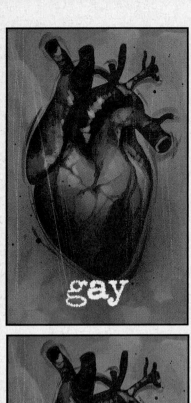

gay

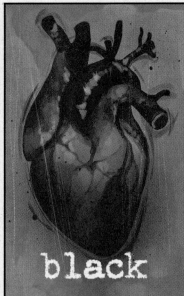

black

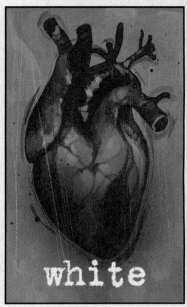

white

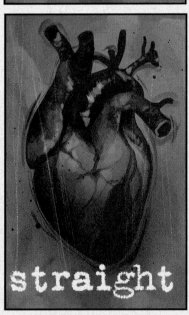

straight

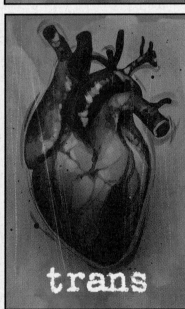

trans

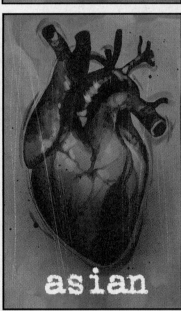

asian

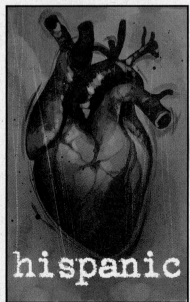

hispanic

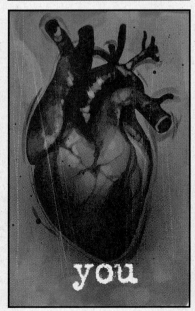

you

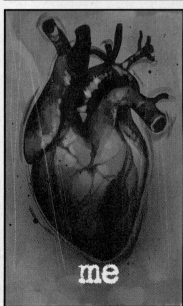

me

Written by Gerry Duggan • Art by Phil Noto

# WUVABLE OAF

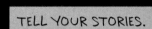

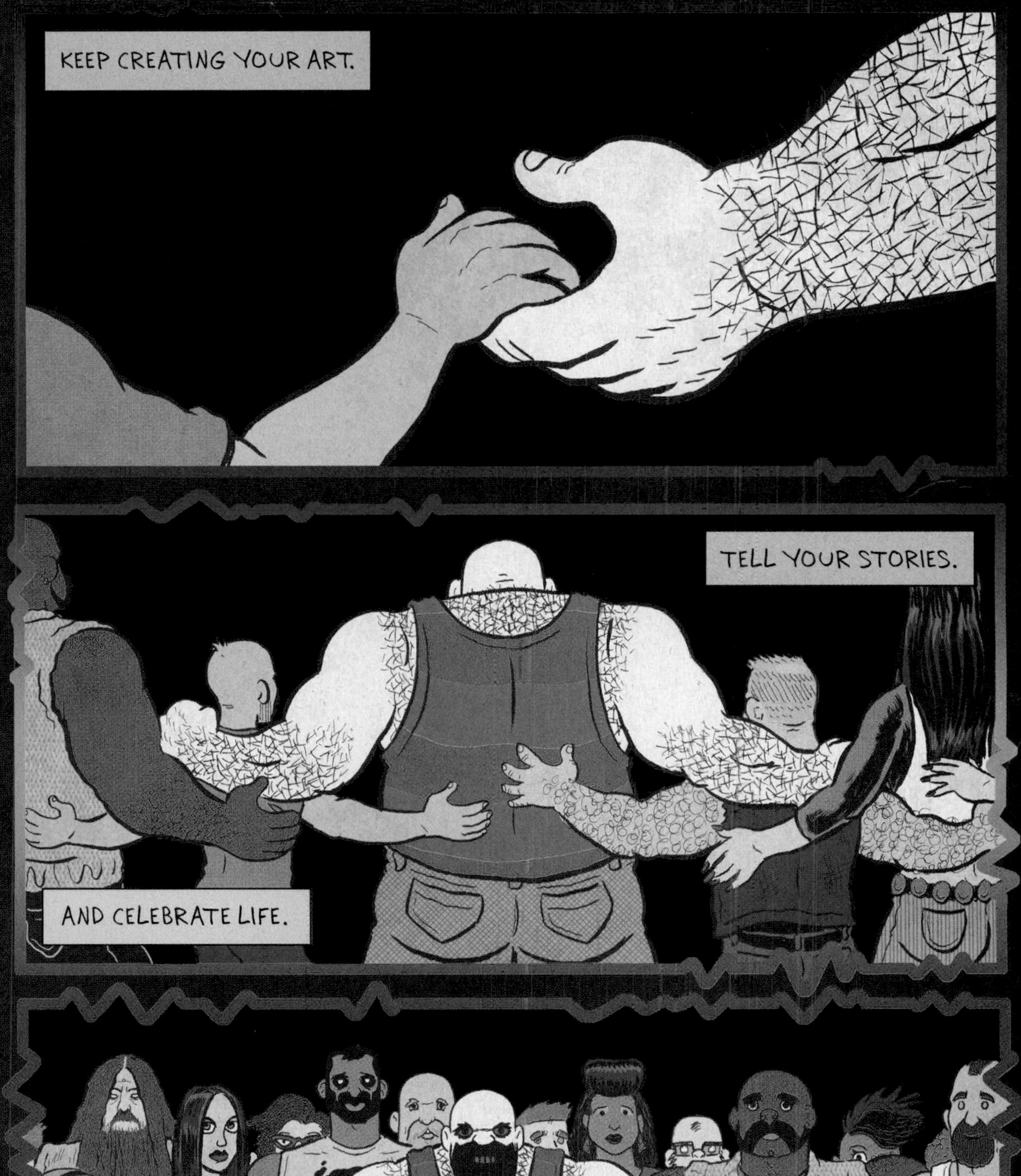

KEEP CREATING YOUR ART.

TELL YOUR STORIES.

AND CELEBRATE LIFE.

BECAUSE THAT'S HOW WE BEAT THIS THING...

MUCH WUV, Orlando!     Written & drawn by Ed Luce

# LOVE IS LOVE

## AFTERWORD

After hearing about the 49 lives lost at the Pulse nightclub in Orlando, Florida, on June 12, I was gut-punched by the horror and loss. And I was not alone. Feeling helpless, I wrote a Facebook post suggesting that the comics community needed to do something—anything. "I'll organize it!" I added, almost as an afterthought.

That was in the morning. By late afternoon, DOZENS of creators had reached out to me to say they were on board. With that, I thought, "I guess we're doing a book."

Over the course of the next few months, I was overwhelmed by the generosity, the passion, the support, and the work all of these talented folks contributed to honor those killed and to help those who survived. Gay, straight, bi, trans, male, female–it mattered not. All of us needed a place to share and express our grief and, most importantly, our belief that love is love.

As a child of "We Are The World" and Live Aid, I believe that artists creating art to raise money and assist in healing is what we are supposed to do. And, as you have seen, hundreds of the best of comics, TV, film, literature, theater, and other media have created deeply powerful art for LOVE IS LOVE. These brilliant, devoted contributors transformed my fleeting idea into a powerful, beautiful reality in four busy, crazy, inspiring, and maddening months.

None of it would have been remotely possible without the generosity of our brilliant, tireless editors Jamie Rich and Sarah Gaydos, DC Entertainment and Diane Nelson, IDW, Chris Ryall and Ted Adams, Archie Comics, and the Will Eisner estate.

And, finally, YOU. Thank you. Know that your support is going to make a difference in the lives of those who survived, those who lost someone, and those who still need help. In a world that seems so divided, the unity and love shown here is what we should all be about every day.

Love creates. Love heals. Love gives us hope.

Love is love.

And my heart overflows with love for you all.

### —MARC ANDREYKO
#### NOVEMBER 2016

Marc Andreyko is a *New York Times* best-selling writer of such works as MANHUNTER, WONDER WOMAN '77, *Torso* with Brian Bendis, BATWOMAN, *Dr. Strange,* and *Captain American & Bucky* with Ed Brubaker, as well as many screenplays, pilots, and directing the occasional play. He lives in Los Angeles with his dog, Frederick. And lots of books.

*Sarah Gaydos would like to dedicate her work on this project to her Aunties Anna Gioello and Ruth Cushing, and to her mother, Susan Butler, with lots of love.*

*Jamie S. Rich would like to dedicate this book to Benrus Madlangbayan, Bob Schreck, Christopher McQuain, Robert Fortney, and all the LGBTQ people throughout his life who taught him by example to accept others for who they are.*

*Amie Brockway-Metcalf would like to dedicate her work on this project to Robyn and Sarah Brody-Kaplan.*